Migrants in Europe

Recent Titles in
Contributions in Family Studies

A Coat of Many Colors: Jewish Subcommunities in the United States
Abraham D. Lavender, editor

Passing: The Vision of Death in America
Charles O. Jackson, editor

Cross-Cultural Perspectives of Mate-Selection and Marriage
George Kurian, editor

A Social History of American Family Sociology, 1865–1940
Ronald L. Howard; John Mogey, editor

Women in the Family and the Economy: An International Comparative Survey
George Kurian and Ratna Ghosh, editors

Revolutions in Americans' Lives: A Demographic Perspective on the History of Americans, Their Families, and Their Society
Robert V. Wells

Three Different Worlds: Women, Men, and Children in an Industrializing Community
Frances Abrahamer Rothstein

Family and Work: Comparative Convergences
Merlin B. Brinkerhoff, editor

Child-Rearing and Reform: A Study of the Nobility in Eighteenth-Century Poland
Bogna Lorence-Kot

Parent-Child Interaction in Transition
George Kurian, editor

The Dutch Gentry, 1500–1650: Family, Faith, and Fortune
Sherrin Marshall

Migrants in Europe

THE ROLE OF FAMILY, LABOR, AND POLITICS

Edited by
Hans Christian Buechler
and
Judith-Maria Buechler

Contributions in Family Studies, Number 12

Greenwood Press
NEW YORK • WESTPORT, CONNECTICUT • LONDON

Library of Congress Cataloging-in-Publication Data

Migrants in Europe.

(Contributions in family studies, ISSN 0147-1023 ;
no. 12)
Bibliography: p.
Includes index.
1. Europe—Emigration and immigration. 2. Europe—
Emigration and immigration—Government policy.
3. Community. 4. Social systems. I. Buechler, Hans C.
II. Buechler, Judith-Maria. III. Series.
JV7590.M49 1987 304.8′094 86-25722
ISBN 0-313-23236-9 (lib. bdg. : alk. paper)

Library of Congress Catalog Card Number: 86-25722
ISBN: 0-313-23236-9
ISSN: 0147-1023

First published in 1987

Greenwood Press, Inc.
88 Post Road West, Westport, Connecticut 06881

Printed in the United States of America

∞™

The paper used in this book complies with the Permanent Paper Standard issued by the National Information Standards Organization (Z39.48-1984).

10 9 8 7 6 5 4 3 2 1

Copyright Acknowledgments

Material from an article by Lazo Karovski, "Macedonia Folk Poetry of Economic Immigration," originally published in *Macedonian Review*, no. 3 (1974), has been reprinted with the permission of *Macedonian Review*.

Every reasonable effort has been made to trace the owners of copyright materials used in this book, but in some instances this has proven impossible. The publishers will be glad to receive information leading to more complete acknowledgments in subsequent printings of this book, and in the meantime extend their apologies for any omissions.

Contents

Figures and Tables

FIGURES

TABLES

Migrants in Europe

1 Introduction

Hans Christian Buechler

Migration studies have gained a degree of maturity. They have moved away from characterizing migrants by certain personality traits (need for achievement, entrepreneurial talent, etc.); away from listing simple push and pull factors regarded as independent of one another; and away from notions of "adaptation" and "integration," popular particularly in the countries of destination where social scientists follow popular apprehensions about assimilation into the host society. Migration studies are even dissociating themselves from the more sophisticated and socially sensitive versions of such studies which focused on the discrimination suffered by migrants in the host countries. In the place of these concerns, with their focus on either the place of origin or the place of destination, other perspectives that encompass the entire trajectory are emerging. Some social scientists even argue that the strategies of nonmigrants can also only be understood in conjunction with those of migrants.

Characteristic of many of the modern anthropological studies on migration is an attempt at creating a balance between a systems orientation and focus on the actors. They stress international, interregional, and intercommunity systems which constrain migrants, without neglecting the creativity given migrants, who not only have a significant impact on their destinies, but in interaction with other migrants as well as nonmigrants, help shape communities, industrial systems, and the political economy.

Finally, the maturation of migration studies can also be seen in an emergent understanding of the complexity of migrant adaptations. The process of migration is viewed as entailing a succession of often temporary adaptations which lead to further ones because of inherent dynamics, reactions on the part of the host society and the society of origin, and wider economic trends.

COMMUNITIES AS OPEN SYSTEMS

A major development in migration studies originated in the reorientation of structural-functional approaches to cultural and social systems. Modern ethnographies have ceased to treat communities as closed and stable systems, stressing regional and national influences. The emphasis is on adaptive flexibility of culture rather than on rigid institutional frameworks. For example, in the field of European studies, Friedl (1974) examines the role of the mercenary draft, tunnel construction, industrial employment, and the provision of tourist accommodations as mechanisms for adapting to a harsh environment in a Swiss Alpine community; Greenwood (1976) analyzes the effect of land speculation for tourist development on a Spanish Basque community; and Boissevain and Friedl (1975) have assembled a series of studies whose specific aim is to place European communities into vaster regional and national contexts.

Within the study of migration, this trend translates itself into a view of migration as an integral part of adaptive strategies affecting not just the migrants themselves, but also those who are left behind. Some such studies have stressed the conservative aspects of migration. For a time at least, migration may permit the preservation of aspects of village life which would otherwise not be possible to maintain in a modern society. The contributions of Gregory and Cazorla (chap. 7), Halpern (chap. 5), and Leeds (chap. 2) all document this phenomenon (see also Brandes 1975). It has also been posited that migration may become a long-term adaptation, manifesting itself in different ways over many generations, an argument made by Barou (chap. 4), Gmelch (chap. 11), Halpern, and Leeds.

WORLD SYSTEMS THEORIES

A second theoretical direction that can be discerned in the recent literature on migration is inspired by world systems and dependency theories as well as other related approaches. This direction stresses the interconnectedness of policy decision making in sender and host countries and the primary role of national and international capital in migration policies. As J-M. Buechler shows in her essay (chap. 12), considerable progress has been made in assessing the impact of migration policies on the lives of migrants. Goodman (chap. 9), Sontz (chap. 8), and Gregory and Cazorla all examine the direct effects of such measures in specific instances. Formal policies, however, are only a particularly salient feature of a plethora of social relationships which cut across local, regional, and international levels to shape migratory flows and through them the areas of origin and destination of migrants. In order to be of use to anthropologists, such approaches must be brought down to a very concrete level and include an understanding of political and economic relationships among communities within the same and different regions. The anthropologist must understand the roles of specific regional and national power elites and the specific mechanisms whereby changes in capitalist production influence the lives of locals on the one hand and migrants on the other.

The articles in this collection document migration fields, which are social systems that include the places of origin and destination of migrants. In such systems social, political, and economic changes that take place in one point in the field have an immediate impact on other parts of the same field. Government policies regarding migration in both sender and host countries, as well as specific treaties between countries, may regulate, or attempt to regulate, movements within such fields. But migration fields have dynamics of their own which sometimes run in opposition to the wishes of bureaucrats and lawmakers. These integrative mechanisms include chain migration; clandestine networks that facilitate illegal movements between countries; the periodic return of migrants to their places of origin; migrant remittances to parts of families who remained behind; payments to boarding schools in the home country where the children of migrants have been sent; and investment in land, construction, and small businesses in the home country.

Barou, Buechler (chap. 10), Gmelch, Gregory and Cazorla, Halpern, Leeds, and Yücel (chap. 6) all analyze migration fields that span two or more continents. Callier Boisvert (chap. 3) examines the nature of a migration field of more limited geographical dimension but where greater accessibility was offset by stringent legal restrictions on migratory movements.

In addition to their geographical dimensions, such migration fields are distinguished by their shape. Already in 1972 Allen found that migrants from certain Canadian communities had an extremely narrow distribution in the region of destination in Maine. They had followed the railroad and concentrated mainly in one locality, although some subsequently spread to other localities. Later, migrants from the same places of origin tended to migrate to the same localities even when the railroad links no longer determined the shape of the migration field. In contrast, migrants from places where emigration began later have a much more diffuse migration field. The examples of such fields in this book illustrate a different contrast, namely between sender communities that—at least until recently—were relatively closed to interregional and even intraregional contacts but which have long been linked to places as distant as Caracas and Rio de Janeiro (e.g., Leeds, Gregory and Cazorla). In contrast, other migrants come from open communities that are highly integrated into the national economy and maintain close ties to regional and national urban centers. In the latter case, rural-urban migration may precede or alternate with international migration.

The concept of ''migration field'' includes migrants and those individuals and institutions that directly impinge upon them in both the place of origin and destination. The field of inquiry extends beyond the migrants themselves but does not ipso facto question the heuristic utility of the concept of migration as a predictor of social relationships. Most of the articles in this book do, in fact, take the concept for granted. However, some anthropologists have gone further in questioning the validity and utility of the migrant-nonmigrant dichotomy. Thus, Sontz finds that the major cleavage between social groups in an industrial German neighborhood is not between migrants and nonmigrants but between skilled workers (which include earlier migrants) and unskilled workers (which include recent migrants). Similarly, Leeds argues that the dichotomy should (at least ultimately) be rejected altogether, for not only are nonmigrant families in the home regions deeply affected by migration, but migration becomes an integral part of the political economy of regions with low emigration rates and of the sender countries as a whole. Indeed, just as on the local level migration may permit the continuation of peasant traditions, it may also diminish resistance against regional and national structures of domination (Gregory and Cazorla, Yücel). Conversely, decisions made to foster internal industrial development—such as damming rivers and flooding agricultural land, reforestation of community lands and channeling migrant remittances out of areas with high rates of international migration (and usually low rates of industrialization) into the regions that are already highly industralized—all have a major impact on migration rates and their degree of permanence. In such a context, nonmigrants are as influenced by migration as migrants, in different but equally important ways, while migrants' options are largely shaped by national and regional economic policies (see also Buechler and Buechler 1975 and Beiras 1972).

We would argue that Leeds's global approach to change should also be applied to indigenous populations in the host countries whose economic options and even conservation of many aspects of their life-style can only be explained by the presence of migrants. Lack of progress in this line of inquiry may lie in the political sensitivity of such a point of view. Migration studies are often funded by the host countries themselves or by countries with similar characteristics, where such views might not be popular.

Such a perspective could lead to a radical reevaluation of assimilation and even adaptation theories, for these theories are still predicated on the assumption that host societies do not change in response to migration. Instead, they take social structure in the host countries as the independent variable and migrant society as the dependent variable. In contrast, a systems approach would lead us to ask what direction certain kinds of social forms in an entire system of interlinked nations are taking. Implicitly at least, Sontz's article constitutes a step in this direction.

SOCIAL NETWORK ANALYSIS

A third major input in migration studies has been the perfection of social network analysis. Although network studies have a long history in the social sciences, they attained a level of maturity only in the late sixties and early seventies.[1] Social networks are in principle bounded by neither space nor time. A focus on social networks thus permits the analysis of interpersonal behavior associated with migratory processes wherever they occur and over any time period over which interpersonal contacts can be traced. Although network analysis is a methodology rather than a theoretical direction per se, this potential has led to the questioning of even fundamental premises of structural-functional studies, particularly their stress on bounded systems and the priority they give to jural rules over behavior. In the anthropology of migration, they have forced analysts to document interpersonal behavior more concretely and have thus provided a welcome corrective to world systems and dependency approaches that tend to view social situations in a rather abstract manner.

In addition to contributing to the understanding of the processes of migration, network analysis is important, perhaps even crucial, to the understanding of household, family, and kin dynamics under conditions of rapid change. It enables the researcher to document precisely the complex adaptations of kin relationships in migratory situations. Such phenomena as the shift from patrilocal residence to matrilocality, the establishment of new temporary residential groupings both at home and abroad during the migratory process, and the manipulation of ties created by the more established migrants on behalf of their kinsmen are readily analyzed in network terms.

The present studies combine systems and actor orientations. Thus Leeds discusses the impact of government policies regarding male and female migration but goes on to acknowledge the creativity of social networks in the migration process as well as in the transformation of Portuguese rural communities. Similarly, Barou, Buechler, and Yücel show that within the constraints on geographical and social mobility imposed by such host societies as France and Switzerland and the limitations in economic opportunities in the regions of origin, Soninké, Galician, and Turkish migrants in interaction with other migrants, individuals in the host countries, and nonmigrants at home have contributed significantly in shaping their own destinies as well as the communities, industrial systems, and political economies with which they have been associated. Perhaps the next step will be to study policy-making and the operation of capitalism in more concrete interactional terms as well, thus permitting us to move from migrants to bureaucrats and elites without switching levels of abstraction.[2]

DYNAMIC MODELS OF FAMILY DEVELOPMENT

Finally, some of the studies presented here have benefited from conceptual advances in family studies. In recent years, the analysis of family dynamics has moved from the construction of models of family cycles conceived as sets of invariant stages through which a family passes over time, to models that pay close attention to the effect of specific historical events on such cycles. Again, the emphasis is on connecting different levels of sociocultural integration (i.e., family, community, region, nation, etc.). Thus Elder's (1978) and Hareven's (1978) concept of *life course* is designed to measure the differential impact of such major historical events as the Great Depression on individuals depending on the stage in their lives they had reached at that time. Similarly, Barou, Boisvert, and Buechler all found that migration played a different role in an individual's life, depending on at what age and at what point in a migration wave he or she first migrated.

To the four types of approaches we have discussed, we should add the recent interest in gathering detailed case studies of particular firms established by migrants (Yücel), individual migrant families as well as life histories of migrants (Goodman, see also Barou 1978 and Cornelisen 1980), and persons indirectly affected by migration (e.g., Buechler and Buechler 1981). Taken together, these approaches complete the interlinkage of all levels of sociocultural integration, both historically and geographically. The present studies constitute a step in this direction. They also outline a program for future studies in the anthropology of European migration in particular and socioeconomic change in general.

NOTES

1. See, however, Leeds's (1964) pathbreaking article that combines network analysis with evolutionary theory already in the mid-sixties.
2. See Leeds (1964) again for a pioneering attempt in this direction.

REFERENCES

Allen, J. P.
1972 "Migration Fields of French Canadian Immigrants to South Maine." *Geographical Review,* 52: 366–83.
Barou, J.
1978 *Travailleurs africains en France: Rôle des cultures d'origine.* Presses Universitaires de Grenoble.
Beiras, X.
1972 *O atraso económico de Galicia.*, Vigo, Spain: Galaxia.
Boissevain, J., and Friedl, J.
1975 *Beyond the Community: Social Process in Europe.* The Hague: Department of Educational Science of the Netherlands.
Brandes, S.
1975 *Migration, Kinship, and Community: Tradition and Transition in a Spanish Village.* New York: Academic Press.
Buechler, H. and Buechler, J-M.
1975 "Los Suizos: Galician Migration to Switzerland." In *Migration and Development: Implications for Ethnic Identity and Political Conflict,* edited by H. I. Safa and B. M. DuTroit, 17–31. The Hague: Mouton.
1981 *Carmen: The Autobiography of a Spanish Galician Woman.* Cambridge, Mass.: Schenkman.
Cornelisen, A.
1980 *Strangers and Pilgrims: The Last Italian Migration.* New York: Holt, Rinehart and Winston.
Elder, G.
1978 "Family History and the Life Course." In *Transitions: The Family and the Life Course in Historical Perspective,* edited by T. Hareven, 21–64. New York: Academic Press.
Friedl, J.
1974 *Kippel: A Changing Village in the Alps.* New York: Holt, Rinehart and Winston.

Greenwood, D.
1976 *Unrewarding Wealth: The Commercialization and Collapse of Agriculture in a Spanish Basque Town*. Cambridge: Cambridge University Press.

Hareven, T.
1978 "Introduction: The Historical Study of the Life Course." In *Transitions: The Family and the Life Course in Historical Perspective*, edited by T. Hareven, 10–16. New York: Academic Press.

Leeds, A.
1964 "Brazilian Careers and Social Structure: An Evolutionary Perspective." *American Anthropologist*, 66: 1321–47.

2 Work, Labor, and Their Recompenses: Portuguese Life Strategies Involving "Migration"

Anthony Leeds

ABSTRACT. Leeds views migration from the country of origin, taking a multi-leveled systems approach. He asks what in the local, regional, and national levels generates migration as an integral part of individual economic strategies. He regards these levels as interdependent but not rigidly so. Each has its own characteristics and logic. Focusing on three communities representing different regions, he first discusses Salazarian economic "policies" and points out their differential effects on the three regions. Then he analyzes economic decision making from the vantage point of his informants, both those who have had migratory experience and those who have stayed at home. He concludes that migration policies of both sender and host countries, differential needs for remittances, and different local opportunities (in part also generated through migration) all influence the rate of migration, the migrant population, and the migrants' economic strategies while abroad.

MIGRATION THEORY: WEAKNESSES

Why go? Why do people leave where they are—perhaps a home place first, and later, some other place of shorter or longer stay—to go to some other place? For the most part, answers to this question in general and in specific cases seem to me gross oversimplifications. First, much of the literature reduces the question to one of *motivations* of *individuals,* more or less abstracted from the structural complexities of their lives. Migrants were "entrepreneurs," "forward-looking," "go-getters," persons wanting to rise in the social stratification system; or they were the less competent, the dumb ones who could not "make it" at home. That whole collection of "explanations" suffered from rank methodological individualism reflected in the impoverished methodological procedures used to try to isolate key, single determinants which governed or significantly influenced such motivation.

Second, another major body of literature—specifically from economics—extracted migrants not only from their social contexts but even from individuals.

Migrants were essentially a reflex of the "differential wage." The outstanding difficulty with this literature was its inability to explain either anomalies (e.g., why some migrants seemed *not* to migrate simply because of the differential wage), or why *some* people *did not migrate* at all (see below). This sort of difficulty is pronounced also in the entire literature on step- and return-migration. It all "accounts," at best, for a highly segmented and abstracted set of data without justifying either the segmentation or the abstraction, much less the decontextualization of the actors from themselves or their social settings.

Third, almost none of the literature, until very recently, dealt extensively, let alone adequately, with the home situation (see, however, works by the Buechlers on Galicia—particularly 1981 and 1983—and data-rich but inadequately analyzed material from Kemper [1977] on Tepotzlan).

Fourth, underlying the oversimplifications above is a conceptual process which, I argue, leads to major confusions, ambiguities, and even falsifications. We observe a change in the standard physical location of persons or of their activities (e.g., commuting as a form of migration) from one place to another, including a change of residence. Commuting does not entail a change of residence, a fact which is usually not made explicit but taken for granted—a point of importance if one wishes to distinguish commutes from migration.[1] On one hand, it is the *relocation* of persons and activities which becomes the defining criterion of the *category*, "migration," effectively disregarding what kinds of persons and activities, not to mention their contexts. By that abstract categorization, on the other hand, a kind of reification takes place. "Migration" becomes a thing with its own (eternal) attributes, separate from social structures and process. This abstraction and reificatory aspect shows up in the almost total *in*attention to the question, When does a migrant cease to be a migrant? or put differently, In what social circumstances has it become irrelevant to our understanding of a societal situation that a person once migrated? We still seem to operate with a sort of ethnicist bias: "Once a migrant, always a migrant."

From the point of view of places from which emigration has taken place, these issues become critical. Let me summarize briefly before turning to more detailed case materials.

First, there is always "motivation." But note: The assumptions in the migration literature have almost universally been (a) that it is *an individual's* motivation, and (b) that that individual is the person who does the migration. Not only is it the case that both of these may be false, but the assumptions themselves eliminate the social processes in and by which migration decisions often, if not always, take place.

Second, the literature standardly orients the *causal* efficacy of the migration "out there": the better wage there, the greater opportunity of life there. But neither of these nor other "out theres" is intelligible without a thorough analysis of "here." Further, the "here"/"out there" dichotomy—standard in the literature (see Uzzell 1976)—is itself a falsification because not only are there, from the point of view of "here," usually *many* "out theres," but "here" can also be seen as an "out there" (if only *some* of the circumstances can be modified, as one hopes to modify circumstances in the other "out theres"). In other words, the analyses and strategies made by the personnel involved are—I hazard a universalistic assertion—*not* simple-minded and dualistic, but complex, multilocal, conditional, and even opportunistic. With respect to such analyses and strategies, the analytic terminology of the social scientists is, in many cases, ill-defined, as in the case of what constitutes standard location and what constitutes a relocation (for example, is a biresidential migration strategy a relocation?).

Methodologically, the implications of the preceding are far-reaching. First, we need a systems model of societal conditions that incorporates a variety of movements of persons from one place to another for activities, work, residence, or combinations of these. (Please note the excision of the term "migration" in that sentence.) The systems *model* of the society, or some sub- or superordinate system with respect to it, should specify the multiplicity of variables and their various hierarchical arrangements in varied subsystems (including socially and geographically differentially located ones) in such a way that body-movements ("migration," "commutes," etc.) can be deduced as consequences of the system operation. We should be able to specify "types" and frequencies of such movements from the system model.

Second, obviously, we need far richer, conceptually more complex descriptions of the social situations in which "migration" occurs—multilocal, multiperson, and multigroup, social structural and processual description of all localities concerned *in* the "migration." Let me illustrate by brief reference to several ethnographic examples and by more extensive description derived from Portuguese materials.

First as to motivation. It may not be the individual who migrates whose motivation is involved at all, or at least, not with respect to the migratory act. The migration literature, its models formulated in a West already highly individualized both in social structural and ideological terms, virtually never conceives of such situations. Rethinking the individualist bias in terms of our *ethnographic* experience of varieties of community process, social decision-making interactions, it seems perfectly plausible to expect to find various sorts of bodies or aggregates of people as the major loci of "motivation" and decision making: an entire village community, extended families, households, networks of friends and family, and so on. So far as I know, this supposition, not having been formulated in migration research, remains to be examined ethnographically, although Lebanese and Armenian family groups are said to have been instrumental in the migration of individuals, and we know that households, extended families, and networks are often involved in financing the trip of a migrant, as in Portugal, Spain, and Somalia.[2]

PORTUGAL: FIELDWORK AND METHODOLOGY

I do not have definitive answers to the questions just posed from the Portuguese fieldwork; much more time and, above all, intimacy with the people involved are needed. However, some interesting perspectives on all these issues come out of examining the locales of heavy emigration from the methodological point of view outlined above. I shall talk mainly about one of the three villages I chose as samples of three of the major regions of Portugal, each characterized by a heavy exodus of people to a multiplicity of elsewheres. From São Martinho people migrated to Brazil from the late 1800s and later shifted to France and Germany; from Lama they went both to Brazil and Venezuela as well as Canada, the United States, and various European countries; while Santa Vitória has been mostly involved in internal migration and, after 1964, migration to Germany and France.

Methodologically, I conceive of any of these villages—or any others which might have been selected—as delimitable ecological units within a much larger system of societal ordering. They are *ecological* in that man-environment relations involve environmental, technological, material cultural and social variables, and relevant knowledge and ideology. They are *units* in that much of the array of activity and conceptualization on the part of the villagers creates recognizable boundary conditions including such aspects as community self-definition (perhaps even *emphasized* by close linkages, such as many marriages, with other, neighboring villages whose otherness is signalized by conceiving such marriages as *across* community borders and even loyalties), high levels of village-bonded work exchanges, there being bureaucratic entities or recognized subdivisions thereof (in Portugal, the *freguesia* and *lugar,* respectively, more or less "township" and "neighborhood" within it).

From the point of view of the last variable, each of the three villages I studied is different. Lama is one of 161 *freguesias* in the relatively small *conselho* (more or less "county") of Barcelos, a major (small) city of Portugal and center of the most significant fair, taking place weekly, of the entire northwest of Portugal, the Minho (see figure 2.1). It has a large number of *lugares,* needed in addressing letters, for example, or mapping, but without clear boundaries among them. São Martinho de Peva in Beira Alta, in central-northern Portugal, is a *lugar* in one of twenty *freguesias* of Moimenta da Beira *conselho* in the *distrito* (roughly "state") of Viseu (see figure 2.1). Moimenta is considerably larger than the *conselho* of Barcelos, hence, of course, the *freguesias* and *lugares* are vastly larger, reflecting radically different population densities, settlement patterns, and land use patterns. Peva, the *freguesia,* has only three *lugares,* in contrast to the eight or ten for Lama which is only about 2 km across. Each of Peva's *lugares,* again in contrast to Lama's virtually continuous distribution of settlement and complex interlocal interaction, is quite separate, distinctive, and nucleated and has a major proportion of the relations of work, family, religion, and sociality taking place in the village itself. Each even has its own patron saint. Nevertheless, *freguesia* officers are scattered among the three *lugares*. One of the villages is even set off from the other two by low, granitic ridges occupied by forests and common lands. The third village, Santa Vitória, in the Alentejo, is itself a *freguesia* with only one other settlement, a depressed, former company town of a Belgian mining company which pulled out immediately after the Republican revolution of 1910. Santa

Figure 2.1 Map of Northern Portugal

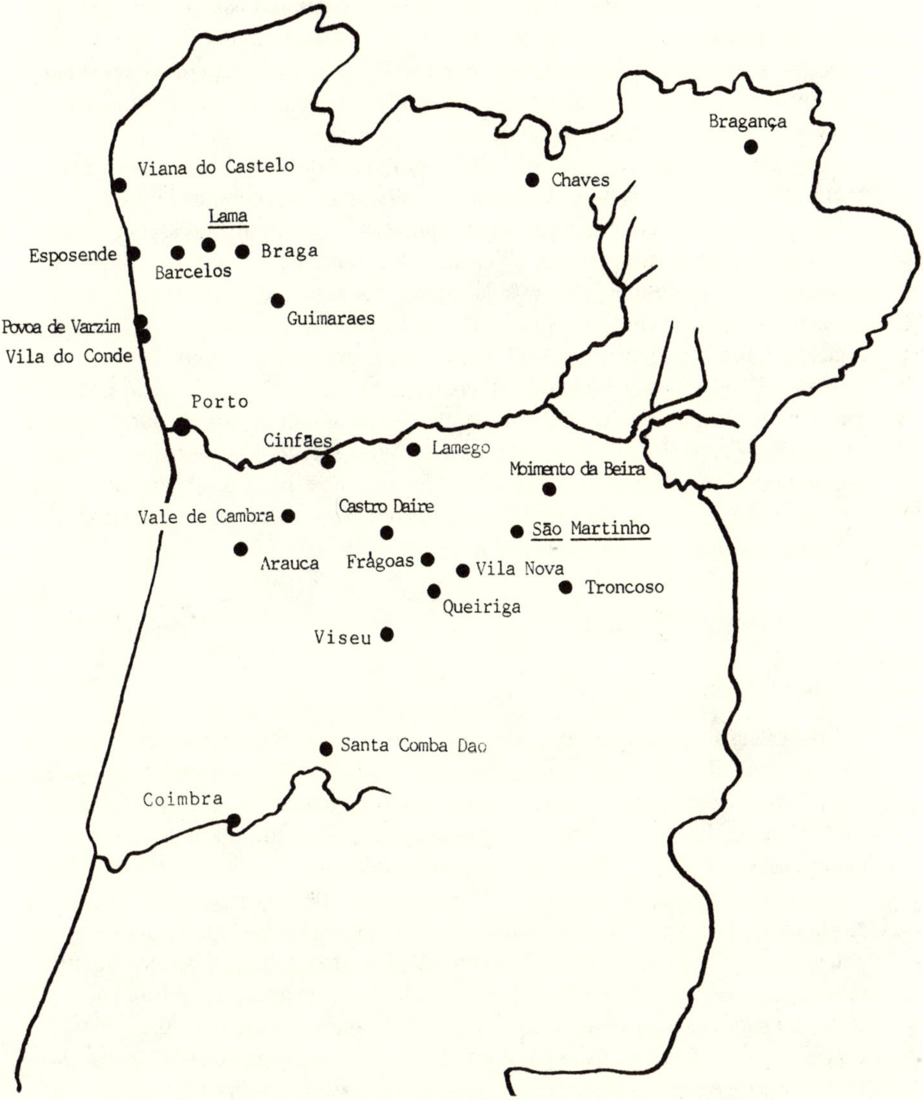

Vitória, like São Martinho, is tightly nucleated and most work and social relations take place within it (see figure 2.2).

Not only are these ecological units subsystems of a hierarchy of interlocked bureaucratic units, but they are also subsystems in respect to various more inclusive levels of economic systems—subregional, regional, subnational, national, and international.[3] These levels embrace not only marketing systems (e.g., the weekly subregional fair in Barcelos and the subnational fish distributions out of Porto going even as far as São Martinho) but institutions for agricultural production and distribution (ranging from local private and cooperative buyers to the [former] *grémios* or agricultural associations, emanating from the Ministry of Corporations of the Salazar epoch).[4]

Any local ecological units, such as the villages discussed here, were interlocked with these and had to take these, as well as the bureaucratic hierarchy, into account when planning strategies with reference to *any* significant aspect of life. Further, both (if indeed they are "two," other than purely analytically) these domains are expressions of the legal system and variously relate to specific agencies of that system (e.g., the courts, also hierarchically arranged). Even the education and health systems are hierarchically arranged, spatially.

None of this is, in itself, new, but there has been very little consideration, in the entire body of literature, of the relation of ecological units to the questions about migrants: Why go? Why stay? Who goes? Who stays? Who decides? Whose motivation? Since these questions have, for the most part, not been asked *together,* and since some have scarcely been asked at all, there has been little focus on places of origin as complex ecosystems.

THREE CASE STUDIES

São Martinho

Like Lama and to a lesser extent Santa Vitória, São Martinho produces most of its own food. Meats come from pigs, sheep, goats, chickens, and some cattle (although cows are mainly used for milk and milk products; as of 1978–1979, there were neither oxen nor bulls in the village). Milk and milk products, especially cheeses, provide subsistence, although milk has been, in recent years, the major source of village cash flows, now being rivaled by eggs and chickens. Horticulture and agriculture provide a rich array of foods—rye, wheat, corn, potatoes—and a wide range of vegetables, several storable for winter months (effectively, December through February). There is also a variety of fruit and nut trees and shrubs and several kinds of berries. A smallish portion of the grains, a very sizable proportion of the potatoes, and occasional vegetables go out of the village into the marketing system, most of the potatoes being sold in Lisbon. Cattle and a certain, now very limited, quantity of wool also move out of the village into trade.

Another product bringing cash into the village is pine resin, and some logging

Figure 2.2 Map of Southern Portugal

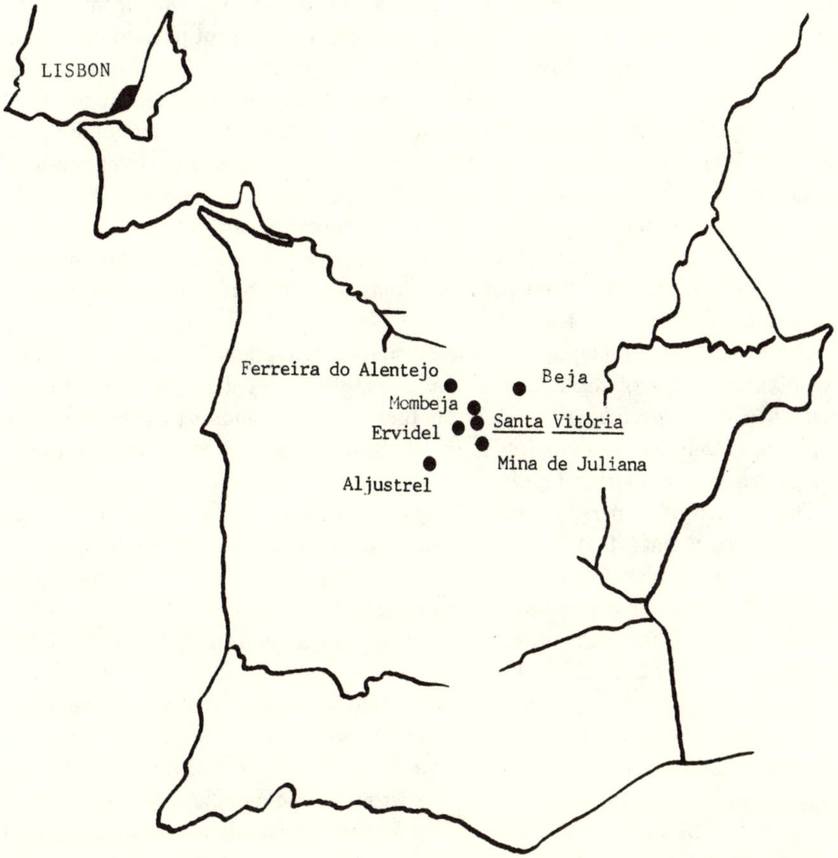

is occasionally done for lumber materials but, as of 1979, seemed to be negligible. The origins and extent of the pine plantings will be discussed below.

All of this is produced on an area not more than 9 km^2 or so, including the barren common lands; the part in crops is probably about 4 km^2 (roughly a square mile, or 640 acres) or considerably less when one calculates abandoned fields (see below). The granitic uplands of the commons are used for grazing sheep and goats; the vegetation here will not do for cattle, which are grazed on stubble, in fallow fields, or in fields planted to a forage crop succeeding the main food crop in the same season in a kind of rotational system involving all of these uses. This rotation is extended to all agricultural and horticultural practice so that, from the point of view of any particular field or garden plot, the crops change from year to year and, with some rotations, from spring to fall (e.g., wheat planted in the fall and harvested in spring, followed by another crop harvested in the fall of the same year, possibly even followed by the planting of forage for late fall grazing).

This complex rotational system of cropping, as well as the grazing not done on the commons, takes place on fields whose *maximum* sizes are rarely over one-half of an acre,[5] but more generally fall within the range of about one-third acre, small ones being about one-tenth of an acre. Garden plots, mostly clustered about the village, itself more or less in the middle of this area, are, of course, far smaller, on the average, ranging from perhaps a maximum of one-tenth of an acre to one-fiftieth of an acre or less.

The system of producing with these microunits of land is made still more complex by virtue of the fact that contiguous plots, for the most part, do not belong to the same owners, or, put another way, the landholdings of a single owner are scattered in microplots over the entire territory of São Martinho (and, occasionally, neighboring *lugares*).

This system of dispersed, tiny holdings has persisted despite attempts by the central government—first, in the Second Development Plan (1959–1964) under Salazar, then under Caetano (1968–1974) through the Lei de Emparcelamento—to consolidate small fields into larger units in part to foster more "economic" bases of mechanization.[6] Such recombinations have been successfully resisted by farmers, a subject I return to below (see Cabral 1974, 559 n.5).

Producing on such tiny, scattered plots itself involves a complex ecological-managerial strategy. Ecologically, the effort appears to be to minimize risk by balancing risk loci against each other via the concurrent use of a multiplicity of microecological niches: if something goes wrong in one, another will more or less cancel it out. Managerially, this means a continuous calculation of where to put which crop and when, taking into account past plantings, present inventories of stored grains, number and kinds of animals owned needing grains and pastures, and so on.

From the farmers' point of view, given this complex mixed farming, it is necessary to control a number of micro "niches," a control which no program of recombination *(emparcelamento)* remotely guaranteed. Hence at least one of the bases of resistance to consolidating land units discussed by Alvaro Cunhal ([1966]

1976, cited in Cabral's footnotes referred to in note 6). Another may have resided in resistance to taxation (see note 5 on the confusion in land measurements). A third may reside in the logic of partible inheritance (see below), whereby *total* value is to be divided into equal parts among heirs so that one lump of value may be a house, another a piece of land, another movable property, etc., all of which can enter into differential marriage exchanges as a way of reconstituting workable units of property and management (e.g., marry off a woman who has inherited a house, including stalls and barns, to a man who has inherited one or several pieces of land so that *property* in land does not become still more dispersed while, at the same time, it is reattached to an operational central place).

The tools of production to operate this complex system come, essentially, from outside the village. The village smiths (two in 1979; three in 1981) can convert metals coming in various forms into simple tools and material objects; the carpenter can make wooden fittings (if a farmer is himself unable to do so), but the metals must come from a larger economy (as was also the case in the so-called closed corporate communities, adumbrated by Eric Wolf (1955), of which anthropologists were so paradigmatically fond). So, too, must any tools and machines using an internal combustion motor—those used for threshing, along with the threshing machine; those used for pumps, along with pipes and cement for their housings; those housed in automotive vehicles (three or four trucks, an occasional car, and, in 1978–1979, two tractors, one of which was used only one month of the year by a migrant home on vacation); and those in such tools as buzz saws, as well as a few tools powered by electric motors. All of these, too, require fuels. Gasoline and diesel fuels necessarily come not only from outside the village and region but from outside Portugal so that, in this respect, all Portugal is a local ecosystem, and any part of it, like São Martinho, is locked into a world system involving imports, exports, balance of payment problems, trade deficits, and foreign exchange problems. *All of these are critical to what happens at local levels in the domain of migration*. Furthermore, it may be noted that the trucks, cars, tractors, and buzz saws are, for the most part, *also* imported into Portugal as well as its regions, subregions, and villages, although some are now assembled in that country. Put another way, although São Martinho is a local ecological unit, that unit is linked by a variety of market and trade hierarchies into the international system of production and exchange itself.

In the context of this production for local use and for local-unit export in exchange for local-unit import; of bureaucratic-legal costs such as tax payments (ultimately, to the next to highest level of social order, the national government), occasional litigations, divisions of properties at deaths (the registration of *partilhas*, "equal parts of total value") vehicle, motor, and group ownership (as of one of the threshing machines) registrations, and so on, villagers make enormously complex cost-benefit calculations. This process was generally evident in São Martinho and the other two villages, but particularly salient in two instances.

In standard ethnographic procedure, I had "participant observed" by helping build a roof for a farmer, who had had to employ the village carpenter to direct the work as a whole. In an animated conversation in the village post office–general store, one Sunday morning, the carpenter, the house-builder, and others discussed the problems and costs of building. The carpenter pointed out to the house-builder that the latter had failed to take into account in his calculations the free labor he was getting from Senhor António (the anthropologist).

The second occurred on a Sunday morning in September 1979, just after the government, late Saturday night, had announced abruptly the raising of all gasoline and diesel fuel prices by 30 percent. The assembled, including the carpenter who owned the only year-round working tractor in the village, analyzed, in great fury, their costs in relation to the incomes from on-farm prices for milk, potatoes, and grains; in relation to the city (chiefly Lisbon) prices for the same after middlemen's markups; and in relation to the amount of each of these produced per hectare. Given the new costs of running the tractor per hour and the amount of work it could do in *area* terms, they concluded that use of the tractor for plowing and other crop-raising and harvesting work would not pay; using the tractor would be feasible only for haulage of rocks, logs and timber, barrels of resins, and the like. This meant, in turn, that agricultural haulage and work would have to be done by cattle. As noted above, in 1979 there were no oxen or bulls in the village—only milk cows, dry cows, and calves. The calculus went on to point out that the use of cows for agricultural work would reduce the milk production, and *that* reduction, in turn, would reduce cash flows into the village—a demonetarization. That recognition was particularly angering to the villagers, a point I return to below.

Careful attention to the discussion revealed that the participants were figuring, as part of their calculations, *usually implicitly or only partly explicitly,* their labor costs at rates equivalent to what they would have to pay if they hired hands to do the work. I encountered this sort of calculation again and again, for example, while participating with one of the threshing-machine owners while he was hoeing his garden. Any excursus of complex calculation which included such implicit evaluations of own-labor costs invariably ended in statements—rhetorical I am convinced—about how the speaker wasn't making anything. These presentations were *not* accompanied by discussions of hypothetical plans—if only they were making *some*thing—to, say, invest what they made either in expanding the farm operation or in some town- or city-based operation. These operations might include an artisanal shop, a commercial venture, an industry, real estate, various forms of monetary investment, professional education involving upward class mobility, etc. Most of the villagers then living in towns and cities were doing some investing. Some of the villagers were reinvesting at home, while some then living in urban areas were also investing in specific ways *in the village* (see below). It is to be noted that most of the people who were "not making anything" (a complaint sometimes accompanied by a hitch of one shoulder, a translation of *é uma vida negra,* "it's a black life") were living *quite* comfortably, some having rebuilt old (17th and 18th century) houses, put on new additions, built new houses, bought electro-domestic equipment and other tools, radios, refrigerators (run by electricity), and so on. That is, the labor costs calculated were not real expenditures for labor, but went to the improvement of living or to investments of various sorts.

This conclusion became quite inescapable when I returned briefly to the village in 1981. Despite further rises in the prices of petroleum products ("we got used to the price rises and learned how to deal with them," said one man), there were by then *four* tractors in the village. There was no evidence that milk production had declined either because of reduced per cow flow or conversion from cows to oxen or bullocks (there was now one bull in the village). There were very sizable new investments in chickens—two quite large new henhouses. Meanwhile, the investment in housing, household and farming tools, and household equipment appears to have continued steadily. There were further reconstructions, additions, finishings of new buildings under construction in 1979, a new café in an old building, etc. In the neighboring village, perhaps a little bit larger, there were eighteen houses *on one side of the village alone,* in various stages of construction, each ultimately worth, it is estimated, about $25,000 (U.S.; in toto about $450,000) when done, mostly being constructed in summer months by persons absent because of emigration: the "suburbanization" of the "peasant village" with what are called in Portugal "casas francesas" (i.e., the houses built by emigrants who went to France).

Despite sharp increases in oil product prices and despite "not making any money" (when labor costs are calculated into production costs), life in São Martinho in 1978, 1979, and 1981 when I visited it ranged from tolerable with reasonable housing and food to quite comfortable with the enjoyment of substantial amenities, even though, it is my impression, ostentation is deliberately avoided in part to avoid envy and the evil eye.

Why leave such reasonable comfort and security, to uproot in a migrational hegira to unknown places and conditions, away from home, family, friends, one's own culture, to face, at best, an only moderately secure "out there"?

The answer is that the situation I have described is not one from which people are leaving (with one or two exceptions), but one from which people have long since mostly left: the attributes of the system I have described are themselves a result of the migration and the relationship between any and all or most of the migrants in their multiple places of migration and this home village in a complex system of strategies. Put another way, the village, as an ecological unit, increasingly became a subsystem of several larger systems and supersystems in which operates a multifaceted set of quite different links. These changing links, or relationships, are what we simplistically summarize in a single term, 'migration.'

The present house-building, investment in machinery, investment in chicken raising and businesses in São Martinho (with parallels in Lama on a lesser scale, except for the housing) and the establishment of small-town factories in the nearby county seat of the neighboring *conselho,* Vila Nova de Paiva, between 1979 and 1981—all these four factories revolving about housing and furnishings—are all products of the differential allocation of emigrants' foreign earnings and remittances to local applications.

This process can only be understood if one examines the state of the local ecosystem at an earlier time. A number of critical points where system states changed could be selected: (a) before and after the promulgation of the Law of Partible Inheritance (Lei de Partilhas) in 1863 which eliminated primogeniture and, with one stroke, began the fragmentation of landholdings so characteristic of northern Portugal;[7] (b) before and after the Republican "revolution" of 1910 which led to some changes in national capital application such that the road system in the area of Vila Nova de Paiva and São Martinho, for example, was developed; old men of the village worked on the roads in 1912 or so, but the railroad which was projected was never built; (c) before and after the rise to power of Salazar in 1928, at which point began a long-term shift in policy, effectively sacrificing continental Portuguese agriculture (whatever the formal plans), accompanied by exploitative development of the colonies to service industrial growth in Portugal itself; and (d) before and after the early 1960s when decolonization movements which had begun in British, Belgian, and French colonies around the world after World War II came to roost in the Portuguese colonies. Even though all of these remain in the memories of informants (e.g., old men actually recall their fathers and grandfathers *talking* about the fragmentation effects of the Law of Partible Inheritance of 1863) and varieties of documentary materials can be deduced, I shall deal here, in detail, only with the last which was generally more accessible to us through many different kinds of interviews. I make occasional references to the earlier significant triggerings of changes of state of the local subsystems and their inclusive systems.

The cumulative effects of land partitions through equal inheritance of value, starting in the last third of the 19th century, combined with limited development of transportation—as in the First Republic (1910–1926), linking these "hinterlands" with important towns and the southern plains region, the Alentejo—and the depressive policies of the Salazar-Caetano regime (1926–1974) towards the agricultural interior; had by the 1940s and 1950s left northern Portuguese microfundiary agricultural populations in most difficult circumstances and almost certainly exacerbated those of the rural proletariat in the Alentejo. In what follows, I give sketches of the linkages with towns, of the depressive policies—the land partitions have already been discussed for northern Portugal—and of the state of agrarian villages up to the early 1960s, using our sample of three villages as examples, although São Martinho will continue to serve as the main one.

In the early decades of this century, the significant towns, from the perspective of any of the three villages, were still relatively small places with agricultural lands surrounding them so that food needs could largely be locally met.[8] That is, "remote" areas, like Beira Alta and Tras-os-Montes were not yet significant as major suppliers of food for the major town markets. In the north, the more important towns, from the point of view of São Martinho, are, today, Moimenta da Beira, the seat of the *conselho* where many administrative matters are taken care of, 18 km away; Vila Nova de Paiva, the seat of the neighboring *conselho* where many service needs are cared for, 5 or 6 km away; Viseu, the *distrito* capital, 40 km away; Coimbra, a *distrito* and subnational capital, about 125 km away; Lamego, a *conselho,* a commercial center, and a subnational religious center (to which men of middle years and older report having made pilgrimages *afoot,* that is, in the early and middle decades of this century), about 40 km away; Porto, a *distrito* and a regional and subnational capital and international port, about 125 km away; and Lisbon, a *conselho,* a *distrito,* and the national capital and an international port, also excercising some regional functions, about 335 km away.

This very widespread network of towns, even at very substantial distances from São Martinho, reflects its highly specialized agricultural aspect and the virtual absence until 1980 or 1981 of *any* significant industrial or medium or large-scale commercial activity in the subregion. Alternatives to the resources, conditions, and constraints of the immediate area all lay elsewhere. In times when transportation was far less developed and the towns themselves afforded far fewer alternative resources, alternatives largely lay outside the country. As will be argued, it is no accident that this area, in fact the whole region, has a history of vast emigration to Brazil from the late 1800s on (see Oliveira Martins 1887). A number of informants described Rio de Janeiro in the 1920s (one made a revisit—to his children—in 1976) and Caracas not long after; one man's grandfather had gone to Manaus in the rubber boom of the 1860s, coming back with nothing but a large bottle (garafão) whence the nickname for the whole family and its elder man who told me the story. My wife and I even found personal names (like Floripes) which we knew from our fieldwork in Brazil but had not encountered in Lisbon or in our other two villages. We also met a few persons who had returned quite recently from long periods in Brazil to settle again permanently in Portugal, specifically Lisbon. We also met several people still living in Brazil who came back for village ceremonies or just for visits. That is, ties with Brazil have been continuous and transgenerational for over 100 years in the São Martinho area. Others, still, told us of reports their cousins from the neighboring village wrote home about Newark, New Jersey (the cousins sent us a Christmas card because we had twice visited São Martinho, and hence were honorarily part of the networks, and I later visited [1983] the cousins). In sum, over the past six or seven decades, partly because of world events such as the Depression and World War II and partly because of the internal, city-based, industrial development of Portugal, the network of significant towns shifted from those in the Americas, especially South America, to those in the more accessible northern Europe—chiefly, for São Martinho, France, and Germany—and to those in Portugal. This shift began to be clearly visible around 1950 or a little later and accelerated throughout the next twenty or more years, specifically till 1973–1974 and applies also to Lama and, to a lesser extent, Santa Vitória.

However, up till the first years of the 1960s, the village remained substantially in the conditions adverted to—relatively isolated from Portuguese towns, largely involved in subsistence agriculture based exclusively on animal and manual labor, extremely limitedly involved as consumers of city-made things, markedly high rates of illiteracy (still today about 80 percent in some parts of Tras-os-Montes), sometimes disastrously bad health conditions, malnutrition, and high mortality rates, especially for infants, and so on.[9]

Lama

Lama, our sample village in the Minho of northwest Portugal, has long been, like all "villages"[10] in that area, more closely linked than São Martinho with cities. These cities were also much smaller in the early decades of the century, in part as a result of national policies from the mid-19th century on, than they are today.[11] It is 18 km from the *distrito* and subregional capital Braga, long a major religious center ("the Rome of Portugal"), near a pilgrimage center, and now also an industrial center and railhead; 12 km from the *conselho* and subregional capital Barcelos, the site of the major fair each week for the whole northwestern sector of the Minho and itself an industrial center and railhead; about 30 km from the *distrito* and subregional capital Viana do Castelo, with a small shipyard and, today, a cellulose plant; 30 km from the *conselho* and subregional capital Guimarães, a major textile-producing town; about 25 km from Famalicão, an important industrial town, and about the same distance or a little more from a series of industrial towns along the coast (Esposende, Vila do Conde, Póvoa de Varzim), themselves outposts of Porto, about 55 km away. It is about 350 km from Lisbon. From Lama, today, there is daily movement back and forth to most of the places listed (excepting Guimarães, Viana, and Lisbon) and less frequent, though still relatively numerous and sometimes crucial trips to the others, especially Lisbon, to which pottery, its major economic base, is—and has long been—sent (we have even seen Lama pottery in the municipal market in Beja in the Alentejo; it is universally known as *louça regional,* "regional pottery").

This network of linkages reflects ties of considerable time depth, a function of the penetration of industry in the 19th and 20th centuries, and earlier (even as early as the 12th century), commercial artisanry, for example, linens, a reduced quantity of which are still produced for the tourist trade, hence, too, a certain amount of labor-intensive flax growing in the region. Despite a fairly long-standing and presently increasing export of pottery and other ceramics, as well as a variety of textiles, metallurgical products, and so on, to Lisbon and to most other cities of the country (as well as abroad), a very large proportion of trade and exchange goes on among villages and towns at the subregional and regional levels. In important ways, all of the towns listed, and all of the villages scattered among them, can be analytically considered part of metropolitan Porto,[12] in part because of a variety of forms of commuting from various hinterland areas in reach of that city. In general, then, the links with the towns are, and have long been, quite different from those of São Martinho, partly because of the almost tiny distances involved (11 miles to Braga, 7 to Barcelos, .6 to the neighboring village, which today has Portugal's largest shirt factory, partly financed by

German capital) and partly because of the penetration of industry throughout the area.

It is important, however, to see this as a *cumulative* process (a point which will be discussed more fully below) and one which accelerated, notably from the early 1960s on. That cumulation over time changed the relation of the agricultural sector to the industrial sector and to the growing, larger industrial towns. On one hand, the agricultural sector in this area came increasingly to be a depressor of and partial substitute for wages[13] and, on the other, a small-scale commercially oriented provider of city needs, especially milk and milk products, fresh vegetables, and chickens and rabbits (the villages, in turn, are on daily fish runs coming out of the Porto area). The pattern of investment in housing we found in São Martinho was paralleled in Lama, especially by emigrant money either brought or sent back. There was also investment by owners of the ceramic shops out of their profits, while their paid workers were limited rather to physical improvements. Some of Lama's *casas francesas* are real mansions.

Santa Vitória

Santa Vitória, in the latifundiary Alentejo, can be partly understood as a "company town" for sundry latifundia which permitted only minimal land use for subsistence. Most of the population does not own land at all but now gets garden areas in the collectively held stream bottomlands, although there are some "medium" peasants there as well. As a result, some of the exiguous cash flows of latifundium workers and members of their families earning cash only via migration outside the region, to Lisbon, or, later, abroad, had to be used for food and household supplies. As in the other two communities studied, earnings are also invested in *casas francesas*.

Santa Vitória has negligible connections with the *conselho* and mining town of Aljustrel about 15 km away; with the *conselho* of Ferreira do Alentejo, an agricultural center about the same distance away; and even with the agricultural center and *freguesia* of Ervidel, 7 km away, except for visits from the padre. Santa Vitória's main connection, for work, supplies, transportation to more distant places, bureaucratic needs, etc., is Beja, 18 km away in a different direction from all these, the capital of both the *conselho* and the *distrito,* and the subregional city whose superordinate city is Lisbon. Other than possibly for limited grains and some meats, it is not, and appears never was, a major supplier of foods to these cities, all of which appear to import large proportions of their food from other parts of the country (e.g., fruit from the Algarve to the south). Major production emanating from the village and its agricultural areas has, until recently, essentially involved agricultural commodities either for use in Lisbon (cattle, swine, wheat, and olives), or for export (cork, and more recently, sunflower seed, cardamom, as well as olives and some wine, and also recently, some baled straw to be used as fodder and bedding in the north; some of the cork went to the Lisbon area, much to the north, the major export-wine producing area of the country).

The ties with Lisbon, only about 180 km away, have been facilitated for Alentejo residents by easier transportation and by the relatively shorter distances, which also made possible in the subregion a considerable internal migration among smaller towns like Aljustrel and Beja and latifundiary headquarters in search of scarce jobs, short-term or part-time—a pattern reconstructible for the 1920s through the 1950s from residence and birth records in the civil registry.

Implicit in the preceding material on Santa Vitória is the fact that it is a very different sort of ecosystem from either São Martinho or Lama. The village itself, with the exception of the few short years since the "Revolution" of 1974,[14] was never the operational center of local production as in the other villages. Local production operations were centered in the latifundiary farmsteads, sometimes under the direction of the owner, sometimes of a relative, sometimes of a representative. Decisions were made, capital—if any—allocated, labor ordered, not by the actual producers—the rural, wage-earning proletariat—themselves but by a class quite separate from themselves, few of whose members, if any, lived in the village.[15] The land, including that in and about the village, belonged to others so that there was even very little subsistence gardening.[16] Farm workers, or rather the farm-worker household, effectively imported foods as, of course, did the village as a whole. The village, then, was mostly a coresidential social system, tied into a more extensive, local production system with other such villages in it (e.g., Mina de Juliana, the old Belgian mining village in the *freguesia* of Santa Vitória; Ervidel, Mombeja, and possibly one or two more).

The linkages with towns reflect very limited abilities for the people to avail themselves of either the service sectors or the sporadic job possibilities during times of seasonal unemployment. The other resource alternatives were extremely limited, only really beginning to appear with the development of Lisbon beginning in the earlier 1940s and on.[17]

EFFECTS OF SALAZAR POLICIES ON PORTUGAL AND THE THREE REGIONS

The Salazar policies which so negatively affected continental Portuguese agriculture, especially in the north, include the 1939 Lei de Baldios (the Law of the Common Lands), which in effect declared the common lands to be property of and disposable by the state, rather than of the communities in which they were located. The state then proceeded to allocate a great part of the common lands, up till then part of the agricultural-pastoral ecosystems of agrarian villages in all northern Portugal (except perhaps the western parts of the Minho and other coastal areas long since ingested into the commercial-industrial system which developed in the 19th century), to forestry uses directed at industry (paper pulp, resins, eucalyptus oils). The *baldios* had already disappeared throughout the Alentejo by the early 19th century, swallowed up by the latifundiary system. Second, the policies produced the corporativist structure of *grémios* (see above), which maintained or strengthened class differences in the areas being discussed. Third was the absence of capital investment in transportation and irrigation (except for a couple of major works in the Alentejo in the 1950s or even earlier) while, at the same time, flooding vast areas of farmlands, mostly in the north, in order to produce hydroelectric power.[18] Finally, there was the program called "As Sobras de Portugal" ("The Portuguese Surpluses").[19]

I shall briefly describe aspects of each of these, recognizing, first, that there were also other negative policies and, second, that there were policies which formally appear to have been positive but operated, intentionally I am convinced,[20] in fact negatively, for example, the Wheat Campaign starting in 1929; the Tomato Campaign some years later; the land reorganization schemes under the Junta de Colonização Interna (Internal Colonization Council), whose few and very limited efforts have long since disappeared back into latifundiary holdings. All these must be treated at length at another time (see Cabral 1974; Cunhal 1966).

The effects of the Law of the Common Lands, *generally,* were not merely to reduce the amount of land available for the pastoral agriculture of the villages but to cut back key parts of the communities' economies. The majority of the *baldios* were used for pasturing sheep, goats, or, if less barren, cattle. Early in our fieldwork, on a side trip, we got into conversation with a man in a street in Bragança, Tras-os-Montes. His comment was one of those revelatory keys which illuminated so much of the fieldwork in the northern rural areas and helped fit oddments of observation into place. For instance, in 1977 when I first drove into Portugal from the north through Chaves to Braga, I saw the endless forestation projects, obviously planned and orderly, of pines and eucalyptus, the oldest, judging from their size, plainly about forty years at maximum (i.e., about 1939).[21] The man in Bragança said that the government, through the then new Junta Forestal (Forestry Council) took over the *baldios* where cattle had grazed to plant them in pines in particular. The results were that certain local individuals, specifically those tied to the Junta, rapidly grew wealthier as the use of these lands was handed over to them, essentially as ownership, while the general populations of the communities which had depended on them suddenly found themselves with part of their subsistence base gone. He explicitly connected this situation with the fact that younger men were forced to emigrate.[22]

This was the general pattern. Pine and eucalyptus forests (both on *baldios* and on private holdings, planted especially by people who emigrated, leaving no labor force behind, but, rather, a permanent crop needing minimum tending) are to be seen throughout Portugal north of the Tejo River, even some south of it in the Alentejo ("beyond the Tejo"), and vast eucalyptus groves in the upper Alentejo—in the central easterly part of the country.

Being Portugal, the outcomes of the law were not so simple as the general case described above would suggest. São Martinho—a fact I did not know when I selected it—did not have its common lands expropriated. This was due to the intervention at top levels of government by a one-time ambassador to Germany and famous historian-novelist, Aquilino Ribeiro, who happened to have been born in one of the *lugares* of the *freguesia* of Peva. Personalism and favoritism saved the *baldios* for the communities of Peva. Another village, Queiriga, about 15 km to the south, was able to keep its *baldios* by the persistence of the local padre who pestered the appropriate ministry till his petition was heard and granted. Still another community, Pendilhe, about the same distance to the west of São Martinho, anticipating the expropriation of the common lands, divided them up equitably among all the heads of households of the village in private holdings, thus outflanking the government. These areas are still in farms rather than forested. Frágoas, about 10 km to the southwest of São Martinho, worked out a deal with the government by which the latter got the major percentage of profit from the forestry crops and the community the minor part (80/20, as I recall, for the first decades and renegotiated in recent years for a better percentage for the village). An improved percentage for the village depended on whether the community took over more of the labor input or administrative responsibility. Labor was already short in the early years due to emigration. In the case of Frágoas and some of the other villages of the area, common lands were in fact converted to forestry uses with corresponding loss of pasture lands and pressure to emigrate as consequences.

One macroeffect (linked, also, to other contributing causes to which I advert below) of this takeover of common lands was the gradual decline of food production in the country as a whole—a cumulative effect leading to the present condition in which over 50 percent of the foodstuffs of Portugal are imported. This, of course, creates major balance of trade problems, a situation directly connected with emigration, as will be seen below.

It is my impression that the Lei de Baldios had much less effect in the area of the Minho and Lama than in the São Martinho area. First, although I think there were still some *baldios* on the hilltops, the agricultural land use has, in part for physical geographical and climatic reasons, long been much more intensive while considerably less dependent on, particularly, sheep and goats. There is a very intensive cattle-crop-stubble-pasture cycling but minimal sheep and goat herding, if any, in some places in the Minho. There are, however, fairly extensive pine forests on the upper slopes of a number of the steeper, low mountains of the area which may have been *baldios,* but do not figure in the awareness of most of the middle-aged and younger people I spoke with in Lama as they do in the Peva and Tras-os-Montes area. Another reason why the *baldios* did not figure so drastically in the local economy underlying migration in the northwest Minho is that the entire area is pervaded by industry (today ranging from artisanal to modern high-tech) dispersed everywhere, making use of a very large labor force potential in the area, whose population density is on the order of 400 per square mile. The area's agriculture essentially operates as subsistence supplier, allowing entrepreneurs to pay relatively low wages (see, e.g., E. Leeds 1984, chap. 3, sections 7 and 8). As already noted, in the Alentejo the *baldios* had disappeared earlier in the context of (in the 18th century) a Church-dominated and, later, a secular latifundiary system. The effects of the disappearance of the common lands in this area long preceded the times under consideration here and require long-term research.

The second area of Salazarist policies which contributed to the difficult circumstances of small farmers was the corporativist structure which created the *grémios*,[23] here, those constituted by agricultural producers called *grémios de lavoura*. Ostensibly, in the corporativist conception, all persons of a similar category of interests, for example farmers, industrialists, etc., were equal members of a corporation or corporative group—the *grémios*—which, *as entities,* represented these interests to and in the government, specifically through the Ministry of Corporations, and, in turn, were "granted . . . representational monopoly and formal access to various advisory and deliberative councils" (Schmitter 1975, 22). The *grémios* became part of the economic and bureaucratic regulatory system of the state, one deliberately aimed at preventing the spontaneous organization of class interest groups (Schmitter 1975, 22).

In fact, and by law, however, the *grémios* operated to maintain striking class distinctions, a phenomenon which has continued since 1974 when the *grémios* were discontinued and various other forms of association such as "cooperatives" were instituted. Schmitter's summary of the *grémios'* mechanisms for creating class distinctions is revealing:

> Once set up by the state or individual initiative in a given *freguesia* [almost certainly *conselho*] or district, membership automatically became mandatory for all. The usual ministerial controls over elections, political activity and financial accounting were imposed. . . . Agricultural guilds could only be created by landowners who paid more than a certain minimum amount of taxes and who were not simultaneously salaried. As if this were not enough to ensure that they would not fall into the hands of the very numerous class of medium and small peasants, access to the general council of these *Grémios* was reserved for "the twenty largest producers residing in a given area" plus some representatives elected by the other producers. (Schmitter 1975)

Persons interviewed added other dimensions to this stratificational process. The larger farmers were almost without exception also literate, as were—for tactical reasons—the persons elected. The structural result was to create fairly marked class boundaries of literate, bureaucratic controllers of the *grémios,* which were concerned with marketing, prices, and supplying (e.g., fertilizers). Reports consistently told of the self-serving advantage held by the controlling council at the expense of the poorer, smaller, and illiterate farmers—for example, in acting as middlemen for the transfer of fertilizers (manufactured largely by the huge national conglomerate of the Melo family, which also controlled other chemical industries and the internationally important Lisnave shipyards in Lisbon) to the rural users.

In brief, whatever the ostensible intent, the effect was a still largely unstudied degree of *exploitation* and *demonetarization* of the majority of small farmers in the northern two-thirds of Portugal.

The third area of Salazarist policies, adverted to above, contributing to the difficult circumstances of farmers generally and microfundiary farmers in particular was that related to the development of infrastructures important to agriculture, specifically transportation and irrigation.

Still in 1986 there are parts of the northeast of Portugal—Tras-os-Montes and neighboring areas of Beira Alta—which have no railroad at all. Where there is a railroad, it is only a meter-gauge track, Santa Comba Dão, not far from Coimbra, being a major transshipment point from the standard European and American gauge railroads of central, coastal, and southern Portugal. Transferring goods, of course, adds to their cost. This archaic and minimal system contributes to the general difficulty of moving goods and services in and out, hence to the general "remoteness" (the word the Portuguese themselves use about the area).

Although a railroad (meter-gauge) goes from Santa Comba Dão to Viseu, it ends there. There was no railroad in any direction to the north of Viseu till one gets to the Douro valley 60 or 70 miles to the north. Thus whole *conselhos* and important towns like Vila Nova de Paiva, Moimenta da Beira, Satão, Castro Daire, Trancoso, Arouca, Castelo de Paiva, Cinfães, Vale de Cambra, Penedono, Pinhel, Sernancelhe, and many others are served by no railroad at all (a distance of about 150 miles from east to west). Thus, São Martinho is 40 km from the nearest railroad. All transportation is by motor vehicle, by animal-drawn cart, or by foot.

The northwestern Minho, as noted earlier, an extremely densely populated area with dispersed cities, towns, and villages, is effectively served by railroads. A major regular-gauge line goes out from Porto along the coast to all the industrial towns to the north and on into Spain, while another line goes north-northeast, dividing into two at Nine to go on, respectively, to the industrial cities of Barcelos (and then on to Viana do Castelo) and Braga, "the Rome of Portugal." Today one can even get direct passenger accommodations from both towns to Lisbon, or, at worst, change trains in Porto. Still another line goes to Guimarães and another to the east-northeast to Penafiel (intimately involved in "pendular" migration to Porto[24]) and to Amarante which has a major furniture factory (Tabopan, one of several by the same name with the same owners in various locations in the north). A spur goes on from Amarante to the northeast for some twenty-odd miles, then stops, leaving the entire area to the north, northeast, and northwest of the railhead without train service up to the very borders of Spain.

Lama itself is, of course, not on a railroad but is close to the railroad lines going to Barcelos and ending in Braga. Getting pottery out of Lama requires trucking (formerly, presumably, cartage). In fact, today, as far as I know, all is done by trucking. Goods and raw materials are brought in by truck (or private car). In earlier years, before the investment in trucks, taxis, cars, buses, goods from outside were far scarcer and more expensive in real terms, while cash was very limited (see below).

The Alentejo is fairly well served by railroads of standard gauge, except for the entire south-central area. Santa Vitória itself is near a railroad which runs through one of the latifundia with which it was connected as the residence place of the labor supply. Clearly, the railroads served chiefly the latifundia in moving produce out and goods and materials in, rather than facilitating working-class passenger movements.

Generally speaking, in Portugal major roads, such as they are, have been developed for some time, some even from the early part of this century, if not before. However, connecting roads range from limited to poor (and are sometimes even left off the road maps, as the perfectly good and important connecting road between the two important subregional centers of Castro Daire and Vila Nova de Paiva was left off one of our maps), while roads leading into the more inward hinterlands range from deplorable to mere tracks (and some are marked as such on the ordinance maps).

This is perhaps most evident not only in the minifundiary northeast and in the Beiras, but also in large areas of the Alentejo. For example, the main road from Vila Nova de Paiva to Moimenta to the north is quite adequate (generally like a two-lane county road in the United States) and well paved. The kilometer of road going off to São Martinho is in partial decay, though once paved and accessible to automobile use at least since 1945 (date of one of the ordinance maps at hand). The road between São Martinho and Póvoa (and Cerdeira and Touro) 2–3 km away over the ridge is a trail, though it is now regularly used by the co-op milk truck on its rounds. From Póvoa on to Touro, the road is improved somewhat; still more so from Touro back towards Vila Nova. The road from the main road to Segões to the east was beaten earth for several kilometers and paved beyond that when we first went there in 1979, but more of it was paved by 1981. (In Beira Baixa the road from Louisã to Pedrogão Grande is marked as a major connecting road on road maps. In fact, much of it is a dirt road, in certain sections wide enough for only one vehicle essentially driving in two ruts.) Some of these secondary and tertiary connecting roads have only recently been "improved," like the ones linking São Martinho to Póvoa and beyond. In other words, they virtually did not exist before 1961. Transportation, at least locally, is almost exclusively described in terms of horses and cattle, saddle bags and carts, or on foot.

In the Alentejo, even today, there are really vast areas—as much as twenty or more miles across—with no formal roads on them, although one can get across the rather flat lands of the plains by truck or car on trails. Santa Vitória is on an important connecting road. Although Mina de Juliana, in the *freguesia* of Santa Vitória, is reachable by a recently paved road of 6 km, that road ends there—as does the electric line which arrived there only in the late 1970s. Anything beyond—to the cork orchards, fields etc.—is over trails, today managed with trucks and tractors, formerly by the same means as those described for São Martinho. This situation is repeated again and again in the Alentejo: even today a large part of the area is accessible only by farm trails, not even a network of dirt roads, properly speaking. The recency of paving and electricity in Mina de Juliana indicates how much worse conditions were before the revolution, and still worse before the development efforts of the mid- and late-1960s.

In the Lama area, the secondary road linking Lama to Barcelos and Braga is well paved and adequate for trucks and buses but is relatively recent. Residents describe the conditions of the dirt road and of hard transit in the early 1960s (before some of the presently operating textile factories were established)—including the need for hostelries because the travel between major towns was so arduous and slow. For that period and earlier—"before slavery ended" (see below) as one respondent said—much local transportation was done on foot, carrying bundles. Although this persists (e.g., in our respondent's fish-delivery service), a great deal is now done with small trucks, cars, and mopeds, as well as with cattle carts.

Even today, some of the roads leading off this main local artery are in various states of marginal passability, a couple virtually impassable after heavy rains by virtue of mud and exposed rock. From residents' descriptions, this appears to have been generally the case in the period under discussion. Under those conditions, moving products or milk to market was exceedingly difficult—especially for the poorer farmers who were more or less, therefore, automatically locked into a subsistence production system.

Another major dimension of Salazar policies respecting infrastructures concerned the use of water resources. As a broad generalization, it may be said that the state appropriated water resources almost exclusively for industrial uses, rather than for agricultural uses. This process began largely after World War II but expanded rapidly in the late 1950s, throughout the 1960s, and continued through the 1970s, even after the "Revolution" of 1974, and into the 1980s. *Still* today, relatively short shrift is being given to the use of water for agricultural programs (e.g., the endless and continuing delays in completing the dam and reservoir of Alqueva which is to be used for irrigation).

Although several major irrigation reservoirs were built in the Alentejo starting perhaps as early as the late 1930s in the lower Sado River basin and east of the Coruche area in the mid-1950s (as a result of the First Development Plan, 1953–1958), most of the capital inputs for water control in the country were invested in hydroelectric power systems, the majority, broadly speaking, in the northern part of Portugal. This phenomenon is clearly to be seen in driving, for example, between Chaves and Braga—dam after dam in deep narrow valleys, with turbines, or again, in the Mondego River valley, as in the recently completed hydroelectric dam between Penacova and Santa Comba Dão.

The effects of putting in these and other dams in northern Portugal are plain to see. Farms went under water, both in the river bottoms and on the hillsides. We saw this process happening on the Mondego River. In 1979, before the huge dam northeast of Coimbra had been completed, obviously after many years of work begun during the Caetano era, the old corrals, farmhouses, and plowed and stubbled fields, both in the valley bottoms and on the hillsides—all abandoned already then—were still visible. By November 1981 these thousands upon thousands of hectares were inundated by an enormous reservoir that served exclusively hydroelectric ends; the land was obviously permanently lost not only to agricultural production but to rural residential-subsistence. More bluntly, the farming population here, as in all the other flooded farming areas over the decades, had to get out. From the late 1950s through the early 1970s, one major option for working-age people was emigration. Presumably, that majority of older and younger people and children (as well as most of the wives who were kept in Portugal by the state's emigration controls) who could not be absorbed on the farmlands of relatives or otherwise in other farming communities went to the industrial towns and cities of Portugal which were to be served by the hydroelectric power as industrial investment expanded. Town growth figures confirm this supposition, as does the rise in official and clandestine emigration, especially beginning with 1961.[25] A related phenomenon, of course, is the increase in foodstuff importation into Portugal, presently over 50 percent of all foods used.

WHY GO?: THE UNTANGLING OF THE WEB

In sum, before the early 1960s the local ecosystems represented by our three villages and their regions were in really quite difficult circumstances—relatively isolated from towns, markets, services, and social welfare benefits (which often did not exist at all in the rural areas): the people impoverished, with minimal access to education (self-perpetuating) or health care and subject to an institutionally reinforced, exploitative class system, appropriating, by various means, "surplus labor value." The Alentejo villages were locked into a highly repressive and exploitative wage system, without subsistence plots, and without formal (if tenuous) representation in the corporativist system. They had experienced dramatic extraction of surplus value in the form of the Sobras de Portugal, disastrous uprootings from at least the 1950s on by virtue of river dammings and farmland inundations with constriction of available lands at the edges of the floodings for those farmers who were able to remain (though these results did not affect our specific villages). Residents of all three villages constantly talk of hunger ("era uma época de fame"), the difficulties of fulfilling basic needs, the intense laboriousness of life in order to keep going, the unavoidability of carrying on sub rosa activities (e.g., hiding grains under saddlebags while traveling from one village to another, described by one man who called all this *a vida de candonga* "the contraband life") to make possible the barest minimum of exchange of necessities. It was critical that activities be concealed from the authorities, specifically the PIDEs.[26] The more one hears these tales, reports, phrases, and metaphors of description, the more gruesome the picture becomes.

The key to understanding the difficult circumstances was given to us in an extraordinary interview with a 24-year-old migrant from a small village in Tras-os-Montes working in a restaurant in Paris. His brother, running a small store in a small community of officially illegal houses (*casas clandestinas*) near the airport in Libson had told us where we could find him in Paris. Eventually we tracked him down to a room in a rooming house where he had a bed, a small table, a chair, a stove, and a new 16-year-old wife with whom he had just returned, along with a smoked haunch of pig, from their wedding in Tras-os-Montes. By their hospitality, we ate of the wedding ham.

There were three major points to the interview. One was his analysis of why the Left would never win power in France because of the general imperial structure of the presidency, its relation to the French National Assembly, its control of the press, its control of other power systems—all assertions whose truth I later confirmed with various French social scientists and officials. This feat of analysis is significant in the perspective it gives of how well migrants and their relatives at home are capable of seeing and interpreting the superstructures with which they articulate—a perspective directly contrary to anthropological paradigms and stereotypes about "closed corporate communities" and "peasant societies." João Afonso was not unique in this capacity, as endless conversations in our three villages bore in on us.

The second dealt with strategies of handling the exchange system—when to hold francs, when to exchange them for escudos, etc.—in order best to build capital, maintain liquidity, take advantage of shifting conditions, and, ultimately, open up a tourist-oriented pizza shop on Avenida Liberdade, the central axial avenue of Lisbon (an excellent plan—there is none now!).

The third part gave us our fundamental clue to many matters about the Portuguese political economy in its relation to migration. "There was no money in the villages," said João Afonso. He made a kind of inventory of his father's roughly seventy holdings of pieces of land and argued that this was ordinarily more than enough to supply food for the whole family, as well as to supply building needs. The problem was *not* lands, food, housing, etc., under ordinary conditions, but lack of cash under extraordinary conditions. No emergency could be met. If, said he, a major storm came over and destroyed a major part of the wheat or rye crops, there was nothing to fall back on, no money with which to buy food. Under the Salazar policies, welfare programs had not reached the rural areas, at least the more remote ones. If one fell sick, there was no money for treatment, hospitals, or doctors.[27] Education was in a worse state then than it is today in villages like São Martinho, Lama, and Santa Vitória, where the whole system of education persists in maintaining sharp class differences and differentiating those few who can, for unique reasons, achieve upward mobility from those who structurally have virtually no means to anything much beyond primary school education.[28] João said, "We left in search of cash."

Cash was the crux. Village Portugal was, by virtue of the operation of the whole set of institutions discussed above, *demonetarized.* There is much evidence for the Salazar period, and if not for earlier ones at least by 1863 when the Law of Partible Inheritance was passed, that this was quite deliberate, one major set of reasons being to have a manipulable labor reserve at the service of various governmental programs and policies. Demonetarization effectively continued till 1961.

It is significant to note that it was this devastating demonetarized condition which supplied so much of the animus in the angry discussion in the post office in São Martinho after the gasoline prices went up. Everyone over 25 or so recalled life without money—the labor, the Sobras (see notes 29 and 30), the *vida de candonga,* the fragility of health and food conditions, the inaccessibility of education, etc. With higher gas costs, they saw the anticipated shift to reducing the number of milk cows, hence the cash flows, as a return to that prior, highly undesirable condition, one which drove people out of their home places, away from their homes and hearths, away from their families and intimates for their own welfare, security, and safety.

Up till 1961, then, according to villagers and other sources, this was substantially the state of affairs not only in São Martinho, Lama (still "the epoch of slavery"; see below), and Santa Vitória, but throughout the country, especially in the small-holding north. As one woman in Lama said (in 1979), "When slavery ended. . . . " "When was that?" I asked. "Oh, about fifteen years ago," that is, somewhere after 1961 up to around 1964 (a date I return to below).

Various strands of information gleaned from interviews and other sources in the villages of our sample and elsewhere made powerfully clear this demonetarized state of affairs and its implications at the village level. João Gomes pulled out a felt mantle used for a raincoat. "This is the last one made in the village [São Martinho]." "When?" "About 18 years ago" (i.e., 1961). Oddments of conversation, partly stimulated by earlier conversations and interviews in Lama about the linen trade and its history, revealed that linen-making also stopped abruptly, just about the same time. From conversations in 1981, when a schoolteacher from Vila Nova de Paiva took me to visit several other villages in this same geographical-ecological region, from a dissertation by Almquist (1977), and from a museum in Ponte de Lima in the Minho which has paintings of the various stages of the linen-making process, I learned that both felt- and linen-making are enormously arduous, labor-intensive activities requiring tools or, at most, relatively simple machines which can be locally made of wood and limited quantities of metal (e.g., felting hammers on cams run by waterwheels in the small felting plants along the Paiva River which runs near most of these villages). All but one of these are now closed down. Not only can the tools be locally made, for the most part, but the raw materials for the product are locally grown—wool and flax in particular. That is, the raw materials of both and the tools for making both—as well as the labor supply—were all part of the local ecosystem demonetarized at the expense of a huge labor input and of security, well-being, and the amenities of life. It will be recalled that all of this was done by hand, or was at most animal- or water-powered work, since electricity, still absent today in many villages of "more remote" Portugal, existed virtually nowhere in rural areas at that time. Not only was life exceedingly toilsome, but also uncomfortable (e.g., in housing and householding conditions), and fragile as in health care.

Many other conversations made quite clear that labor-intensive activities, in the absence of cash, were enmeshed, necessarily, in an in-kind system of exchange given some specialization ecologically, occupationally, and in terms of land tenure and use. Not all users of land were owners; some rented. This meant that the full array of ecologically specialized field locations was not always available to them. Similarly, not all farmers were able to carry out the full array of agricultural tasks for total self-subsistence.

Further, given how the partible inheritance worked, there were some households which did not have land or had wholly inadequate areas and varieties of land. This was the case, for example, of Don Alfredo, a man who had married into the village, bringing with him almost exclusively portables, while losing connection with his home village to the north. The wife was one of a number of siblings. Even in the cashless times, they became traders, and virtually all of their trade was in-kind. He described exchanges of produce from the village, for cloth, for items for the fair, for foods—all of it virtually without cash.[29]

In the mid- or late-1930s, Don Alfredo also became a contractor for agricultural laborers and, for one period, for laborers to work on the irrigation system on the Sado River in the Alentejo. These laborers sought cash by going to the Alentejo, especially the rice fields in the Alçácer do Sal region along the lower Sado. Don Alfredo's wife was one of the women migrants, as was her sister. One of their sons—through whom and whose wife I originally got to São Martinho—was born virtually in the rice fields where migrants worked literally from dawn to dusk standing in water while sleeping nights in separate barracks for men and for women and small children where all were fed from a sort of soup-kitchen food line. (The men, the women, and the lads were even transported down to the Alentejo in separate trucks.) These internal, rural-to-rural migrations were called *ranchos* and are reported as early as the mid-19th century (Silva Picão 1903). They ended, significantly enough, about 1961. The migrants were called *ratinhos* (mice). The contracts usually were for nine months, occasionally a month more or less.

Many people from São Martinho and other villages in this and neighboring subregions were trucked down to the Alentejo. One suspects this was one of the reasons for the road improvements in the earlier part of the century and on.

With increasing man-land ratios—particularly after 1863 when the Law of Partible Inheritance was passed as a measure *calculated* by the elites to keep a now independent yeomanry on the farms and out of the cities where their aggregating might create a parallel to the proletariats which had so disturbed northern European urban centers in 1848, and again after 1936, when the Law of the Common Lands initiated constrictions on subsistence uses of land, exacerbated between 1939 and 1945 by the forced extraction of grain "surpluses" (the so-called Sobras de Portugal) by the government—and with consequent rises in adult and infant mortality and disease rates as well as consistently reported assaults and robberies, to get out of these horrifying conditions to get some cash was an effort often to save life itself, even if under terrifying circumstances.[30]

A number of people we knew in São Martinho got their start this way. It provided a means for an accumulation of cash or petty capital just enough to get a person out of the trap. Señor António, who owns a string of butcher stores in Rio de Janeiro, bought his ticket in the 1950s and thus got his start to his present considerable wealth. So did others. In fact, the trader-contractor and his wife have both been, for quite a number of years now, *feirantes*—fair people—circulating regularly among a set of street markets or fairs located around greater Lisbon and into the northwestern Alentejo around Alçácer do Sal. Others, too, got the cash for migration abroad by means of the earnings from the *ranchos*.

There were also *ranchos* which went to the Douro Valley among whose major wine products are the world-famous ports. However, the need for large numbers of laborers—men and women—occurred only during the *víndima,* the annual collecting of grapes, carting them to the wine-processing areas of the farmsteads, and carrying out the then necessary processing steps. The whole period lasts for not much more than a month or so in mid and late fall. The distance, hence transportation cost, is relatively small, on the order (from São Martinho) of forty to fifty miles. The short-term migrants picked up a small bit of cash for some minimum flexibility in larger life strategies. In any case, money was the key.

A number of things are to be noted about the foregoing. Migration in those years can be seen as part of a strategy to generate cash flows and all they might bring into the villages and households. For that end, several very limited options were available: formal, legal migration abroad, very much constricted by government policy and action until, perhaps, 1961 or so; clandestine emigration abroad; short-time, short-distance *ranchos* to the Douro Valley for an extremely limited sum of cash; long-term, long-distance *ranchos* to the Alentejo, also for quite limited amounts of cash, though in sum, of course, larger than those earned in the Douro, but at far greater personal sacrifice; very limited sales of agricultural products through the *grémios;* some local work for bureaucrats, the state, persons of the elite (doctors, padres, lawyers—all interlinked with the bureaucrats as a class). All local work was so limited that no cumulation of money for even reasonable welfare, much less for any sort of investment, was possible. Generally, then, the only sources beyond the most marginal were elsewhere. Hence the removal we call migration, intimately linked with the place from which removal occurred in a single system of goals and strategies.

In Santa Vitória, as noted, the work cycle in cork and olives was about four months. One man in another village of the same ecozone, when asked what they did the other nine months, said, "We stood on the streetcorners and starved." Some sought temporary work in the very limited alternative sector of mining, particularly around Aljustrel. Others, especially women, got temporary work in Alentejo areas specializing in other crops, especially tomatoes, whose labor absorption occurred in seasons other than olive and cork times. In Beja and lesser towns virtually no industry existed (or exists) to absorb labor. The alternatives were to move permanently to industrializing Lisbon or (after 1964) to get longer-term work in agriculture each year in northern Europe or to go there for an indefinite number of years.

Lama, also with an elaborate history of migration, presents a different picture from the other two villages in that its major source of cash has been the dispersed if relatively large-scale (as well as artisanal) manufacturing and the basically subsistence agricultural base with some sales and exchanges, even though *visually* the area *looks* agricultural and is generally, stereotypically, so conceived. But wages were deliberately depressed and the expansion of the number of jobs did not correspond to the size of the labor supply (see note 37). Also, people began to find out from the experience of previous migrants, returning from northern Europe with greater industrial skills, that they could get better and higher-paying jobs in Portugal by emigrating. In sum, these are the answers to the question, "Why go?"

WHY GO? AND WHY STAY?: THE STRATEGIC BASES OF THE TRAJECTORY OF A MIGRATION SYSTEM

But clearly the answer is much more complex, for two reasons: a) not everyone went, and b) those who went, went in different ways at different times. There were *choices* of strategies based on conditions in a multiplicity of places ranging from the home places, to the towns nearby, to the national capital, to other rural areas, to foreign meccas, each with different weightings, at different times, in different villages, and for different households and individuals in the villages.

The differential phenomena of migration lead directly to the question: "Did those who stayed, or those who chose short-term *ranchos*, need money less than whose who went on the long-term *ranchos* or went abroad?" At one level, obviously not—they were as subject to the welfare difficulties and to the dangers of climatic disasters as were those who went; they were also immersed in a poorly recompensatory, labor-intensive production system of local subsistence goods; they certainly wanted most or all of the externally available things which the villagers, including those who migrated, wanted. "Why *not* go?" or put another way, "What was there to *stay* for?"

The answer lies both in the character of the property at home and its actualities and potentialities *and* in the monetarization of the villages by remittances of money from the migrants or by the cash they brought home when returning from in-country migrations. The migrants' possibilities of sending money back, and their doing so, became *part* of the multilocal strategy of deciding who stayed at home. Migrating and staying at home were—and, I would suggest, almost always *are*—part of a *single* complexly conceived strategy.[31]

Obviously, the answer lies, too, in who were the employables in the places to which migrants went. Who was employable or nonemployable was, of course, crucial but by no means entirely determinative of who migrated and who stayed. In general, in the past several decades of Portuguese history, those employable abroad have ranged in age from late youths to early middle-aged persons, perhaps predominantly men. That it was only men who were employable is by no means clear, however. When women got to France, Germany, and, on a lesser scale, other countries of northern Europe, they appear to have found employment as readily as the men.

In fact, the hurdles for women were in Portugal rather than up north. It is reported, for example, that men were heavily favored in terms of getting visas from the Portuguese officials for official emigration, while women experienced great difficulties. Reportedly, it was government policy to keep women—especially married women and still more especially those with children—at home.

That fact is, itself, of vital importance because it appears to have been a *deliberate* policy in order to assure flows of foreign exchange to Portugal.[32]

Monetarization of villages by remittances also necessarily means the flow of foreign exchange to Portugal, through the village to the banks, to investment corporations, to the central Bank of Portugal, etc. That the government was thoroughly aware of this is indicated by several changes—effectively liberalizations made between 1961 and 1963. According to all estimates, official and unofficial, there was a drastic rise in clandestine emigration, that is, an effluence of persons without exist visas, contracts, or other formal documents for leaving Portugal.[33] This started in later 1961 and rose very markedly in 1962 and each year thereafter until 1966. Though clandestine emigration had existed previously, from 1961 on the underground system to help people get out of the country expanded greatly. It included specialists, called *enganchadores*, who arranged for falsified papers or got would-be migrants physically across the borders into Spain. In return they were paid handsome fees for their services, up to several thousand escudos, according to reports of informants.

The migrants had to cross through both the Portuguese borders and the contiguous Spanish borders, and then, after crossing Spain clandestinely, to cross the Spanish-French frontier, going into France as illegal entrants. The Portuguese-Spanish borders, it is reported, were guarded on the former side by the notorious PIDEs and after 1939, by Franco's Guardia Civil. Both could be and, it is reported, were alerted to attempts at illegal border crossings. Arrests of would-be migrants on both sides resulted, followed by their being sent back, imprisoned, and put on trial.[34]

Around 1961–1962, the alerting of border guards appears to have been eased—that is, the central state called off its watchdogs and those of its neighbor, Spain, in order that more would-be migrants could succeed in becoming actual migrants. The estimates of clandestine migration (see note 33) confirm this success and the likelihood that that success was a function of intentional government policy, although the indications are that the migration continued to be predominantly of men, while women stayed at home.[35]

A second phase of this first liberalization started in 1962 and accelerated thereafter. This consisted in legalizations by the Portuguese authorities of illegal emigrants (Sousa Ferreira 1976, 56.). Legalization, of course, officially recognized the migrant's status as such and also (usually) permitted him to return to Portugal without legal penalties. Even though the numbers were at first small, as one would expect, the *shift* of policy is of the highest significance, especially taken in conjunction with the border openings described above. Among other things, it made it less necessary for migrants to hold their savings in the country of emigration and, by the same token, more likely to send them back or reinvest them in Portugal. The legalizations increased yearly (see note 35), undoubtedly, in part at least, a function of information spreading among communities of migrants abroad, such as the *bidonvilles* (shantytowns) of Paris and elsewhere in France, then still existent.

The second major liberalization occurred beginning in 1964 with the establishment of the Serviço Nacional de Emprego (SNE—the National Employment

Service). Among other things, it initiated a system of formal contracts with workers wanting to emigrate (as well as contracts for work in the internal labor market); these were especially important for emigration to Germany and to some extent Switzerland, with which the SNE established formal ties allowing it to act as agent for supplying both short- and long-term contractual labor. We know a number of persons both in the north (from São Martinho) and the Alentejo (from Santa Vitória and in the collective farm in the *conselho* of Serpa where we did considerable fieldwork) who went to northern Europe by means of such contracts—some for long-term industrial work, some for short-term agricultural work as in the sugar beet harvests, thereby supplementing seasonal work in the Alentejo. In one case in Sáo Martinho, the man had, in fact, gone to Germany earlier (around 1962), since, he reported, the Germans had already made representation to the Portuguese authorities who allowed a certain number of people to slip out (see above). He later regularized his status by means of an SNE contract. Clearly, the Portuguese government was both expanding the legal forms of emigration and relaxing still further the controls on clandestine emigration.

It is significant, in this connection, that Portugal joined the European Free Trade Association (EFTA) in 1965. One supposes that the establishment of the SNE was a step taken in anticipation of closer, complex ties of exchange of materials, goods, and labor with EFTA countries. The opening of the EFTA period coincides with the breakdown of the nationalist development program of the Salazar regime (aspects of which I return to below) and the early phases of the opening up of Portugal to capital-intensive multinationals.[36]

The third major liberalization occurred shortly after the end of Salazar's term (1968) and the accession to office of Marcello Caetano who had, some years before, been Salazar's minister of the colonies (Ministro de Ultramar, 1944) and later (1945) president of the Câmara Corporativa (the Chamber of Corporations) and then (1955) deputy prime minister. Though, in a very general way, the policies concerning the development of the political economy were similar to those of Salazar, nevertheless some significant changes were attempted. These related especially to the development policy respecting industry with a strong expansion of incentives for multinationals to invest, a strong departure from the nationalist industrial policy which, until the mid-1960s (as noted above regarding EFTA), had dominated Salazar's thinking and action, including the economic, political, and jural relations to the colonies. Multinational investment was, as remarked, capital-intensive, bringing in foreign capital resources but *not* producing any significant increase in labor demand.[37] In this third period, not only did legalizations increase rapidly, not only did controls over clandestine emigration relax still further, but the Portuguese government finally established a complex accord with the French government concerning the status in work and welfare in that country of Portuguese workers numbering close to one million (1971). Both the relaxation and the *convénio* with France permitted a massive increase of emigration of wives and children of migrants (see note 35 for increases in family emigration for this period).

The results of this set of liberalizing actions were a comprehensive legalization of formerly illegal migrants and a still further surge of migration, most of it (but not all) now legal. Demographic statistics for some *conselhos* and *distritos* even show net population losses, most of those declines being evacuations from rural areas. The surge of emigration continued until the economic recession caused by the OPEC price increases of 1973 and the "Revolution" of 1974 made possible the return of a considerable number of migrants (especially to the Alentejo where rural wage workers collectivized farms after occupying them) and opened a whole new phase of Portuguese history by virtue of 'granting' independence to the colonies.

Corresponding to the surge in emigration, remittances increased sharply, reaching a peak in 1973 of 15 percent of gross national product, roughly two billion dollars (Banco de Portugal, *Relatório* 1973). Remittances became the largest single source of foreign exchange, well beyond tourism (Banco de Portugal, *Relatório* 1973) to which some of that capital went via great investment funds, heavily involved in construction, such as FIA and FIDES. The latter, of course, employed considerable numbers of rural-to-urban migrants.

Clearly, the combination of the pre-1961 conditions described at length above and the post-1961 liberalizations had the effect of drastically evacuating the countryside, especially of personnel most capable of physical labor. The result of this decrease in the rural work force meant abandonment of fields—different stages of which an observer can clearly see in their degree of overgrownness, some with furrows still visible, some with weed overgrowths, some with high brush. Still other fields, starting already in the early 1960s (or even earlier), were planted with trees, as noted before. My estimate for all arable lands removed from production in São Martinho is about 40 percent. The connection of such removals, in Portugal generally, with the increase of food imports has already been noted.

Yet this depopulated, deactivated agrarian sector is precisely the one described in the early part of this chapter which has cash and comforts, a substantial degree of security—one in which those who are there stay and to which some of those who are away wish to (and more than occasionally do) return. It is a situation of *relative* stability with many amenities, unlike the uncertain state of affairs, increasingly tense as the recession beginning in 1973 intensified, for emigrants in the countries of emigration.

Two major themes are to be extracted from the above. First, the present situation in the rural villages in Portugal is itself a processual result of—a continuous historical reconstruction by—the multiple strategies of networks of people including migrants *and* stay-at-homes. (In varying degrees, it is crucial to note, the two "categories" are interchangeable, a point usually missed by virtue of the reification of "*the* migrant.") Clearly this proposition, even though here exemplified by a specific set of cases during a specific time, is intended as a generic assertion. It needs only minor changes in wording to take on the form of a general proposition whose validity is being asserted: "*Any* present situation (i.e., *any* given time of "observation," past or present) in the rural villages (of

Portugal; *any* society) is a processual result of—a continuous historical reconstruction by—the multiple strategies of networks of people.''

Methodologically, this implies, of course, equivalently detailed study of all persons and their contexts associated with a local ecosystem, whether or not they left or leave it for shorter or longer periods, or permanently, as what are conventionally called migrants. In the cases of São Martinho and Lama, such detailed study involves a number of major variables, some of which may be described as external and some as internal. Many of the former have been discussed above; external job markets and their histories; the action of the state through economic organizations; bureaucratic agencies, the police, the military, such institutions as taxation and laws such as that of partible inheritance. One might add other countries as locations of political asylum, for example, France for Spaniards after 1939 and for Portuguese seeking to escape military service in the colonies, or the political repression of the opposition by the Salazar regime, or the United States for Haitians escaping the Tonton Macoute of the Duvalier regimes.[38]

The internal variables have only been alluded to indirectly in the preceding pages. They include the fact—for Lama and São Martinho, at least—that *some* amount of subsistence, even in the worst and most repressive of times, could be gained from the land. It might be a resource of last resort, even if in such a bad way that life became shorter, nastier, and more brutish—as in the period of the Sobras de Portugal when the mortality and illness rates rose and near starvation was felt by most people. However, the land nevertheless was and remains a resource to resort to in *a general structural situation which remains permanently equivocal*.

The post-1973 oil-induced crisis and recession in the foreign labor markets made this sharply apparent, and migrants home on vacation in São Martinho and Lama (and elsewhere where we had conversations) were acutely aware not only of the insecurity that crisis implied but also described specific efforts by the French and German governments to push migrants out, respectively the Plan Barre (of the Minister of Labor Barre) to give migrants a lump sum of 10,000 francs to go home and *never return* again as workers and the Germans' making eligibility requirements for welfare benefits much more stringent. Both of these efforts changed the name of the game for persons from the villages already abroad and for anyone in the villages thinking of going abroad—the situation there was much less secure, much more equivocal than before. Plainly, such equivocality is not unique; in fact, in a capitalist society one may assert that it exists always, though the degree will vary.[39] Under such circumstances, a major strategy involves maintenance of resources of last resort.

In fact, more inclusively, the strategy is to improve ''those'' resources continuously so that ''they'' are not resources of *last* resort but ''ones'' which are, at least generally, feasible, reasonable, and providers of some comforts and amenities. This is precisely what I have described as happening between about 1961 and the present. Indeed, to do just exactly that was the intent in the first place, whether one migrated or stayed.

This is clearly exemplified, using São Martinho as an example, by any number of important pieces of data: a) the purchase and ownership of a tractor by a migrant living in Germany, used only (by him) during the vacation month, *taken at harvest time;* b) his extending, improving, and building new additions to his house; c) the purchase of a pool and game room in the hotel of Vila Nova de Paiva as an investment by another migrant to Germany; d) generally the radical rebuilding and improving of old houses or building of new ones, all with garden spaces for food production around them; e) the establishing of a café by return migrants from France; f) returning not only for the month's vacation at harvest time but on brief vacations, such as at Easter, to tend, for example, to spring planting and other chores, thus keeping some of the fields not only in production but as ancillary sources of income. Parallels were found in Lama and Santa Vitória in investment in comfortable houses with modern infrastructure, but also in other small investments such as shops, restaurants, or trucks. A grand strategy embracing all of the above is indicated by the radical decline in the emigration to Brazil which had surged up again rapidly after World War II, once postwar reconstruction in northern Europe had occurred and job markets expanded there. The decline of emigration to Brazil is paralleled by an almost vertiginous rise of migration especially to France, especially from 1955 on (see Sousa Ferreira 1976, chart p. 50). Succinctly: one can *drive* from France to Portugal in twenty-four hours (generally, or, for example, in response to an emergency telephone call). France becomes an ecological extension of the home place ecosystem.

The question of who was employable abroad, though important in determining who went, leads us to only part of the answer of who went, however. Persons equally employable did *not* go—for example, the carpenter in São Martinho, some men perhaps further along in years but still eminently employable, and the owner of the tavern–general store–post office who had married into the village. The variables concerned involve the maintenance and ownership of arable property, the necessity to maintain agricultural production when possible (see vacation behavior mentioned above) as both a subsistence and insurance system; the requirements of attending to bureaucratic exigencies such as paying taxes, answering to land surveys (such as was in process during our fieldwork of 1979); taking care of death and birth registrations and marriage licensing, census responses of various sorts (population, electoral), school registration for children not with their parents abroad for whatever strategic reason (e.g., cuts in welfare benefits in Germany), decedents' legalities, property partitions and their registrations, as well as the claiming of any limited part of the decedent's property which the law allows to be left as bequest, etc.

As a rule, though this would require extensive detailed study in both São Martinho and Lama, the ones who stayed at home were either the more significant property holders [40] or those persons with more direct potential access to property and its disposition (either by adding properties by inheritance or purchase or by marital exchanges involving land, houses, and machines), as well as those persons most directly involved in decision making and management of production and marketing. They were and are constructing for themselves—but also for children, siblings, and other collaterals—limited chiefly by the labor supply for production (hence land abandonments). A second category of people who stayed is that of skilled tradespeople—in São Martinho, the stonemason, the carpenter, and the blacksmith. In Lama, there were, of course, many skilled artisans in the ceramic enterprises, most of which were at least several generations old. A number of workers and owners involved had never emigrated, while a number had, to Canada, Venezuela, Brazil, France, Belguim, and Mozambique/Rhodesia.[41] A third category, almost nonexistent in São Martinho but more prevalent in Lama and Santa Vitória, consists of service people such as café owners, retail storekeepers, the post office ladies, schoolteachers (nonresident in São Martinho), the priest and his housekeeper(s), bakers, tavern keepers, etc. [42] A fourth quasi-category was itself determined by Portuguese policy and by possible imbalances in employment ratios abroad—more women stayed home. I call it a quasi-category because women, like men, are holders of property (though, it is reported, in the division of values to heirs, women are more likely to inherit a house while men inherit land—allowing for the marital exchanges alluded to above). Women are quite as important in the work of agricultural production as the men. A few women are also involved in marketing arrangements, but only limitedly, aside from major involvement in operating retail stores in all three villages.

WHY RETURN?: MINHA TERRA

Beyond all the home interests which determine who stays and who returns or wants to, all of the strategies involved in migration, especially insofar as they revolve around improving the "resource of last resort" to the point of its being a relatively secure and comfortable place to be, if not, in fact, a pleasure dome, are informed by a structure of meanings and values (loosely designated as "culture" in our anthropological lingo). These meanings and values are attached to locality, various forms of social life, and one's own history. These sorts of variables, I would assert, apply generically to those situations we designate under the term "migration," but have their particular forms and flavors in Portugal (see Leeds 1987) which help us understand going, staying, and returning.

All three villages have major features of *community:* many family lines, often intricately interlinked, living in a common place with common experiences over generations, making many kinds of exchanges, and giving variegated forms of mutual support endlessly (and having *characteristic* fights, envies, jealousies, and accusations of witchcraft and evil eye—an ethnographic tale of community woes which must be dealt with elsewhere). The *community* experience involves, among other critical experiences, the reproduction of life itself—pregnancy, childbirth, and child care—in the context of mutual support, family and friends, *not* in the isolation of, say, a Parisian rooming house or *bidonville*. It involves support and security for the aged, those no longer able to do anything, and those limited to light tasks. (The distribution of these age groups in the São Martinho age pyramid was *visually* most striking.) In short, the home place, an ecosystem and community, remains strategically critical to major aspects of the domestic cycle for many (even aside from questions of property and production).

The community is, from the point of view of any actor, *minha terra*, a term with no semantic equivalent, significantly enough, in the English of long capitalistically organized America with its drastic geographic mobility. I have rendered it above (see also "Minha Terra é Lama," Leeds 1987) as (my) 'home place'—the place where I was born, where my first meanings were learned, where the foods I like best are raised and cooked, where the landscape is beautiful and friendships and kin ties deeply meaningful (even if the place is a disaster, not to be returned to). For the man through whom we got to Lama, it is the place of the conventionalized concept of *saudade* (nostalgia, longing, the sense of being absent from). For the wonderful young woman through whom we originally got to São Martinho (see "When the Gulls Fly, the Tempest Comes," Leeds 1987), who was not even born there (but in the city of Coimbra) but came to it through her husband (who was also not born there but while his mother was on one of the *ranchos* to the Alentejo rice fields), it was the place she wanted eventually to move to for its peace and calm and because the chestnut trees are beautiful. It is a place of which she has become part; she, like her husband's family, is known there; she "belongs" there (*pertencer* is the word used). (The anthropologist *não pertence a ninguem,* "does not belong to anyone"—as a boy, with whom I had done threshing, responded to the tractor driver from the neighboring village who was plowing his father's land as he kept an eye on him.) It is a place where her in-laws—the *feirantes* spoken of earlier—are reconstructing and modernizing their whole house, obviously as a vacation and retirement place. For all of these—and so many of the others, including those who have businesses or who work in Lisbon, Vila Nova de Paiva, or elsewhere—it is the ultimate place of the familiar and the meaningful, of rootedness, of identity. One stays if one can, one returns if one can (except for a few), one visits when one can—and one's strategies are constructed accordingly.

In sum, "who stays?," "who goes?," and "why come back?" are one and the same question, the answer to which lies in a multilevel view of the ecosystem in which migrants are generated. That multilevel model includes, at its most fundamental level, the local ecosystem, but from the point of view of the *same* actors with their multiplicities of concurrent and interlocked contexts, it includes also intranational, regional, and multiregional levels, the national territory as a whole, and the international system *as various extensions of the local ecosystem,* conceptually and in practice, always, of course, with "imperfect" information.

SYSTEMS: SUBSYSTEMS, SUPERSYSTEMS, VARIABLES, AND INTERACTIONS THROUGHOUT THE HIERARCHY

Further, from the point of view of each of these levels, there are also actors—individuals, groups, or agencies—who make strategic decisions: the Junta Forestal, bureaucrats of the Wheat Campaign, the minister of corporations, the director of the SNE, the minister of finance, the prime minister, major corporations, various international bodies (like EFTA or the International Monetary Fund—see "The F.M.I. Helps Portugal," Leeds 1987), the policy-making bodies of other countries, etc. In one way or another, to many of these, the local ecosystems, such as rural villages, often collectively conceived, as in "the agricultural sector," may constitute important variables in *their* strategies. This point has been exemplified by the history of the use of remittances by the Portuguese state.

In this view, all levels are always in motion. Since this is so, the overall structure and its subsystems are also always changing—*any present situation is itself a historical reconstitution,* especially in such dynamic circumstances as those involving migration, even though the rates of that reconstitution may vary greatly over time.[43]

This matter of the interaction of levels is a second major theme of my story here. Each of the levels has organizational characteristics of its own—geographical bases, territorial markers, institutions, intergovernmental linkages, even, perhaps, "cultural traditions." As partially *and varyingly* autonomous levels, they can interact in varying degree and in varying ways with each other. It is theoretically and methodologically critical to think, both empirically and in terms of models, about the varying degrees of autonomy or linkedness ("loosely-coupled" versus "tightly-coupled" in general systems theory language).

This issue is powerfully emphasized by my deliberate choice of transformations occurring in the early 1960s in Portugal—in fact, specifically, in 1961. The reader reviewing the case material will recall major symptoms of change, of discontinuities, of transformations, of restructuring, some so clean-cut that they can be dated to so brief a moment as—1961. Plainly some major perturbation, reverberating through all levels of this complex system, must have occurred.

That specific perturbation was the beginning of the Angolan war of independence in March 1961, probably inevitable, given the decolonization movements in general after World War II and specifically that of the neighboring Congo in 1960. The Angolan war had a virtually immediate effect on continental Portugal. The vertiginous rise of military expenditures generated, in what had been a virtually stable value of money for many years, if not decades, a marked inflation which rose even more sharply from 1964 on when the Mozambiquan independence war began (Gonçalves 1972; Cadilhe 1974), the year in which the SNE was established.

That inflation meant, immediately, a rise in the costs of foreign exchange and increasing difficulties in the balance of payments. The balance of payments problem was severely exacerbated by the gross increases in importation of military equipment. The military budgets in the next few years reached about 50 percent of the national budget (Banco de Portugal, *Relatórios* [annual], for respective years) or more if one adds in the emergency special military budgets. Further, there was, from the beginning of the war, clearly no short-term solution—if any at all—to this problem for a small country like Portugal carrying on a war many thousands of miles away in a territory ten times or so its own size.

This situation worsened exponentially in 1964 when the Mozambiquan revolutionary movement began—at roughly the same time as that of Guinea Bissau. Portugal now tried to carry on, in effect, three separate wars, the one in Mozambique in another territory roughly ten times its own size and, taking the three colonies together, a population several times larger than that of the "parent" country.

The system changes which are symptomatically expressed in what I have described for 1978 in São Martinho, Lama, and Santa Vitória can be clearly understood in terms of the radically and almost instantly transformed conditions of the higher-level systems of the Portuguese political economy, those too of the intermediate levels, and, therefore, the changed strategic contexts, at the local level, of all those persons who strategize about staying home, migrating, returning, or combinations of these.

The Portuguese state, for some twenty or thirty years prior to 1961 committed to a nationalistic, import-substituting industrialization policy, suddenly found itself in that year in a situation of major fiscal danger. The response to that danger has been described in the foregoing text—the liberalizations, the founding of the SNE, the development of international agreements, the opening to multinationals, joining EFTA, the proposed joining of the EEC, etc. In short, a radical transformation of policy and of the entire political economy took place with great rapidity and clear sequential exemplifications.

A major feature of the transformation was the transformation of work, of labor conditions in multiplicities of locales, of the recompenses of work and labor. One major aspect of these changes was a rapid monetarization of rural Portugal—with the most far-reaching consequences in terms of patterns of production, investment, multilocal economic strategies by villagers (some of which we describe as "migration"), the disappearance of older "modes" of production, of older institutions of labor use and abuse (e.g., the *ranchos),* in fact of the corporativist system itself (although that disappearance is also linked to the unwinnable colonial wars and that other major processual perturbation, the "Revolution" of April 25, 1974).

Arbitrarily starting with 1961 and coming on to the present, or starting with any point in time, we see, first, a very complex system with multiple loci of choice and action comprised in it. One need not physically be in all the loci, even if this were possible, in order to think strategies and tactics, but one must have information about other loci to be assessed in terms of one's role in the locus of the present moment. (Increasing flows of migration meant increasing flows of information.) Second, we see that the system is not fixed—the structure changes, so that the loci in it take on different strategic meanings over time if they do not in fact also change as a result of, or in conjunction with, change in the system as a whole. Examination over very long periods of time would show that the *rates* of system change vary greatly, sometimes appearing as virtual stagnation, sometimes as almost a flash of reorganization, triggered by some event or "force."

In conclusion, the events or behaviors we entitize as "migration" dissolve, in the present approach, into a multiplicity of quite different sorts of concepts, strategies, and relationships of individuals and groups, located in and locating themselves with respect to many different places and institutions. Because of this multilocal and multileveled, interwoven reference system, which includes indefinitely large numbers of differentiated other actors who, for the most part, we do *not* speak of as migrants—the bureaucrats, the industrial investors, the professors who study economic and social systems, [44] even if, in pursuit of these kinds of work, they had moved from place to place, the abstractions we call "migration" and "migrants," as standardly conceived, tend to be highly misleading. They do not allow us to explain the differential movement of individuals (or groups). For the most part, the standard models of migration do not give us much of an understanding of societal process or of individuals as social beings and actors. They are so abstracted and reduced—in the technical sense of reductionist paradigms—that a richly textured view of social and cultural process is automatically excluded: work, labor, and their recompenses become denatured, abstracted, categories rather than complex processes of human life—material, social, and value-laden as they are.

NOTES

1. The question is not merely one of taste, convenience, or convention, but an important theoretical one. Commutes can be considered parts of a continuum in the *degree* of migrancy, an idea, so far as I know, not in the literature at all, but theoretically undoubtedly critical. Note the range from a daily commute between (a) a suburban residence and a center-of-city workplace, to (b) the same suburban residence and a three-to-five-day-a-week job in another city or town reachable in, say, one to three hours of travel each way, to (c) the same residence and a five-day-a-week job in a city involving major travel and travel costs, for example, between Boston and New York, Cincinnati, or Los Angeles. The latter two kinds of commute involve a second residence in addition to the regular residence used on weekends and holidays. The arrangement is customarily called 'commuting,' but is obviously not different in principle from a removal not of 5-day periods but of say weeks, months, or year periods (see also note 24).

2. Portuguese examples came up in our fieldwork. Buechler (1983) and Buechler and Buechler (1975, 1981, 1983) refer to such aid in their works on Spain. The Somalia case was reported by Professors Allan Hoben (anthropology) and John Harris (economics), both of the African Studies Center, Boston University.

3. There are even cases where the subregional system operates *over* national boundaries, for example, the northwestern Minho with adjacent parts of Galicia in Spain or parts of easternmost Alentejo with adjacent parts of Spain. Labor and commercial exchanges take place over the national boundaries in a complex regional system of organization.

4. The *grémios* were elements or units of the corporativist structure of the Portuguese state set up under António Salazar, the prime minister–"dictator" between 1932 and 1968. There were commercial and industrial *grémios* as well as the agricultural ones, representing "organic" interest groups.

5. These estimates of size were made, mostly, by pacing off widths and lengths. The range and distribution of field sizes need detailed study, taken together with crop rotation, land ownership, and land usership, including renting. That the problem is of greatest difficulty is reflected by the fact that the total land area calculated from the figures collected by the government's land tenure survey team in 1979 were reportedly equivalent, for this general area of Portugal, to about half the area of vastly larger Spain. No doubt, ownership, use, usufruct, renting, possibly sharecropping, and other categories of relation to land were conflated by the surveyors—possibly, perhaps probably, on the basis of deliberate obfuscation by villagers, who may delay for many years registering the inherited parts *(partilhas)* in order not to disturb their ecosystemic strategies of agricultural exploitation worked out over years. Although this must be checked by intensive research, it is supposed that de facto, or folk, "ownership" of land and ownership actually registered in the land registry offices are widely different because of the time delays in registering the parts inherited from a decedent. Since the land survey was to be the basis for the revised system of taxation, based on standardized estimates of land worth for various categories of land (woodlots, improved arable, abandoned, pastures, etc.), but *not* an income tax since farm incomes are so difficult to calculate, obfuscation of actual property relations was of a certain interest to the locals. A history of taxation with respect to local strategies in agrarian Portugal (and, of course, other societies) desperately needs to be done.

6. See especially Cabral (1974, pp. 549, 552–57, 557–58 n.1, 559 n.5).

7. But not in the Alentejo. I have inquired about the "anomalies" of the Alentejo of agricultural economists, historians, and village residents, especially in Santa Vitória, but have not received a satisfactory explanation as to why the latifundia did not fragment. From bits and pieces, I hypothesize (if feebly) that the Alentejo was eminently suited for very extensive, long-term crops, such as olives and cork, which are not only transgenerational capital holdings but the individual trees live for as long as 800 or 1,000 years. The crops (and profits) collected are labor-intensive but need labor for only a few months of the year. The long historical inheritance, continued in significant degree in the present, especially in its renovation after the Barreto Law of 1977 modifying the Lopes Cardoso agricultural reform law passed after the "Revolution" of 1974, has severely damped population growth generally—reflected in net declines of some districts in recent decades as well as in steady and rather sharp declines in family size, especially after foreign emigration opened up in the 1960s, on one hand (see note 25 and appendix), and on the other, a cash profit system which allowed absentee ownership with minimum outlays for permanent stewardships. Since the anticlerical movements of the earlier 19th century (including running monks and monasteries out of the region), the area has also been relatively secular. At the priest's advice I did *not* do my census of under 18-year-olds from parish records but rather from the civil registry, because only about half the relatively few children are baptized. In general, *both* in the working and owning classes, the families appear to have been smaller than in the north (i.e., fewer heirs to divide value among). The total value, given absenteeism, was divided among city properties—real estate, possibly factories, commercial establishments, etc.—and land, so that even if there was a number of heirs, the lands could remain *relatively* undivided. Informants reported, further, that lands were reintegrated by siblings' buying each other out—one got money capital, the other reconstituted a large enough piece of land to make substantial cash profits from the extensive farming, while keeping open huge hunting preserves *(coutadas)*. In other cases, several large parts appear to have been managed as a single enterprise by one sibling, while the others developed other activities in the city (chiefly Lisbon, of course)—a kind of migration, in point of fact, but not discussed at all in the literature. The managing itself may

have allowed for accumulating capital with which to reconstitute lands once owned by an ancestor or to constitute new large holdings by purchase. Where cork plantations were the major use of land, it was desirable to have *at least* enough land so that one could keep a permanent, if small, work force on the latifundium. Since cork is cut only once in nine years, this means one-ninth of the orchards are cut annually. If the holdings are too small, cork cutting must skip a year or more, since the cash return is too small to allow annual cuttings (Branco 1983)—and then labor retention becomes a looming problem. A solution is to increase holdings.

8. At the conference, "Portugal Contemporâneo—1900–1980," held in Lisbon, December 1981 *(Análise Social* 1982, 1983), the papers of one session described this transference of agricultural lands into urban uses in and around Lisbon—already, at the time here discussed (1950s–1960s), a city very much swollen by industrial growth—a growth starting during World War II and accelerating afterwards. That is, the population increased drastically, while the land areas devoted to agricultural uses have disappeared into what has become the greater metropolitan area of Lisbon, necessitating increasing imports of foods from other parts of the country and from abroad.

9. Numerous sources confirm each other on these statements. See for example da Gama 1940 and the various novels about the region by the great Portuguese novelist, Aquilino Ribeiro, born in Peva, the same *freguesia* in which São Martinho is located. Informants' comments and statements, along with parochial records from São Martinho and Lama, frequently gave pieces of evidence. A further possible evidence is the stature and body proportions of Portuguese, especially from northern Portugal, whose late childhood-adolescent growth periods occurred at the time of the Sobras: they tend to be short with particularly reduced leg length, a quite possible result of major nutritional deprivation. On the whole, children of these people are considerably taller and with more "normal" leg/trunk length proportions.

10. The Portuguese term is *aldeia,* with the implication of rusticity and rurality, much as "village" in English conveys those ideas. Actual *aldeias* range from Everyanthropologist's dream Peasant Village—clustered stone houses on a hillside, like São Martinho—to what are in fact complex small city-places like industrial, multiservice, class-divided Lama, even without gross differences in population size (though Lama, the *freguesia,* has perhaps eight or ten times the number of people of São Martinho, the *lugar,* one of three, *in* a *freguesia).* Phenomena of this sort are not limited to Portugal and, indeed, involve some major theoretical and methodological problems of greatest import to anthropology—including the deromanticization of "peasantries" and their "villages," with their alleged closednesses, inturnednesses, etc.

11. Mid-19th century government policies in Portugal, especially after the proletarian upheavals of 1848 in northern Europe (with some counterparts such as the rebellions of Maria da Fonte and of the Patuleia in Portugal; see Riegelhaupt 1982), were directed explicitly against the growth of urban proletariats. This was one of the rationales for the Law of Partible Inheritance

12. I believe a convincing theoretical and empirical argument can be made for considering all the *"aldeias"* (see note 10) within perhaps 50 or 60 km of Porto, as well, of course, as the "towns," as a single metropolitan area (on "towns" and "villages" issues, see Leeds 1980). Porto operates as *the* northern Portuguese center for national planning (e.g., the Commissão de Planeamento da Região do Norte), central bureaucratic decisions (e.g., certain kinds of construction permits even for the outlying villages), specialized health care (e.g., electrocardiograms at the Hospital São João), regional organizations (e.g., the

Movimento de Apoio aos Rendeiros do Norte [The Northern Tenant Farmers Support Movement]; the Associação Industrial Portuense), etc.—even where lesser cities may have parallel, but smaller, and subsidiary organizations (e.g., the Associação Industrial do Minho in Braga). Porto is, of course, also the major port for the entire north. Further, as research by José Madureira Pinto, economics professor at the University of Porto, and his team has been showing (personal communication), there is an elaborate system of "pendular migration" (his term) from as far away as, for example, Penafiel, some 35 km—essentially a system of daily, work commuting. (Given Portuguese roads and transportation, the 21 miles involved is equivalent to a much greater distance in American terms, perhaps as much as 40 miles.) All these relations to Porto as a central city are fundamentally different from those of, say, a São Martinho to Porto, which involves some occasional long-distance trade (e.g., the fish truck I saw there once), Porto's exports of national and imported products (e.g., Dutch aluminum to the window and door-frame factory in Vila Nova de Paiva) to the hinterlands, major labor transfers by residential change (migration), and so on.

13. See E. Leeds 1984, chap. 4, for interviews with textile industrialists in the area described above on the subject of subsistence agriculture as partial wage substitutes, thus cheapening cash wages.

14. After the "Revolution" of 1974, most of the Alentejo latifundia were "invaded" by the rural proletariat, mostly under the auspices of the Portuguese Communist Party, and set up as collective farms. In Santa Vitória, a medium-sized collective farm was constituted of a number of properties around the village and had its headquarters there, so that the village, for the first time perhaps, became the center of major farm operations. The *unidade colectiva de produção* (UCP), the collective farm, has since been destroyed by a complex political process starting in 1977 with the Barreto Law during the Socialist government of Mário Soares; António Barreto was the minister of agriculture. The destruction of this and other UCPs in the Alentejo has been accompanied by marked recrudescence of seasonal unemployment and internal migration. Evidence can be adduced that some of the funding backing up the return of UCP lands to former owners came from agricultural credit loans from the United States for corn imports (to feed cattle in the north) attached to certain policy positions counter to the existence of the UCPs.

15. There were some "small holders" in the Alentejo (e.g., in Santa Vitória), with lands in the range of 50 hectares, who lived in the village. They had better houses—and graves, through which, in part, I discovered their presence one day as I ate my lunch in Santa Vitória (itself a reflection of the closedness and difficulty of fieldwork). The history of the acquisition of such small holdings is itself a research subject of greatest interest, almost untouched, so far as I know, in the literature.

16. After 1974 the state saw to it that some lands immediately next to the watercourse running through Santa Vitória were made available to residents for gardening, resulting is substantial improvements in household economies and nutrition.

17. Why population has always been so low in the Alentejo is not entirely clear; some suggestions appear in note 7 above. Plainly, given the major forms of agricultural production, the carrying capacity for human population was limited. The land tenure system, of course, tended to reinforce those forms. There is also a lack of information as to if, when, and where emigration went in the 19th century and the earlier part of the 20th—a subject for further research.

18. See Jorge Dias's study of Vilarinho das Furnas (1948) and a movie of the same

name made about that community during the time of making decisions about leaving it forever. The process was still to be observed in 1979–1981.

19. We have as yet not been able to find published sources on the Sobras. They were reported to us by villagers of Lama and São Martinho, in quite independent areas of the country. We checked with the eminent historian Victor de Sá, who confirmed the information generally and specifically spoke about the system of rationing at the time.

20. Intentionality I reconstruct as the best logic to explain a great variety of events and their *sequence* of occurrence. If one denies intentionality, the overall order, which seems to me quite apparent, could only have happened by accident. The probabilities of an accidental hodgepodge creating so complex a system, one so relatively orderly, seem infinitesimal. Intentionality can, in part, be reconstructed from public statements of key figures (e.g., Salazar, especially *before* he got into major office when he spoke more analytically and directly and less politically [see Salazar 1954], Caetano, and many others); from discussions in the Câmara Corporativa; from statements in the various development plans from 1953 on; from semiunderground and underground publications which existed throughout the period; from censored materials from newspapers (some of which kept files of what was censored); from informants' recollections and understandings, and so on. In this connection the following quotation taken from the cover of *O Salazarismo,* volume 1 of Lucena's work on corporativism (1976), is most striking (my translation):

> Always contradictory, the corporative institutions often begin by "not existing," later "they exist but they don't function," and finally it becomes evident that they in fact became consistent, but are the opposite of what the people who depict them say they are. However, looking at the matter more closely, one suspects that they were more or less planned this way from the beginning. And that, moreover, the Salazarist project is powerful, without failing to be ridiculous.

21. About 1938 or so, we planted a grove of pines on a farm we then owned in Clinton Corners, N.Y. Revisits through the mid-1970s gave me visual cues as to tree sizes at various ages.

22. See Pereira da Silva 1973 on popular resistance to the programs of the Junta Forestal in west-central northern Portugal, near the Vouga River.

23. Even though one may speak about class differences among minifundiary farmers, the structure of that system of class is fundamentally different from that of the southern latifundias (and also from seigneurial and other estate owners in the north, especially in major wine-exporting areas like the Douro). In the south there were essentially two classes, each with one or two subfragments: the latifundia, with a lower-status small-holder fragment; and the wage-earning proletariat, including a very unstable and varying number who held small subsistence areas on sufferance of the latifundia in a form of clientage—a way for the latter to maintain a reserve labor force without paying them. In the north there was a *set* of class fragments, differentially distributed in different areas, depending on kinds of crops, seasonality of production, presence of seigneurial and other large (by northern standards) holdings, etc.: a) tenant farmers *(rendeiros),* b) sharecroppers *(meeiros),* c) some permanent rural proletarians *(trabalhadores rurais),* d) impermanent ones as in the *ranchos,* e) caretakers *(caseiros)* on estates, f) freeholders ("peasants," *camponeses, lavradores, agricultores*). These categories were (and, to some extent, are) not clear-cut because some tenant farmers also were freeholders, for example, or some who went on *ranchos* may also have been freeholders or tenants. Looked at from the point of view of an extended family, mutually supporting members may have been involved in several of these categories at once. The consequence of these vastly different organizations

of rural class systems for the *grémios* is that, in the south, they were totally in control of a small, virtually exclusive one-class group—the larger latifundia, with a correspondingly major influence in the government, and a total exclusion of the rural laborers, many active in the underground unions and Communist Party. In the north, in areas like that around São Martinho, the *grémios* were in control of a much less clearly delimited set of people, with a considerably wider (though perhaps not *effective*) membership, more interlaced in each other's interests. Though the northern *grémios* in such areas are reported to have sharpened class differences, they nevertheless seem to have reflected political-economic values relatively widespread among a large number of the people.

24. See note 12 on "pendular" migration.

25. The larger, especially coastal or near-coastal cities are the significant industrial ones, with two secondary interior ones, Covilhã and Viseu respectively, in the districts of Castelo Branco and Viseu. Towns like Vila Real and Bragança, in Tras-os-Montes, typify provincial centers largely related to agrarian interests. Note the following figures for a number of northern cities (see Serrão [1972] 1974):

	1950	1970	Net Growth, 20 Yrs.	%	Ave. per Annum
Porto	284,847	310,437	25,590	9	1,278.5
Braga	83,777	101,877	18,000	21	905
Viana de Castelo	68,991	71,254	2,263	3	113.2
Vila Real	46,483	44,286	-2,197	-4.7	-109.8
Bragança	38,070	33,928	-4,142	-11	-207.1

The agrarian cities show an absolute decline. The same picture is given by figures for districts (Centro de Estudos de Planeamento 1976, 23):

	1950	1960	1970	Growth 20 yrs./%	
Coastal industrial districts					
Aveiro	477,191	524,592	545,230	+68,000	+14.26
Braga (a bit inland)	541,377	596,768	609,415	+68,000	+12.57
Coimbra (a bit inland)	432,044	433,656	399,380	-33,00	-7.56
Leiria	389,182	404,500	376,940	-12,000	-3.77
Lisbon	1,226,815	1,382,959	1,568,020	+342,000	+27.81
Porto	1,052,663	1,193,368	1,309.560	+250,000	+24.40
Setúbal	324,185	377,186	469,555	+145,000	+44.84
Viana de Castelo	274,532	277,748	250,510	-24,000	-8.75
Inland industrial districts					
Castelo Branco	320,279	316.536	254,355	-66,000	-20.58
Viseu	437,182	482,416	410,795	-26,500	-6.04
Inland agrarian districts - north					
Bragança	227,125	233,441	180,395	-47,000	-20.57
Guarda	304,368	282,606	210,720	-93,500	-30.77
Vila Real	317,372	325,358	265,605	-52,000	-16.31
Inland agrarian districts - south and central					
Beja	286,803	276,395	204,440	-82,500	-28.71
Evora	219,638	219,916	178,475	-41,000	-18.74
Faro	325,971	314,841	268,040	-58,000	-17.77
Portalegre	196,993	188,482	145,545	-51,500	-26.17
Santarém	453,192	461,705	427,995	-25,000	- 5.56

The liberalizations after 1961, discussed in the text, are clearly reflected in the figures showing population declines in the agrarian districts.

26. After Salazar's accession to power in the late 1920s, the already existent secret police were reorganized as the Polícia Internacional e da Defesa do Estado, the notorious

PIDE, trained in the early 1930s by the Gestapo. Even though their name was again changed after the accession of Caetano in 1968, no significant change in their functions or operations, including murder, torture, and assassination, took place. After April 25, 1974, the PIDE was abolished, and curiously all the PIDE files disappeared. It is alleged that people in the PCP (Partido Comunista Português), the Armed Forces Movement, as well as all the old forces of the Salazar-Caetano right, had had various involvements with the PIDE, which no one wanted to have come to light.

27. Although there was a general substantial improvement during the 1960s and early 1970s and vast improvement after 1974 when clinics and health posts were opened in many rural towns and "villages" (e.g., Lama), often in association with the former Salazarist Casas do Povo (People's Houses, a kind of corporativist community center giving limited services), many areas are still without local doctors and, in the larger immediate areas, without any significant specialized medical care. My friend Mário of São Martinho spent six months in traction for a disk problem, isolated from family and friends in a Lisbon hospital. A child from the northeastern Beira Alta area, having suffered a complex leg fracture, went through a succession of local and subregional hospitals with limited facilities, ending up in the Porto hospital. What is almost more significant is that the *class* relations of medical care often still persist today. Villagers and people we knew in Lisbon *bairros de lata* ("tin can neighborhoods," or "squatter" settlements; see Leeds 1981) who had come from such villages described the bowing (literally, with hat-tipping) and scraping and kowtowing to "Senhor Doutor" (Sir Doctor) to make sure that the status relations were in proper order to help guarantee the doctor's goodwill in case of emergency or other need.

28. Though most villages have primary schools, taught by teachers with the very low-level training afforded by normal schools, secondary schools are, for the most part, only to be found in the *conselhos* or the larger towns and district capitals. In São Martinho, this meant Viseu, 40 km away, at least an hour's ride each way, plus transportation costs, a set of constraints most villagers and their children found prohibitive. The alternative was the *internato* or boarding arrangement in Viseu, where per month cost, including school fees, came to well over a month's minimum salary. Since villagers generally don't have *cash* incomes (whatever they get in kind) of that scale, they cannot afford *internatos*, except, for example, the owner of the store-tavern-post office and a few others who have managed several sources of income. One sees, then, a sort of spatial distribution of education, corresponding to class relations—less and lower as one gets further towards the villages and away from the cities. Circumvention of this structure of class via the education system and education policy (from monarchy times to the present), which kept education out of or limited in the hinterlands, was sometimes achieved by families for their boys by getting them into Catholic seminaries as prospective priests. This was often a ruse to use the Church and its support while having no intention of entering priestly office. We know several such persons in Lama (which has such seminaries nearby, especially in Braga), particularly one of a working-class artisanal family who eventually got higher schooling, "through the padres," in Barcelona, while at least one of his brothers has had or is continuing university education (in history) at the University of Porto.

29. How value equivalences of items in-kind were set requires further research.

30. While we were doing fieldwork in squatter settlements *(favelas)* in Rio in 1968, we met in one of the most depressed *favelas* Ruth Ferreira, a man who had immigrated some years before from the Minho. He described working for a storekeeper in a town (Viana?), where he was afforded living space: his bed was under the sales counter. This was probably in the early 1960s. Perhaps he used the cash he earned to get to Brazil. Descriptions of the

living and working conditions for the *ratinhos* were even more hair-raising, as indicated in the text. Disease and death accompanied the whole experience; informants spoke specifically of bronchitis from working knee-deep in the water of the rice fields.

31. It will be noted, if this idea is accepted and checked against research results cross-societally, that virtually all "explanations" of migration based on the motivations of the migrants alone and all statements of the type that it is the bright ones or the talented ones or the ones who could make it who leave, collapse at once.

32. In his dissertation in the early 1920s, Salazar reportedly spoke of the necessity of emigration for Portugal in order to maintain flows of remittances for foreign exchange. Clearly this foreshadows a conscious policy. See E. Leeds 1984b.

33. Sousa Ferreira gives several tables (1976, pp. 55, 61, 67). The first, table 5, reproduces the figures from Portugal's Instituto Nacional de Estatística (INE) for legal *e*migration, the figures from France's Office National d'Immigration for *im*migration of workers and their families, and the total of these two. The difference between that total and the INE number of legal emigrants is taken to be the number of clandestine emigrants. Table 6 (displaying some minor disparities with table 5) gives the number of legalizations of emigrants from 1963 through 1969; these had been included among the "legal emigrants" in table 5. Table 10 puts all these figures together for the years 1950–1970, as in the chart given in table 2.1 in the appendix. These figures are, of course, for France alone—a twenty-year total of 625,480. Table 2.2 in the appendix gives only legal emigration for all countries for the years 1948–1974. The continuing sharp rises, first of legal emigration, (1961–1964, 1969) then of clandestine workers (1961–1966, 1969–1970), and then of families (1963–1970), are striking. Sousa Ferreira's figures and those given in table 2.2 agree for France between 1950 and 1960, then the latter go wildly higher for several years (1961–1968) and then agree again. I cannot account for this difference. The total emigration for 1948-1974 given in table 2.2 is 1,313,284.

34. Rodrigues Português 1977/78 et al., under the direction of the historian Victor de Sá (see note 19), did a study on court cases involving apprehended clandestine migrants.

35. See sources given in note 33 and the tables in the appendix (families would, of course, be mainly women and children).

36. See Pereira 1971; Pereira 1972; and Rolo 1977 on multinationals.

37. If anything, the capital-intensive investment, along with general technological advances in older industries, produced a net *de*crease in labor demand. At the same time, there was a steady, if not very large, increase of the Portuguese population, with a dip in the few years around the 1970 census. The population went up hugely after 1974 with the influx of *retornados* (see note 41) fleeing the colonial wars and perceived postindependence dangers in the former colonies. Thus there was an increasing "excess" of labor supply.

38. The very removal of political refugees abroad may create conditions of change, or at least pressures for change, in the home countries over shorter or longer periods by virtue of the refugees' political action or propaganda.

39. The recent state of the American political economy is an example of major dislocation, insecurity, perceived danger, experienced uprootings, hunger, homelessness, and unemployment, including strong pressures on the usually relatively comfortable middle classes.

40. The largest property holders in São Martinho had moved to Viseu where they were in law and medicine; they rented out their lands in the village. A somewhat similar pattern existed in Lama, apparently with greater historical depth; a seigneurial family was in-

volved, although their castle in the village had been sold to a lawyer from Porto. In the Santa Vitória area, property owners of the latifundia were generally absentees in any case, involved in city occupations in Lisbon. The whole question of latifundia and seigneurs as "migrants" requires further discussion (see note 44).

41. I speak here of people who had been to and returned from the colonies *before* colonial independence was proclaimed by Portugal; after that date in 1975, a vast influx of "returnees" *(retornados)* came to Portugal from the colonies, although many had fled considerably earlier because of the colonial wars—a total of nearly a million persons returning (not counting the troops, perhaps another 200,000) under highly special conditions. The population went up to just under 10,000,000. The persons referred to in the text are those who, on various grounds, had gone to the colonies—"migrated," "colonized," served in the military—then returned to continental Portugal, also for various reasons (e.g., one man I met in Lama (1981) had spent twelve years in Mozambique, then thirteen working for the British on the Rhodesian railroads, then returned about 1972 to Portugal to care for his aging father).

42. Some officials of the *freguesias* had not been emigrants. Others had, notably in Lama, where at least two in office during our fieldwork had spent considerable time in Venezuela, but had returned and were running sizable (by Lama standards) enterprises, one an artisanal ceramic factory inherited from his family and the other a cement tube–making establishment).

43. What governs the variability of rates needs theoretical, systematic thought; today we mostly treat changes of rate as empirical givens rather than as theoretical problems. We speak of very slow rates as (periods of) "stagnation" and rapid ones as "dynamic" (periods), but the terms are merely descriptive labels, not theoretical terms. In principle, I think, the theory would be one of multiplicity and saliency of linkages among systems; among subsystems, systems, and supersystems; among variables of systems—degrees of closeness and interaction as opposed to relative autonomies. Thus an event of the magnitude and linkage characteristics of the initiation of the colonial war is likely to ramify rapidly at all levels and to all subsystems.

44. At a symposium on Mexican migration at the annual meeting of the American Anthropological Association some years ago, a very eminent anthropologist remarked during the discussion period, "Academics don't migrate; they move." Since I see no theoretical or empirical difference between academicians' moves (in the United States, say) and laborers' moves to other work places, I suggest that the statement is a class-centric one without theoretical content.

APPENDIX: SOME FIGURES ON PORTUGUESE EMIGRATION

Table 2.1 Official and Nonofficial Emigration to France[1] (corrected)[2]

Year	a Official Emig[3]	b Immig. Workers[4]	c Immig. Families[4]	d Total (b+c)	e Clandestine (d-a)
1950	319	72	242	314	—5
1951	67	260	158	418	351
1952	261	472	178	650	389
1953	414	438	252	690	276
1954	568	459	288	747	179
1955	985	949	387	1 336	351
1956	772	1 432	419	1 851	1 078
1957	3 102	4 160	480	4 640	1 538
1958	4 694	5 054	1 210	6 264	1 570
1959	3 542	3 339	1 499	4 838	1 296
1960	3 593	4 007	2 427	6 434	2 841
1961	5 303	6 716	3 776	10 492	5 189
1962	8 051	12 916	3 832	16 798	8 747
1963	13 587	24 781	5 062	29 843	16 256
1964	19 949	43 751	7 917	51 668	31 719
1965	17 200	47 330	12 937	60 267	43 000
1966	18 500	44 916	18 695	63 611	45 000
1967	13 512	34 764	24 833	59 597	46 085
1968	5 760	30 868	27 873	58 741	52 981
1969	27 234	80 829	29 785	110 614	83 380
1970	21 962	88 634	47 033	135 667	113 705
	169 384	436 147	189 333	625 480	456 096

Note: The big leap forward in 1969 is due to the amnesty for illegal emigrants signed by Caetano on December 21, 1968.

[1]Apparently, only France kept summary tallies of illegal immigrants, workers, and families alike; comparable calculations for other countries, thus, cannot be made so that the total figures for *all* emigration are probably still larger than the maxima published.

[2]Corrected means that the numbers from 1961 on are the total given as "official" by the Instituto Nacional de Estatística, minus those emigrants legalized or amnestied in the respective years, i.e., persons already migrants then, not *new* ones in that year.

[3]These are the corrected legal emigration figures.

[4]Office National d'Immigration, *Statistique de l'Immigration, 1970*, Paris, 1970. The figure in column b for 1970 is from the OECD's *Portugal*, Paris, 1971, p. 17.

Source: Adapted from table 10, Sousa Ferreira (1976, p. 67).

Table 2.2 Total Portuguese Emigration for All Countries

Year	Fed. Rep. Germany	S. Africa	Argentina	Australia	Brazil	Canada	United States	France	Holland	Luxemburg	United Kingdom	Sweden	Switzerland	Venezuela	Other Countries	Totals
1948	n	295	814	n	8 770	n	637	n	n	..	n	..	n	738	1 089	12 343
1949	n	208	1 067	n	11 974	n	1 505	499	n	..	n	..	n	795	1 248	17 296
1950	1	232	1 865	8	14 143	7	938	319	4	..	20	..	2	3 077	1 276	21 892
1951	2	351	1 994	41	28 104	14	676	67	2	..	22	..	2	1 416	973	33 664
1952	4	355	1 477	13	41 518	23	582	261	2	..	32	4	1	1 668	1 072	47 018
1953	..	313	784	16	32 159	275	1 455	414	3	..	67	..	1	3 504	695	39 686
1954	4	559	818	42	29 943	1 380	1 918	568	4	..	93	..	6	5 508	168	41 011
1955	..	1 025	583	70	18 486	1 147	1 328	985	4	1	67	2	7	5 718	373	29 796
1956	6	1 225	463	46	16 814	1 612	1 503	772	8	..	97	4	4	3 773	690	27 017
1957	5	757	518	37	19 931	4 158	1 628	3 102	8	1	60	..	14	4 324	813	35 356
1958	2	647	662	57	19 829	1 619	1 596	4 694	6	..	103	4	9	4 073	729	34 030
1959	6	729	385	41	16 400	3 961	4 569	3 542	2	2	76	..	8	3 175	562	33 458
1960	54	688	190	98	12 451	4 895	5 679	3 593	3	2	84	5	8	4 026	542	32 318
1961	277	1 126	434	110	16 073	2 635	3 370	5 446	55	20	137	1	49	3 347	446	33 526
1962	483	739	790	110	13 555	2 739	2 425	8 245	70	4	163	12	20	3 522	662	33 539
1963	1 039	699	368	112	11 281	3 424	2 922	15 223	152	115	239	27	53	3 109	756	39 519
1964	3 868	1 437	207	175	4 929	4 770	1 601	32 641	297	328	331	21	193	3 784	1 064	55 646
1965	11 713	2 802	159	164	3 051	5 197	1 852	57 319	480	363	421	62	171	3 920	1 382	89 056
1966	9 686	4 721	225	288	2 607	6 795	13 357	73 419	1 308	462	597	267	205	4 697	1 605	120 239
1967	2 042	1 947	192	347	3 271	6 615	11 516	59 415	401	205	631	284	191	4 118	1 327	92 502
1968	4 886	921	124	381	3 512	6 833	10 841	46 515	467	215	537	118	176	3 751	1 175	80 452
1969	13 279	713	139	446	2 537	6 502	13 111	27 234	420	361	783	99	276	3 044	1 221	70 165
1970	19 775	702	124	360	1 669	6 529	9 726	21 962	393	269	506	227	362	2 927	829	66 360
1971	16 997	339	55	435	1 200	6 983	8 839	10 023	338	175	303	103	344	3 500	766	50 400
1972	14 377	274	17	249	1 158	6 845	7 574	17 800	149	529	309	23	527	3 641	612	54 084
1973	31 479	359	18	672	890	7 403	8 160	20 692	394	2 870	586	22	1 246	4 294	432	79 517
1974	3 049	452	19	643	729	11 650	9 540	10 568	278	2 123	666	8	735	2 550	387	43 397

[1]The noncorrespondence between the French figures for 1961–1969 given in table 2.1 and table 2.2 has been discused in the text. Whether similar noncorrespondences of numbers exist for other countries is not known, since as noted in table 2.1, n.1, only the French had the necessary data.

Source: Adapted from Secretaria do Estado da Emigração, *Boletim Anual*, *1974*. Lisbon, 1974, table 2.8 (pp. 21–22).

REFERENCES

Almquist, Eric

1977 "Mayo and Beyond: Land, Domestic Industry, and Rural Transformation in the Irish West, 1750–1900." Ph.D. diss., Boston University. Ann Arbor: University Microfilms.

Análise Social

1982 *A Formação de Portugal Contemporâneo, 1000–1980*. Special volumes nos. 72–74, 77–79 (1983).

Branco, Fernando

1983 Personal communication, February 28.

Buechler, Hans

1983 "Spanish Urbanization from a Grass-roots Perspective." In *Urban Life in Mediterranean Europe: Anthropological Perspectives,* edited by M. Kenny and D. Kertzer. 135–161. Urbana: University of Illinois Press.

Buechler, Hans C., and Buechler, Judith-Maria

1975 "Los Suizos: Galician Migration to Switzerland." In *Migration and Development: Implications for Ethnic Identity and Political Conflict,* edited by H. I. Safa and B. M. DuToit, 17–31. The Hague: Mouton.

1981 *Carmen: The Autobiography of a Spanish Galician Woman*. Cambridge, Mass.: Schenkman.

1984 "Four Generations in Spanish Galicia: A Developmental Analysis of Socioeconomic Options." In *Culture and Community in Europe: Essays in Honor of Conrad Arensberg,* edited by O. Lynch, 150–72. New Delhi: Hindustani Press.

Cabral, Manuel Villaverde, ed.

1974 *Materiais para a História da Questão Agrária em Portugal—Séculos XIX e XX*. Lisbon: Inova.

Cadilhe, Miguel

1974 "O arranque da inflação portuguesa." Reprint from *Boletim* no. 91. Banco Nacional Ultramarino, Porto.

Centro de Estudos de Planeamento

1976 "Contribuição para um Estudo da Evolução da População Portuguesa." No. 8 of *Estudos Urbanos e Regionais* (October).

Cunhal, Alvaro

1966 *Contribuição para o Estudo da Questão Agrária*. Lisbon: Edições Avante! 2 vols. 1976.

da Gama, C. Manuel Fonseca

1940 *Terras do Alto Paiva; Memória históricogeográfica e etnográfica do concelho de Vila Nova do Paiva*. Lamego: Voz de Lamego.

Dias, Jorge

1948 *Vilarinho das Furnas*. Porto: Instituto para Alta Cultura.

Gonçalves, Oehen

1972 "A Política Monetária e Financiera em Portugal no Ultimo Decénio." *Simpósio sobre a Política Monetária e Creditícia como Instrumento do Desenvolvimento Económico*. Porto: Banco Português do Atlántico.

Hoben, Alan and John R. Harris

1983 "The Use of Anthropology in Development Planning: The Case of Somalia.'' Colloquium, Department of Anthropology, Boston University, February 2.

Junta de Emigração
1969 *Boletim de 1969*. Lisbon.

Kemper, R.
1977 *Migration and Adaptation: Tzintzuntzan Peasants in Mexico City*. Beverly Hills: Sage Publications.

Leeds, Anthony
1980 ''Towns and Villages in Society: Hierarchies of Order and Cause.'' In *Cities in a Larger Context,* edited by Thomas W. Collins, 6–33. Athens: University of Georgia Press.
1981 ''Lower-Income Urban Settlement Types: Processes, Structures, Policies.'' In *The Residential Circumstances of the Urban Poor in Developing Countries,* 21–61. United Nations Center for Human Settlements (HABITAT). New York: Praeger.
1987 *Minha Terra, Portugal: Poems of Lamentation and Celebration (The Growth of an Ethnography and a Commitment)*. Luso-Brazilian Center, Brown University. Providence: Gavea-Brown.

Leeds, Elizabeth R.
1984a *''Labor Export and Development: The Political Economy of Portuguese Migration.''* Ph.D. diss., Massachusetts Institute of Technology, Cambridge.
1984b ''Salazar's ''Modelo Economico'': The Consequences of Planned Constraint.'' In *Portugal in Development: Emigration, Industrialization, the European Community,* edited by Thomas C. Bruneau and Alexander Macleod, 13–51. Ottawa: University of Ottawa Press

Lucena, Manuel de
1976 *A Evolução do Sistema Corporativo Portugues*. Vol. 1: *O Salazarismo;* Vol. 2: *O Caetanismo*. Lisbon: Perspectiva e Realidades.

Madureira Pinto, José
1977–1978 Personal communications in various interviews.

Office Nacional d'Immigration
1970 *Statistiques de l'Immigration, 1970*. Paris.

Oliveira Martins, J. P.
1887 *Fomento rural e Emigração*. Lisbon: Guimarães Editôres (reprinted articles from the early 1880s on), 1956.

Organization for Economic Cooperation and Development
1971 *Portugal*. Paris: OECD.

Pereira, Miriam Halpern
1971 *Livre Cámbia e Desenvolvimento Económico: Portugal na Segunda Metade do Século XIX*. Lisbon: Edições Cosmos.
1972 *Assimetrias de Crescimento e Dependência Externa*. Lisbon: Seara Nova.

Pereira da Silva, Armando
1973 *Ocupação Sem Limites: História Breve da Reacção Popular contra os Abusos de Autoridade Practicados na Serra de Talhadas do Vouga*. Lisbon: Prelo.

Ribeiro, Aquilino
1918 *As Terras do Demo*. Lisbon: Livraria Bertrand, Círculo de Leitores, 1974.
ca.1942 *Volfrámio*. Lisbon: Livraria Bertrand, 1965.
1946 *Aldeia*. Lisbon: Livraria Bertrand, 1964.
1958 *Quando os Lobos Uivam*. Lisbon: Livraria Bertrand, 1974.
Riegelhaupt, Joyce
1979 "Peasants and Politics in Salazar's Portugal: The Corporate State and Village "Nonpolitics." In *Contemporary Portugal The Revolution and Its Antecedents*, edited by Lawrence S. Graham and Harry M. Makler, 167–90. Austin: University of Texas Press.

Rodrigues Português, Ernesto Pedreira, José Rodrigues Afonso, José Rodrigues Lima, and Manuel António Domingues
1977-78 "A Emigração no Alto Minho (1960–65)." Paper for the course "History of Contemporary Portugal," Prof. Victor de Sá. Braga. Xerox.

Rolo, José Manuel
1977 *Capitalismo, Tecnologia, e Dependência em Portugal*. Lisbon: Editorial Presença.

Salazar, António de
1954 *Discursos, Notas, Relatórios, Teses, Artigos, e Entrevistas, 1909–1953*. Lisbon: Editorial Vanguarda.

Schmitter, Philippe C.
1975 *Corporatism and Public Policy in Authoritarian Portugal*. Contemporary Political Sociology Series, vol. 1. Beverly Hills: Sage.

Secretariado de Estado da Emigração.
1974 *Boletim Anual, 1974*. Lisbon: Ministry of Labor.

Serrão, Joel
1972 *A Emigração Portuguesa*. 2d ed. Lisbon: Livros Horizonte, 1974.

Silva Picão, José da
1903 "Os Ratinhos" from *Através dos Campos. Usos e costumes Agricolo-Alentejanos. Concelho de Elvas*, 2 vols. (the second published in 1922). Reproduced in Cabral 1974, 361–376.

Sousa Ferreira, Eduardo
1976 *Origens e Formas da Emigração*. Lisbon: Iniciativas Editoriais.

Uzzell, J. Douglas
1976 "Ethnography of Migration: Breaking Out of the Bi-polar Myth." In *New Approaches to the Study of Migration*, edited by D. Guillet and J. D. Uzzell, 45–54. Rice University Studies, no. 6/3. Houston: Rice University Press.

Wolf, Eric R.
1955 "Types of Latin American Peasantry." *American Anthropologist* 57:452–71.

3 Working-class Portuguese Families in a French Provincial Town: Adaptive Strategies

Collette Callier Boisvert

ABSTRACT. Boisvert views migration from the point of view of the country of destination. Her case complements that presented by Leeds, for she is dealing with migrants who plan to remain abroad and therefore bring their families to France (although the early migrants also regarded migration as temporary). France's former migration policies appear to have caused or at least facilitated this trend: Faced with an aging population, the nation wished to expand the lower age groups. Because of the time depth involved, three generations of Portuguese migrants are already present in France. Kin and fellow Portuguese migrants in general play an active role in adapting to life in France. For example, close kin often regroup in the same neighborhood.

In spite of the long-term nature of migration, contacts with the home country have remained important. Migrants purchase vacation homes in Portugal and many plan to retire there. Few, however, have actually returned permanently, although Portuguese were among the migrant groups who took most advantage of the government's incentives to return home. We will encounter a similar group of host country–oriented migrants (but from an earlier period of migration) in Sontz's article.

INTRODUCTION

The literature on the importance of social networks (both kin and coethnic networks) in the migratory process is quite extensive. Especially in the case of Portuguese migration, the role of kinship and neighborhood ties in chain migration has been emphasized (Trindade 1965; Poinard 1971, 1972; Anderson 1974; Brettell and Callier Boisvert 1977; Lamphere et al. 1980). All these studies report that kin and friendship networks are used widely during the period of initial migration and settlement in the new society.

In this chapter, based on qualitative research,[1] I propose to examine some variations on the theme of the adaptation of migrant families to another society.

The sample is constituted by thirty-five rural Portuguese families settled in Poitiers, a French provincial town.[2] The methodology is based mainly on structured and unstructured interviews. I study the migrants' use of their kin network and family role relationships as an adaptive strategy for Portuguese migrants to improve the family's standard of living. I examine the role of kinship and relationships among members of the same ethnic group in the migrants' adaptation through the study of the migratory process, housing, and employment patterns. Are these social networks maintained after the initial process of settlement? Do the migrants develop ethnic enclaves with a marked sense of community in the host country? Or, on the contrary, is group solidarity not perceptible, because individual families pursue a more assimilationist strategy in their new environment (Graves and Graves 1980)?

In her study of Portuguese families settled in New England, Lamphere shows that "the nature of a local economy and the couple's work position within it directly shape and transform both conjugal roles and kin networks" (1980, 221). Similarly, I propose to see how the adaptation to new labor contexts changes conjugal roles, kin relationships (with parents, siblings, and children of a married couple) and other social networks (within the ethnic group or with the receiving society). Finally, I wish to examine the relation of these adaptive strategies to the receptivity or prejudice of the host society. For the migration policy of the receiving country has a strong influence on the importance of social networks among migrants.

MIGRATION POLICY IN FRANCE

In her study of Italian families Schnapper (1974) showed how cultural centralization in France contributed to weaken social life among migrant families. French society is a centralist and assimilationist society for European migrants as it was for the mass of French peasants who flocked into urban centers in the 19th century. Nevertheless, migration policy has changed in the last decade.[3] Migrants are now assisted in retaining their language, religion, and ethnicity. At the same time, publicity campaigns are organized to sensitize public opinion to migrant problems. Some opinion polls (Girard et al. 1971, 1974) noted that French attitudes with respect to foreign migrants vary markedly according to the latter's citizenship: "A decided opposition appears between on the one hand, the Italians, the Spaniards, and the Portuguese, all of whom encounter few problems, and on the other, black Africans and Maghrebians" (1974, 1058).

Foreign minorities have long existed in France (George 1976), but migration policy has never clearly evolved, following instead the vagaries of labor needs. After World War II, a new migration policy was formulated by the *Office National de l'Immigration* (March 1946) for the reconstruction of the country with the aid of foreign labor. Different phases followed one another (Tapinos 1975) with an acceleration in the annual rate of migration in the decade of 1961–1971, waves of clandestine migrants until 1974, and an abrupt decrease thereafter when

France closed it doors to new migrants as a result of worldwide inflation and unemployment. Now migration policy tends to better employ its human capital (Kayser 1977), using different means to integrate foreign workers (mainly of European origin) and young members of the second generation.

PORTUGUESE MIGRATION TO FRANCE

It is estimated that nearly one million individuals left Portugal in the decade of the sixties (more than 10 percent of the total population of Portugal) to work in Western Europe and especially in France. Migration of Portuguese workers to France came after the Italian and Spanish waves. In the decade of 1961–1971, there was a rapid increase in the annual rate of migration (from approximately 40,000 to 80,000 per year) with large numbers of clandestine migrants. After 1971, as a result of an agreement signed between Portugal and France, the annual rate of Portuguese workers was limited to 65,000 and began to drop. After 1974 migration was limited to members of the nuclear family still residing in Portugal. A new agreement between the two countries was signed in 1977. It guaranteed some occupational, educational, and social rights to Portuguese workers and their families, as well as the maintenance of their ethnicity through language and culture. They also received long-term residential and work permits (ten years, renewable).

Portuguese migration to France has been characterized by two distinctive features: a high level of clandestine migration, and, increasingly, its involvement of entire families (Poinard 1971; Leloup 1972; Antunes 1973; Godinho 1974; Sousa Ferreira 1976; Serrão 1977). Clandestine migration was facilitated by the proximity of France and the ease of legalization after arrival by French authorities. It was also due to the rigid migration laws in Portugal and the threat of military service during the African colonial wars. Approximately two-thirds of all Portuguese migrants to France in the twenty years between 1950 and 1970 came illegally.

Like Galician migration (Buechler and Buechler 1975), Portuguese migration is an age-old movement and traditionally was a male experience. But the proportion of families moving to France increased rapidly. More and more women and children accompany the household head or follow him soon after. Between 1964 and 1974 the proportion approximated 50 percent (*Boletim anual* 1975). This tendency for family migration strengthened with the new migration policy of "family regroupment" established by the government to encourage permanent settlement. This shift of migration policy is related to the "natalist" population policy, designed to expand the rate of demographic growth. So Portuguese migration presents a third distinctive feature: a "rotating" phase followed by long-term or permanent settlement. Conjunctural migration became structural (Poinard 1979).

The foreign population of France amounts to 7.7 percent of the total population (January 1976). The Portuguese are among the most numerous (858,929), surpassed only by Algerians (884,320), and greatly exceeding the Italians (558,205) and Spaniards (531,384). They have settled everywhere in the country, but are more concentrated in some urban centers, heavily industrialized areas (the "région parisienne," Lyon, Clermont-Ferrand, Toulouse), and because of the proximity to the border, the Lower Pyrénées. The small town of Poitiers (81,313 inhabitants in 1975) represents an area with relatively few foreigners (1.5 percent of the total population). But the Portuguese form the most numerous minority: one-third of the foreign population.

PORTUGUESE FAMILIES IN A PROVINCIAL TOWN

The thirty-five nuclear families in the sample originated from the rural areas of northern Portugal. The husbands were previously employed in agriculture or in craft industries (masons, painters, carpenters). A few of them were coal miners. The wives and daughters were engaged in agriculture or were employed as maids. Some worked in the textile industry. Most arrived between 1963 and 1972 as clandestine migrants. The town of Poitiers is located on the railroad between the border and Paris. It offers housing facilities and an expanding labor market in construction and public works. For these reasons, Portuguese male workers have settled there, followed by their wives and children. In 1978 the average length of residence in France was approximately thirteen years for men and eight years for women in the sample. The average age was 41.8 for men and 37 for women. The average number of children per family was 3.2.

As others have pointed out in studies on migrant communities, kin networks are vital in helping couples solve instrumental needs like arranging for migration and finding housing and jobs. Here I will consider the nature and frequency of this kin support among Portuguese families settled in a small town, both during the initial phase as well as in the long term.

The Migratory Process

Kinship and friendship networks are the most usual channel of migration in the spontaneous and illegal movement of Portuguese migrants. The husband usually migrates first with kinsmen or fellow villagers and after a few years asks his wife and children to join him. But other alternatives are possible. The couple may leave their children in Portugal in the care of the maternal grandmother (Brettell 1979), so the woman can help her spouse to earn money in order to be able to return definitively to the homeland at an earlier date. This "conjugal couple strategy," as Brettell called it, and as Buechler and Buechler observed among Galician migrants in Switzerland (1975), was usual at the beginning of Portuguese migration. But it was increasingly dropped in favor of family migration. A man may arrange for other primary relatives—siblings or children—to migrate. The father may help his son who wants to escape military service, his daughter who wants to work as a maid in France. Even women may migrate first and then call the spouses to join them. Whoever initiates it, the migration of the head of household usually means that the entire nuclear family is united sooner or later.

Maria and Manuel's case is an example of family strategy in the migration process. Manuel arrived *a salto* (illegally) in 1967 with a cousin who had heard about work in Poitiers. The two men found employment as manual laborers in a company of public works and have remained there to this day. Two and a half years later Manuel asked his wife and their seven children to join him. The oldest daughter, Augusta, was engaged to a second cousin, Joaquim, who followed her *a salto* one week later. They married in Poitiers and the young man worked in the same company as his father-in-law. Two years later Joaquim called his single sister. She, however, was not able to find the kind of job she wanted and returned to Portugal. At the request of his wife, Manuel found work in the same company for her brother Francisco, who arrived in Poitiers alone. Later Francisco was joined by his wife and children and they settled in a neighboring house. Recently, the fourth daughter of Maria and Manuel married a fellow villager during vacation in the homeland. She returned to France with her parents and subsequently called her husband, who arrived two months later as a legal migrant.

Housing and Employment Patterns

Because of the relative ease in finding lodgings and work, and because of the mobile nature of male and female employment (see below), kinship and friendship ties are the determining factor in the choice of residence. Portuguese families in Poitiers are quite dispersed. Some of them live in ancient lodgings in the center of town; others in old farmhouses in the suburbs, leased to them in exchange for certain services—guarding the property or maintaining the house of the owner. Most, however, live in low-cost public housing (*Habitation à Loyer Modéré,* HLM) in the peripheral neighborhoods, mixed with French families of modest means. Recently, migrant families have been buying individual houses in housing estates surrounding the town, or old houses which they renovated. At present one-fifth of the sample is engaged in the process of buying a house.

This dispersal does not, however, preclude the formation of small groups. Primary relatives—parents and siblings of a married couple—tend to regroup in the same area, sometimes even the same building.[4] Maria and Manuel's family may serve as an example: Maria and three married daughters presently live in the same neighborhood. Maria broke relations with her sister-in-law, who now lives in another neighborhood. When Maria decided to move from the first house, two married daughters moved as well, and the third moved to an adjacent building upon her marriage. Thus certain kinship ties—mother-daughter bond, bonds between siblings—are activated not only in the initial process of settlement, to arrange lodgings for the newcomers, but also later when living conditions improve and the migrant family resolves to move house. A married daughter, for instance, wants to live near her mother just as in Portugal (Callier 1968).

Housing conditions vary according to the length of residence in France and plans for the future. As migrants strive to amass "a bundle" in the least amount of time, living conditions are not greatly improved in the first years. But as their stay lengthens, and their plans change, living conditions improve. The settlement pattern of Portuguese families is similar to that of French rural families of modest means: they begin in old lodgings in the center, followed by low-cost public housing in the peripheral neighborhood, and for the most successful, end in their own individual houses. This process is the same in many localities in France (Poinard 1972) and shows the gradual assimilation of Portuguese migrants.

The local labor market presents migrant men and women with a narrow range of occupations because of the weak industrial development of the town.[5] Work as employers in the commercial sector is nearly closed to them by French authorities and by lack of training, except in crafts industries. Most of the work available is work that the French do not want to do (Granotier 1970; Minces 1973; Viguier 1972).

The construction and public work sector employs most of the male population, 25/33 men of the sample. A few industrial enterprises accept and train a small number of young workers, migrants and members of the second generation. Some light manufacturing firms employ a dozen or so young women. They are also employed in lower-level jobs in hospitals and in the commercial sector. However, a woman who is older than 25 at the time she enters France, who does not know the language and possesses no professional skill, has no other option but work as a domestic—21/35 women of the sample. If she is single, she may become a maid in a family; if married, a chambermaid in a hotel, a waitress, or a cleaning lady in a private home or public building. The women usually arrange hours of cleaning around their family life, in order to work as long as they can each day: for female employment is an essential part of a family's economic strategy.[6] Migrant families have a stable income, even though they may change employers because of low hourly wages and such common abuses as overtime work at standard rates, unpaid premiums, and systematic lowering of positions (Granotier 1970; Minces 1973; Viguier 1972). But Portuguese workers are now well informed of their rights. They look for the highest hourly wages and the chance to do overtime even if the job is very hard.

Kinsmen and friends act as an employment agency to find a job or a new employer, often at the request of the employers themselves. This results in the concentration of kinsmen in the same firm.

Since 1975 an increasing number of Portuguese craftsmen have established their own small construction firms, using family or coethnic labor.[7] Thus workers became employers in the only occupational sector where they could acquire locally some ability: construction. Some of them had already been craftsmen in Portugal, but they needed to practice and assimilate new techniques. After approximately ten years of residence, they were able to enter the construction market. They cannot avoid the difficulties resulting from a period of economic depression. In such a context, family or ethnic solidarity remains indispensable to overcome uncertain economic conditions.

In short, family solidarity is an important factor in housing and employment patterns, even when individual families pursue an assimilationist strategy in their new context. This leads us to the question of whether the existence of small family groups means that the Portuguese form ''ethnic enclaves'' in the receiving society. In other words, we must ascertain whether family solidarity can be extended to group solidarity.

Ethnic Community

Two forms of Portuguese ''urban villages'' have existed in France. The first, the *bidonville* (shantytown) such as the one which cropped up in the sixties in Champigny, a suburb east of Paris, no longer exists. The majority of migrants living there under miserable conditions were men. It was a temporary settlement, with a high degree of turnover. In contrast, other urban villages near Paris, in the Pyrénées (Trindade 1965), in Puy-de-Dôme And Rhône (Poinard 1979), presented better living conditions—decent old lodgings, ancient farmhouses—and were characterized by a stable settlement. This type gathered together entire families who wished to re-create the previous social networks. Both forms of ethnic enclaves were constituted by migrants who originated primarily from the same village.

These two forms seem to correspond to the first steps of the Portuguese rush to France. Later, the Portuguese settlement changed. French migration policy did not encourage any form of residential segregation. In fact, the subsequent waves of migration of Portuguese workers in the last two decades and their settlement all over France did not entail the creation of increasing numbers of urban villages. As Brettell and Callier Boisvert have noted:

> The unorganized character of Portuguese migration, its individuality and initially high degree of illegality works against the formation of strong community ties. So too does the assimilationist character of French migration policy. Finally, there is little political or economic advantage to the formation of strong community or ethnic ties among Portuguese migrants in France. (1977, 168)

In the sample, except for members of extended families, migrants did not originate from the same village, but from the entire northern half of Portugal, and they do not constitute residential communities in the host town. But this does not necessarily mean that there is no community feeling. As we shall see, migrants identify with others through a more or less complex network of social relations which link related and unrelated families together to compose an ''unstructured community'' (Brettell and Callier Boisvert 1977).

THE HOUSEHOLD AND RELATIONSHIPS AMONG PRIMARY RELATIVES

Because family migration, both legal and clandestine, increased rapidly in the last two decades, the most common form of household composition today is the nuclear family.[8] In the sample, thirty-three families out of thirty-five are complete nuclear families. The remaining two households are headed by women, one separated and the other a widow. Only two cases include other kin as permanent members: an old married woman's father who cannot live alone in Portugal, and a married woman's single sister who is a precious aid to her for housework.

The migrant household is not a simple reconstitution of the family unit in Portugal. In most rural areas of northern Portugal, members of nuclear families are dispersed for economic reasons (Callier 1966; Goldey 1975). Male labor migration is traditional (Godinho 1974; Serrão 1977; Pereira 1981). They migrate to urban centers or to foreign countries, returning home on weekends or for holidays. Children usually leave home when they do not find work in the fields or in the village. At the age of 12 or 13, girls are placed as maids in urban middle-class families or in factories, and boys become apprentices or messengers in businesses. In contrast, in the receiving country, the family unit is stable and complete throughout the year.

The family unit may be affected by migration at different periods of the family cycle. A couple may begin life together in France. They may migrate just after marriage—it is usually a second stay in France for either the husband or the wife—or they may marry in France. However, the couple may also have spent the first part of their married life in the homeland. When they migrate, the oldest children would then be teenagers, the youngest born or educated in France. The head of the household has often spent a more or less lengthy stay in France alone, acquiring an experience which may have had a marked effect on him. Such families face problems which are different from those in which the couple migrated more or less at the same time and at the beginning of their conjugal life. They need to exert greater efforts of adaptation to succeed in their family life. But in either case the greater stability of the nuclear family among migrants strengthens both conjugal and filial bonds.

Migration and urbanization necessarily involve a new distribution of conjugal roles. The two spouses contribute to the resources of the household: the husband by means of a stable salaried job, the wife to a lesser degree, because of child care responsibilities. Thus she may work part-time as a cleaning lady. She usually manages the family budget, and although she does not account for daily expenditures, she does discuss and solicit the advice of her husband for major purchases. The husband takes from his wage what he needs for personal expenses—gasoline, tobacco, café, and frequently, betting on the horse races.

The sharing of daily chores between spouses varies according to the wife's work. As Lamphere et al. (1980) emphasize, the couple's work position in the local economy and the nature of the wife's paid employment change the degree of conjugal role segregation. When the wife does only a few hours of cleaning, the husband's aid is occasional and involves mainly caring for young children, shopping, and cooking. The daily participation of the husband becomes a necessity for young couples when the wife has a full-time job. Nevertheless, he rarely engages in doing the laundry and housework, which he considers feminine tasks.

Traditionally, the husband has the authority and power of decision making in Portuguese households. As a proverb says: "In the house she rules but I rule her" *(na casa manda ela e nela manda eu)*. In practice, it is increasingly common for informants, especially young couples, to say that husband and wife share authority. The couple exercise their power of decision making together, mainly with regard to future plans. They share the responsibilities of educating their children but in a somewhat unequal fashion. Authority is in the father's hands, whereas the mother is responsible for transmitting traditional values and for handling all the administrative questions with respect to children about education, health, social life, etc.

The tendency for joint activities is more accentuated in a family's social life. The spouses spend much of their leisure time together—except in cafés, catering only to male migrants—relaxing at home, watching television, and hosting or visiting relatives and friends on Saturday nights and Sundays.

In short, complementarity and dependence characterize the conjugal role relationship among Portuguese couples in France, as Buechler (1975) notes for Gallego couples in Switzerland. Following Bott's terminology (1971), migration and urbanization change the segregated roles of peasant couples to complementary and dependent, then joint roles.

The relationships between parents and children may vary according to the age of the children when they arrived in France. The youngest who received all of their education there are more influenced by the receiving society and want to live like their schoolmates. The oldest children, arriving as teenagers, are marked by their rural childhood and have learned to behave according to traditional rules of conduct. Faced with this threat of a split within the family, many parents strengthen their control over the children's behavior and demand their respect. Every family has a television set. Some informants say that they bought it to keep children at home. Parents do not discriminate between sexes with respect to schooling. Other variables influence both parents and children. For instance, birth order and the age of the child upon arrival are both significant. The oldest are often disadvantaged. Frequently they arrive too old to follow French schooling at their age level and thus rapidly lose interest in studying. Instead, they leave school at 16 to work and contribute to the family income. The most gifted child, boy or girl, is encouraged to study in order to find a good job.

Intergenerational conflict exists, but it diminishes rapidly when a young person who is in conflict with his parents begins to work and marries. Portuguese society encourages individualism (Dias 1971). At any rate, children have aspirations similar to those of their parents, that is, to start a new family and work hard to live decently within the ideal of family self-sufficiency. This ideology of family self-sufficiency is strong among all Portuguese peasants. Lamphere (1980) also observed it among Azorean migrants settled in New England.

In conclusion, migration of nuclear families involves a greater dependence of family members on one another and self-reliance in the face of a foreign society which was chosen for economic motives. Adaptive strategies are family strategies. The search for material and social success leads each family unit to retreat into an individualism which is enhanced by urban life and industrial civilization. Nevertheless, migration does not lead to a break with the extended family. In economic migration, only the productive sector of the population comprised of two generations migrates. Because of the length of Portuguese settlement, three generations now coexist. The third was born in France. In a foreign context, a new family bond—grandparents-grandchildren—is developing through daily contacts. The grandmother, preferably maternal grandmother, takes care of her grandchildren or she looks after them when they come home from school until the parents return, in order to make it easier for the mother to work.

In the extended family the kin ties predate the migration experience, but they are also intensified by it, as only a few members are in France. They are reinforced by ritual bonds: kinsmen are chosen as godparents. The deliberate regrouping of parents and siblings of a married couple in the same neighborhood shows how important sources of aid and support primary relatives are both on the practical and affective level. However, this approximation does not lessen family self-sufficiency, especially financial autonomy: "Everyone in his own home" *(cada um em sua casa)*. Family solidarity is based on reciprocity and respects the independence of each household. Sisters, for instance, exchange goods and services, child-care services, and hours of cleaning. The ties are closest when the kinship network is established by women, a fact which can be generalized to other cultural groups (Firth, Hubert, and Forge 1969). Outside of mother-daughter and sibling bonds, the strength of kinship ties varies from family to family.

SOCIAL NETWORKS

Informants carefully distinguish between kinsmen and nonkinsmen in the social network. Their small number, dispersal, and the lack of a consulate or Portuguese priest are inimical to a strong sense of community.[9] Ethnic affiliation is still defined according to place of origin for the most part (Buechler and Buechler 1975). Reserve and mistrust are common attitudes towards unknown compatriots. In the beginning of migration, many newcomers were victims of unscrupulous compatriots. "The Portuguese mistreat one another" *(os Portugueses são ruins uns para com os outros)* is a frequent comment among migrants. But the length of residence and the small size of the town, which facilitates interpersonal relations, alter this negative attitude. Each family has a good knowledge of other Portuguese families in the neighborhood and in more distant areas, even without regular frequentation. Women make new acquaintances in the street and in the marketplace; men, on construction sites and in cafés. The Sunday open-air market serves as a preferred context for male and female socializing. As in many other cities in France (Nizier 1977), migrants flock to traditional markets where they feel at home. The continuity of interpersonal linkages is also maintained among migrants through voluntary associations.

Two voluntary associations were recently created, in 1974 and 1977. These are a sports association and a folkloric society. Both include only a small number of members, but they involve the entire family as active supporters and have a great impact on the local Portuguese minority. Voluntary associations are excellent contexts to observe ethnic solidarity (Callier Boisvert 1978). It is true that they provide an arena for envy and competition between families. But this competition for personal assertion is also a factor in ethnic identification. It creates interpersonal linkages, even if its negative aspect is emphasized. It shows the great interest of coethnics in gaining social prestige.

The awakening of a sense of community in the migrant milieu is hindered by frequent "comings and goings." The geographical proximity of Portugal to France facilitates these movements. At the beginning of migration, most Portuguese families were oriented towards eventual return to their homeland. As did Galician migrants (Buechler and Buechler 1975), they built a house in the native area where they passed their vacations, providing for the definitive return. Trindade (1973) and Poinard (1979) emphasize the renewal of villages and the artificial prosperity carried by returning migrants.[10] Many families still consider their stay in France to be temporary and expect to return one day to their homeland. The goal of return is stronger in the parents' generation. They plan to retire there when old and out of work. It is part of the Portuguese cultural ideology of return migration as Brettell describes it (1979). In fact, the rate of actual return is low, and as Godinho notes (1974), it has always been low. At present, it no longer seems realistic to build a nice house in the homeland. The high cost of land and construction since the Revolution of April 25, 1974, and the severe economic problems of Portugal—among which unemployment and competition with the *retornados* in the labor market are particularly important for returning migrants—are dissuasive factors.[11] So the homeland appears more and more as a vacation setting, and the receiving country as a permanent place to live.

One can say that migrants now have two communities of identification: their native village during holidays and their neighborhood in the host society. The migrant family measures its accomplishments against the native community, as well as against migrant and French neighbors. At first, relations between French and Portuguese communities were characterized on the one hand by paternalism and on the other by a mentality of assisted people, reproducing the system of relationships in Portugal between haves and have-nots. These relations are still in effect with employers, doctors, officials, etc. However, both in the occupational and residential milieu, interethnic relations on the same economic level have improved. At least for young migrants and for the most successful families who are interacting more and more with French society through neighborhood associations, social relationships have become increasingly egalitarian or reciprocal. As a result of this greater approximation, mixed marriages and the adoption of French citizenship are rising.[12] During the initial settlement in France, marital partners were chosen among fellow villagers. Now there are three alternatives: the traditional choice in the native village, and more frequently coethnic or French partners. Maria and Manuel's married children serve as an example: Augusta, the oldest, married a second cousin, who migrated soon afterwards to join her. Eugênia married a Portuguese who worked in France with her father. Fátima married a French boy she knew through her employment. Noemia's spouse is a fellow villager she frequently saw during holidays; and the fifth child, a boy, became engaged to a French girl whom he knew at school.

The number of adoptions of French citizenship is still low compared with the number of Portuguese in France, but it increased rapidly in the decade 1969–1978.[13]

CONCLUSIONS

Kinship networks are widely used as an adaptive strategy by Portuguese migrant families in the initial phase of settlement, because of the spontaneous character and high degree of illegality of the movement. Later, primary relatives are still required for some instrumental tasks and on the affective level. Nevertheless, these close bonds do not really affect the strong ideology of family self-sufficiency. Migration and urbanization strengthen conjugal and filial bonds. The greater dependence of members on one another constitutes the family adaptive strategy in the new context. Migrant families are part of a mass society, the French working class, at the lowest level of the local economy. The wife's paid employment is an economic necessity of the family strategy. Because of the structure of the local economy, many wives obtain only unskilled jobs or remain underemployed. But they nevertheless succeed in improving their social position both within and outside the household. The integration of these families is not merely functional. In a small town, the system of relationships is very close to that which the migrants knew in their own country: a provincial way of life intermediary between rural life and the life of a large city. So migrant families have gradually become involved as consumers in the receiving society. Their social aspirations are rising and displacing their goal of eventual return. As a result, social mobility and competition among families for social prestige are directed not only against fellow villagers—who call them *Os Franceses*—but also against coethnic and French partners in the receiving society. This competition enhances the process of assimilation. So the aims of migrants converge with those of the host society that wishes to settle the most hardworking families permanently, following its selective migration policy.

NOTES

1. The research was conducted intermittently between 1973 and 1978. It was partially supported by the Calouste Gulbenkian Foundation.

2. I still maintain contacts with one-half of these families.

3. See *La Nouvelle Politique de l'Immigration,* Secrétariat d'État aux Travailleurs Immigrés, Paris, 1977.

4. When a family buys a house in another neighborhood, such a regrouping would seem difficult. However, it may occur anyway. One informant—a married woman who is engaged in buying a house—says that she intends to rent a part of her future house to her parents and young brother.

5. Portuguese workers present some characteristics which differ from those of other labor migrants in France: (1) Weak qualifications, with the highest rate of laborers and the lowest rate of technicians and managers of all foreigners (*Statistique du Travail,* 1980). (2) A high number of active women. In 1977, 40.2 percent of Portuguese workers were women. Portuguese women had the highest rate of female foreign work in 1975 with 30.8 percent of the total—13.3 percent for Moroccan and Tunisian women—but they are usually employed only as menial laborers or in cleaning services (Taboada Leonetti and Levi 1978). (3) The extent of undeclared or overtime work for men during their leisure time—*biscate*—and for women as cleaning ladies in private homes, during the entire week.

6. A few of the women who do not work say that they consider the family allowances given for children as their contribution to the family income. For six children, the total of family allowances approximates a man's wage. The family allowances were of course a strong stimulant to the reconstitution of families in France.

7. Portuguese migration follows the paths of previous migrations. In Poitiers the two most important buildings and public works enterprises belong to men of Italian and Spanish origins. Between 1975 and 1981, 36 Portuguese workers—approximately 6 percent of the male Portuguese population—established their own firms: 29 are masons, the others are painters, carpenters, or plumbers. In the same period, only 5 tradesmen were registered, 2 in the construction sector. Before 1975 the number of Portuguese employers was insignificant (source: Prefecture of Vienne).

8. The new distribution of conjugal roles and social networks was the topic of my two previous articles on Portuguese families (1977 and 1978–79). So I will deal only with those issues that were not covered in my earlier articles.

9. Others pointed out the priest's role among rural Catholic migrants (Trindade 1965; Béteille 1972; Brettell 1979). The priest's support is crucial to promote a sense of group identity.

10. In 1977 a form of financial aid, *o milhão* (of centimes = FF 10,000) was granted to all those migrant workers residing in France for more than five years who wished to return home. Between 1977 and 1979 only 5 percent of Portuguese accepted this aid to return. But it is true that the Portuguese were the most numerous among all migrants to accept such financial aid (Poinard 1979), which ended in November 1981.

11. *Retornados* are the Portuguese of Angola, Mozambique, and Guinea, who returned to their homeland at the end of the colonial wars.

12. As the Consul of Portuguese for the concerned area says, mixed marriages now represent one-half of all marriages celebrated in France (both French woman/Portuguese man and Portuguese woman/French man). Children are automatically French.

13. The minister of labor provides the following figures for naturalization of Portuguese citizens for the decade 1969-1978:

1969	1,365
1970	1,947
1971	2,780
1972	3,233

1973	3,800
1974	4,784
1975	5,263
1976	5,552
1977	6,224
1978	8,603

At the local level, the number of demands of naturalization is rising in a parallel manner. It rose from six in 1974 to thirteen in 1979 (source: Préfecture of Vienne).

REFERENCES

Anderson, Grace M.

1974 *Networks of Contact: The Portuguese and Toronto*. Waterloo, Ont., Canada: Wilfrid Laurier University.

Antunes, M. L. Marinho

1973 *A Emigração portuguesa desde 1950. Dados e Comentários Cadernos*. Lisbon: Gabinete de Investigações sociais.

Béteille, Roger

1972 "Les Rouergats à Paris (19e et 20e siècles). Un phénomène socio-religieux mal connu, le rôle du clergé dans l'émigration." *Études de la région parisienne* 33: 9–18; 34: 12–20.

Boletim Anual da Secretaria de Estado da Emigração

1975 Lisbon.

Bott, Elizabeth

1971 *Family and Social Network*. 2d ed. London: Tavistock.

Brettell, Caroline B.

1979 "Emigrar para voltar: a Portuguese ideology of return migration." *Papers in Anthropology* 20, no. 1: 1–20.

Brettell, Caroline, and Callier Boisvert, Colette

1977 "Portuguese Immigrants in France: Familial and Social Networks and the Structuring of Community." *Studi Emigrazione/Etudes Migrations* 46: 149–203.

Buechler, H. C., and Buechler, J. M.

1975 "Los Suizos: Galician Migration to Switzerland." In *Migration and Development: Implications for Ethnic Identity and Political Conflict,* edited by H. I. Safa and B. M. DuToit, 17–31. The Hague: Mouton.

Buechler, Judith-Maria

1975 "The Eurogallegas: Female Spanish Migration." In *Being Female: Reproduction, Power, and Change,* edited by Dana Raphael. World Anthropology. The Hague: Mouton.

Callier, Colette

1966 "Soajo, une communauté féminine rurale de l'Alto-Minho." *Bulletin des Etudes Portugaises* 26: 237–78.

1968 "Remarques sur le système de parenté et sur la famille au Portugal." *L'Homme* 8: 87–103.

Callier Boisvert, Colette

1978 "Minorité et groupe folklorique." *Arquivos do Centro Cultural Português*. Paris: Calouste Gulbenkian Foundation, pp. 741–57.

1978-79 "Immigrés portugais en France: rôles masculins et rôles féminins au sein du groupe domestique." *Bulletin des Etudes Portugaises et Brésiliennes* 39/40: 273–97.

Dias, Jorge
1971 *Estudos do Carácter nacional Português*. Estudos de Antropologia Cultural, no. 7. Lisbon; Junta de Investigações do Ultramar.

Firth, Raymond; Hubert, J.; and Forge, A.
1969 *Families and their Relatives*. London: Routledge and Kegan Paul.

George, Pierre
1976 *Migrations Internationales*. Paris: P.U.F.

Girard, Alain
1971 "Attitude des Français à l'égard de l'immigration étrangère. Enquête d'opinion publique." *Population* 26: 827–75.

Girard, A.; Charbit, Y.; and Lamy, M. L.
1974 "Attitude des Français à l'égard de l'immigration étrangère. Nouvelle enquête d'opinion publique." *Population* 29: 1015–69.

Godinho, Vitorino Magalhães
1974 "L'émigration portugaise du XVe siècle à nos jours. Histoire d'une constante structurale." In *Conjoncture économique et structures sociales*, pp. 253–68, The Hague: Mouton.

Goldey, Patricia
1975 "Emigration and Family Structure: A Case Study from Minho." Communication to Symposium on *A Família no contexto do fenómeno migratório*. Lisbon; U.N.L.

Granotier, Bernard
1970 *Les Travailleurs immigrés en France*. Paris: Maspéro.

Graves, Theodore D., and Graves, Nancy B.
1980 "Kinship Ties and the Preferred Adaptive Strategies of Urban Migrants." In *The Versatility of Kinship*, edited by Linda S. Cordell and Stephen Beckerman, 195–218. New York: Academic Press.

Kayser, Bernard
1977 "L'échange inégal des ressources humaines: migrations, croissance et crise en Europe." *Revue Tiers-Monde* 18, no. 69: 7–20.

Lamphere, Louise; Silva, Filomena M.; and Sousa, John P.
1980 "Kin Networks and Family Strategies. Working class Portuguese Families in New England." In *The Versatility of Kinship*, edited by Linda S. Cordell and Stephen Beckerman, 219–48. New York: Academic Press.

Leloup, Yves
1972 "L'émigration portugaise dans le monde et ses conséquences pour le Portugal." *Revue de Géographie de Lyon* 42: 59–76.

Minces, Juliette
1973 *Les Travailleurs étrangers en France*. Paris: Seuil.

Nizier, Stéphane
1977 "Le marché de Villiers: le Portugal, un dimanche." *Autrement* 11; 44–5.

Nouvelle Politique de l'Immigration
1977 Secrétariat d'État aux Travailleurs Immigrés. Paris.

Pereira, Miriam Halpern
1981 *A Política Portuguesa de Emigração 1850–1930*. Lisbon: A Regra do Jogo Editor.

Poinard, Michel

1971 "L'émigration portugaise de 1960 à 1969." *Revue Géographique des Pyrénées et du Sud-Ouest* 42: 293–304.

1972 "Les Portugais dans le département du Rhône entre 1960 et 1970." *Revue de Géographie de Lyon* 47: 35–58.

1979 *Le Retour des Travailleurs Portugais.* Paris: La Documentation Française.

Schnapper, Dominique

1974 "Centralisme et fédéralisme culturels: les émigrés Italiens en France et aux Etats-Unis." *Annales* 29, no. 5, 1141–59.

Serrão, Joel

1977 *A Emigração Portuguesa, sondagem histórica.* 3d ed. Lisbon: Livros Horizonte.

Sousa Ferreira, Eduardo

1976 *Origens e formas da emigração.* Lisbon: Iniciativas Editoriais.

Statistiques du Travail

1980 "Enquête sur la main-d'oeuvre étrangère effectuée en octobre 1976." Supplément au *Bulletin Mensuel.*

Taboada Leonetti, Isabel, and Levi, Florence

1978 *Femmes et Immigrées.* Paris: La Documentation Française

Tapinos, Georges

1975 *L'immigration étrangère en France, 1946–1973.* Paris: P.U.F., I.N.E.D.–Travaux et Documents.

Trindade, Maria Beatriz Rocha

1965 *Immigrés Portugais.* Lisbon: Instituto Superior de Ciências Sociais e Política Ultramarina.

1973 "Sobrevivência e progresso de uma aldeia despovoada." *Geographica* 9, no. 35: 3–25.

Viguier, Marie-Claire

1972 "Les travailleurs Portugais à Toulouse: migration, travail, vie collective." *Annales de l'Université de Toulouse le Mirail* 9: 115–132.

4 In the Aftermath of Colonization: Black African Immigrants in France

Jacques Barou

ABSTRACT. The Soninké, who migrated to France from sub-Saharan Africa, have had a much more difficult time in the host country than the Portuguese migrants. In part, this may be due to the timing of their migration, but probably to a larger extent to racial attitudes. In contrast with the Portuguese migrants, who appear to be regarded as more readily assimilable, they are regarded as difficult to assimilate. Barou shows the extent to which a migrant group with a very different cultural background from most migrants in Europe can set up a migration field with characteristics all its own. Among the most significant features is the importance of community elders, reminiscent of Cohen's Hausa traders in Ibadan, Nigeria (*Custom and Politics in Urban Africa*, Berkeley and Los Angeles: University of California Press, 1969) who establish diaspora communities in dominantly Yoruba cities; the chaneling of remittances to community projects in the home village and to in-laws as bride wealth; the (at least initial) continuation of caste distinctions in the migratory setting; and the role of storytellers (*griaules*) and craftsmen specialized in the production of African jewelry to be sent back home as gifts. These traits are not just continuities of African village life but are often prior adaptations to interethnic contexts, especially interregional trade. Barou views these unique migrant processes as undergoing constant transformations under considerable pressure from the host country as well as the emergence of new but often frustrated expectations on the part of the younger migrants.

INTRODUCTION

In the period between 1950 and 1970, France, like other industrial European countries, needed to import labor. According to the 1975 census there were about 4 million foreigners in France, or almost 6.5 percent of the total population. This was not a new phenomenon, since France had been a very important host country, even before the Second World War.

In 1936 the percentage of foreigners was almost the same as today. In real numbers they amounted to 2.5 million persons, but the proportions of different nationalities represented among the immigrants have changed significantly. Then, most immigrants came from European countries, especially Italy, Poland, Spain, and Belgium. Only a small number—less than 200,000—came from non-European countries. Of these, almost all came from French colonies, mainly Algeria. Natives from other colonies were very few: some Moroccans and Tunisians, a few Indochinese, but almost no people from sub-Saharan Africa.

In 1975 the nationals from European countries still represented about 60 percent of the foreign population. After other West European immigrants, almost one million Portuguese migrated beginning in the early 1960s. Then, with the demise of French colonial rule, people from the newly independent countries of the Third World arrived. Today there are almost 800,000 Algerians, 400,000 Moroccans, 150,000 Tunisians, about 120,000 Black Africans, and about 100,000 Indochinese (Vietnamese, Cambodians, and Laotians) in France.

With the exception of the majority of Asians and some Africans, who enjoy the status of political refugees, and about 50,000 students and apprentices, almost all these immigrants are guest workers, who often live in France without their families and are engaged in unskilled and poorly paid labor.

It is surprising to note that the immigration of these peoples reached major proportions only after their countries had gained independence. The question immediately comes to mind as to why the French government did not attempt to recruit labor from its colonies on a large scale at a time when North African and sub-Saharan African countries were still under its direct rule. The answer is both economic and political. Before World War II there was no real competition for labor among the industrial European countries. For Great Britain, Ireland remained an important source of cheap labor, while Germany was undergoing a deep economic and political crisis and could not absorb immigrants. So France was the only country which tried to attract guest workers from the formerly underindustrialized South European and East European countries. After 1960 the competition for foreign labor increased. West Germany, Switzerland, Belgium, the Netherlands, and the Scandinavian countries all needed migrant labor in order to fulfill the needs of industry in a period of significant economic growth. The high wages that these countries were able to offer attracted many of the Italians, Spaniards, and Greeks who had worked previously in France.

As the labor needs of France grew, it became increasingly necessary to draw on the labor resources represented by former colonies. In the North African colonies, emigration was delayed for a long time because of the claims of French settlers who needed local labor to farm their large landed properties and to develop their newly formed industries. As these countries became independent, expatriates as well as capital returned to France and spurred investments there. This in turn heightened the need for labor. Simultaneously, the exodus of French settlers led to unemployment among North African industrial and agricultural workers who formerly had worked for them. The situation was further aggravated by the economic consequences of the French-Algerian conflict. Thus, the stage was set for a major migratory wave.

In the former sub-Saharan African colonies a similar situation led to migration on a smaller scale. The Africans employed by the French army and navy sometimes preferred to remain in France rather than return to Africa. This early settlement was the beginning of a larger migratory movement which became significant only some years later.

In the early 1960s, with Algerian immigration uncertain because of the military and political conflict, Black African immigrants came to be seen as a cheap substitute. So agreements concerning the flow of workers were arranged between France and some of the newly independent African states. As a result, the French government attempted both to catalyze and to regulate a new migratory movement. The agreements concluded with the Senegalese, Malian, and Mauretanian governments in 1962 provided for the recruitment of workers in Africa by the French National Immigration Office (O.N.I.), which had the sole right to issue immigrants' visas and working permits. But during the 1960s the greater part of the African workers entered France without O.N.I. documents and the office could do little more than legalize their status of guest worker after they had already spent some time in France. Such legalization was necessary to preclude the increasing illicit exploitation in housing and working conditions.

Although legal immigration was stopped in 1974, and in spite of growing difficulties, many African newcomers continued to attempt to enter France in search of even badly paid or illegal employment. Many were expelled by the police on the basis of the new restrictive immigration acts.

At present, thanks to the more liberal immigration policy of the socialist government, Africans continue to enter France in order to try to turn the present "regularization" of undocumented migrants to their advantage. The effect of this legislation appears to be paradoxical. The already settled undocumented workers do not show much interest in being "regularized" because they risk losing their illegal jobs, which often have not been declared; in contrast, unemployed newcomers who have nothing to lose, do everything they can to take advantage of these laws in order to obtain the right to remain in France. Since family immigration is again permitted, many married African workers, recognizing the advantages of education and social security benefits in France, seek to have their wives and children join them. This family immigration constitutes a very recent phenomenon among an African population previously constituted only by men. Another recent development is the fact that immigration is no longer confined to the three traditional sender countries (Senegal, Mali, and Mauretania) but includes many other former French and even English and Portuguese colonies.

The number of Black Africans has increased from 20,000 in 1960 to around 120,000 today. The French government has clearly succeeded in initiating large-scale immigration from Africa but has entirely failed to regulate it. At present, the rate of African immigration to France no longer corresponds to labor needs. The reasons for this lie in the fact that since 1973 the economic conditions in the poorer African countries have deteriorated even more than in France. As a result, migrant remittances to their native countries cannot be invested in productive activities which could generate wealth and employment, but are consumed by immediate social needs. This in turn decreases the opportunities of resettling at home. In addition, social and cultural pressures also impel Africans to migrate to France. The younger generations of Africans have been educated in an educational system reflecting French cultural patterns, and this education has led to a degree of identification of modern African values with the French way of life. Thus their new behavior creates conflict with the elders and increases the young people's desire to flee from the traditional society and its constraints.

We are thus justified to assert that African immigration in France has largely exceeded labor demands and that it appears to have become more a historical and social phenomenon than an economic one. In other words, we can characterize it as a belated aftereffect of colonialism.

HISTORICAL BACKGROUND

Black African immigration to France is linked to internal African processes. Since the beginning of colonization and probably before, peoples living in the arid Sahelian savannah used to move south in order to work in the richer countries of the western coast. For instance, the Mossi of Upper Volta worked as agricultural laborers for the native farmers and European planters in Ghana and the Ivory Coast. The Hausa of Niger and northern Nigeria practiced their trades in the Yoruba towns of southern Nigeria.

Many other Sahelian ethnic groups represented among the African immigrants in France also have long traditions of migrating within Africa. Such was the case of the Soninké, who are the most numerous African group living in France today. There are about 70,000 Soninké in France, representing over 60 percent of the entire Black African immigrant population. In Africa the Soninké number about 500,000 and are settled in the Senegal River Valley located between the boundaries of Senegal, Mali, and Mauretania.

In spite of the fact that they are citizens of three countries, the Soninké always express an acute consciousness of their common ethnic identity. They have kept alive the memory of their long and prestigious history which helps them to strengthen their sense of unity. In the 11th century they furnished a royal dynasty to the kingdom of Ghana, which occupied an area near their present territory in eastern Senegal. In that period they acted as middlemen in the trans-Saharan trade as they were located between the southern end of the caravan routes and the countries that furnished gold and slaves to the camel drivers coming from Northern Africa. This enabled them to exact taxes. The Arabic chroniclers of that time described them as a rich and well-ruled people. They converted to Islam early on, and today they remain very proud to be one of the most ancient Muslim people of sub-Saharan Africa.

Due to the decline of the trans-Saharan trade in the 19th century, the Soninké progressively lost their wealth and power and began to emigrate as tradesmen throughout the whole of West Africa. Until 1965 Soninké communities were established in the Congo and in Zaïre, where they were often engaged in the gold and silver trade. They were expelled for political reasons by the governments of these newly independent states.

Another migratory movement developed during French colonization: seasonal laborers used to go to central Senegal to work in the peanut fields, a crop encouraged by the French administration. Others were employed as coal trimmers in steamships sailing on the Senegal River. From the river fleet they were transferred to oceangoing vessels which gave them the opportunity to establish contacts in Europe and elsewhere. At the same time many Soninké were enlisted in colonial troops and were often moved to other African countries as well as to France.

After the Second World War other events created the basis for migration to France. The French navy was technically modernized and steamships disappeared. The coal trimmers lost their jobs and sought employment as dockers in French ports. Many African soldiers were demobilized in 1945 and in 1954 after the war in Indochina. Some stayed in France and joined their countrymen working in the ports. Small Soninké communities were established in Marseille and Le Havre. Soon, some Soninké were attracted to the Parisian region, where there were opportunities for better jobs.

Soninké tradesmen returning from Zaïre after Independence brought back capital and were able to lend money to those of their fellows who wished to emigrate to France. As we shall see later, their role as brokers and informal credit-bankers was to become very important for Black African migration to France. They introduced the only element still lacking to create the conditions for massive migration: the financial means to travel and to enter France.

As the Soninké area remained agriculturally very poor and opportunities for seasonal employment in peanut farms became rarer due to the mechanization of agriculture, emigration rapidly became the main source of income. In 1962 agreements concerning the movement of workers were concluded between France and the three African states in which the Soninké were living. This was the first attempt to control an already growing phenomenon. The emigratory process was extended to other ethnic groups—first to the close neighbors of the Soninké, the Toucouleurs in Senegal and the Bambara in Mali, and little by little to many other groups in West Africa: the Ouolof and Diola in Senegal, the Mossi in Upper Volta, the Hausa in Niger, the Khassonké in Mali, etc.

The establishment of a number of Soninké brokers in Dakar launched many of these peoples on the trek to France. Not only did the brokers lend migrants money to pay for their trip, but also helped migrants to acquire forged documents with which to enter France. Connected as they are with the underground network of forgers and smugglers engaged in labor trafficking, the Soninké brokers in Dakar are specialized in illegal migration. This fact explains why the Soninké still predominate among African migrants in France; although they lend money to members of all ethnic groups, they prefer to deal with their fellow ethnics.

These Soninké brokers who have established lucrative activities of usury in

Dakar conduct their business with the help of an important network of relationships formed by their kin and fellow countrymen living in France and in the villages of their different regions of origin. This enables them to bring pressure on their debtors wherever they may move. They also often receive and manage the earnings sent by the migrants, thereby adding banking and financial brokerage to their other activities.

Thus, immigrants in France remain dependent on these brokers for long periods of time. It can take them several years to pay back the money they have borrowed for forged documents, for the assistance of smugglers to enable them to cross borders, and for the trip itself. Since so much of their earnings go to their creditors, they must be prepared to put up with very poor living conditions in order to save enough additional money to send to their extended families.

Sometimes they send remittances directly to their families, but often they depend on the same brokers to make the transfers. This contributes to the dependence of the migrant on the broker but protects the remittances from frequent attempts at misappropriation by corrupt postal clerks. As in many other situations, informal mechanisms set up by Africans involved in the migratory process were necessary to overcome deficiencies in the public services. In France, unemployed migrants who cannot enjoy public welfare because they have not yet found employment or were not declared by a former employer use similar mechanisms to survive. Immigrants in such situations—often newcomers—are condemned to incur greater and greater debts, making them more and more dependent on their elders and through them on the entire hierarchical system of migration, which is ultimately dominated by the few who control lending.

Generally unskilled and often illiterate, the newcomers are able to obtain only irregular and/or lowly paid jobs. Presently, most of them are casual laborers intermittently employed by subcontractors. Those who are still undocumented are often not declared by their employers and cannot benefit from welfare. Among the newcomers, young single men generally experience the worst conditions because they must save in order to pay the bride price for a future wife. As a result, they sometimes lose their autonomy entirely.

In comparison to the newcomers, the early immigrants, who entered France in the 1960s and were regularized before the employment situation deteriorated, seem privileged. They enjoy regular employment as sanitation workers for the transportation department in Paris or as unskilled workmen in the motor car industry. Today it is more difficult for a foreigner to land such jobs. As a result, the difference in economic power between younger and older migrants continues to increase. Ultimately, this dependence becomes intolerable for both the elders, whose economic power is no longer sufficient to cover the increasing need for loans, and for the young themselves, who are increasingly reluctant to accept the social constraints involved. So the stage is set for a crisis encompassing both the immigrants in France and those who remained behind in the regions of origin.

Before we describe the crisis in the African system of migration, we must first consider the traditional organization of the communities of immigrants in France.

TRADITIONAL ORGANIZATION AND COMMUNITY LIFE

Because of their frequently illegal status in France, the African immigrants were led to establish a network of enduring social relationships in the host country in order to provide for public welfare. Self-reliance was also fostered by the defensive attitude against a hostile environment, for particularly as Africans, they were often the victims of racist attitudes on the part of their French hosts. Thus they were led to live together and to establish large communities. Today almost 70 percent of them live in the Paris area. If they choose to live there, it is because they have a better chance to be admitted to a cosmopolitan population and also because the opportunities to find illegal jobs are better in Paris than in other localities in France.

These communities gather men from the same Soninké villages. Initially, they lived in old blocks of flats converted into dormitories. These houses were purchased with money lent by the Dakar brokers. Sometimes a broker owned a building directly, controlling it by means of an administrator who occupied one of the apartments. The agent collected the rent but did not maintain the building. These settlements were generally also overcrowded, and then became real slum dwellings, condemned by public decree. Thereupon, the inhabitants were rehoused in large public housing projects for single men called *foyers* and managed by public housing associations. Since the immigrants requested to be rehoused together, the village communities succeeded in maintaining themselves. However, they often had to share the *foyer* with other communities from other Soninké villages or even with members of other African ethnic groups.

Today, a *foyer* may include a Soninké village community of around 300 individuals and perhaps 200 to 300 additional persons from other Soninké, or Toucouleur, Bambara or Khassonké villages. Nevertheless, in the Paris area the Soninké are dominant in every African *foyer*.

The organization of these African enclaves is not an exact reproduction of the original patterns in African villages, for they face new internal and external constraints. The migrants had to adjust their traditional customs and develop new ones, employing traditional symbols, norms, and ideologies to enhance their cohesion and distinctiveness and thus to assist them in maintaining the consciousness of their common interests and identity.

The first major adjustment they had to make was to organize themselves as an exclusively male community. In Africa there is a sexual division of labor. In France the immigrants had to assume both masculine and feminine roles, so they had to devise a new allocation of tasks.

Since this new division of labor was based on preexisting structures in the original society, we must first briefly describe the traditional social structure. Sahelian peoples, including the Soninké, employ a single concept to describe both kinship and ownership. The Soninké word *kimu* refers to a consanguineous extended family whose members work on collectively owned fields, share its products, and obey the same elder who is generally polygamous.

The *kimu* is organized according to a seniority system. The patriarch makes decisions concerning the distribution of tasks and wealth as well as those concerning marriage. Work is also organized according to seniority. For instance, the eldest son must work for one day in the patriarch's fields. The second son must allocate one day to the fields of the patriarch and one to those of the eldest son. The third son has the same obligations as the second, but in addition he must spend a third day working in the latter's fields. The system extends to grandsons and great-grandsons. Such a system always gives more power to the oldest and exploits the youngest.

The different *kimu* belong to larger kin groups called *kaa*, a word which can be translated as "clan." The members of the *kaa* bear the same patronymic and claim descent from the same illustrious ancestor. Each *kaa* has a headman, the *kaagumme*, generally a prestigious elder of a *kimu* selected by his equals.

The different *kaa* have different social statuses inherited by their members. The Soninké system of ranking is similar to the caste system in India. There are three castes among the Soninké. Some *kaa* are called *hoore,* a word we can translate as "noble." Their members are free from any bondage and they hold the dominant position in the society. The *hoore* are divided into three categories. The *wogi* have access to chieftainship. The *marabouts* hold religious Islamic power. Even though they have no access to the chieftainship, they nevertheless remain politically influential. The third category, the *miskin,* are noble but they have no particular privilege except freedom.

Other *kaa* are called *nyakamala.* They include the different categories of craftsmen: the blacksmiths and jewellers, who are called *tage,* the weavers and tailors, or *jaare,* and the shoemakers, or *garanke*. The *gesere* are a typical African category whose job it is to eulogize people from noble or royal descent by relating the history of their illustrious ancestors. The third caste is that of the *komo,* which includes the slaves and the persons whose ancestors were reduced to bondage during the tribal wars of the past. Although slavery was officially abolished at the time of French colonization, the descendants of the slaves still have the same relationship to the noble clans as in earlier times. These castes are hereditary and endogamous. Intermarriage between members of different castes is forbidden. So the social status inherited by members of the same clan is always the same.

In France common residence encourages the development of a social hierarchy similar to that in the native country. Seniors continue to rule over the migrant communities, regardless of the occupations they may have. Junior members must hand over all their earnings to the elders, who alone decide how much they will send home to the family and how much will be left for the young earner.

The elders constantly supervise the junior members and even organize their leisure time which—just as at home—is spent in endless discussions dealing with problems affecting the native village. Any leisure activity that would distract from communal life is discouraged. Thus, going out with European women, particularly prostitutes, is deemed unacceptable for religious and above all economic reasons.

Each *foyer* is governed by a council of elders who collect the rent and pay the lodging association. This body also manages communal funds destined for the sick and unemployed. Each member of the villages represented in the *foyer* must contribute to the common fund regularly.

The ascetic life they must lead leaves the young people with few opportunities to enjoy themselves. They find their dependency on the elders more difficult to accept in France than in their native country. At least in the traditional society young men are organized in age-grades which give them a degree of collective strength and autonomy, but in France they must face the power of their elders singly.

The social stratification system of the native country also undergoes modifications in France. Most of the *nyakamala* engage in their traditional crafts after the day's work. The tailors set up sewing machines in their bedrooms and produce traditional clothing, especially embroidered tunics called *boubous*. The blacksmiths and jewellers often claim the right to equip a forge in the basement flat of the *foyer* to produce typical African jewelry. These products are not sold outside the community, for example to European customers interested in exotic goods. Most are sold to members of the community living in the *foyer* who buy them as presents to be brought back to their kin and friends upon their return home. They represent tangible proof that the returning migrants have succeeded in becoming wealthy during their stint abroad. Those who bear no gifts are looked down upon as inadequate and are condemned to lose all social prestige. In particular, young migrants who wish to marry buy large quantities of artifacts from the Soninké craftsmen in France; for the marriage portion they must bring to their wives consists, in part, of traditional clothing and jewelry.

Sometimes a *geseru* visits the *foyers* and in a one-man show eulogizes the noble members of the community and chants the heroic feats of their ancestors. The *geseru*'s stories enhance the prestige of particular noble clans in the eyes of the entire *foyer*. As a result, members of different clans compete with one another to induce the *geseru* to favor their ancestors' names over those of their rivals. Such rivalry sometimes leads noble men to cede almost all their earnings to the *geseru*. Consequently, the *gesere* enjoy a degree of wealth and power in France unequaled by their fellow *kaa* members at home.

With respect to the economic aspects of communal life, the noble clans tend to monopolize the most profitable activities such as the kola trade and management of collective funds. The latter include a general Soninké fund, common to all members of this ethnic group living in France. Its nature is mainly symbolic. In theory, all Soninké migrants must contribute to this fund. In practice, most pay irregularly or not at all. The treasurer in charge of the coffer is an elder of royal descent belonging to the *wogi* clan. His duty is an attribute of the headman's authority to represent the unity of the group and has no real economic or political significance.

The royal funds are another matter. The old Soninké country was divided into different territories called kingdoms, each of which was headed by a king selected by his equals. The immigrants from these different kingdoms formerly collected funds to invest in their territories of origin. Because the original kingdoms now correspond to districts in the three nations in which the Soninké live, the immigrants speak about Malian, Senegalese, or Mauretanian funds which are used to assist nationals living in France or sometimes to help finance highway construction and maintenance in their native countries.

Immigrants from the same village also have their own collective funds. Indeed, these are the most important ones. They are used as insurance against unemployment and illness as well as investment in mosques, schools, post offices, etc., in the home village. The managers of these funds always belong to the *hoore,* or "noble" caste. The nobles also enjoy the monopoly on political power in the *foyer*. Indeed, each *foyer* is governed by a council of wise men formed by the elders of the noble clans. Although they are not the official chiefs of the *foyer,* they hold moot courts to arbitrate disputes within their ethnic community and act as intermediaries between their own group, the community leaders of the other communities living in the *foyer,* and the clerks of the lodging association. Thus their political role appears to be more informal than it was in Africa.

In contrast, the relations between the *hoore* elders and the members of the other castes have not changed. Even though the occupational position of a slave is higher than that of a noble, the slave must still obey the noble in the *foyer*. The domestic tasks devolve upon the slaves and the junior members. They prepare traditional African meals served following ancient Soninké customs: the members of the entire clan eat from the same collective dish, the elders first and then the juniors, according to age-grade. When the nobles are satisfied, they give the dish to their slaves, who generally have cooked it and must content themselves with the scraps. Even if a noble is a street sweeper in his trade life, he will never sweep in the *foyer*. As a result, there is a clear differentiation between the occupational sphere (around Paris, trade unions and political organizations are quite active) and the traditional world reconstituted and adjusted to the *foyer* with a hierarchical system more rigid than in the original society.

This contradiction is sometimes difficult to live with for some individuals, who may even suffer severe depression. We encountered the case of a young Soninké of slave origin who committed suicide because the noble members of his community refused to let him study.

Many young men have attempted to split from the community and join French society as individuals. However, they are often rejected by the host society. Thus most of them, while suffering from the contradictions between the occupational and the private life, recognize that they are condemned to live in a community which is both coercive and reassuring. Nevertheless, the impossibility of escaping the social constraints of communal life and the feeling of lagging behind the society they are living in are already inciting to rebellion some who suffer most. Such rebellions will create a crisis in the traditional communal life of the African immigrants in France and may well transform the entire organization of the migratory movement. Considering that this crisis is occurring in the context of major economic deterioration affecting both the sender and host countries, we are led to the conclusion that the migratory process from Africa to France is bound to change substantially in the coming years. Let us now deal with this brewing crisis and its potential effects on the future of Black African migration.

THE CRISIS IN THE TRADITIONAL SYSTEM

There are two types of crises among the African immigrants in France: the first involves individuals; the second, the communities. Some individuals, principally young men, find it difficult to cope with the hard working conditions they must face and with the ascetic life forced upon them by communal living, often involving sexual abstinence. Many exhibit different kinds of frustration behavior. We have encountered a number of cases of depression among young African immigrants. Depression is often associated with psychosomatic symptoms for which these individuals are hospitalized. One of the best solutions in these cases is for the patient to return to his original milieu. This fact underlines the differences in the social constraints in Africa and in the immigrant communities in France. In France the greater rigidity of the familial and social hierarchy on the one hand, and the attempts by the receiving society to adapt the immigrants to their new milieu on the other, often exacerbate the contradictions faced by the migrants.

As indicated earlier, individuals rarely succeed in assimilating to French society. Nevertheless, some do manage to leave their community, without too many psychological problems, by joining a trade union or political organization where they again find some kind of unity and assistance. The case of Bassirou, a young Soninké who lived for a long time among his fellow community members in a *foyer,* may serve as an example. He was working in a factory where French workers were numerous and was elected to the position of shop steward. Thereafter, he joined the C.G.T. (Confédération Générale du Travail), the largest French trade union, and then became a member of the French Communist Party. Eventually, he left his community and the *foyer* where he lived. At present he is living in a tenement block in a suburb among French worker families, most of whom share his political ideas. He looks happy and well-adjusted in his new surroundings, where he can play a more satisfying role than before. When he speaks about himself, he usually says "I am of Malian descent" rather than "I am Malian," although after ten years in France, he has still not requested French citizenship.

However, Bassirou's case is exceptional. Most of the African immigrants who attempt to assimilate to French society are rejected by it, and when they no longer belong to a group, they feel uprooted. The resulting identity crisis engenders psychological difficulties that can manifest themselves either as mental confusion leading to hospitalization or as deviant behavior leading to imprisonment.

These individual crises also affect their communities. The individuals who are inclined to leave their group, mostly young ones, become progressively more conscious of the difficulties they will encounter. Many are therefore attempting to gain power within their own communities.

Certain factors may explain this attempt to upset the existing balance of power. As a consequence of the growing economic difficulties—the Soninké are associated with the enduring Sahelian drought—people are forced to emigrate in larger numbers. So the proportion of young immigrants in France is constantly growing. As a result, they sometimes succeed in reinstituting the traditional age-grade organization in the *foyers*. In the last year we have even noticed the existence of collective funds in some *foyers* managed and used only by young men belonging to the same age-grade.

These young newcomers are often more literate than the older ones. They are thus more able to take an active part in democratic representative organizations, which the French government encourages the immigrants to form. They often use such new organizations as the tenant committees, recently introduced in the *foyers,* to protest against the lodging associations and claim better accommodations and lower rents. Because they generally speak better French than their elders, they are selected as spokesmen for the community vis-à-vis the public authorities, which in turn increases their power vis-à-vis their elders.

Gradually, the meaning of communal life is taking a more satisfying form for the young. The *foyer* is no longer the bastion of rigid hierarchies dominated by the elders. It is becoming an African enclave whose organization is based on a new system of values. This new system sets itself against both the sociocultural patterns of the host society and the former seniority system of the traditional community.

Islam is the central value of the new system. The *marabouts* are becoming more and more influential in the *foyers*. The leaders of the tenant committees are persons who are respected throughout the *foyer* communities as much because of their Islamic education as their ability to speak good French and deal with public authorities.

Ethnic differences are considered to be of minimal significance by the young immigrants. The informal organization controlled by the elders was based upon kin relationships. In contrast, the new formal organizations, such as the democratically elected tenants committees, are often interethnic. In this context, Islam becomes a way to reach a new common consciousness, for it is a value which is shared by the elders and juniors as well as by the different ethnic groups living in the *foyer*.

However, these immigrants are Muslims in a typically African way. They are mostly members of the Tijani brotherhood. So they have no regard for the orthodox religious observances of the North African Muslims living in France, and they are themselves often rejected by the latter. Religious conflicts frequently erupt between the two groups of immigrants. Consequently, they rarely dwell in the same *foyers*.

Thus, Black African Islam is presently becoming the common basis for a new ethnicity among immigrants from West Africa. The communal life is maintained under a new order. However, the formerly dominant groups do not always tolerate the erosion of their power. This is turn is engendering new migratory processes from Africa.

FAMILY IMMIGRATION AS AN ANSWER TO THE CRISIS OF THE COMMUNITY?

As their power grows, the young become more and more reluctant to undertake the domestic tasks in the *foyer*. So it becomes necessary to call upon the women's services in order to prepare the meals. Today women often come into the kitchens of *foyers* to do the cooking for a modest fee. This in turn alters the traditional system of collective meals. Now people eat individually from dishes specially prepared for them.

These women are often married to men who formerly lived in the *foyers*. The meals they cook are a good source of income for the household. Their success in turn encourages the married men of the community, particularly elders, to bring their wives to join them. For the elders, communal life has become less and less satisfying. Because their juniors no longer obey them as in former times, they feel that they are losing their social prestige. Formerly, the high rank they held in the community compensated for the ascetic life they were obliged to lead. Now they can no longer play a role commensurate to the self-image they would like to maintain. From this vantage point, bringing their wives to live in France is a way of heightening their social rank in the community again, rather than a form of escape.

"I feel better since my wife is here," says Babacar, a 45-year-old Soninké belonging to the *hoore* caste. "I can invite my equals to dinner at home. She prepares the meals and waits at table." The ability to entertain persons of one's own rank has an important value with respect to social conventions in Africa. Thus Babacar's statement expresses a sense of regaining social prestige among the immigrants, for the arrival of his wifc enabled him to be regarded as a "society man."

Often the married men living in France attempt to bring only their wives to join them and leave their children at home. "Children must be reared in the village and educated by the elders," says Babacar, who has just married a second wife because he wanted to leave the first one in Africa to take care of the children. So, as a result of the recent family immigration to France, polygamy is spreading again in Soninké country.

Couples who bring their children to join them in France often experience enormous difficulties. These difficulties in the cases where the children are born in France or have moved there as infants are different from those where older children have joined their parents. Kinship structures in Africa are very specific. Children raised in Africa form lasting bonds with many adult caretakers. In many West African societies, special close relationships are maintained between grandchildren and grandparents, between the mother's brother and the sister's son, and joking relationships between cousins descended from the father's brother or the mother's sister. In contrast, the relationships between children and their agnatic kin are characterized by respect or even fear. When children come to France, they move from an extended to a nuclear family. They deal with only two and, during most of the day, only one caretaker. Indeed, the mother often has to assume the principal care of the dependent children. Most of the father's life takes place outside the home among his fellow workers and in his former male immigrant community. Thus the mother has to play all the different roles at the same time. She seldom succeeds in assuming so complex a task. Young mothers in France often lose all consciousness of their duties towards their children. Each year many African children are given up to public assistance. Disagreements and divorces are also frequent among African households in France.

Conversely, when families find a way to live in harmony by adopting the French way of family life, they have to deal with problems of readjustment when they go back home. "I was ashamed of my children last summer when we spent our holidays in our village," says Safyatou, a Malian mother whose children were born and bred in France. "They were unable to behave properly towards their aunt on their father's side. This made her angry and it was a scandal in the family." The behavior of these children towards their kin in Africa was the same as towards close friends of their parents in France. This was perceived as almost indecent in the society of origin. So, when family immigration "succeeds" in one sense, it may lead to permanent settlement, however strong the parents' desire to return home in the future may be.

CONCLUSION

African immigration to France has not ceased completely, in spite of the present economic crisis in Western Europe. Illegal immigration of male newcomers remains important, and so does the reuniting of families. The new arrivals take place in a context of readjustment of the traditional structures of social organization of the immigrants. Male communities and extended families both have adjustment problems today.

The problems mentioned in this chapter are likely to become worse and more prevalent before they improve. In a few years problems will emerge with regard to the second generation, some of whom are growing up in troubled families. Although French society is succeeding in absorbing the second generation of European immigrants, it is not the same with the second generation of immigrants from the former colonies. Today there are signs of a generation of unhappy and rebellious Algerian youth. Will the African children now growing up in France have a similar future?

5 Yugoslav Migration Process and Employment in Western Europe: A Historical Perspective

Joel Martin Halpern

ABSTRACT. Similar to the preceding chapters on migration to France, the following four chapters on migrants to Germany complement one another. Halpern, like Barou, examines the cultural background of migration, which he views in the context of specific historical developments in Yugoslavia, in particular Yugoslavia's singular brand of socialism with open borders. Here, too, long-term migrant adaptations included cultural dimensions. Craftsmen migrated to distant places in order to ply their trade, and semiskilled or unskilled workers temporarily abandoned their villages for places as distant as Istanbul—all formally instituted practices marked by rituals and supporting symbols and ideologies. Other precedents of modern migration include migrations caused by war that displaced large numbers of people. The migration stimulated by the more rapid growth of West European economies is thus based on a rich variety of precedents. It is a process which is already so prevalent that it has generated its own mythology and oral tradition.

INTRODUCTION

Movement of peoples, whether on the part of individuals, families, larger kin units, or whole ethnic groups, has long been a creative process in social history. Absolute stability in place, like absolute stability in culture, is a negation of the dynamics inherent in human relationships. It is not possible to understand the significance of the postwar movement of Yugoslavs to Western Europe in search of better economic opportunities without comprehending the cultural baggage they carry. This accumulation of traditions and experiences profoundly influences the processes of their adaptation and the impact that the new settings have on the lifetime perspective of the migrant. All peoples are influenced by their traditions, but among groups such as the Yugoslavs, past values, perceptions, and cyclical time perspectives tied to a still viable oral tradition constantly influence current behavior and future plans.[1] This perspective forms the basic point of departure for this chapter.

Yugoslav migrants within the past half century have emerged from a civil war which questioned the ethnic basis of the Yugoslav state. The consequences of this civil war remain prominent in folk memory. Time is compressed within a cyclical framework, and decades past become yesterday. A more recent experience has been that of a socialist revolution whose results have been ongoing. Unlike perceptions tied to ethnicity and identity in cylical time, the socialist revolution, so strongly tied to societal modernization processes, exists in linear time, in which past events do not recur but are projected into a developing future which is conceived of as differentiated from the past.

The ethnic conflict and the socialist revolution were both internally generated through military struggle in World War II, in which the civilian population was involved intimately in both the fighting and the suffering. The results of this struggle form the basic charter of legitimacy for the contemporary Socialist Federated Republic of Yugoslavia. The federated structure of the state reflects the fact that these developments have taken place among a diverse group of South Slavs (Yugoslavia is "Land of the South Slavs" in Serbo-Croatian) as well as among the other resident ethnic minorities.

This crucible of events, an intermixture of linear and cyclical time processes, has occurred just prior to intensive industrialization and urbanization. In the 1950s and early 1960s these were determined partially by central socialist planning. They took place within the framework of a society which had been overwhelmingly peasant in social structure and largely agrarian based. These events formed the background to the large-scale migrations to Western Europe.

Yugoslavia is unique among the socialist states of Eastern Europe in maintaining open borders. This conscious policy decision has made large-scale migration to Western Europe possible.

GENERAL PERSPECTIVES

Migratory processes are seen, in part, through the prism of cultural history, in cyclical time. They also exist in linear time and can be seen as an innovative mechanism within a socialist society. Clearly, the two aspects are not exclusive but interactive in complex ways which are explored in this essay. Since past is present in so many of the ways in which Yugoslavs see the world, historical dimensions are stressed. This chapter, like others in this book, reflects the movement of workers in Europe over the last quarter century from the less industrially developed nations of Southern and Southeastern Europe (as in the case of Greece and Yugoslavia) to the more economically developed countries of Northern and Western Europe. There have also been related movements from North Africa and the Middle East to these same European areas. (Yugoslavia has been directly involved in these other movements in that Greek, and especially Turkish, workers drive through Yugoslavia on their way to Western Europe and have a significant impact on highway traffic and not infrequent fatalities.)

These long-term trends involving individuals and close kin are paralleled by other kinds of short-term and a lesser number of long-term movements from Northern and Western Europe to the South on the part of individuals and their families seeking vacation spots and retirement sites. One interpretation of these movements, which have very much affected regions throughout Yugoslavia, is that one part of Europe is a good place to work and another part is favored for nonwork time and, to a degree, for retirement. This bifurcation of preference for place of work and place of rest and recreation has a precedent in our recent past, with the onset of the complex class stratification of industrial society in the 19th century. At the same time its vast scope on a European-wide basis is new in world history, promoted by the unprecedented economic prosperity of the 1960s and early 1970s. The limits on economic growth so painfully obvious over the last decade will probably constrict these processes, but their vast significance will remain, both in the ways in which individual and community lives have altered and the ways in which the landscape has permanently changed. Tourism as an industry does impose long-term ecological change (Halpern and Kerewsky-Halpern 1973). One cannot fully appreciate the role of migrant workers in the Ruhr heavy industry without its counterpart of hotel complexes, for varying income groups, in Dalmatia.

It is only since World War II, then, that these long-distance population movements for tourism and retirement have become mass middle-class prerogatives. Formerly, they were clearly the domain of the economic and social elite. Labor migration is, however, of long duration in the Balkans (Halpern 1975). Understanding the process of migration is not possible without considering the significance of the point of departure and the place of destination as fixed entities. The history of the Balkans is, in no small measure, a history of migrations up to recent times. Connected with these migrations is a transformation of the natural environment. The South Slavs adapted from settled agricultural patterns to seminomadic pastoralism under the pressure of drastic political changes resulting from Ottoman imperial expansion in the medieval period. They readapted to more settled farming ways beginning with the end of the 18th century, when the Ottoman empire began to contract.

The impact of these processes, and subsequent modernization in the late 19th and 20th centuries, varied in intensity on a regional basis within Yugoslavia. Changes resulting from migrations in the preindustrial period were particularly marked in the central and southern parts of Yugoslavia: Serbia, Montenegro, Bosnia-Hercegovina, and Macedonia. As a distinguished Yugoslav ethnologist phrased it, "Each generation of my ancestors lies in a different soil." Thus by examining briefly the historical bases of migratory movements in a Balkan context, we are, at the same time, raising questions about the kinds of values associated with residential and occupational stability, as contrasted with mobility, from a long-term perspective.

A Yugoslav villager deciding to move to Western Europe—often by migratory stages, to a Yugoslav town and then on to Western Europe—clearly carries with him the cultural baggage of his ancestors in cyclical time perspective. These migratory processes within Yugoslavia, especially in the southern parts of Yugoslavia, were initially described by the Serbian human geographer Jovan Cvijic, publishing his major work in French in time for the deliberations of the Versailles Peace Conference (summarized in Cvijic 1918a, 1918b). He himself was a temporary migrant, having obtained his graduate education in France before returning to Yugoslavia to establish the discipline at the University of Belgrade.

How does the cultural baggage described by Cvijic and others affect the recent decisions of migrants? One can suggest that perceptions of the advantages in geographic mobility are not simply conditioned by perceived economic opportunity but are evaluated through an associated cultural screen in which implicit covert values based on historical experiences play a key role. Migration can be seen as part challenge, part adventure, and a form of natural adaptation to changing circumstances as well as necessary utilization of economic opportunity.

HISTORICAL PERSPECTIVES

A description of the historic migration process for the Serbian regions of Yugoslavia is summed up by Cvijic (1930/31; 666–668):

> From the 16th century onwards there have been a series of movements that have lasted right up to the present time. The liberation of Serbia at the beginning of the 19th century checked them temporarily; but only in Serbia itself. The population increased extraordinarily quickly. . . . Serbia, in fact, had obtained a fresh population of very mixed origin; and there is hardly a village that does not contain emigrants from two or three different districts.
>
> The settlers who came from the Dinaric [Mountains] area were an almost exclusively stock-breeding population; but when they had settled in Serbia they changed over to agriculture. . . . streams of migration established themselves in Serbia after the Liberation [from the Turks], because every immigrant to Serbia was allowed to take land freely—and there they mingled with each other. Each group had some effect upon the rest, and an amalgam of the various qualities was formed. People grew to know men of different character from themselves, they learnt from each other about the different Serbian lands through which they had traveled, and they made a common stock of their knowledge and experiences in the quickest and most easy way possible. . . . forests were to a great extent cut down; this and the cultivation of the land changed its appearance and even its climate to a certain extent. Out of this process of ceaseless change and modification, the Serbian state was emerging.

Migration involved psychocultural as well as ecological adjustments. To be successful in surviving meant to adapt to new social situations as well as to change agricultural practices. Adaptation had cyclical time characteristics of precedent and predictability, but simultaneously there was an element of linear time in the transformation of the environment which resulted in the cutting over of the forests when the lowlands were resettled (earlier habitations had dated from neolithic times), but this now occurred with great population increases. Movement to lowlands was also taking place elsewhere in the Mediterranean, as the social historian Braudel observed (1972; 415–16).

Contemporary migrants from central Yugoslavia to Western Europe have not come, then, from an area in which there has been long-term stability but rather from a region of relatively recent settlement, one which has experienced intense ecological changes within the memory of the past few generations. Peasant background and the continued viability of oral tradition represent continuity in the sending society.

Another aspect of the interplay of cyclical and linear time processes (in addition to that of recurrent migration, social adaptation, and long-term ecological change) has been the premodern seasonal rhythm of occupational alteration. Braudel cites Saint George's Day in April and Saint Demetrius's Day at the end of October as two times in the year when an apprentice could enter the service of a master. In April migratory craftsmen departed for distant jobs and laborers entered contracts. This was also the time for brigands to gather. In October the Ottoman armies ceased their campaigns and the laborers and craftsmen returned home. It was then, too, that the shepherds left the mountain pastures with their flocks and the highwaymen disbanded (Stoianovich 1967; 66–67). It should be added that trade also involved movement. For example, commerce in pigs, which was characteristic of Serbia from the late 18th century, did involve many village merchants. They traded their livestock from Ottoman-controlled areas in the south across the Danube into what was then a province of Austria-Hungary. This trade continued through the 19th century, becoming, along with prunes and plum brandy, a principal export of the new Serbian state.

LONG-TERM, TEMPORARY MIGRANTS: THE *PECALBARI*

Traian Stoianovich, a student of Braudel, comments on Balkan mountaineers who were involved in brigandage, crafts, and trade and who frequently migrated (1960; 276):

> The Greek and Vlach highland inhabitants of Thessaly, Epirus, and Macedonia present another example of the free but wretched who make fortunes. The pastoral folk of these highlands obtained a livelihood from five principal occupations: the men were herdsmen, brigands, seasonal migratory workers and mercenary soldiers, and muleteers, while the women were skilled weavers. The people of the Pindus often did not dwell in a fixed place throughout the year. Seeking green pastures, they climbed the mountains in summer and descended into the lowlands and approached the sea in winter. Since small numbers of individuals can supervise large herds, men tended to become superfluous. Men unable to earn a living through the exercise of economic functions consequently turned to banditry. . . . the expansion of towns in the 16th century subsequently opened other occupations to the pastoral rural folk. Younger sons and men who lacked herds or the urge to highway robbery departed from their homes for a season or a year to work as pecalbari

or semiskilled and unskilled laborers in distant towns, even in the Ottoman capital [Istanbul].

In the medieval period national boundaries as we know them today were, of course, not marked. Clearly defined national entities did not exist, nor did consciousness of national differences. Distinctions up to the 18th century tended to be expressed in religious terms or in regional or local perspectives. It is clear, however, that moving long distances and changing occupations, either temporarily or permanently, involved a need to be flexible in social relationships. People made use of a variety of social networks.

In the early 1930s Louis Adamic, the Yugoslav-American writer, found the institution of temporary migration, the *pecalba,* functioning in Macedonia in southern Yugoslvia (1934; 115–24):

> The village of Galicnik—nearly three thousand feet above sea-level in the barren and not easily accessible mountains. . . . is a village of grass widows. For approximately eleven months out of the year, no men—aside from a priest or two and a few octo- and nonogenarians—live in the hundred odd homes. . . . Their husbands and older sons [if more than fifteen years of age] are scattered over Central and Western Europe, Greece, Rumania, and Yugoslavia, the north coast of Africa, parts of Asia Minor, Russia, and the United States, where, during the building seasons, they work at highly specialized trades of masonry, stonecutting, and wood-carving, cabinet-making. . . .
>
> Once a year, between the first and fifteenth of July, most of the men return from the big world. Those working in Europe, in Asia Minor, or in North Africa get home yearly; those in America and the distant parts of Russia return but every two or three years. . . . The communal wedding day, when all the couples married that year are wedded simultaneously . . . occurs on July 12th. When we were there, sixteen couples entered matrimony. All of the bridegrooms were from Galicnik. All but two were regular pechalbari. The other two were sheepmen whose flocks' grazing-ground was several hours distant from the village.

Recent Yugoslav statistics record the demise of this community due to migration. From a population of 948 in 1953 the village declined to 644 in 1961, and to only 17 people and 9 households in 1971.[2] The community had originally been settled in the 14th century. The demise of the mountain village of Galicnik in recent times is symbolic of the ultimate consequences of prolonged migration: the place of origin ceases to exist. If the community scatters abroad and merges with other groups, this can be seen as a development in linear time, although the processes of adaptation have cyclical time perspectives since many cultural elements, even under these circumstances, reappear in new forms.

The rituals involved with the *pecalba* tradition were important in that they stressed ties with the place of origin. The cognitive map of kin ties and obligations to those left behind by the migrant was reinforced. A man continued to be of the village even while residing physically outside of it.

While working in Macedonia in 1962 I obtained an account from an Orthodox peasant of the process of going on *pecalba* as viewed from the village community (Halpern and Kerewsky-Halpern 1975, 6–9). This description refers principally to the period before the First World War, when villagers from Macedonia, then under Turkish rule, went to work in Serbia, Romania, Bulgaria, and Turkey.

The pecalbari used to travel to their jobs on horses provided by *kiradzije,* Moslem men who specialized in renting horses and guiding and escorting the workers. With their help, workers could travel to Belgrade in 17 or 18 days [from southern Macedonia]. Two poorer workers would hire one horse. A more prosperous man would rent one for himself and his bags, bedroll and food including bread.

The kiradzije, being Moslem, could best communicate with the Turkish police guards, who were posted at every important place. Each pecalbar would give a guard a small bribe to avoid delays and baggage checks. In times of need, the families of the workers would borrow money from the Moslem carriers; the kiradzije trusted them and would get their money back when they visited Belgrade or wherever the men of those families were working. Thus there was great confidence between the Moslem kiradzije and the Christian pecalbari.

As for migrant workers who were Moslem, they did not travel far on pecalba. The furthest they would go was to Bitola [a nearby provincial town]. Most Moslem men worked at home. They were carpenters and also built houses and made farming tools such as rakes, pitchforks and plows, and also tables and looms. Among the Christians only elderly men, those over 60, stayed home.

It is revealing to put these attitudes in present-day perspective. Following the lifting of immigration restrictions in postwar Yugoslavia, many Macedonian-speaking Moslems declared themselves to be ethnic Turks and migrated to Turkey, some to Istanbul.

The account continues:

On the side of the water jar [used by the family] they attached a piece of jewelry of the kind brides wear on their bodices, and they would also fasten on a sprig of dogwood. When this was ready and the young man was about to set out, the container was placed on the threshold of the house. He was supposed to kick it with his right foot, making sure that he did not overturn it. Bread and water represented luck and fortune in the coming work. The dogwood stood for the good health of the worker, and the bride's jewelry to ensure that he would think of his young wife or fiancee, be true to her and return home one day. This is done even today.

After the pecalbar left his house he was accompanied to the edge of the village by the older men and women. They made jokes so that he would not pine for his beloved.

At a point a few kilometers from the village they would separate. At this place there is still a pear tree. At the moment of leavetaking the relatives would weep near this tree, and this spot is called the weeping pear tree. According to local belief not only the people but the tree wept at the sight of the young men leaving.

Upon their return from pecalba, workers would bring gifts for members of their household, close relatives and friends. In those days, as now, it was shameful if a man did not bring presents for all. A returning worker was visited by all his kin in the village, who welcomed him with a large flat bread and a wooden flask of wine. The returned worker would talk about the others who remained abroad and of his own work plans, what to do with his money, and how long he would stay. Even today before workers set out on pecalba, the custom with the water jug, bread, jewelry and dogwood is still practiced, but today there are no more kiradzije.

THE VIEW OF FOLK POETRY

The still viable oral tradition interprets changes through the cyclical time framework of folk poetry which functions primarily in an oral, not written, context. The pecalba of the turn of the century is reflected in the Macedonian poem "Weep, Manda, Let Us Weep" (Karovski 1974, 296, 298):

The young woman:

Our men in alien lands,
the one in wretched Egypt
the other in Muscovy!
....
Our companions light-hearted,
we two to be lamented,
to be lamented without our masters.
Our companions with boy-children,
we two with empty hands.
Our companions stroll abroad,
we two are imprisoned,
imprisoned in our gaols.

The young man:

I will go to alien lands, my soul,
to alien lands to work
and stay three whole years there.
I will send to you a paper white,
a paper white, a letter sad—
for you to read and weep.
I will send to you a necklace fine
for you to wear and weep, my girl!

This view of traditional sex roles obviously is linked to expectations which were even then idealized for a folk society. But a study of contemporary migrant workers in Sweden carries the title from a Macedonian folk poem on its title page, "Labor Migration (Pecalba) Is a Big Sorrow" (Meurle and Andric 1971). On the flyleaf there is a quote from a worker:

It's not that I hate this country:
It's not that this country hates me,
But the stamp of import brands me.
From the butcher's shop to union chair,
'Made in Sweden' people prefer.

The second poem focuses not on the home village but on the problems of contact and integration with the receiving society. A contemporary option is the possibility of integration into a non-Yugoslav West European setting rather than the *pecalbar*'s return to his home community. Permanent migration to North America has been occurring since the end of the 19th century and has continued up to the present, but large-scale assimilation into West European societies has really been significant only during the past few decades. There are indications that such a solution has been increasingly less viable with the recent economic downturns. At the same time, these developments increase the appeals of certain home communities.

A Danish anthropologist, Carl Ulrik Schierup, in his report on two villages in eastern Serbia from which migrants have come to Denmark, mentions the migrants' referring to the superior customs they have in their own country, a counterpoint to the view of the Yugoslav in Sweden cited above (Schierup 1973, 49). They told him that if there were factories near their homes they wouldn't have to go so far abroad to seek jobs. Schierup stresses that these Serbs feel tied to their native community's way of life, its associated value system, and the kinship network through which indispensable affect is manifested.

WARTIME MIGRATIONS AND THEIR CONSEQUENCES

The wartime migrations impacted strongly on a Yugoslav society which was then still primarily peasant and also in various ways created a readiness for the contemporary West European migration experience. Some of this experience in both World Wars was extremely traumatic, but there were aspects which were viewed as positive, especially when it was possible to learn new techniques which could be incorporated into the home community. These experiences were, of course, massive in scope, involving millions of both soldiers and civilians.

An elderly Serbian peasant recalled in the 1950s (Halpern and Kerewsky-Halpern 1972, 65):

I first served in the army in 1914. I was taken as a young man into the army when the Germans invaded our country. The president of the village council took a group of us by oxcart to a town near Valjevo [in central Serbia], where we trained for three months. . . . After we succeeded in throwing the Germans [Hapsburg armies] out of Serbia in 1914, we went to the Bulgarian frontier. There, when the Austrians and Germans invaded again in 1915, we were defeated. King Peter returned to Salonica [Greece] and I was taken prisoner by the Germans. But in 1916 I was interned in Czechoslovakia where I worked in a factory. Later I was sent to work for a farmer in Hungary. There I worked as a peasant. In most ways it was like here. But I was impressed by their use of scythes. Here before the war we used sickles to cut wheat. Our people thought that cutting wheat with a scythe would scatter it. They used to grab a few stalks of wheat and cut them. It took many people 10 to 15 days to cut the wheat. I told my father, "Let's go reap the wheat." He said it would scatter. I said it wouldn't. So this is the way we changed.

Other kinds of innovations were introduced into villages as a result of wartime imprisonment. A woman from southern Serbia, who subsequently migrated abroad, recalled her father's innovation in their village as a result of his experiences during World War II (Halpern 1980, 252):

When he returned home from Germany he built himself an outhouse with a seat. It was kept very clean and it was a good idea as well as practical for him to be able to sit since he had rheumatism. But this was regarded as a terrible idea in the village. People just began gossiping and saying how something was wrong with my father, that he was out of his mind. "Just look what he built, why don't you go there and see, go to his house and see the nice seat he has in his outhouse!" For days and days people didn't talk about anything else. But even though they gossiped, all those who came found it was really comfortable, clean and much neater this way. Lots of people built their own. But my cousins resent it. Somehow because they are younger and one of them is working in town, they feel more educated. So they never built one. But they live next door to us and come into our yard.

INTERWAR ECONOMIC MIGRATIONS

Migrations in the period before World War II were due not only to political conflicts but also had as a major cause rural overpopulation engendered by continuing high birthrates at the same time that initial sanitation measures were bringing down death rates, although there were many regional variations. A consequence was progressive fragmentation of peasant holdings as available common land in forest was used up. Within what is now Yugoslavia more prosperous lowland plains areas in the north and west had opportunities for temporary seasonal agricultural laborers. This was quite separate from the opportunities for skilled craftsmen such as the *pecalbari*.

Such movements were also separate from the late 19th- and 20th-century emigration from the southern and central parts of Yugoslavia (Macedonia, Bosnia-Hercegovina, and Montenegro) as well as the western and coastal areas of Croatia and Slovenia. Young men often tended to stay abroad, while married men generally returned home. There were also those who emigrated with their families. This tripartite pattern continues. The movements were very significant in numerical terms; for example, in the three decades from 1880 to 1910 a group equal in size to virtually the entire natural increase in the population of Slovenia immigrated to North America.

From the perspective of the concerns on which this chapter focuses, modern voluntary labor migration of Yugoslavs to mainly industrial as well as some agricultural work in Western Europe began before the First World War, especially to the mining areas of Belgium, France, and Germany.

In 1935 a young Yugoslav economist, Rudolf Bicanic, who was a member of the Croatian Peasant Party and newly released from prison because of political opposition to the government, made a trip to the coastal and mountain regions of Croatia and Bosnia. He wrote a small book about his experiences (Bicanic 1981). Some of his chapter headings graphically express the situation as it then existed during the height of the Great Depression: "Water! Give us Water!" and "Three Fourths of the Croats Have No Beds of Their Own." His chapter on the peasant worker describes how 4,500 peasants from just one region were doing agricultural labor in Belgium, France, and Holland. He describes the villagers' absolute dependence on their remittances (Bicanic 1981, 132):

> Everything we possess is from them. . . . How strange is the fate of our passive regions. Their land is barren and poorly cultivated; floods inundate the fields and wash the good soil away. At every step one sees the need for many willing, hard-working hands to wretch it out of neglect. Yet its sons must water another's land with their sweat and blood. Is it not possible that their own fields could be made fertile with their labor?

A partial answer to this question some four decades later is to be found by glancing through the 1971 Yugoslav census where the 1971/1948 population growth index is found to vary from 1,200 to 1,300 for parts of major cities (overall, the cities themselves average from 180 to 500). By contrast, many rural communities do not exceed 100 and fall below the average for all of Yugoslavia (130). Some villages are as low as 12, representing a drastic loss. Even within the agricultural regions the rate of increase is almost always greater for the towns.

Bicanic saw the villagers as faced with dire alternatives:

> Necessity drives the peasant to become an industrial worker. The great majority of our working class are impoverished peasants. Some 83% of our miners are peasants; 68% of our lumberjacks, 69% of construction labor, and 73% of the cement production force. The lot of these peasant-workers is desperate. They do the heaviest work, live in the worst conditions, and receive the lowest wages. . . . The inhabitants of our passive regions desire above all things freedom, and after freedom, the opportunity to earn a tolerable living. They do not believe that agriculture alone will be able to support the rapidly increasing population. They, therefore, demand that industries be started in their areas so that people can earn a living at home and not be forced to scatter their bones throughout the wide world, or rely on charity after every meager harvest. (Bicanic 1981, 138)

From the perspective of almost half a century later, it seems that the ultimate solution for some villages has been partial or total abandonment. This is particularly true in relatively remote areas where the land is marginal or difficult to work. At the same time, some areas have industries located nearby and others have become tourist resorts. Many areas Bicanic surveyed have contributed proportionately the highest numbers of workers who have emigrated to Western Europe in the postwar period. It seems that their bones are ultimately being scattered, not because of need but from preference.

MIGRATION AND RURAL DEPOPULATION

Rural depopulation in the postwar period has been a voluntary process. The policies of socialist Yugoslavia with respect to the dominant private agricultural sector may have played a role as a negative incentive, but living standards have risen for all, and a wide range of services are available even on the village level. The example of the demise of the village of Galicnik can be viewed in this light. Depopulation has been particularly acute in mountainous regions where people have had a long history of migration. Overall, in the last few decades the home community progressively has begun to lose its attractiveness as a place of eventual return. Current economic limitations may, to a degree, reverse this trend.

It remains difficult to sort out the various factors: economic motivation, the desire for education, the presumed attractions of city life, and the conscious policies of the socialist government which have promoted all these factors. At the same time politically based restrictions on the size of individual agricultural holdings (formerly set at ten hectares) and other restrictions can be seen as motivating in a negative sense. A primary factor has been the greatly expanded primary educational opportunities now available in every rural community. Schooling can be seen as providing the main incentive for those of some ambition to leave rural areas. When the aroused wishes are not fulfilled in an urban Yugoslav setting, there exists the further motivation for both students and workers to seek opportunity abroad, a pathway that recently has become increasingly difficult.

During the last several decades Yugoslavia has become an exporter both of unskilled labor and trained technicians and professionals. These people are the products of a greatly expanded secondary and higher educational system. In a sense, the socialist government of Yugoslavia has subsidized the professional training of many who now permanently work in Western Europe and North America (Klemencic 1978). While it is true that in the same period Yugoslavia has received grants and loans from the West, this reciprocal subsidy has not been seriously analyzed. At the same time the absorption of trained personnel outside a Yugoslav state which has no place for such people does greatly relieve pressures for much potential dissatisfaction with the system.

WORLD WAR II POPULATION TRANSFERS AND THEIR POSTWAR SUCCESSORS

The massive movements which were direct consequences of the war can be divided into two categories. The first is wartime population transfers from 1939 to 1944. The second encompasses the evacuations of those seeking refuge at the end of the war, many of whom feared the consequences of the policies of a socialist-communist revolutionary government. The largest group in the first category are some 400–500,000 Yugoslav prisoners of war and forced laborers who were sent to Germany and Austria in the period 1941–1944. Most numerous in the second category were approximately 160–350,000 Italians then resident in Yugoslavia and a lesser number of Yugoslavs who went to Italy right at the end of the war in 1945–1946. A significant number in the first category and most in the second were permanent migrants who eventually settled in Western Europe and North America. In the period 1945–1950, some 280,000 ethnic Germans either fled Yugoslavia with the retreating German armies, were expelled, or sought to leave voluntarily. Approximately 100–200,000 Yugoslavs also went to Western Europe as political refugees in 1945. Some of these were people who had actively fought the communists; a number of them had been in groups allied with the Germans. The categories are approximate, and they overlap.

A separate category, the most tragic of all, was that of some 58,000 Jews who were deported to German death camps. There was also the resettlement of some 100,000 people of Hungarian nationality in Hungary, 60,000 of whom went during the war and the remainder immediately afterwards. A smaller group of 10–15,000 Russians who had left the Soviet Union at the time of the Bolshevik Revolution left Yugoslavia between 1945 and 1961. It is difficult to determine the proportions of those who stayed in Western Europe and those who went on to North and South America and Australia, but it appears that the latter category was significantly larger (Kosinski 1982).

Since many of the prisoners of war returned home, the net outflow was about a million persons, not including Jews and other deportees who were killed in the concentration camps. After 1950 the type of migrants changed, consisting mainly of those who moved temporarily or permanently, primarily for economic reasons.

It is important to keep in mind, however, that even though Yugoslavia is the only East European state with a policy of relatively open borders, immigration to Western Europe and North America continues to be plagued by the actions of violent political extremists. Many of the extremists are supporters of groups that were tied to the Nazi-supported Croatian fascist state that existed during World War II (e.g., the Ustashi). They have hijacked planes and murdered Yugoslav diplomats and Yugoslav migrants. Some have returned clandestinely to Yugoslavia and engaged in random acts of bombing and murder. Some of those involved in these activities grew up in postwar Yugoslavia and left after the economic migration had begun. The activities of these terrorists are so widespread throughout Western Europe and North America that they have given a unique cast to the Yugoslav emigration and instilled fear among many of the migrants.

Explanations for this kind of activity can at least partially be traced to the fact that the Yugoslav state as it is now constituted lacks legitimacy for persons who believe in an irredentist Croatia, Macedonia, or Serbia. During World War II, at the same time that the communist partisans and Serbian Royalist Chetniks were fighting the Germans, they were also fighting each other. The conflict was particularly bloody, both for military and civilian participants.

There have been other conflicting groups. In the 1980s problems have developed with respect to the large Albanian minority within Serbia. The legacy of all these historically based conflicts remains to motivate violence among the few. Given all of these factors, it is indeed no small matter that the Yugoslav state continues to maintain relatively open borders. The other East European governments have been much more repressive in their internal policies than the Yugoslavs, but they are, without exception, composed of one nationality which is largely or overwhelmingly dominant, and so there is no questioning by emigrants of the essential legitimacy of these states as corporate units. Politically motivated personal violence has been largely absent among these other groups, even though many of the migrants from those countries feel themselves to be enemies of the socialist government in power.

Another way of thinking about politically motivated violence is with respect to its ties to cyclical time and oral tradition. The firm sense of location within a region, an ethnic group, and a national history can also increase the sense of threat from events in a linear time such as political revolutions with their attendant changes. This sense of threat can also be transferred into a desire for dominance, for expansion into what are presumed to be historically legitimate areas (e.g., the idea of a "greater" Croatia, Macedonia, or Serbia). These perceptions are very much related to the migrations to Western Europe. In France, Germany, Sweden, or Great Britain, violent dramas of national identity are being played out. (Identity traumas of the South Slavs, Libyans, Iranians, Armenians, Palestinians, Sikhs, and others attract national attention at different times.)

POSTWAR YUGOSLAV URBANIZATION AND MIGRATION TO WESTERN EUROPE

The most massive migratory movement in recent Yugoslav history has been from villages to urban centers. It is important to note that Yugoslavia has no overwhelmingly dominant metropolitan center as, for example, Athens is for Greece. As a result of this general pattern of rural exodus and urban growth, between 1921 and 1961 the percentage of the agricultural population of Yugoslavia declined from 79 to 49. At the same time the total population increased from 12.5 to 16 million with the most intensive development taking place since 1950. By 1960, out of a totally agriculturally based population of 9.2 million, some 1.3 million people living in rural areas commuted to jobs outside of their villages. In the 1950s over 2 million Yugoslavs left rural communities for urban areas. Almost a fifth of the total population had either moved from villages or were working outside their native place by the beginning of the 1960s when the substantial migration to Western Europe began (Halpern 1975, 86).

This migration is linked to the restructuring of the Yugoslav economy under a series of Five Year Plans which emphasized growth in industrial production. Industry was relatively dispersed, being located in all the major cities, the capitals of the most populous of the constituent republics—Ljubljana (Slovenia), Zagreb (Croatia), Belgrade (Serbia), Sarajevo (Bosnia-Hercegovina), and Skopje (Macedonia)—as well as in the smaller provincial towns. During the 1960s some 400,000 new jobs were created in industry. The status of private farming had initially been undermined by abortive collectivization campaigns which followed the break with the Soviet Union in 1948. The limitation on private landholdings and the taxation structure which favored the newly organized social sector in agriculture also aided this process, as did the universalization of education. Schools in the villages stressed the glamour of industrial work and urban jobs as an explicit part of the communist ideology, which emphasized the implicit glamour and socially progressive tendencies of the worker as opposed to the conservative peasant. Even with services in education, health, and transportation increasingly available in rural areas, the desire to "get out of the mud" became overwhelming among the younger generation. Remaining behind was, in a sense, failure or, at best, a situation which required rationalization. An increasing number of peasants did combine living in villages with town employment. For many this was a preliminary step to permanent immigration to towns. The idea that their children could receive a superior education in town was a particularly potent factor motivating mature workers. From town residence it was then an easier step to temporary or permanent migration abroad although ties with kin already in foreign countries made it easier for villagers (Thomas 1982).

NUMBERS AND CHARACTERISTICS OF MIGRANTS TO WESTERN EUROPE

While some villagers did move directly to jobs in Western Europe, it was generally as unskilled labor. As noted by Ivo Baucic (1977), a geographer from the University of Zagreb and one of the major Yugoslav researchers in problems of external migration, there were approximately 860,000 Yugoslav workers and 250,000 dependents among the 13 million migrants in Western Europe before the economic crisis began at the end of 1973, marking a time when this type of international migration had expanded to its maximum dimensions. Citing an increasing number of dependents, especially children, among the migrants, Baucic hypothesizes that a significant proportion of these migrants will end up taking permanent residence in the receiving country.

The number of Yugoslav migrant workers in Western Europe increased drastically from an estimated 14,000 in 1965 to 210,000 a year later. By 1969 the number had reached 420,000 and grew to 660,000 in 1971. Given the rapid turnover in some jobs, there was a much larger number of the population who had had a migratory experience, since these numbers do not all represent the same people. This situation had a parallel with earlier immigration to the New World, especially in the period before World War I, where there were large reverse flows. Constant movement was made much easier in the postwar period by geographic closeness and fast, convenient transportation, usually by train or private car. The long periods of separation which marked the life of the *pecalbari* of an earlier period were absent.

As a result of the economic slowdown and constricting opportunities, as well as the long existing desire of many migrants to return home to settle permanently, some 130,000 emigrants returned to Yugoslavia in 1974 and 1975, while in the same time only 20,000 left for jobs in Western Europe. At the end of 1975 there were about 770,000 migrants in Western Europe. Some 200,000 more went overseas to Australia, Canada, and the United States. When this group of 970,000 is compared to the total Yugoslav labor force of 4.7 million, it is apparent that for every 100 persons employed in Yugoslavia there are some 20 who work abroad.

According to data from the 1971 census, women made up approximately 31 percent of the migrants, representing a radical change from earlier times. This percentage was approximately equal to the proportion of women in the Yugoslav labor force. One quarter of the migrants were in the 20-24 age group and 83 percent were under 40. With respect to formal education, 42 percent had completed at least eight years of schooling, compared to 33 percent of the total Yugoslav population. Some 6 percent had finished university or high school, relative to 8 percent of the total population. With respect to degree of skill, the difference is more dramatic: 17 percent of the emigrants were educated or highly skilled, almost double the average of 9 percent. The migrants, then, were young, relatively well prepared, and also appeared to be among the best educated of those coming from Southern Europe.

Emigration to Western Europe has not been distributed evenly with respect to region either of origin or of destination. Again according to 1971 data, Croatia, which had only 28 percent of the total population, provided 34 percent of the emigrants. In contrast, the major population center in central Serbia, with more than a quarter of the population (27 percent), sent less than a fifth (18 percent) of the migrants, following a pattern from earlier migrations abroad. Croatia had a migration rate of 6.1 per thousand, Serbia 2.5, and Kosovo, the least developed region in Yugoslavia with a large Albanian population, had 2.1. The less developed republics of Bosnia-Hercegovina and Macedonia had rates of 4.8 and 4.4 respectively, with the overall Yugoslav rate being 3.9 (Baucic 1977).

The reasons for this differentiation are not immediately clear. While ecological limitations have been significant for some areas, as was illustrated by the situation of the *pecalbari* in Galicnik and is the case for the mountainous Republic of Montenegro, some of the most prosperous agricultural areas in Croatia and Vojvodina—of flat plains to the north of the Danube in Serbia—have historically been important sending regions. A high degree of industrialization and closer contacts with Western Europe can be influential, as has been the case for Croatia and Slovenia. Albanian Moslems, perhaps the poorest segment of the Yugoslav population (mainly from the southern Serbian region of Kosovo), have recently increased immigration abroad, following their earlier pattern of migration from Kosovo to more prosperous areas of Yugoslavia such as Slovenia. The notion of ethnic succession is relevant: the Albanians came to Slovenia when Slovenes were leaving for Western Europe and North America. Following from different circumstances, mountaineers from Bosnia and Montenegro replaced German settlers in the fertile plains of the Vojvodina after World War II, when these people left for their ancestral home in Germany. Contacts with the West, degree of economic development, and ecological and ethnic marginality are all factors which have entered into this process.

Countries of employment represent an uneven distribution. Overhwelmingly, the most important has been West Germany with 55 percent of the migrant workers residing there, many from Croatia. On the other hand, Serbs have tended to favor Austria and France. In the latter cases there are clear historic connections, although it is not easy to assess their current influence. Germany was the enemy in World War II, and many of the Yugoslavs are employed in menial industrial and service jobs; for those focusing on a short stay, with the main desire to save money in order to build a house in the home community, it has not been difficult to accept marginal living quarters and temporary low status. This type of adaptation is familiar to those who have examined American immigration history at the turn of the century and the role of boarding houses.

Complexities in processes of chain migration are exemplified in a case history cited by Schierup (1973, 31). The purported first migrant to Western Europe from the Eastern Serbian village that he studied was a man who had previously been in jail for seven years, possibly for political reasons. He then escaped across the border and made his way to Germany. (His illegal emigration was presumably necessitated by the fact that he could not get a passport. Such cases were more frequent in the 1950s and early 1960s. By 1964 official Yugoslav agencies were involved in cooperative efforts with foreign employers.) Later, when he lived in Sweden, he sent for his brother who had been associated with the Communist party organization in the village. This brother was subsequently killed by Croatian terrorists in Sweden. He then returned to his native village and built a large house. He reportedly also had enough money to open a café on the Yugoslav coast.

While politically motivated murder has not been a common experience, the triumphant return home to construct a large house has been so prevalent a national experience that the government has tried to encourage returnees to invest in enterprises in return for long-term employment as well as trying to make bank savings attractive and thus to avoid what the government has considered unproductive investment in construction. The symbolic value of a big brick house has, however, remained an important value.

FILM IMAGES AND SOCIAL SCIENCE ANALYSES

The journey of Yugoslav village emigrants to Northern and Western Europe has had the consequence of bringing into close contact people with contrasting values and life experiences. This interaction is portrayed in the film *Montenegro* by the Serbian expatriate film director Dusan Makavejev. His films have been concerned with the sexual aspects of class and cultural conflicts. *Mysteries of the Organism,* an earlier film set in Belgrade, dealt with the stormy love affair of an ethnic Hungarian telephone operator and a patriarchically obsessed ethnic Albanian rat exterminator. Her relative freedom from social and sexual constraints contrasts with his expectations for a wife's proper role. Their conflict eventually leads him to murder her, with all the details graphically portrayed. Both were migrants lacking supporting kin in Belgrade, seeking unsuccessfully to find a new life with each other.

Montenegro is set in Stockholm. It is a tale of a neurotic and bored Swedish housewife living with her husband and children in an elegant villa with all possible creature comforts. He becomes aware of the extent of her disturbance when she sets the bed afire. Calling in a money-hungry psychiatrist doesn't seem to help. In the confusion of an attempt to join her husband on a trip abroad, she is accidentally whisked off by Serbian immigrants to their contrasting ethnic enclave, the "Zanzi" bar and distillery, near the railroad tracks. In allegorical fashion a lusty Montenegrin lover is portrayed as a keeper at the Stockholm zoo. A subplot chronicles a Montenegrin peasant girl whose roast pig and plum brandy gifts for her friends in Sweden are not allowed past Swedish customs. Her transformation is chronicled from "innocent whore" who serviced Scandinavian tourists on the Yugoslav coast to stripper in the "Zanzi" bar. The uninhibited sex and free-floating life at the bar are set against the housewife's family home, where her children efficiently take over the distaff chores in her unlamented absence. The stark contrasts between the two stereotypes would appear as approximating the truth to some superficial observers of the migrant scene. Or, from another view, they are fantasies which each group has of the other, revealing more than a bit of envy on both sides, with their illusions of order versus free sexuality. One is tempted to conceive of a film where the order is reversed on the pattern of the *Mysteries of the Organism,* and where a libertarian Swede is substituted for the Hungarian telephone operator and a moralistic Montenegrin for the Albanian exterminator. This reveals, in part, how cultural stereotypes can be totally reversed depending on whether one has a Yugoslav or Swedish audience in mind.

The actualities are more complex. There is certainly a large stratum among the Yugoslav migrants who are closely tied to their peasant origins yet migrate as single men. But many of the migrants have their families with them and their wives work. Child care and school facilities for the children then become a crucial problem. Sometimes a grandmother is along to help. At other times children are sent home if the situation becomes difficult. Working-class migrants may live in marginal housing but their passion for saving to return home would seem to limit much connected with a "Zanzi" bar type setting even for single men.

Most working-class migrants go to Western Europe with a consciousness of Yugoslavia's technological and economic inferiority to the West, but they also travel with a prideful sense of self which enables them to maintain their identity while accepting low social status. This situation contrasts, in at least some respects, with their relatively egalitarian homeland. There are, of course, politically powerful groups in Yugoslavia, and authority is to a degree centralized and certainly hierarchical in terms of the Communist Party's dominant role in economic and social institutions. However, Yugoslavia does not have the diversity of economic and class-linked life-styles found in the West. The stresses involved in playing the subordinate role of the migrant are offset by reliance on kinship and friendship links with other migrants and thoughts of a future return home, especially on the part of the unskilled workers, or the expectation of a degree of mobility possible in the receiving society. The latter has been particularly important for professionals and highly skilled workers who plan to remain abroad permanently.

A negative feature of life abroad, especially for the workers, has been the Croat-Serb conflict. Professionals have more alternatives and resources to deal with this problem, but they are also affected. This conflict is implicit in the very name of the language they speak. Some Croats, for example, would call it Croato-Serbian. When Yugoslavia was originally constituted as a result of the Versailles Conference after World War I, the Croats ceased living in a province of the Austro-Hungarian Empire. They joined the Serbs to become one of the two main ethnic constituents of the new Yugoslav state. The Serbs were, however, numerically dominant and had a prior history of approximately a century as an independent state and so became the dominant group in the new union under a Serbian king.

Hostilities from the interwar period, inflamed during World War II by the Ustashi massacres of Serbs and Jews resident in Croatia, continue to be played out among the migrant workers. The importance of the Ustashi is found not only in individual ethnographic accounts such as that cited by Schierup (1973) but also those reported by Meurle and Andric (1971). They refer to the role of the Ustashi in terrorizing Yugoslav, especially Serb, workers in Sweden, using various methods including murder. They cite incidents of Croatian workers, recruited in churches and clubs by Ustashe, appearing with blankets over their heads and singing taunting songs outside a barracks housing Serbian workers. Subsequently, individual workers who supported Socialist Yugoslavia were threatened with death but were too terrorized to report the threats to the Swedish authorities.

Meurle and Andric also cite other problems such as the alienation of young Yugoslav workers from the mainstream of Swedish society. Such isolation intensifies the ethnic conflicts. It makes safe enclaves such as a "Zanzi" type bar more appealing, where it is not hedonistic sexuality which is prime but a psychologically comfortable atmosphere.

CLASS AND MIGRATION

While professionals are in a minority among the immigrants to Western Europe, their importance is disproportionately evident in the statistics. They tend to stay longer, many permanently. Their much higher incomes make their remittances that much more significant. Most physicians, dentists, engineers, architects, and computer specialists received their initial training in Yugoslavia. Much of their technical education is comparable to the background of their Western colleagues. A number have become very successful, such as the film director Makarejev, or affiliated with universities, as in the case of the sociologist Mile Andric.

While no migrants are free from the consequences of ethnic conflict or the potential of emigrant terrorists, professionals tend to live in a much less ethnic environment than do workers. Many continue to maintain extensive kin networks reaching as far back as the villages of parental origin and frequently visit their homeland. A number have vacation homes, especially on the Dalmatian Coast. Some free professionals may have a Yugoslav clientele and most retain Yugoslav friends, but their important relationships are within the host country. Intermarriage with nationals of the host country is frequent, and many have a life-style in which extensive international travel is frequent. Anthropologists meeting such professionals while they themselves are on vacation have a qualitatively different experience than that of interviewing workers in the field. Getting acquainted with such individuals is clearly a matter of studying "across" or "up" as opposed to the more conventionally "down" approach to workers. In compiling a kinship network for a given Yugoslav residing abroad or for a village family, one frequently encounters a wide range of class settings. These networks continue to function actively regardless of ways in which the participants become differentiated through education, occupation, and country of residence. Class differences can result in the attenuation of such networks over time, but this is usually a matter of generations. Networks also function to enhance possibilities of upward class mobility for village youth and workers.

ONLY POOR WORKERS AS MIGRANTS?

A limited perspective is reflected in the photo montage text of John Berger, who treats all migrant workers in Western Europe from a Marxist perspective. He overlooks the varied ways in which kin from different socioeconomic settings interact (Berger 1975, 108): "Just as agencies now in Istanbul or Athens or Zagreb arrange contracts whereby workers go to Cologne or Brussels, so in early nineteenth century Britain, agents were set up by the Poor Law Commissions to recruit the unemployed in the villages of the South-Western Counties of England and dispatch them to Manchester."

He also points out that though Yugoslavia had one of the highest growth rates in the world from 1945 to 1965, the wages Yugoslavs now receive abroad are four times what they earn at home. Berger cites the comments of a Yugoslav worker:

> To go home? Of course, as soon as I can. You can see I live out of a suitcase. I buy nothing. What should I do with the things I bought? You can't cart them around from lodging to lodging. It would be different if I were going to stay here, if we were going to settle. But I could never do that. I'd always choose the life at home in my own country. One day it will be better at home than abroad and, when I go back there, I'll be able to work for myself and I'll build myself a house. It'll be a kind of paradise. If only the wages at home were a bit higher and if everyone could find work there, nobody would leave to go abroad. (Berger 1975, 214–15)

This quote is followed by several pages of photos of Yugoslavia showing peasants selling cattle near a parked diesel locomotive, making mud bricks, and using simple wooden wheelbarrows, and village children posed with sheep and a horse near a cornfield. The adjoining photograph is of New York City at night. It is perhaps indicative of the confusion that such contrasts engender that I had to double-check the photo credits to make sure it was not a Yugoslav city.

While no one need doubt that migrants have endured much pain and suffering in the course of their journeys, the fact that these migrations occurred in the latter half of the 20th century, often under intergovernmental agreements with calculated social benefits, is important. While it is true that it is the professionals from Yugoslavia and not the workers who reside in the high-rise apartments of Munich, Paris, and New York, it is also true that peasant grandmothers are not unfamiliar visitors in these settings. When seeing a Yugoslav now working in Western Europe driving a Mercedes down a Yugoslav village lane, one thinks of alternatives for that investment in terms of long-term improvements in the worker's life. But that is clearly the worker's decision and not the anthropologist's.

A COMMUNITY CASE HISTORY

How has the emigration of workers affected a specific community and permanently altered the lives of close kin? At what point do ties with the village begin to disappear? The author has worked intermittently since 1953 in the village of Orasac in central Serbia, visiting that community eight times for periods ranging from a few weeks to over a year, the last visit occurring in 1978.

Especially during the summer a visitor to this community would immediately be aware of the number of cars with German, Austrian, and Swedish license plates. Since this is not a tourist area, the cars can safely be assumed to belong to local villagers who are now working abroad and have come home to visit on their vacations. Many are involved in constructing new homes along the main road. Following the village pattern, construction proceeds intermittently as money becomes available. The official statistics for 1971 list 800 workers abroad. Providing a variation from the Serbian pattern, the largest number are in West Germany (40 percent) followed by France (25 percent), with smaller numbers in Austria and Switzerland.

A composite picture of the members of one agnatic lineage illustrates the kin links. An engineer in Chicago maintains ties with relatives who include faculty members in France, a surgeon in Germany, and workers in Switzerland. The worker in Switzerland has already built a house in the village for his family. The engineer in Chicago travels frequently to Yugoslavia to visit his parents and brother who have remained farmers. The brother's son is studying at the University of Belgrade but plans to take time off to visit his uncle in Chicago "to see what it is like."

A niece has just returned from a stint as an architect in Paris and moved to the local market town after marrying an engineer at the local firebrick factory. Everyone has had a chance to visit the new house, which cost about $60,000 in Yugoslav currency. There is great pride in the parquet floors and a complete set of appliances imported from Switzerland.

The engineer's aunt, although she continues to farm with her husband, does enjoy visiting her daughter in Switzerland. This aunt has also learned how to manage a foreign currency account at the bank in the local town since her daughter provides her with money for child care and associated expenses. It is expensive to have their child with them in Switzerland; besides, they would like the child to have a local education since they plan to return home soon; her husband is counting on his Swiss experience to qualify him for a skilled job at the local insulator factory.

Across the road two brothers who are stonecutters on vacation from jobs in Austria are completing a large brick house in which there will be separate apartments for each of their families and for their parents. Their father is on pension, having contracted silicosis while working at the local marble quarry.

Not all experiences are pleasant. The engineer has brought with him photos of a murdered cousin. This man had moved from a job as a skilled worker in Germany to Chicago to be near his relatives. After marrying a member of the local Serbian community, he borrowed money and opened a restaurant. A little over a year later, he was murdered in a holdup. The photos attest to the fact that all proper ritual was carried out at the funeral and that it was performed in the proper style. This experience is compared by villagers with a recent highway accident in which a farmer was crushed by his overturned tractor.

CONCLUDING THOUGHTS

The experience of migrations to Western Europe is easiest to view from its impact on a delimited village community. Yugoslav peasant subcultures were historically strongly linked to state activities. As the *pecalba* experiences illustrate, contacts with a distant world have a long historical precedent. The key difference from today was that the outside world was then the prerogative of men only. But even then men carried the village with them to distant lands, for it was only when they brought their money home to the village that their experience was truly meaningful. While major investment in building a house in a village today has something of that element, it occurs in a very different context. The village may still be a good place to live in or retire in, but it is not work in agriculture which is the occupation to which most now return. Further, while most intend to reside in these homes for the rest of their lives, it is possible that the houses might be sold at some point if a move to town seems more appropriate. Options within the village community are now open.

The role of women in migration is now important. They accompany their men abroad. Sometimes they work or go abroad as single women. Even the villagers who remain as farmers occasionally go abroad to visit kin. The present situation is one of great mobility for all concerned, and while sex-specific roles continue to exist, they are not overwhelmingly dominant as in the era of the *pecalba* at the turn of the century.

A continuing sense of ethnicity and historical heritage remains important and is linked to the social reinforcement received from the maintenance of a locally based kin network. Orientations to a cyclical time framework help to balance the pressures of linear time omnipresent in a world environment of technological innovation and inherent in the adjustment, by those who live abroad, to a diverse cultural setting.

While economic conditions since the early 1970s have restricted opportunities for migrants, processes set in motion in the 1950s and 1960s have a momentum of their own. Limitations are increasingly evident, but travel and contact continue and opportunities still exist. There is an optimism inherent in the experience of these migrants. Few are bitter about having made the trip although degrees of success vary greatly. Political terrorism, though it continues, has affected only a relative few.

Prejudice of North and West Europeans against those from the South and East still exists, but it is much modified from earlier times. Economic stringencies can bring "Zanzi" bar stereotypes to the fore, but it seems unlikely that there will be a return to the former norm in these matters.

It is possible to view the current period of economic constraints as positive in that these limitations provide a time for adjustment to the radical cultural transformations of the early postwar decades.

NOTES

1. This chapter is based, in part, on field experience in Yugoslavia over a period of three decades beginning in 1953. Specific community data is from a Serbian rural community which has been studied for the same period: Halpern 1967 and Halpern and Kerewsky-Halpern 1972. Research has been sponsored by grants from the National Science Foundation, the National Institutes of Health, and the National Academy of Sciences. Research in Yugoslavia was carried out under official exchange agreements between the National Academy of Sciences and the Council of Yugoslav Academies. See Halpern and Kideckel 1983 for detailed references.

2. Statistics used were published in multivolume series by the Savezni Zavod Za Statistiku (the Federal Bureau of Statistics) in Belgrade.

REFERENCES

Adamic, Louis

1934 *The Native's Return*. New York: Harpers.

Baucic, Ivo

1977 "Regional Differences in Yugoslav External Migration." In *Population and Migration Trends in Eastern Europe,* edited by H. L. Kostanick, 217–44. Boulder: Westview Press.

Berger, John

1975 *A Seventh Man, Migrant Workers in Europe,* photographs by Jean Mohr. New York: Viking Press.

Bicanic, Rudolf

1981 *How the People Live: Life in the Passive Regions (Peasant Life in Southwestern Croatia, Bosnia and Hercegovina: Yugoslavia, 1935),* edited by Joel M. Halpern and Elinor Murray Despaltovic, translated by Marijan Despalatovic. Research Report 21, Department of Anthropology, University of Massachusetts at Amherst.

Braudel, Fernand

1972 *The Mediterranean and the Mediterranean World in the Age of Philip II,* vol. 1. New York: Harper and Row.

Cvijic, Jovan

1918a "The Geographical Distribution of the Balkan Peoples." *Geographical Review* 5: 345–61.

1918b *La Peninsule Balkanique*. Paris: Colin.

1930/31 "Studies in Jugoslav Psychology, II." *Slavonic and East European Review* 9: 662–81.

Halpern, Joel M.

1967 *A Serbian Village*. New York; Harper and Row.

1975 "Some Perspectives on Balkan Migration Patterns." In *Migration and Urbanization, Models and Adaptive Strategies,* edited by Brian DuToit and Helen I. Safa, 77–115. Chicago: Aldine.

1980 "Memories of Recent Change: Some East European Perspectives." In *The Process of Rural Transformation, Eastern Europe, Latin America and Australia,* edited by Ivan Volgyes et al. New York: Pergamon Press.

Halpern, Joel M., and Kerewsky-Halpern, Barbara

1972 *A Serbian Village in Historical Perspective*. Prospect Heights, Ill.: Waveland. Reprinted 1986.

1973 "The Anthropologist as Tourist, An Incidental Ethnography of the Impact of Tourism in a Dalmatian Village." *East European Quarterly* 7: 149–57.

1975 "The Pecalba Tradition in Macedonia, A Case Study." *Journal of the British Yugoslav Society* no. 2, pp. 6–9.

Halpern, Joel M., and Kideckel, David A.

1983 "Anthropology in Eastern Europe." *Annual Review of Anthropology* 12: 377–402.

Karovksi, Lazo

1974 "Macedonia Folk Poetry of Economic Immigration." *Macedonian Review* 9, no. 3: 295–301.

Klemencic, Vladimir

1978 "The Character, Causes and Effects of Emigration from Yugoslavia." In *Iseljenistvo Naroda i Narodnosti Jugoslavije i Njegova Uzajamne Veze so Dominom, Zbornik*, 709–714. (Results of a Conference of Yugoslav Emigration Held in Zagreb, 1976.) Zagreb: Zavod za Migracije i Narodnosti.

Kosinski, Leszek A.

1982 "International Migration of Yugoslavs during and Immediately after World War II." *East European Quarterly* 16: 183–98.

Meurle, Kristina, and Andric, Mile

1971 *Background to the Yugoslav Migration to Sweden, Case Study of a Group of Yugoslav Workers at a Factory in Sweden*. Department of Sociology, Lund University, Sweden.

Schierup, Carl Ulrik

1973 *Houses, Tractors, Golden Ducats, Prestige Game and Migration: A Study of Migrants to Denmark from a Yugoslav Village*. Moiesgard, Arhus Universitet, Institut For Etnografi og Socialantropologi, December.

Stoianovich, Traian

1960 "The Conquering Balkan Orthodox Merchant." *Journal of Economic History* 20: 234–313.

1967 *A Study in Balkan Civilization*. New York: Alfred Knopf.

Thomas, Colin

1982 "Migration and Urban Growth in Yugoslavia." *East European Quarterly* 16: 199–216.

6 Turkish Migrant Workers in the Federal Republic of Germany: A Case Study

A. Ersan Yücel

ABSTRACT. Like Yugoslav and Soninké migration, Turkish migration has deep historical roots. The decline of the Ottoman Empire, colonization by the capitalist West and, in the last quarter of the 19th century, major famines led to large-scale migratory moves from rural to urban areas and from the eastern half to the western half of the country. Indeed, most of the early migrants to Germany had previous migratory experience.

Yücel used the method of participant observation to its fullest potential. He entered Germany illegally as many of his fellow migrants did and found employment and cheap housing for his wife and himself in the same manner as his compatriots. His vivid case analysis permits us to visualize the difficulties faced by migrant workers and their ingenious means of overcoming them through the judicious (and sometimes exploitative) use of their social network of fellow migrants. In the process he shows what migrant status in Germany entails. Foreign workers in Western Europe have often been called an "underclass." The term does indeed highlight the relationship of Turkish workers to German society. They are a category of individuals who do not enjoy the same rights as indigenous workers and, because of restrictive immigration policies, must frequently forego even the limited benefits granted to legal migrants. However, the label does not take into account the fact that the migrants have other reference groups as well. Their cohort of migrants may give more recognition to such factors as relative age than to legal status in Germany or even to the type of work and size of earnings. Ultimately, most migrants view their standing in their place of origin, where they eventually plan to return (or fear that they may be sent back to), as much more important than their temporary migrant status. As Yücel shows, however, these divergent identities are not entirely independent. A successful migrant entrepreneur may be forced to adopt the same discriminatory practices vis-à-vis his less fortunate countrymen that his hosts use.

INTRODUCTION

Human spatial movements have always generated tensions and problems of a demographic, social, psychological, economic, political, and environmental nature. These problems, in their turn, have attracted the attention of social scientists, creating a tremendous amount of published research in the field of human migrations. Today the literature continues to grow on an increasing scale just as improved communications make it easier for people to gather information on opportunities elsewhere and move.

Most of this literature relies heavily on census data, official statistics, surveys, and similar quantified data. Such macroscopic approaches can expound the dimensions and general characteristics of large-scale migrations but fail to provide insight into the actual process of migration. In addition, they often ignore the social and cultural diversity within a migrant population. One of the main claims of this article is that Turkish workers in the Federal Republic of Germany (FRG) are a heterogeneous social group and that this heterogeneity follows certain parameters which include differences of education, regional origin, skill, sex, age, and marital status. There is no migrant type; Turks may be perceived in Germany as one distinct group among the *Gastarbeiter* (guest workers) but the differences among Turks, at least for the Turks themselves, are far more significant than the similarities. It is all too easy to create a false migrant type that exists not in the field but only in the minds of those who created it.

Writers like Descloitres (1967), Rose (1969), and Castles and Kosack (1973), for example, who are regarded as authorities on European labor migrations, have created such general and false types. Basing their generalizations on macrostatistical indicators about the sending societies which stress their underdeveloped characteristics, like high rates of population increase, low levels of education, high unemployment and low per capita incomes, these scholars have arrived at typologies of migrants that portray them as classic peasants: unskilled, uneducated, impoverished, tradition-bound, and hopelessly ignorant of industrial urban life (Rhoades 1976, 69).

In the case of Turkish migrant workers, who are regarded as the most backward of all the migrant groups in Europe, such a view is grossly oversimplified and is not representative of the great majority of migrants. Because of the highly organized nature of present-day European labor migrations and the specific demands of the industrial countries of Europe, the migrants constitute, if anything, comparatively more educated, skilled, and urbanized segments of the labor-sending countries and respresent "a kind of working class brain drain" (Rhoades 1976, 70). Turkish migrants are young, better educated, economically active and likely to be married with large families, and likely, therefore, to have strong family ties and commitments in Turkey. Turkish labor migration has been predominantly male, although on a decreasing scale. As the migration stream matured (Böhning 1972b), the proportion of women increased to 19 percent in 1967, and finally to 24 percent in 1973.

Some of the concepts developed by anthropologists have helped greatly in gaining better insight into migration. The application of network analysis has been one of the most widely used and successful in this respect. It has been especially useful as a tool in explaining how small groups of migrants behave in specific contexts; how the social norms operate; how the information, opinions and attitudes, goods and services are transmitted; and how people are socialized in one direction rather than another (e.g., Mayer 1961; Barnes 1954; Bott 1957; Mitchell 1969).

Intrinsic to the concept of networks are the elements of choice and decision making by the actors. They are required to choose who to recruit to their networks, how many links to utilize to achieve a particular end, whether or how much to reciprocate to other persons in the network, for how long to operationalize a network, how frequently to interact with their links, etc. When network analysis is applied to the study of migration, the migrants are no longer aggregates of numbers who flock into the industrial centers because they are all 'pushed' out of their rural homes or 'pulled' by the urban centers because of economic imbalances (although they are very important), but people who make rational decisions—within the structural limitations of their social situations—about whether or not to migrate, how and when to migrate, which channels to use, which part of their total networks to utilize, where from among many possible destinations to go, etc.

Turkish migrant workers operate within social networks which might be described, following B. S. Denich, in terms of concentric spheres (1970, 137). An inner core consists of relations with *yakin akrabalar* (close relatives, including affines as well as kinsmen), with whom mutual binding obligations are acknowledged. Around this are graduated spheres of relations with more distant relatives *(uzak akrabalar)* and *hemşehriler* (fellow countrymen) and *arkadaşlar* (friends) who are not specifically obligated to a person but who may be called on for specific services. The relationships within the social networks are very much "instrumental" in character (Wolf 1966, 12). Each member of a person's network is a potential link with other persons who may be in a position to help him but who are not personally known to him. Because of the severely limited structural positions of the migrants on the margins of German society, their achievements in the FRG depend on the success of their manipulation of their categorical and personal relationships. These relationships are governed by what M. D. Sahlins called "generalized reciprocity" (1972), which is a form of exchange based on the assumption that returns balance out in the long run and are supported by norms that are believed to be "Turkish." Relatives and *hemşehriler* of friends are frequently called upon to find jobs and accommodations or to provide other services either for oneself or for another friend. Those who are approached in this way feel obliged to do what they can and help, for not doing so would be un-Turkish *(Türklüge yakişsmaz)* and would entail, in repeatedly proven cases, being ostracized by the Turkish community, the source of recognition and status for an overwhelming majority of Turkish migrants. In this chapter I will analyze social networks which facilitate and shape Turkish migration to Germany in the context of a specific network of which I and my wife were ourselves members, during fieldwork in Germany in 1972–1973. In addition to participant observation my research included a survey of 767 Turkish migrants drawn from various industries in different parts of the FRG. The survey was intended to exemplify and illustrate rather than be statistically representative of all Turks in Germany.[1] Before we proceed with the analysis we must first provide the historical, geopolitical, and economic background in which these networks operate.

THE HISTORY OF TURKISH MIGRATION

Turkey has a long history of migration. The disintegration of the Ottoman Empire beginning in the mid-16th century and its simultaneous colonization by the capitalist West led to the rise of richer peasants while the poorer ones started to lose their land. At the same time, more and more European goods began to infiltrate the empire, with the consequent disintegration of traditional craft forms and institutions of production. These developments resulted in internal migration from rural areas towards the cities, where former peasants and craftsmen became laborers in the modern sense after the full separation of the labor force from the means of production.

The migration of peasants to urban centers gained momentum after the famine years in the last quarter of the 19th century. Hundreds of thousands of people abandoned their homes in Central Anatolia, in and around Ankara, Kirşehir, Yozgat, Çankiri, and Sivas, and came to cities like Adana, Bursa, and Istanbul in 1874 and 1891 (Sencer 1969, 116–18). This migratory movement has continued unabated to the present, fueled by the large-scale introduction of tractors into Turkish agriculture since the 1950s.

The general trend of migration is from the eastern half of the country towards the western half. Most of the migrants go to the big cities like Istanbul, Ankara, Izmir, Adana Zonguldak, and Samsun. The general pattern is for the young men to migrate first and bring their dependents only after they feel secure in their new environment. The men constituted 62 percent of the total migrants in both the 1935 and 1960 censuses and 61 percent in 1965 (Tümertekin 1968, 5). Of course, some men never bring their families to the cities: those who have some land and animals to be looked after and those with dependents too young or too old to work in the city prefer to leave their families behind—a factor found to be true for some of the migrant Turkish workers in West Germany. The aim of the majority of the men in this category is to save enough money in as short a time as possible and go back home to better their life there by buying some land or animals. However, most of them can never achieve this goal and become permanent workers in the cities. When another member of the family becomes old enough to work, he either joins or replaces the one already in the city.

Among the many important effects of internal migrations in Turkey, the one concerning us the most is that the majority of the early Turkish migrant workers in Germany were the people who had once migrated to big cities in Turkey and used them as jumping-off grounds for their venture into Europe. Abadan found in a sample survey that 53.3 percent of the Turkish workers in the FRG indicated that their permanent places of residence were the three big cities (Istanbul, Ankara, and Izmir), but only 23.5 percent of them had been born there (Abadan 1964, 50).

TURKISH MIGRATION TO GERMANY

After the war most people predicted that Germany would become a land of emigration. The country was in ruins: the industrial complexes and the transportation system had been demolished and the male work force decimated. There were 8–10 million refugees from the former German territories and nobody thought that Germany could provide for all these people in the near future. However, the resulting exodus from Germany in the first years after the war was much smaller in magnitude and shorter in duration than had been expected. The reconstruction of German industry was begun immediately after the war, and with the help of the currency reforms of 1948, the economy recovered rapidly. The refugees were quickly absorbed into the labor force. Meanwhile, another source of labor was provided by refugees from the German Democratic Republic throughout the 1950s. Until the construction of the Berlin Wall in 1961, more than 3 million people had come to the FRG from the East. This group was also integrated into the economy very quickly, and by the late 1950s labor shortages started becoming very serious (Rist 1978, 60–61).

Germany turned once more to the migrant laborers for the expansion of its economy. A number of labor agreements were signed with countries in Europe that were experiencing labor surpluses. The first agreement was signed with Italy in 1955 for the recruitment of workers for the construction industry and agriculture. Other agreements followed: with Greece and Spain in 1960, Turkey in 1961, Portugal in 1964, and Yugoslavia in 1968. These agreements have governed the growth of the migrant labor force in the FRG. In 1960 there were 389,356 foreign workers constituting 1.5 percent of the total labor force. By 1973 it was 7,595,000, or 11.9 percent of the total labor force. In 1973 Turkish migrant workers had become the largest group of migrants, representing 23 percent of the migrant labor force (Rist 1978, 52-66). Subsequently, migration dropped considerably. Thus, while there were 600,000 Turkish foreign workers in Germany in 1974, in 1978 only 514,000 remained (Siewert 1980, 1065).

The impact of Turkish migration was felt not just in Germany but in Turkey as well. Migrants retain their links with Turkey and the remittances which they send back are an important source of foreign currency for Turkey. Migrant remittances constituted 56.7 percent of Turkish imports in 1973 and made an important contribution in reducing the deficit of Turkey's trading account (Hale 1978, 67, 68). At the same time, labor migration has reduced the supply of labor in Turkey itself, with significant consequences for the level of unemployment there. However, the long-term consequences are likely to be less benign: Turkey has increasingly exported skilled workers, and there is growing evidence that on their return the capital they have accumulated in the FRG is not used in a way which promotes real development.

THE RECRUITMENT PROCESS

The selection, transportation, and placement of workers are carried out by the authorized institutions in Turkey and the FRG. For Turkey this institution is the Turkish Employment Service (TES). In Germany the German Federal Labor Bureau and the Unemployment Insurance Institution cooperate for this purpose and are represented in Turkey by the German Liaison Office (GLO) in Istanbul.

A German employer who wants to hire foreign labor contacts the local Employment Bureau and asks for the necessary papers. He fills in the required information for each job: the required skills and the wage and working conditions offered for that job as stated within the last agreement between employers and trade unions. If there is no agreement, the average wage and working conditions of the region are written down. Employers have the right to choose the foreign workers they want to employ from among the Turkish, Greek, Spanish, or Portuguese nationals. One precondition of labor import is that the employer provide accommodations for all the workers he wants to import and that he pay a fee for all the recruitment expenditures. In the early sixties this fee used to be only 165 deutsche marks (DM) per person. Later it was increased to 300 DM and on September 1, 1973, to 1,000 DM per person in the hope of discouraging employers from recruitment of foreign labor, which had reached a disconcerting level.

The labor migration from the FRG is highly selective. The prospective migrants who are rejected include those who have criminal records, those who are denied passports for political reasons, those who are illiterate, and those who have ill health or are above certain age limits. The age limits are 35 for unskilled and 40 for skilled workers.

After the first selection the TES sends for the selected applicants to the German Liaison Office. The final selection is conducted by the German Liaison Office (GLO) in Istanbul. The prospective migrants are medically examined by German doctors. Those who pass the medical tests are subjected to skill tests, either personally by the employers or by their representatives. Officially recruited migrants are required to submit a primary school diploma which is obtained after five years education between the ages of 7 and 12. Illiterate people and those with only a formal three-year village primary school education are not eligible as migrants. Therefore, these people either give up hope of official recruitment or try to get a primary school diploma.

The skill requirements are another barrier for prospective migrants. The needs of German industry determine who goes there first. Most of the applicants are unskilled workers. As the demand for skilled workers is higher, the number of unskilled workers on the waiting list is increasing every year. When compared with the other labor-exporting countries, Turkey is found to be increasingly exporting the largest numbers of skilled labor; in 1974, for example, 46.3 percent of the migrant workers sent to West Germany were skilled.

Failing to meet any one of these requirements means an end to the hopes of official recruitment. Therefore, individuals may also resort to bribery at any stage of the recruitment procedure. The head of the GLO, von Harasovski, stated when interviewed in May 1972 that 20 percent of the workers they handled were being refused for medical reasons and an additional 15 percent were failing for other reasons.

The successful candidates sign a contract with German firms. The contracts are countersigned by the employers or their representatives and endorsed by the TES and the GLO. The duration of the contract is usually one year, after which the worker is free to change his job, renew his contract, or return home. With the signing of the contract, the long waiting period—up to ten years for some unskilled workers—and the following "rites de passage" (all the inquiries, tests, bureaucratic formalities) are over.

Transport to Germany is arranged by the GLO. The workers are usually sent by train. They are informed of the departure date and requested to be at the station in Istanbul at a certain time. There they are given their tickets and food packages to last them for three days (or the money to buy food for the same period). Then they are put on special labor trains and sent to Germany in special second-class sleeper compartments. The journey lasts two days and three nights. The train is met in Munich by the representatives of the German firms.

The bulk of labor migration from Turkey to Europe is through official channels. The number of workers sent by the TES between 1961 and 1971 amounted to a total of 478,441 with a peak of 58,142 in 1973. The total number of registered workers in West Germany reached 528,414 in 1973. Of those in my sample, 86.1 percent had used official channels, and 13.9 percent had come to Germany as "tourists." Among those who had used official channels, 75.7 percent had waited for their recruitment, and the other 10.4 percent had jumped the queue by either receiving personal job offers—through their relatives already in West Germany (6.7 percent)—or by enrolling in a village producers' cooperative (3.7 percent).

The prospective migrants who are rejected on the grounds of failing to satisfy official requirements, or those who have no hope of recruitment within a short time, may resort to the alternative of spontaneous recruitment.

In 1973, during my fieldwork, an estimated 50,000 Turkish workers were working in the FRG "illegally." People who come from other than EEC countries, usually with a tourist's passport, and work in the FRG without a work and stay permit are called illegal workers by the German officials. Rather than using the term "illegal" in referring to this group, I will use the term "spontaneous migrants," as adopted by the Netherlands United Nations Association (van Houte and Melgert 1972).

Some employers have taken advantage of spontaneous migration as a cheap source of manpower. By employing spontaneous migrants they were avoiding both the social security contributions and the recruitment fees that would be paid to government agencies, which by 1973 were 1,000 DM per person. These employers also did not have to bother with the legal requirements for accommodations. As a result, most of the spontaneous workers occupied the worst accommodations in West Germany. They also received the lowest wages.

There were many agencies *(Arbeiterverleihfirmen)* in the FRG whose main business was to recruit and employ foreign workers for the purpose of leasing them to other firms for short periods. Most of these firms were run by a small staff from a tiny office. They had on their books an average of 500 workers, sometimes as many as 1,500, consisting mainly of spontaneous workers. In Frankfurt alone there were about a hundred firms whose only assets were a single office and whose only business was to hire out migrant workers to other firms. There is evidence that some of these firms took advantage of spontaneous migrants by not paying them proper wages.

The spontaneous workers were a headache for the German trade unions. The legal foreign workers with their tendency to keep wage levels low were bad enough, but the spontaneous workers were intolerable. They were ready to accept any job on the employer's own terms, at the lowest rates. They did not, and could not, become members of trade unions. They were thus regarded as a threat to the organized workers and their unions.

The most interesting aspect of spontaneous migration for the anthropologist is that it provides a dynamic example of how the social networks are manipulated in achieving certain ends. It is true that officially recruited migrants are also engaged in network manipulations, but unless they get a personal job offer from the employers of their relatives which brings them near their relatives, official migrants go through a period of transition of up to a year from the moment they step on the special labor train to the FRG. During this period most of these workers are sharply removed from their social networks and placed in a strange environment. They start to rebuild their social relationships there, and if they are unlucky enough to be the first Turks in that region, they may find it extremely difficult to establish any contacts and end up in total cultural isolation. For the spontaneous migrants, however, there is, in most cases, no such severance of social relations as all the stages of migration, from taking the decision to migrate to finding a job abroad, are performed within the actor's social network extending from home to the country of immigration.

The decision to migrate is taken after careful consideration of the information that is received through a worker's social network extensions in Europe, which supplements and often helps in evaluating the general facts about migration that the worker learns from the official sources, newspapers and radio or television. Communication between migrants in the FRG and their relatives or friends in Turkey is very effective. Letters are exchanged regularly, presents are sent on *bayrams* (holidays) and birthdays, and most of the migrants go home regularly at least once a year during the holidays. Migrants write about their work, accommodations, recreation, and the new environment. In turn, they receive news about their families, friends, political events, and the economic situation at home. When the migrants come home for holidays they are the center of attention. They bring suitable presents of western goods for all the relatives and friends and relate their experiences at length in endless chats.

The information and encouragement received from migrant friends and relatives are the primary factor in deciding to be a migrant. The importance of the social networks in the migration process becomes obvious here. Over 77 percent of my sample workers had from one to seven relatives already working in the FRG.

When a determined prospective migrant, probably after doing all he can within the official framework, comes to the conclusion that there is no hope for official recruitment in the near future, he will look for recruitment. In the 1960s, during the early phases of the migration process, the easiest and most widely used type of spontaneous recruitment was to go to the FRG as a tourist and obtain work there either through one's relatives or friends or through certain agents and migrant worker dealers.

The main disadvantages of spontaneous migration are its high economic cost, the economic and legal insecurity, and the uncertainties it involves. Spontaneous workers can only get tourist passports which cost £T 1,000 (£ 28) and are valid for one year. Unlike officially recruited migrants, they must pay for their own travel. Furthermore, if they cannot get into West Germany at their first try, the travel expenses may double or treble. Official migrants are met in West Germany by the representatives of their employers and taken to their final destinations, where they are provided with accommodations. Spontaneous migrants are met in Germany by the police and the customs officers, who are extremely suspicious of Turkish tourists, and are searched and scrutinized thoroughly. The slightest suspicion that they are not 'real' tourists is enough to deny them entry. If they succeed in getting through the customs, they scatter and head for their respective destinations: relatives and friends working in various parts of the country. The fares, food, and temporary accommodations may become very expensive if they are unable to locate their contacts very soon.

Those who fail to persuade the customs officers and the police that they are 'real' tourists are returned immediately. If they have come by airplane, they are out on the next flight back. Those who travel by train or by bus or car meet more difficulties and earlier on in their journey. The first confrontation with foreign police and customs officials comes at the Austrian border. As a labor-importing country, Austria has the same migrant labor–related problems as the FRG, although on a smaller scale. Many suspected 'tourists' are returned to Yugoslavia, where most of them try to get to the FRG via another route, and some fall victims to the spontaneous migrant dealers and are robbed mercilessly.

Those who are not allowed into Austria while traveling by train or bus usually gather in large stations like Ljubljana or Zagreb before they make their next move. Here they meet other Turks and try to find some fellow countrymen *(hemşehri)* whom they can trust. They exchange information and evaluate the facts. Contacts are made with 'guides,' Turkish, Yugoslav, or Austrian nationals who, for a large sum of money (between 200 to 500 DM—Atsiz in *Cumhuriyet,* Nov. 29, 1974), undertake to lead groups into Austria and the FRG along tracks through uninhabited areas in the Alps.

The experience of Yusuf was typical. Yusuf was a men's tailor in a large central Anatolian town when he decided to go abroad and make some money to enlarge his tailor's shop and possibly move to a large city. As there was little demand for men with his qualifications, he decided to go as a tourist. As a cousin of his wanted to go abroad too, they decided to go together. They obtained tourist passports and left Turkey by train. Their destination was Belgium, where they had an uncle. Two days later, they were duly stopped at the Austrian border and returned to Yugoslavia. They went back to Ljubljana, where they learned from other Turks that it was possible to go to Belgium via Italy and France. They bought two tickets to Paris and got on the next train. Some hours later the train arrived at the Italian border; this time they were stopped by the Italian officials on the grounds that they did not have visas for France. They returned to Yugoslavia to try to get French visas. Two days later they learned from the French Consulate that Turkish nationals, as member citizens of the Council of Europe, did not need visas for stays of up to three months. Equipped with this knowledge, they boarded the train once more. On the train they met a Turk who was returning to his work in France after a holiday at home. With his help and knowledge of French they succeeded in persuading the Italian and French customs officials that they were genuine tourists and thus got into France. They headed straight to the north, to a village near the Belgian border that they had learned of from their friend on the train. There, they waited until dark and crossed the border during the night by walking 27 km through a wooded area. The next morning they took a train to Brussels, where their uncle worked and lived. They stayed for forty days with their uncle. He succeeded in finding a job for Yusuf's cousin on a building site, but could not find a suitable job for Yusuf. Finally, his uncle decided that Yusuf should try his luck in the FRG. They contacted a fellow countryman who was known to be a spontaneous migrant dealer, and talked with him about the chances of getting into the FRG and finding a job there. They were assured that he could take Yusuf into Germany and find a job for him there. He would charge 300 DM for his services and the risks involved. If Yusuf wanted to become a legal worker in the FRG, that too was possible but would cost 1,500 DM. Since he could not afford 1,500 DM, Yusuf decided to go in as a tourist. On the arranged day, the man came to take Yusuf into the FRG in his car. They drove to the German border, and saying that they were only passing through on their way to Turkey, they got into Germany without much difficulty. Once in the FRG, he took Yusuf to the nearest town, bought a train ticket to Frankfurt, and gave Yusuf the address of a fellow countryman in a village near Frankfurt where he had a small dressmaking business. He put Yusuf on the train and said that he was expected there.

The next day Yusuf was working in his first job in the FRG. He worked there for eight months until the place was closed down because of financial difficulties.

THE ADAPTATION TO THE LABOR MARKET

As I have already mentioned, the migrants are brought into the FRG to fill specific gaps in the labor market, to fill low-rank manual occupations that have been left open by Germans. Therefore, the migrants tend to concentrate in certain occupations, industries, and regions of the country. A great majority of the migrants work in the manufacturing and construction industries. The work migrants do in these industries is strictly regulated, routine, monotonous, and tiring. It is carried out in noisy, dirty, often smelly surroundings in large, impersonal firms. For the majority this is an experience that they had not been subject to before. For those who came from the rural areas, farming backgrounds, or a nonworking life like that of students and housewives, this is an experience that transforms them and incorporates them into the lowest stratum of the working class where everybody else in the society is above and beyond them.

In response to these conditions, Turkish migrants have developed behavior patterns which include a strong economic rationality, a dual value system (see below), "uniplex relationships" with the members and institutions of the host society, and "multiplex," intense relationships with other Turks which are based on social networks formed around kin and ethnic relationships in which "individuals are prepared to honor obligations, or feel free to exercise the rights implied in their link to some other person" (Mitchell 1969, 27).

Through a well-developed economic rationality they try to get the most out of their employment situation. This is reflected in their attitude to work itself: the frequency with which they change jobs, for example, indicates their readiness to change employment purely for financial gain. To achieve this they are prepared to move hundreds of miles, provided that they are within social distance of their social networks.

Like the officially recruited migrants, spontaneous migrants too could not afford to be choosy about their first jobs in the FRG. They gratefully accepted any job that was offered or found for them. Once the migrants started working or felt secure in the new environment, they quickly reminded themselves that they were "target workers" (Böhning 1972, 62) and needed better jobs (e.g., those where overtime and bonus opportunities were present) in order to earn as much money as possible, as quickly as possible, so that they could return home as soon as possible.

It is interesting to note that even some of the officially recruited migrants, who had gone to the FRG after signing annual contracts, had managed to change their jobs before their contracts expired. Although the job changing rate was much higher among the spontaneous migrants during their first year in the FRG (59.4 percent of the spontaneous migrants who had held more than one job), more than one-third (34.3 percent) of the officially recruited migrants who had held more than one job had also changed their jobs within one year.

The tendency in changing jobs seems to be towards less arduous, less dangerous, higher paying, and relatively more secure factory jobs. While the number of people working in factories increased from 56.9 percent in the first job to 100 percent in the seventh job, the numbers working in construction went down from 21.3 percent in the first job to 9.1 percent in the sixth job, and the numbers working in mining similarly went down, from 16.9 percent in the first job to 8 percent in the fifth job. Over 7 percent in their fourth jobs and 4 percent in their fifth jobs had realized what is regarded by most migrants as the ultimate in achievement and had become self-employed.

In this context it is important to consider how job changes are effected. When this is done it becomes clear that the economic rationality of the migrant worker is possible only because of the networks of kinship and friendship of which he is a member.

These kinship and home-based social networks play an important role in finding new jobs in the FRG. Of the migrants in the sample, 77.2 percent had found their first jobs through TEX, and 18 percent through their relatives, *hemşehris,* and friends who were either instrumental in having them invited by a firm personally, from Turkey (9.4 percent), or finding them jobs once they were in the FRG as "tourists" (5.2 percent). The social networks are even more important in finding the second and subsequent jobs. Over 62 percent of the Turkish migrants in the sample reported that their relatives, *hemşehris,* and friends had found them their second jobs.

An important outcome of utilizing the social networks that are largely based on kinship and ethnic ties in finding jobs and accommodation has been the colonization of certain factories, towns, and villages in Germany by groups of Turks who are related by kinship (including marriage) or common geographical origin in Turkey.

Another aspect of the role of kinship and social networks in job mobility concerns the question of place and distance of employment from current residence. It seems clear from my data that the attractiveness or otherwise of particular geographical locations is not an important consideration in itself. What matters in changing jobs is whether there is help available in the new situation, that is, whether the social networks extend to the new area.

Geographical mobility involves changes in social networks. Unless the move is voluntary and to a location where there are many relatives and friends, it could involve considerable modifications and uprooting in social relationships. Some of the difficulties involved in such changes were exhibited in the experiences of Kemal, one of my respondents. Kemal had been working in the Mercedes-Benz factory in Stuttgart for the previous six years when he came with his wife, Ayla, and 3-year-old son to open a dressmaking factory in Hausen, near Offenbach. Hausen was over 200 km from Stuttgart, where Kemal had many relatives, in-laws (he had met his wife in Stuttgart, through his father-in-law who was a workmate in the Mercedes works), together with German and Turkish friends. Kemal and Ahmet, who were the owners of the factory we worked in, were friends from Turkey. They had both been first *girak* (apprentices) and then *kalfa* (assistant masters) under the same tailor in Istanbul. In one of Kemal's visits to Offenbach to see Ahmet he had learned from his friend that a dressmaking business in Hausen was up for sale at 15,000 DM. Since he had been looking for such an opportunity for some time, he decided to buy the business and move to Hausen.

As Kemal did not know anyone in Offenbach or Hausen, he was counting on Ahmet's help in establishing himself there. At the beginning Ahmet was very helpful: he introduced Kemal to the owner of the business, a German, and helped in the negotiations of the terms. However, soon after Kemal bought the business their relationship started to deteriorate. While Ahmet was an ambitious, hard-working man with a strong capitalistic outlook and little time or patience for people not connected with his business ambitions, Kemal was a rather passive, timid man with a traditional outlook, relying heavily on his wife (whose character resembled Ahmet's) for the running of the business. As they were both in the same line of business, taking orders from big factories in the region and employing the same type of workers, they were potential business rivals. Ahmet became less and less forthcoming with his help. He regarded Kemal as an incompetent business-man, expecting everything to be done for him by others. Kemal regarded Ahmet as overambitious, selfish, and jealous, with no respect for ethnic and friendship ties. Finally they stopped visiting each other. The result was terrible isolation for Kemal and his family. They had no relatives or friends in the vicinity of their work or accommodations (which were in another village about 10 km away). The nearest people they could turn to for financial or moral support were over 200 km away in Stuttgart. Since Kemal and his wife were both working in the factory for very long hours (from very early in the morning until very late in the evening), they had neither the time nor the opportunity or strength to make friends and socialize in their new setting. The only people they were in touch with for any length of time were their ten workers, two of whom were Mudmet and Yusuf, two spontaneous Turkish workers who used to work for Ahmet until they were sacked by him and who in fact were in a more precarious position than their new employer. The rest of the workers were German women with whom conversation was strictly limited to work matters. Kemal and Ayla's effective networks (Epstein 1969, 111), which were made up of kin and friends, both Turkish and German, and who were linked by multistrand (or multiplex) relationships (Mitchell 1969, 22) in Stuttgart, had shrunk and were reduced to a single, common network which contained their employees and was made up of single-strand (or uniplex) relationships (Mitchell 1969, 22) based on work. On more than one occasion, Kemal complained that had he known Ahmet would behave like this and abandon him when he most needed Ahmet's help and advice, he would probably never have gone there and ventured into business. On another occasion Kemal stated: "But wait until I go to Turkey next summer. I'll show him! I'll tell our master [the tailor who taught both Kemal and Ahmet their trade] in Istanbul about what he did to me. He won't be able to show his face again in Istanbul for shame!''

SOCIAL RELATIONSHIPS IN THE PLACE OF WORK

The importance of social networks and the intensity and multiplexity of the relationships in these networks will become more apparent after an examination of the process of migration as it affects the lives of a small group of Turks in the FRG, including my wife and myself.

What I aim to do is describe something of the interpersonal world of Turkish migrants and their experience of work itself. The methods of anthropological research which rely heavily on participant observation and on case studies of particular people are very well suited to achieve such an aim. They make it possible for the researcher to gain access to the subjective realities of a social group and to appreciate what it feels like to be a member of a particular group. The subtle nuances of social interaction and social perception which define the social relations of Turkish communities in the FRG in fact can only be grasped, as it were, from the inside using these techniques.

CHOICE OF LOCALITY

For my fieldwork in the FRG I had decided to experience migration first hand and go to Germany as a migrant worker using the ''normal'' recruitment channels and procedures. As I had neither technical skills which were in demand in the FRG nor the time to wait in the queue for unskilled workers, the only channel open to me in the end was the unofficial one. My wife, Oya, was also coming with me, so we decided to go as ''tourists.'' The next step was to draw on the resources of our own social networks to establish a bridgehead in the FRG. We thought about the people we knew in the FRG and chose Gül, a close school friend of my wife's who was also known to me. About a year previously she had married Erkan, a lithographer, and both had gone to the FRG. Erkan was working in Frankfurt and they were living in a flat in Offenbach, about 8 km away from his work. They were ideally situated in the heartland of Hessen, which had one of the highest foreign worker concentrations in the FRG. In 1972, 12.2 percent of all foreign workers in Germany were living in this state (Şenel 1975, 20) and over 10 percent of the Turkish workers were also living there (Bundesanstalt für Arbeit 1974, 21). We wrote a letter to our friends explaining our intention to go to the FRG and to stay there for about eighteen months as spontaneous workers to gather research material concerning Turkish workers. Within a fortnight we received a reply inviting us to their place, urging us to stay in Offenbach, close to them where there were many Turkish workers.

We traveled in our right-hand drive car with British license plates and got into Germany without any problems, saying at the border that we were returning to England. We arrived in Offenbach one Friday evening and met with a warm reception from our friends. Erkan thought that there were at least 1,500 Turkish workers in Offenbach and some thousands in and around Frankfurt. (The real figures were 2,596 in Offenbach, 3,865 in Hanau, and 15,611 in Frankfurt [Bundesanstalt für Arbeit 1974, 102].) He said that he could introduce me to his friends in the area and that he could help us find accommodations and jobs if we decided to stay in Offenbach. When I said that Offenbach seemed an ideal place for us, Erkan replied that he would get to work the following day to look for accommodations.

The next day we went to see two of Erkan's friends, Riza and Hüseyin. Riza was an interpreter in one of the banks in Offenbach; Hüseyin was a skilled electrician working in Frankfurt. They had both been in the FRG for more than nine years and had their families with them. We told them that we were looking for accommodations and jobs and asked for their help. Two days later Hüseyin turned up with an address he had got from a friend. We went to see the place but it had been taken. Riza went to see some estate agents for us, but all the available flats were beyond our means. Meanwhile, Erkan and I were following up the advertisements in the local papers and visiting the local estate agents. Some of the advertisements had notices saying "No Foreigners," but although most of the flats had no such advertised restrictions, when we went to see them the landlords refused to show us the flats, some saying bluntly that they did not want any foreigners and others offering various excuses.

Within four days of our arrival in Offenbach, five of Erkan's friends were looking for accommodations for us. The information kept coming in. At the end of the week we found a pleasant flat in Mühlheim, about 5 km from Erkan's flat. Two days after that Riza came to say he had found us temporary jobs: cleaning offices for three hours each evening in a nearby electronics firm. The next day he took us to the factory to introduce us to the person in charge. Riza promised that he would continue to look for more suitable jobs for us; we were to work there in the meantime. The implications of these patterns of helping one another are very important. They are the basis of complex patterns of reciprocity and social obligation which, over time, hold the Turkish community together (see Leach 1954).

Two weeks later, Gül introduced my wife to a Turkish woman, Nermin, who had a small dress repairs and alterations shop in the main street of our village. Nermin offered my wife a part-time job in the shop. She started working there the next day. I met Nermin and her husband, Nuri, the same evening. Nuri was working in a shoe factory near Frankfurt. They were both from Istanbul and had been in the FRG since the early 1960s and had worked in various jobs until Nermin opened this shop. They lived in the same village, in a flat about fifty yards from the shop. The shop seemed to be the center of social activities for the Turks living in the village. A Turkish lady who lived in the next house spent most of her time in the shop, bringing tea, coffee, and cakes from time to time. Some other Turks living in or near the village also visited the shop during the day. The men usually called in after work when Nermin's husband would be present, whereas the ladies usually called in during the morning when they went out shopping. Subjects of conversation ranged from gossip about other Turks to fashion, shop prices, news about Turkey and the situation of the "tourist" workers, and employment opportunities and work conditions in the region.

Both Nermin and Nuri could speak German. Apart from the customers, who were all Germans, there were three German neighbors, two ladies and a man, all of whom were in their sixties, retired and widowed, who visited the shop almost daily to sit and chat.

As the Turkish residents who had lived longest in the village and as owners of a business, Nermin and Nuri were the focus of interest and respect among the other Turks who lived there. People sought their advice and help from time to time. One of the frequent visitors to the shop, Muzaffer, who was a tailor in Turkey and working as an electric welder in a nearby factory, for example, brought a *hemşehri* of his one day, explaining that he had recently arrived in the region and as he wanted to bring his wife soon they were looking for accommodations for him. They had heard that there was an empty flat in the village and had come to ask Nermin to go with them to speak to the landlord on their behalf. They all went to see the landlord but came back disappointed: the man had refused to let his flat to a Turk. Muzaffer's friend later found a flat through an estate agent.

When Nermin and Nuri went home on their annual holidays, they left the shop to my wife, Oya. She would get 50 percent of the earnings she realized. Now she was in direct contact with the customers who were almost all Germans. She started to feel the insecurity of being a spontaneous worker. She was constantly asking herself questions: What if the next German who comes in is a policeman? What if he asks for my work permit? What can I tell him? What if I am arrested? She felt very nervous and uncertain while she was working in the shop by herself. Every German customer was a potential threat to her stay in the FRG. She could only relax in the company of other Turks when they visited the shop. Although Nermin's three German friends continued to visit the shop frequently and were friendly towards Oya, she could not be sure that they were not on very friendly terms with the local police chief as well and would tell him about this new Turkish lady who worked in Nermin's shop. The fact that one of these ladies often greeted her jokingly when she came in the shop with "Heil Hitler!" did not make Oya feel very comfortable or welcome either.

These feelings point to a more fundamental theme, that of insecurity and of how migrant workers, particularly spontaneous workers, cope with it. That they do is clear; they develop an outlook which is simultaneously fatalistic and hopeful. They do not worry too much about the risk of being caught and believe that their luck may hold out to avoid this.

Soon after Oya took over the shop some new Turkish men started visiting it. They were living in rooms in a converted barn and stable across the street from the shop. They had noticed that I was present at the shop most of the time and started visiting. There were eleven Turks living in three rooms. One of the rooms was occupied by Ali, his two sons, Osman (16) and Ömer (18), and two "tourist" relatives. Since the room had only four beds, Ali was trying to find accommodations for one of the relatives. Ali was a man of 50, of Kurdish origin and from the villages of Ankara province. He had an air of quiet respectability, authority, and congeniality about him. When we met him he was working in a slaughterhouse, but a couple of months later he changed his job and became a street sweeper in Frankfurt, working for the municipality.

One of the other rooms was occupied by three men from Konya who worked in a metal factory nearby. They all had temporary stay and work permits *(Duldung)* and were preparing to go to Turkey to legalize their position. They worked very long hours and kept to themselves; therefore, I could not get to know them better.

In the third room stayed two men, Selim and Selim *Hoca,* of Kurdish origin from the villages of Erzurum province in eastern Turkey, and one man from Konya who was working in the same factory as his *hemşehris* who lived in the next room—indeed he spent all his time in their company. Both Selim *Hoca* and Selim were working in a tire company outside the village. Selim *Hoca* was 39 years old. He had been a visiting village imam in Turkey, hence his title *Hoca.* He had come to the FRG about ten months previously as a "tourist" through a migrant dealer in Turkey. He had arrived in West Berlin, where he had a brother, via Yugoslavia–East Berlin, and found a job in a construction firm using his brother's passport. After a couple of months he had heard from friends in Hanau that the authorities in Hessen were granting stay permits to the "tourists" and had come to Offenbach, where *hemşehris* had found him a job in the tire factory and accommodation in this house.

Selim was 53 years old. He was a stock farmer in Turkey. He had also come as a "tourist" with the help of his cousin who was a migrant dealer in Hanau. He had been unable to find a job in Hanau for nine months and had been looked after by his cousin during this period. About two months previously he had managed to get a job in the tire factory and, with the help of Selim *Hoca,* accommodations in the village, so had moved there. Both Selims had managed to get temporary stay permits with the help of their employer and were planning to go to Turkey that August to regularize their positions.

Our conversations usually revolved around the problems of spontaneous workers, economic conditions in Turkey, and life in Germany. Both Selims were strict Muslims: they did not drink alcohol and would not touch anything containing pork. They found the Germans highly immoral and their women too scantily dressed. However, they appreciated the Germans' industriousness and thought they were clever, hardworking people. Both Selims were also aware that there were some unscrupulous employers among them, ready to exploit the vulnerable spontaneous workers. They thought their employer was one of them. They were working in very bad conditions, among plastic and rubber fumes, in close contact with high temperatures, but they were being paid only 5.50 DM per hour. They were planning to leave the factory as soon as possible once their status was regularized. Selim *Hoca* wanted to join his brother in West Berlin, where he thought the earnings were much higher. Selim was hoping to find another job in the region where he had relatives.

AHMET'S WORKSHOP: A MARGINAL BUSINESS

One day Selim stated that he was going to find us permanent jobs. They knew that Oya was working in Nermin's shop part-time and not earning much. One of their neighbors, Osman, who was Ali's younger son, was working in a small dressmaking workshop in a nearby industrial village. Selim had asked Osman to talk to his boss, who was also a Turk, about us and see if he could employ us. In a couple of days Selim came with the news that Osman's employer, Ahmet, wanted to see us. The next morning Selim and Osman took us to Ahmet's workshop. They were making jeans for a large factory in the region. Ahmet explained what the work involved. He was getting the already cut material from the factory and making it into jeans. Each worker was doing a particular job, such as sewing the side seams, putting on the pockets, zips, or belts, etc. He asked Oya if she had experience on industrial machines and this type of work, which she had, for she had studied dressmaking at college in Turkey and had worked as a supervisor in a garments factory in England. Ahmet then asked her to do some sample work on one of his machines and after seeing this asked her to start work immediately. He explained that if she worked fast she could earn good money and that some of the workers were earning up to 1,800 DM per month.

I explained that I was a student in England and was doing research in the FRG on the Turkish migrant workers. I started to spend most of my time in the workshop, helping out with the manual jobs like sorting the jeans into different sizes, helping Ahmet to load or unload them from his van, etc. A couple of days later I learned to use a simple machine that made loops for the belts, so I started helping with those. Ahmet noticed that I was being helpful in the workshop and offered me a part-time job at 4 DM per hour.

From an anthropological point of view Ahmet's workshop was of considerable interest. In the first place it exemplified several features of Turkish entrepreneurs in the FRG: their marginality, their reliance on ethnic relationships for their operation and success, and their position as cultural brokers operating within both the German and Turkish migrant systems and providing bridges for the exchange of goods, services, money, and information between these systems. Ahmet's problems of labor recruitment illustrate, too, the extent to which spontaneous migrants fill a real gap in the labor market. The logic of the labor market was such that without spontaneous workers Ahmet could not have exploited the opportunity he was given in that section of the garments industry. They gave him sufficient flexibility to establish his business on a more certain footing. And as I shall show, at the point when a shortage of spontaneous workers and the increased penalties of using these workers forced him into official recruitment channels, spontaneous migrants were the first to be dispensed with. In a real sense, they bear the burden of business uncertainties.

The workshop was situated in the middle of a growing industrial village about 8 km north of Offenbach. It was housed in a converted barn in a small yard. There were eighteen sewing and special-purpose machines (like overlooking, button hole, and loop machines) in a space of approximately 5 by 10 meters, arranged in three rows of six machines. The place was lit by fluorescent lights placed on the walls and ceiling. There was one window at the back. The only ventilation was through the front door and back window, which were kept open on warm days. There was always an overwhelming smell of starch and dust from cloth fibers in the workshop. During our first weeks there we suffered severe irritation of the eyes, nose, and throat, but eventually got used to it.

When we started there were nine Turks (seven men, one woman and a young girl) including Ahmet, the owner, and his wife, Işik, and three Yugoslavs, one Greek, and one Italian woman working in the place. The Italian woman and the young Turkish girl, Semra, who was 14, were part-timers. Semra was working two to three hours a day examining, cleaning, and folding the finished jeans according to size. She often brought her 4-year-old sister with her and worked while her sister played in the yard. Their father was said to be an alcoholic, working only intermittently and spending all his money on drink. Their mother was working two shifts in a factory and leaving Semra in charge of the sister when she was at work.

Ahmet, a man of 36, had been in the FRG for twelve years. After working in various jobs for five years he had opened a dress alterations and repairs shop in this village. About eight years previously he had married Işik in his hometown of Urfa in Turkey and brought her over to Germany. Soon after her arrival she started working in a dressmaking factory and remained there until they opened the workshop. Ahmet worked in his shop for seven years, saving money and waiting for an opportunity to enlarge his business. He knew some Turks in the nearby villages who owned dressmaking workshops producing for the large factories around Offenbach and making simple garments like jeans and overalls. He was hoping to open a similar workshop himself one day.

The opportunity came when the German owner of the present workshop wanted to sell the place. He had apparently been unable to find enough workers at low enough wages for him to make a profit so had closed the place. Ahmet bought the machines and took over the business. He was introduced to a factory where he could get work making jeans. Rather than close his old shop, Ahmet put a trusted Turkish tailor friend there and started recruiting workers for the workshop. The previous owner had recommended three of his hardworking employees: a Greek, a Yugoslav, and an Italian woman living in the village. He contacted them and they agreed to work. His wife also left her work for the workshop. Ahmet had been promised as much work as he could cope with provided his quality was satisfactory. He was getting denim material already cut in various sizes, together with zips, buttons, cotton, etc., and being paid a certain price (he would not divulge how much) for each pair of jeans delivered. The factory also suggested how much to pay his workers on a piecework basis.

Since he could not guarantee the productivity of the workers, Ahmet decided to recruit on only a piecework basis with no guaranteed minimum wage. He soon realized that the only workers he could find without paying a basic wage would be spontaneous workers. He started visiting and phoning Turkish friends in and around Offenbach, Frankfurt, and Hanau who either owned dressmaking workshops and dress alteration shops or worked in them. He told them that he was starting a business and that he needed good, hardworking, and fast workers. He told them that he was prepared to employ "tourists" and that they should send any person considered suitable.

Within a month he had found two Yugoslav women, both friends of Ahmet's first Yugoslav worker, and five Turks: Semra, the 14-year-old girl; Osman, the 16-year-old boy who introduced us to Ahmet; Sami *usta,* a tailor in his fifties with a temporary resident permit *(Duldung);* Rasim *usta,* a "tourist" tailor in his late thirties; and Nezih, a tailor of 29 who also had a temporary residence permit. Sami *usta* had been working in a dress alterations shop, while Nezih and Rasim *usta* were employed in a garments workshop in the region and had come to our workshop in the hope of higher earnings. Their previous employers were also Turks. For Semra and Osman this was their first experience of employment. Sami and Rasim *ustas* had had their own tailor shops in Turkey, hence their title *usta* (master). They were both from western Turkey, Sami from Denizli and Rasim from Sakarya. Sami had left his shop to his *kalfa* (assistant master) and *çiraks* (apprentices) and had come to the FRG to try his luck about a year previously. He had found a job in a *hemşehri*'s dress alterations shop and had worked there until he came to Ahmet's workshop. Rasim, on the other hand, had applied to the Turkish Employment Service together with his wife to go to the FRG, and when his wife's turn came up a year previously, he sold his shop and accompanied her to the FRG as a "tourist." His wife had been recruited by a food-processing firm near Offenbach. Her firm had helped to find them a small basement flat in a modern block not far from the factory. They had made friends quickly and through them he had found a job in a garments factory.

Ahmet was pleased with his workers, for they were fast and efficient. His suppliers were also pleased with the quality and quantity of the work he delivered each week. They kept reminding him that he could get more work if he found new workers. In his second month two more Turkish tailors, Mehmet and Yusuf, joined the workshop. They were both spontaneous workers in their early twenties. Mehmet was also from Denizli and had learned his craft in the workshop belonging to Sami *usta,* who was a distant relative. Mehmet had been in the FRG for eighteen months. He had come by plane and had managed to get into the country without any difficulty, it was believed on account of his looks. He was a well-dressed young man with long, light brown hair who could easily have passed as a German. From Frankfurt he had headed straight for Essen where he had two uncles working in the metal industry. In a few days one of his uncle's friends had found him a job on a construction site, where he had worked for one month, while his uncles were trying to find him a better job. At the end of the month he was placed in a *hemşehri*'s dress alterations shop in Düsseldorf. Although the work conditions were much better, the wages at 4 DM per hour were very low. He knew that Sami *usta* was working somewhere near Offenbach, so he wrote and asked if Sami *usta* could find him a better job there. One week later Mehmet received a reply from Sami *usta* stating that he had found Mehmet a job as a machinist in a dress workshop. After only one month in Düsseldorf Mehmet moved to Offenbach and started work in a jeans workshop owned by a Turk. He also moved into a flat rented by his employer for his workers, where he shared a room with three other Turks.

Mehmet worked there for about nine months until his employer declared himself bankrupt and closed the workshop. Although the legal workers received their wages in full, the ten spontaneous workers, among them Mehmet, were not paid their last month's wages (about 1,000 DM each). While they felt very bitter about this and thought that their employer's bankruptcy was fraudulent, they could do nothing but look for new jobs. Mehmet knew that Ahmet had opened a new jeans workshop in the same village. Two of his friends, Rasim *usta* and Nezih, had started working there a couple of weeks previously. He went to see Ahmet for a job and started work there the same day. The next day he moved into the flat rented by Ahmet for his workers, where he again shared a room with three other Turks.

Mehmet's arrival in Offenbach illustrates well the importance of social networks in finding work. It illustrates, too, the determination and the high economic rationality on the part of migrants to move readily to better conditions. The kind of work he had to do was less important to Mehmet than the wages he earned. Although his second job in the dress alterations shop was more creative and less monotonous, he did not hesitate to change this job for a monotonous, much more tiring but much more lucrative one as a machinist in a workshop.

As we saw earlier, Yusuf had arrived in Offenbach after an adventurous journey and started working in a *hemşehri*'s workshop where Mehmet was also working. He worked alongside Mehmet for about eight months until his employer declared bankruptcy. During this time he had been living in a flat supplied by his employer, sharing a room with Mehmet and two other Turks. When the workshop closed he went to see another *hemşehri* who owned a similar workshop in the village and was immediately accepted. Since his new employer had no special accommodations for his workers, he asked Yusuf to stay in the basement of the workshop until he found a room for him locally. Yusuf agreed and joined five other "tourist" Turkish workers living in the basement. This was a dark, damp, and dirty place which Yusuf had to endure for forty days. When he realized that his employer had no intention of finding them a decent place to live in, he left the workshop and went to work for Ahmet, who also offered him a bed in the flat he had recently rented for his workers.

There are many points of similarity in the experiences of Mehmet and Yusuf. However, Yusuf's experience prior to his arrival in Ahmet's workshop highlights an additional feature of the spontaneous migrant experience, namely, very poor accommodations. In addition to the awful living conditions there is the powerlessness of such men in being able to do anything about it. Being spontaneous workers gives their employers a great deal of power over them. They cannot protest for fear of detection. Their only option is to move on.

When Oya and I started working there, Ahmet had more or less organized himself. He had appointed Rasim *usta* as *Meister* (foreman) and when Ahmet was out Rasim *usta* was in charge of the workshop. He was the fastest and most able man in it. Apart from helping Ahmet to organize the work and spending most of his time sewing, he also distributed work to the other workers and repaired the machines. He was the general trouble-shooter. Other than Rasim *usta*'s position there was no formal organization or hierarchy in the workshop. Except for Semra, everybody was working at a machine, doing a particular job such as sewing the side seams, putting in zips, etc. Ahmet and his wife, Işik, were also working at machines when they were in the workshop. Ahmet had to be away frequently to take or deliver orders, material, etc. After our arrival, Işik started spending more and more time away from the workshop at home. They were looking for a new flat to rent, for they had been living in an old one with no bathroom and wished to change. Soon they found a modern flat and moved in. After this, Işik came to work only if we were pressed for delivery and needed an extra machinist—once or twice a week.

Ahmet was constantly searching for new workers. When he realized that he could not find any more workers locally, he decided to recruit officially from Turkey and applied to the local employment bureau in Offenbach for four Turkish workers. Since he had to pay 5.50 DM per hour minimum basic wage to each officially recruited migrant on top of the recruitment fee of 300 DM per worker, he was rather apprehensive about the efficiency of the workers he might get without seeing the quality of their work, and he did not want to commit himself to more than four workers at once. He also had to provide accommodations for the officially recruited workers, and there was not room for more than four in the flat.

SOCIAL RELATIONS AMONG WORKERS

Until the officially recruited workers came there were no regulations governing work routine in the workshop. People started and finished work or had lunch breaks at different times. Since everybody except myself was working on a piecework basis, this did not matter. Ahmet usually picked up the Turkish workers from the flat, which was about a mile away, and brought them to the workshop in his car just before eight o'clock in the morning. The other workers arrived between eight and nine o'clock. Around twelve or one o'clock we had our lunch break. Workers usually brought their lunch from home and heated it in the workshop, or brought fish and chips (usually on Fridays) or sandwiches from the local shops. The Turks usually had their lunch break at the same time and ate together. The food each person brought was put on a table and shared. If some of the Turks did not stop working while others were eating or drinking tea or coffee, they were always invited to share the food and beverages. This invitation did not usually extend to workers of other nationalities, symbolizing the limitation of intimate relationships to their own group, thereby heightening the consciousness of solidarity within the group.

The relationship among the Turks in the workshop was close and multiplex. They had a shared culture that they had carried over to Germany. All the men had learned their craft under similar circumstances in Turkey. They had all started as apprentices *(çirak)* in tailor shops and, over the years, had become assistant masters *(kalfa)* and finally master tailors *(terzi ustasi)*. The important structural elements in Turkish society like sex, age, and *hemşehrilik* that guide social behavior had been strengthened and supplemented in their case by additional similar rules through their occupational socialization from an early age. This was much in evidence during their daily communication both at the workshop and outside it. Although the workshop organization contained no formal hierarchy, for example, all the Turks there, including the employer Ahmet, addressed Sami as Sami *usta,* indicating respect. This was partly due to his age—he was the eldest man in the place—and partly to his position in Turkey where he had been a master tailor with his own shop and where he had trained many tailors, including Mehmet. Sami *usta,* on the other hand addressed everyone by their first names, except Oya and Işik, the wives of Turkish colleagues, whom he addressed as either *yenge* (sister-in-law) or *hanim* (madam, Mrs., Miss, lady, indicating formality, distance, and respect). All the other men addressed Oya and Işik similarly—except of course their husbands.

Ahmet was addressed by all the Turks, except Sami and Rasim *ustas* who addressed him by his name only, as Ahmet *usta* or Ahmet *Abi* (from *Agabey,* elder brother, indicating respect but also familiarity with connotations of protection). Ahmet addressed all the men by their first names and Sami as *usta*. Ahmet and Sami addressed Rasim *usta* by his name, but all the other Turks called him either *Meister* (German for foreman or master) or Rasim *usta*.

The younger Turks—Mehmet, Yusuf, and Nezih—called each other by first names, indicating friendship and similarity of status, while the youngest Turks, Semra and Osman, called them *Abi* (elder brother) and Işik and Oya *abla* (elder sister), indicating respect.

I was addressed by the Turks, including Ahmet, as Ersan *Bey* (Mr., Sir—a title reserved for urban, educated men or officials, indicating social distance, formality and respect). They all knew that I was a postgraduate student in England and was doing research on Turkish migrants. They appreciated the fact that to be able to learn about them I was prepared to work in similar conditions and they were keen to talk to me and regarded me as one of them. However, deep-rooted cultural values prevented them from calling me just by my first name, and they automatically supplemented it by the title *bey*.

The workers of other nationalities, the three Yugoslavs, one Greek, and one Italian woman, were addressed by their first names. While the relationships between the Turks and other workers were uniplex, pertaining to workshop only, the social relations among the Turks were multiple, covering their whole life in the FRG. They not only shared a common Turkish culture and work experience in Turkey but also a common presence in Germany. They had similar problems, worries, and expectations.

AUTHORITY AND REWARD IN WORK

Ahmet's relationship with his Turkish workers was not simply an employer-employee relationship, restricted to the workshop. Frequently their relationship continued after working hours as well. He was also landlord to most of them. They paid their rent to him, and he transferred it to the owners of the block. He often visited them in the flat to see if they needed anything and to talk to them. Sometimes he ate and drank with them. He also invited them to his house from time to time. Workers saw him as one of them, a friend who had made it good and achieved what they all hoped to achieve one day: self-employment and, ultimately, industrial production. To achieve this he had worked hard for many years and proved himself to be a competent and clever man by making right decisions at the right times and not missing the opportunities he came across. This brought him respect and admiration from his workers. For most of them he was a model migrant and a model too of success, therefore a natural leader. His preferential recruitment of Turkish workers, and especially of spontaneous Turkish migrants, whereby he was taking a risk of having to pay several thousand DMs fine if found out, and his sharing in their intimate social relationships like eating and drinking, joking, playing cards, visiting bars and brothels together, created bonds of mutual trust and solidarity between Ahmet and his Turkish workers which guaranteed him a loyal and productive work force.

Since Ahmet had an abundant source of work, he was always keen to produce as much as possible. We always had more work than we could handle during a normal working day of eight hours. Although the other workers left the workshop after eight or nine hours, the Turks considered it *ayip* (shameful, indecent, unmannerly) to leave the shop before Ahmet did. Therefore, our working day usually stretched to eleven or twelve hours and occasionally to fifteen hours. This was made bearable by the informal system of prestige connected with work that existed in the workshop group. Working hard and fast and producing more work than the others brought prestige and satisfaction. Therefore, workers were keen to work hard and long hours to produce more work. To be known as the fastest and the one who produces most work was to be known as the best worker in the workshop. At the center of this system was, of course, Ahmet as the ultimate source of acknowledgment. His comments, like "well, friends, Yusuf has beaten you all this week. He's produced the most . . . ," created an atmosphere of competition and kept the system, and the workshop, functioning effectively.

The successful working of the system was probably due to the fact that it served both Ahmet's and the workers' ends. As they were all working on a piecework basis, the more they produced the better they were paid. Since most of the workers were spontaneous and in constant fear and expectation of being caught and deported by the police, they liked nothing better than to work as fast and as long hours as humanly possible so that either they could save as much as possible before they were caught or they could accumulate their target savings as quickly as possible and leave the country before they were caught.

THE STRUCTURE OF MARGINALITY

Towards the end of 1972, the public attitude against foreign workers in the FRG was intensifying every day, creating political pressure on the federal and local governments, employers, and other institutions connected with the migrants. Since most of the migrants were officially recruited workers with guaranteed economic and residential rights and, more importantly, were filling positions that were essential for the operation of large firms and the German economy, one way of reducing public pressure was to do something about the spontaneous workers who were generally in marginal jobs and firms.

The authorities started tightening their control and taking stringent measures against spontaneous migrants. They introduced laws increasing penalties for these workers and their employers. On October 12, 1972, for example, the fines for employing spontaneous workers were increased to 10,000 DM, and it was also declared that the deportation charges would be taken from the firms employing such workers. In December 1972 nearly one hundred firms had been fined between 3,000 and 10,000 DM for employing "tourists" *(Tercümen,* Dec. 16, 1972). Police raids on factories, construction sites, workers' hostels, and private residences suspected of harboring spontaneous workers became more and more frequent. The Turkish daily *Hürriyet* on January 17, 1973, for example, reported on the front page, with pictures of police raiding the Turkish residences in Berlin, that the police in Berlin had declared war on spontaneous workers and were hoping to catch and deport most of the estimated 20,000 Turkish "tourists" from the city. That day they had caught 253 Turkish workers who did not have any stay or work permits and had detained them for deportation.

These developments were affecting our region and our workshop as well. We started hearing of the police raids in the region more often. The social networks of the Turks in the region were very effective in communicating information. Whenever the police raided a work place, the Turkish workers there or the owners immediately informed, either by telephone or by visiting in person, the other work places in the region where they had Turkish friends. When this happened all the Turkish employers and workers in the region became involved in a big intelligence network. The progress of the raids was followed very carefully. Information like how long the police spent in a factory, which direction they came from, and in which direction they went next, was carefully evaluated. The workshops in whose direction the police were moving sent their spontaneous workers away for safe periods until the raid or the possibility of it was over.

During our stay in Ahmet's workshop we were warned four times about the raids in the region. When the police moved closer to the village we left the workshop and spent two to three hours away in the shopping center of the nearby town. On the last occasion the raids continued for two successive days and we stayed at home. While there had been three months between the first two raids (one in September and the other in December of 1972), the last two had taken place in January 1973 and within three weeks of each other. Ahmet became very apprehensive about the situation.

Meanwhile, in November 1972 Ahmet received his first two officially recruited workers from Turkey. The *Arbeitsamt* (employment service) informed him that the other two would be coming in three weeks time. He had also found a Turkish woman worker, a distant relative of his who had been working in Berlin. Since she could not stay in the flat with all the other men, she was staying in a small room in Ahmet's flat. Now all the machines in the workshop were occupied and there was no room for new ones. Ahmet started looking for a new and larger place to move into and soon found one in a nearby town about 5 km away.

We moved into the new place in early December. It was a modern factory building at least four times bigger than the previous one, with proper ventilation and toilet facilities. Ahmet bought some more machines for the new workers. With the arrival of legal workers the workshop started acquiring a formal organization. Since Ahmet had to pay a minimum wage of 5.50 DM per hour to the officially recruited workers, it became necessary to have regular working hours. To prevent confusion and provide a steady flow of work, all the workers were asked to start at the same time, eight o'clock in the morning, have a lunch break at 12:30 P.M. and finish work at 5:00 P.M. (for the official workers). Anyone who wanted to do overtime could stay and work on piecework after this time. Rasim *usta* started spending less time sewing and more and more time organizing and supervising the work. Ahmet by now had stopped working on the machines and was devoting his time to managerial functions like finding orders and new workers. He had applied for six more Turkish workers to be recruited from Turkey; two of these were personal job offers for the wives of two of his legal workers, Nezih and Camil. He had also secured a new order from another factory, again making jeans.

By the end of January 1973, after only nine months, Ahmet had established himself as a successful businessman. After six months in business he had moved into a better and more modern flat, his wife had given up manual work and become a housewife; after eight months he had moved into a bigger and better factory building, sold his old Ford car and bought a van for the business and a new Mercedes for himself, and given up manual work in the workshop. By then his spontaneous workers had served their purpose and become a liability rather than an asset. Now he could afford to hire legal workers but could not afford, especially after the substantial increases in fines, to keep his spontaneous workers and run the risk of financial disaster. Now he had much at stake. So, after several days of preparing the ground, during which time he consistently conveyed his anxieties about employing "tourists" and the dangers of detection, he finally sacked them all after the last police raid in the area, which had come within three weeks of the previous one. The fact that he had never been the subject of a raid himself did not matter. The dangers were there, and the realities of business life forced him to take this action. He was now at a point where several forces converged and pressured him, some from without, like the political decisions regarding spontaneous workers and ever-increasing police raids, and some from within this business, like the developmental stage of the workshop from a marginal small business to a bigger enterprise which is starting to integrate with the garment industry. However, the rationality of the decision for Ahmet to sack the spontaneous workers was not much consolation for those of us who were sacked. We felt rather used and abandoned. Mehmet and Yusuf complained bitterly that up to just two months previously Ahmet was continuously telling them that they were his two best workers, and now he did not want to know them. They thought Ahmet had recently become a very selfish man, thinking about nothing but money and showing no regard for friendship or social obligations. Although he told them that they could stay in the flat until they found a new place or until his new workers arrived from Turkey, they did not wish to stay there any longer than was necessary.

We started looking for jobs and accommodations for Mehmet and Yusuf. We visited several workshops and migrants' hostels. The owners of established firms did not want to employ spontaneous workers. They all stated that the police were putting too much pressure on them these days and advised us to wait for some time and then call again. Then we went to see Kemal, Ahmet's friend who had come from Stuttgart to open a workshop in Hausen. He was very keen to employ Oya, Mehmet, and Yusuf. He had started in business about a month previously with only eight German women workers, all transferred with the workshop from the previous owner. Some of these were part-timers and one was pregnant, and none of them worked after five o'clock in the evening. Kemal was in great need of Turkish and spontaneous workers, but since he was new in the area and his only friend Ahmet had abandoned him, he had found himself in a social desert and had been unable to recruit anyone. We came as a great relief for him. He often stated that when he found more Turkish workers he would dismiss all the German ones because of their unproductiveness and unwillingness to do overtime.

Mehmet and Yusuf asked Kemal to find accommodations for them in the village, which Kemal soon did through newspaper advertisements. They were to share a room in the house of an elderly German lady.

Within four days of being sacked by Ahmet, Oya, Mehmet, and Yusuf had found other jobs in a garment workshop similar to Ahmet's when it was in its early stages. Once more they were involved in a Turkish entrepreneur's efforts to break into self-employment and industry through the utilization of ethnic ties and social networks in a workshop on the margins of industry. Since, by this time, I had started doing my survey and was visiting other towns, I was unable to spend much time in Kemal's workshop. However, Oya worked there for about two months and I was able to follow the progress of the workshop through her. It seemed that Kemal was having more difficulties in developing his business than Ahmet had had when he started. Most of Kemal's difficulties came from the lack of social contacts with which he found himself as a result of his venture outside the geographical boundaries of his social network, which was localized in and around Stuttgart. When Oya left his workshop two months later, he had still not been able to recruit any more Turkish workers.

When Kemal's experiences and difficulties are considered in comparison with Ahmet's and our own experience and relative success, the importance of social networks in the migration process becomes clear. Turkish migrants operate within social networks in which relationships are based on kinship, place of origin, and friendship; these relationships are instrumental in character in that each individual in the network is a sponsor of and a potential link to others who are unknown (Wolf 1966, 12). The successful operation of the networks depends on the traditional values of Turkish society in which *sayqi* (respect) is paid towards those who are older and/or in authority; *sevqi ve koruma* (affection and protection) given to those who are younger or in need, and of course to females. Free support for friends and generous hospitality to others are also important elements in this value system. In Germany these values are upheld and can be explained by the notion of "generalized reciprocity," which is defined as a form of exchange based on the assumption that returns will balance out in the long run (Sahlins 1972). Individuals help each other not because they expect something in return directly but believe that when they need help it will be given to them freely by other Turks. Indirect sanctions are applied to those who do not follow the rules of the game, who evade their responsibilities and do not help their friends. Such men will be branded as selfish, as exploiting others, as not being real Turks. These are ostracizing accusations which can effectively exclude those so condemned from the interlocking ties of generalized reciprocity (Denich 1970, 138).

Ahmet, for example, although very successful in the beginning in operationalizing his network connections and meeting his obligations, was becoming more and more reluctant to help friends in need of his support and, therefore, incurred the criticism and the curses of his friends like Kemal, Mehmet, and Yusuf. Kemal's comment that he would complain about Ahmet's selfish behavior to their master in Istanbul, with the expected result that Ahmet would not be able to show his face again in Istanbul for shame, shows the depth of feeling Ahmet's unsocial behavior created in Kemal and the possible extent of the damage this might cause to his social relations.

However, the more successful Ahmet became, the less important such interpersonal sanctions became. Seen from Ahmet's point of view, his steady integration into the official economy and business success in the FRG—both developments conferring on him a status which did not depend solely on the recognition of fellow Turks—meant that he could afford to be selective about whom he would help. At the same time, the importance of the opinion of Ahmet's former master *(usta)* in Istanbul had, for him, considerably lessened. The "opinions" which were at the center of Kemal's threats can be seen as symbolizing the essential values of the Turkish community. But it was precisely this community from which Ahmet was gradually breaking away. His relationships with his new legal Turkish employees were also of a more formal and specific (or uniplex) kind. His gradual integration into German society and his acceptance and observance of the rules and regulations were putting strains on his relationships within the Turkish community, whose interests were basically opposed to those of the German one. He was gradually losing his identity as a group member (as "one of us") whose interests and problems were similar and was becoming identified as an employer (as "one of them") whose interests and problems were in their turn different and often in conflict with those of the Turkish community which consisted primarily of workers.

CONCLUSION

The picture which emerges from this case study, though by no means complete, lends weight to the following more general points.

First, there is no account here of trade unionism. It is in the nature of being a spontaneous worker that formal membership in a trade union is not possible. They could not in fact exist "officially" in any institution in German society except perhaps in the records of the police. Their access to employment and accommodations, therefore, depended entirely on unofficial, informal contacts through the social relations and networks of the Turkish community.

Second, it is clear that, like many of the official migrants, the work that spontaneous workers were doing required less skill than they in fact possessed. Two aspects of this need to be emphasized. The first is that they do not suffer a loss of social status as a result of this deskilling. No one in the workshop, for example, thought of himself as a mere machinist. They were all tailors, some older, more experienced and respected, therefore *usta,* some younger with less experience—but still they were all tailors. They all recognized themselves and others in these terms. What they did in the FRG did not confer higher status like *Meister*. The second point is that they could tolerate the tedium of their work because they believed it to be temporary and a step towards self-employment in the future. This is an aspect of the migrants' economic rationality. But there were aspects of their work which did give them status, and this connects with the third general point, namely, that the authority structure of the workshop rested, in part, on an informal competitiveness among the workers. Those who worked well were well regarded both by the employer and by the other workers.

The fourth point concerns social obligation. Migrant workers depend very much on one another for help. The values of Turkish society reinforce a sense of the need to help one another which, in my view, is stronger in Germany than in Turkey itself. The subtle norms of reciprocity which operate in this context have to be respected. Those who do not respect them are ostracized because their behavior threatens the whole community in what is, after all, a basically hostile environment.

The final point concerns marginality. It is clear that the situation of spontaneous workers is an insecure one, that the risk of their losing their jobs is high. But they do not function in an impersonal market; the risk of job loss also carries the risk of a breakdown of very supportive social networks. This kind of insecurity can be borne, but the psychological costs of doing so are high. In the end it is the spontaneous workers who bear the heavy costs of the business success of small entrepreneurs and, through them, of large German manufacturers.

The social relationships of spontaneous workers in the work situation in other sectors of the German economy (e.g., in construction, where there is a heavy concentration of spontaneous migrants) will be different from those described here. The size of firms, the ethnic mix of the labor force, the nationality of the employer, and the sector of the economy are some of the factors which will shape many different types of work situation for both official and spontaneous migrants.

NOTE

The research on which this chapter is based was carried out in Turkey and in the Federal Republic of Germany between April 1972 and October 1973. It was funded by a grant from the Turkish Ministry of Education.

1. Since conducting a statistically meaningful sample survey was out of the question, given the time and resources at hand, I decided to cover a cross section of the Turkish migrants which would be illustrative of the general population. However, since access to certain types of workers was more difficult than to others, some categories are overrepresented and others underrepresented in the survey. For example, in 1974 41 percent of the Turkish migrants in the FRG were in the iron and metal industries. In the survey they are represented by 125 Opel workers (46.8 percent of the sample). The next largest group of Turks were working in other manufacturing industries (25 percent). They are represented in the survey by 59 Dunlop, 37 A.E.G. (Allgemeine Elektrizitäts-Gesellschaft), and 9 other factory workers (39.4 percent of the sample). Seven percent of Turkish migrants are engaged in the mining industry. In the sample there are 37 miners (3.9 percent). While the rest of the Turks in industry or services constituted 34 percent of the total, they were represented in the survey by only 9 workers (3.4 percent). Women are also underrepresented because of difficulties in obtaining access to the hostels where they were lodged.

REFERENCES

Abadan, N.

1964 *Sati Alamnya' daki Türk Iscileri ve Sorunleri*. I.C. Başbakanlik Devlet Plamlama Teşkilati, Ankara: Başbakanlik Devlet Matbaasi.

Abadan-Unat, N.

1981 "Turkish Migration to Europe and the Middle East, Its Impact on Social Legislation and Social Structure." Paper presented at the conference on Social Legislation and Social Structure in the Contemporary Near and Middle East, Rabat, Morocco, September.

Barnes, D. A.
1954 "Class and Committee in a Norwegian Island Parish." *Human Relations* 7: 39–58.

Böhning, W. R.
1972 a *The Migration of Workers in the United Kingdom and the European Community*. London: Oxford University Press.
1972b "Problems of Immigrant Workers in West Germany." In *Immigrants in Europe,* edited by N. Deakin, 18–24. London: Fabian Society.

Bott, E.
1957 *Family and Social Network*. London: Tavistock.

Bundesanstalt für Arbeit
1974 Ausländische Arbeitnehmer, Nürnberg.

Castles, S., and Kosack, G.
1973 *Immigrant Workers and Class Structure in Western Europe*. London: Oxford University Press.

Denich, B. S.
1970 "Migration and Network Manipulation in Yugoslavia." In *Migration and Anthropology,* edited by R. E. Settle, 133-45. Seattle and London: American Ethnological Society.

Descloitres, R.
1967 *The Foreign Worker: Adaptation to Industrial Work and Urban Life*. Paris: Organization for Economic Cooperation and Development.

Epstein, A. L.
1969 "The Network and Urban Social Organization." In *Social Networks in Urban Situations: Analyses of Personal Relationships in Central African Towns,* edited by J. C. Mitchell, 77–116. Manchester: University of Manchester Press.

Hale, W. M.
1978 *International Migration Project, Country Case Study: The Republic of Turkey*. International Migration Project, Dept. of Economics, University of Durham.

Leach, E. R.
1954 *Political Systems of Highland Burma*. Boston: Beacon.

Mayer, P.
1961 *Townsmen or Tribesmen: Conservation and the Process of Urbanization in a South African City*. Cape Town: Oxford University Press.

Mitchell, J. C., ed.
1969 *Social Networks in Urban Situations: Analyses of Personal Relationships in Central African Towns*. Manchester, England: Manchester University Press.

Rhoades, R. E.
1976 "Guest Workers and Germans: A Study in the Anthropology of Migration." Ph.D. diss., University of Oklahoma.

Rist, R. D.
1978 *Guestworkers in Germany: The Prospects for Pluralism*. New York: Praeger.

Rose, A. M.
1969 *Migrants in Europe: Problems of Acceptance and Adjustment*. Minneapolis: University of Minnesota Press.

Sahlins, M. D.
1972 *Stone Age Economics*. Chicago: Aldine.

Sencer, M.
1969 *Osmanli Toplum Yapişi*. Istanbul: Ant Yayinevi.
Şenel, Ş.
1975 Federal Almanya'da Yabani Istihdam, I.I.B.K. (Turkish Employment Service) Genel Müdürlüğü Yayini no. 121, Ankara.
Siewert, P.
1980 "Zur Entwicklung der Gastarbeiterpolitik und der schulpolitschen Abstimmung der Kulturminister Konferenz." In *Bildung in der Bundesrepublik Deutschland: Data and Analysen,* 2, Max Planck Institute für Bildungsforschung, 1053–12. Stuttgart: Ernst Klett.
Tümertekin, E.
1968 *Türkive'de ic Göcler*. Publications of Istanbul University No. 1371, Geographical Institute No. 54. Istanbul: Fekulteler Mathassi.
Van Houte, H., and Melgert, W., eds.
1972 *Foreigners in Our Community*. Amsterdam: Keesing.
Wolf, E.
1966 "Kinship, Friendship and Patron-Client Relations in Complex Societies." In *The Social Anthropology of Complex Societies,* edited by M. Banton, 1–20. New York: Praeger.

7 Family and Migration in Andalusia

David D. Gregory and José Cazorla

ABSTRACT. Gregory and Cazorla address the political-economic reasons for migration, then show why migration did not solve Andalusia's economic problems. They argue that development has occurred only in the already overdeveloped tourist localities and in industrial cities in the north. In contrast, migrant remittances have generated few local employment opportunities. This situation may be attributed to the Andalusian class system where an elite controls large-scale mechanized farms and olive groves kept under production with low-wage seasonal labor.

The specific impact of migration on the family depends on the stage of family development—as the household expands, its members increasingly compete for living space—as well as on fluctuations in the demand for foreign workers.

INTRODUCTION

To understand the effects of intra-European labor migration upon the economy and structure of the family in southern Spain it is necessary to consider the interplay of variables at two levels: international and local. At the international level, migratory flows are determined by economic considerations, in particular, by the demands of production in the host countries. It is at the local level, however, where the decision to migrate is ultimately a family matter, in which the social position as much as the economic conditions of the family impels some or all of its members to seek a new livelihood far from their native home.[1]

SPAIN: NATIONAL CONTEXT

In thirteen years Spain broke out of the stagnation of the post–Civil War and was transformed into the tenth industrialized nation in the world. Its gross national product (GNP) increased annually by 7.3 percent from 1960 to 1973. The two most salient characteristics marking this period of "modernization," however, were a violent rural exodus that left many of Spain's provinces deserted and an overall aging of the population.[2]

Between 1960 and 1977 its population grew less than 1.1 percent, achieving a total of 36.3 million inhabitants by mid–1977. Its birthrate declined from 21 per 1,000 in 1960 to 18 in 1977, representing a change of −14.3 percent. Crude death rates remained unchanged at 9 per 1,000. Between 1900 and 1970 nearly 14 million Spaniards abandoned their natal communities. Beginning in the 1950s one out of every ten migrants left not only their homes but their country as well. By the 1960s over 1,000 people a day migrated to the urban areas of Spain or the industrialized zones of Western Europe. During the decade of Spain's most rapid economic expansion (1961–1971) around 80,000 workers emigrated annually with the assistance of the Spanish Institute of Emigration; 80 percent went to France, Germany, and Switzerland. The volume of nonassisted and clandestine movements oscillated between 57 percent and 35 percent of the controlled movement from year to year (García Fernandez 1965, 16). Some investigators believed that nearly 100,000 migrants departed clandestinely each year (Trivino 1963).

This dramatic restructuring of the Spanish economy was clearly visible in the redistribution of its active population. Between 1960 and 1977 the active population engaged in agriculture declined from 42 to 19 percent, rose in industry from 31 to 42 percent, and rose in services from 27 to 37 percent. Between 1960 and 1970, however, the labor force grew by only 0.2 percent; it climbed feebly to 0.9 percent between 1970 and 1977. Obviously, it was the heavy internal migration out of the rural areas that provided the labor.

Spain's rapid economic growth and changing active population, however, did not significantly retard intra-European migration. The program for rapid industrialization was designed to benefit the capital-intensive sectors. It did little to create sufficient jobs even for Spain's slowly growing population. The 19 percent yearly average rise in employment between 1960 and 1974 was due largely to demands in construction and services. The rate of employment growth in industry actually fell from an annual average of 1.8 percent between 1960 and 1968 to 0.8 percent between 1968 and 1979. Demographically, the male working-age population increased by 906,600 in the decade of the 1960s, while the actual male labor force grew by only 151,000. The decrease of over 1.5 million male workers in agriculture (with another 1 million leaving the farm sector between 1970 and 1977) was paralleled by 889,000 new jobs in industry and 727,000 in services. The rest of the available labor force of over 700,000 men either found work by emigrating abroad or remained jobless. Throughout this period the participation rate for women in the work force declined. Their exodus from the countryside was not offset by a rise in their participation rate in the cities (OECD 1977, 32–33). In fact, it has been estimated that 90 out of every 100 working Spanish women leave the work force immediately upon marriage.

Such a violent uprooting of the population had drastic effects upon Spain's traditional family structures: the separation of couples, children left with grandparents, the increase of births out of marriage, people marrying later or not at all, the weakening of obligations between spouses and of ties with kin and community (FOESA 1975). But it is important to remember that Spain has maintained a high level of emigration since the 16th century, different regions of the nation being directly affected more than others during particular historical periods. For centuries the survival of rural peasant agriculture in all of Europe, not just the Mediterranean, necessitated that the surplus population move off the land. High rates of geographical mobility were present in most of Europe long before the beginning of the 19th century's drive toward industrialization.

Charles Tilly, reviewing five centuries of European migration patterns, demonstrates how rural households repeatedly used migration in the short run to adjust their relatively inelastic labor requirements, in which demand and supply were often badly matched. He illustrates how during times of surplus population the extra family members moved into the armies or domestic services, became peddlers, etc. During periods of unusually high mortality the same households made up the shortages by employing servants or kinsmen from adjoining regions. This type of individual, local, short-distance, often circular migration was the prevalent pattern up to the age of industrialization. From the mid-19th century up to the Second World War the trend shifted to a type of chain migration, over greater distances, becoming a type of permanent family migration which marked a more definitive break with the place of origin (1978, 66–67). As we shall see in the case of southern Spain, an ambiguous mixture of these two earlier patterns developed in the 1950s in response to the new demand for temporary workers—not families—in the expanding economies of Western Europe.

Since the turn of the century there has been a wide divergence between the development of Andalusia and the rest of Spain in just about every area: economic development, birth and death rates, migration patterns, family structure, etc. Considering the important economic role Andalusia played in much of Spain's history, it might be better to refer to it as a "depressed region" where the rate of development failed to keep up with the national economy and shows signs of falling farther and farther behind.[3] Like many other traditional areas of out-migration in the Mediterranean, it is a "stagnant agricultural zone" with intensive peasant farming in the mountain areas and extensive capitalist farming on the plains. Its service-oriented cities are no longer able to offer sufficient jobs, even in construction, and unemployment in the 1980s is the worst in all of Spain. Natural population increase once again exceeds the rate of out-migration. The ratio of population and potential savings is worsening. Indigenous savings (especially those of the migrants) have been channeled out of the region by economic institutions that have consistently ignored both national and regional developmental policies for the area. None of the national economic reforms of the 1960s or the political reforms of the late 1970s and early 1980s have been able to redress this fundamental disequilibrium between Andalusia and the rest of Spain. For a time it was hoped that the geographical selectivity for migrants from this overcrowded and economically backward region might reduce the social pres-

Table 7.1 The Evolution of the Andalusia Population since 1900

	1900	1950	1975
Almeria	359,013	357,401	386,776
Cadiz	439,390	700,396	952,328
Cordoba	455,859	781,908	717,005
Granada	493,460	782,953	736,045
Huelva	260,880	368,013	400,104
Jaen	474,490	765,697	645,524
Malaga	511,989	750,115	919,251
Sevilla	555,256	1,099,374	1,375,540
Total	3,549,337	5,605,857	6,132,573

Source: Instituto Español de Emigración.

sures and marked inequalities. In Andalusia, however, the traditional imbalances have actually increased.

ANDALUSIA: REGIONAL CONTEXT

Andalusia is the second largest cultural-historical region on the Iberian peninsula, accounting for 17.3 percent of Spain's land mass. Its 6 million inhabitants are spread throughout an area of 87,218 km^2, with 812 km of coastline, nearly as large as Portugal (88,608 km^2).[4] Since the beginning of the century, the population of Andalusia's eight provinces evolved as shown in table 7.1.

The four provinces of Eastern Andalusia (Almería, Granada, Jaén, and Málaga) initially registered a greater population than Western Andalusia (Cádiz, Córdoba, Huelva, and Sevilla). Due to its "relatively" greater prosperity, Western Andalusia grew more rapidly after 1919 until by 1975 it composed 56.2 percent of the total Andalusian population. From 1900 to 1950 the population rapidly expanded by 36.7 percent. The following twenty-five years it grew by only 8.6 percent. This difference, however, is not attributable to a declining birthrate, which is the second highest in Spain, averaging 22 per 1,000. In this century over 3 million Andalusians have migrated out of the area. During the 1960s it lost 14 percent of its total population. Of the 2 million Spaniards who participated in the intra-European migrations between 1959 and 1973, Andalusian emigration oscillated between 30 percent and 40 percent of the total (see table 7.2).

The reasons for this massive outpouring of people are not hard to discern. What resists logic is why, after all these years, Andalusians still have the lowest living standard (measured by per capita annual consumer spending) in Europe. Its varied natural resources in mining and agriculture, tourism, the easing of its population pressures through emigration, an inflow of over one-third of workers' remittances from Western Europe, and ample cheap labor have not radically changed the

Table 7.2 Assisted Emigration to Europe According to Regions in Spain (percentages)

Regions	France 1964-1972	Germany 1962-1972	Switzerland 1962-1972
Andalucia	43.2	33.9	19.2
Valencia	17.4	4.9	5.6
Murcia	10.5	4.7	4.1
Galicia	6.1	21.2	32.8
Leon	4.2	5.1	10.4
Cataluna	3.8	2.2	2.1
Castilla la Vielja	3.7	6.4	4.5
Extremadura	3.0	7.7	6.1
Castilla la Nueva	3.0	10.3	9.6
Aragon	2.2	0.4	1.2
Vascongadas	1.5	0.7	0.6
Navarra	0.7	0.4	0.8
Asturias	0.4	1.2	2.4
Canarias	0.1	0.2	0.2
Baleares	0.1	0.1	0.2
Ceuta y Melilla	0.1	0.5	0.2
TOTAL	100.0	100.0	100.0

Source: Instituto Español de Emigración.

region. Its agricultural production is the lowest in Europe. In 1964–1965 two-thirds of all family incomes were less than 5,000 pesetas ($89 a month). In 1979 per capita incomes in Andalusia remained 27 percent below Spain's national average, and 58 percent below industrial areas like Catalonia. All the figures indicate that while the Andalusians have a higher income than in the past, they are not keeping up with the national average and have been falling steadily behind. In terms of infant mortality, illiteracy, and unemployment, Andalusia also continues firmly entrenched at the bottom of all of Spain's regional rankings.

Andalusia's total active population declined between 1950 and 1975; in some cases as much as 4.6 percent, as in the province of Cádiz. Table 7.3 shows that during this period there has been a steady decrease in the primary sector, as much as 30 percent in Málaga and Sevilla. Other provinces, like Almería, Granada, and Jaén, maintain an agricultural population similar to Spain's national average at the beginning of the century.

In 1977, 1 percent of the farms still occupied 54 percent of the land, while 58 percent occupied only 4 percent of the land. The agricultural wealth of Andalusia is in the hands of around 20,000 large landowners (.3 percent of the population). Three quarters of the farm workers are still classified as *jornaleros* or "casual laborers"—hired and fired on a daily basis. Migration has not raised agricultural

Table 7.3 Active Population in Andalusia, 1950–1975, Primary Sector

	1950	1975
Almeria	64.2	45.8
Cadiz	41.7	20.1
Cordoba	60.9	37.1
Granada	67.8	42.7
Huelva	53.1	29.6
Jaen	68.8	44.4
Malaga	55.4	25.1
Sevilla	51.1	21.3
Spain	48.8	22.9

Source: Cazorla 1965, Banco de Bilbao 1975.

wages. What raises there have been are the results of political decisions in Madrid. Migration has actually accelerated the mechanization of agriculture, which has primarily benefited the larger farms and squeezed out many of the medium-sized ones that cannot afford to invest in modern agro-industrial techniques.

The active population engaged in industry has only increased significantly in Sevilla, Huelva, and Cádiz, and here only in the urban centers. In the rest of Andalusia, the population officially classified in the industrial sector for the most part is employed in small workshops not truly involved in industrial production. During Spain's boom years, attempts were made to create industrial "poles" of development in the south. Unfortunately, the politics of creating "poles" was not markedly successful.

As in most of Spain, the service sector grew the fastest in the south, especially jobs in administration and tourism. For example, in Eastern Andalusia (an area greater than Belgium), the largest employer is the University of Granada. Tourism, restricted to a few of the provincial capitals and the coastal fringe, has emptied many of the mountain areas and built up heavy concentrations of the population around the capitals and along the coasts. These economies are precariously dependent upon the vagaries of the international tourist trade.

The lack of capital has often been held responsible for Andalusia's poor development record. When national figures of tourist receipts and migrants' remittances are considered, as well as the predominant role played by Andalusia in both activities, this excuse no longer seems acceptable. Much of the earnings from tourism have been poured back into tourism in areas of the south that were already severely overdeveloped. Inflation and severe environmental degradation have been the results. The remainder of tourist earnings, like the migrants' remittances, are reinvested in the industrial areas of the north. For example, the largest savings bank in the south, the Caja de Ahorros de Ronda, invested only 1.5 percent of the money deposited in its fourteen branches in Andalusia.

While easing population pressures, migration has done nothing to create badly needed jobs. Year by year there has been a progressive selection for the younger age groups. Until the late 1970s this trend left an aging, uneducated, less productive work force in the countryside and a large youthful unemployed proletariat in the cities. At the end of Spain's economic expansion and the virtual cessation of large-scale migration into the rest of Western Europe in 1975, John Naylon succinctly outlined a problem that has grown worse in the 1980s:

> With at least 25,000 new young workers coming into the Andalusian labor market every year, of whom some 10,000 are destined to be casual laborers, rural unemployment is not only seasonal but permanent. Altogether there are some 400,000 surplus hands (still) in agriculture alone. Unemployment on such a scale warps the social and moral outlook of Andalusia's laboring population, dissipates energy and enthusiasm, and represents a tremendous economic loss. (1975, 18)

PLACE OF ORIGIN: DECISION TO EMIGRATE

While the migratory flows of the 1950s and 1960s emptied many of the smaller villages and towns with 5,000 or fewer inhabitants, it was not a new experience totally altering the traditional lifeways and family structures throughout all of Andalusia. For generations people left their communities in search of a better life. In fact in some areas, especially on the rich fertile plains, migration and tradition were closely linked. The maintenance of tradition in many of the communities with 10,000 and more inhabitants was actually made possible by emigration, alleviating population pressures on culturally defined scarce resources. In other areas, closer to the mountains, the contemporary intra-European movement of "temporary" workers had a greater effect. Here there was a more direct feedback relationship between changes in the patterns of emigration and the local economic system.

In many of the towns of the plains the political economy had been controlled by the gentry for centuries. For a long time, regardless of the usual problems of underemployment and unemployment created by the total dependence upon one crop, the traditional system relatively supported all groups. After the Civil War, however, the gentry were the first to leave the towns of fewer than 10,000. They mechanized agriculture wherever possible in order to bring down labor costs; this was especially the case where the main crops were grains rather than olives. Soon larger numbers of the day laborers were also forced to come and go on almost an annual basis. Migration started to become a tradition. In these towns, *yo soy emigrante* (I am a migrant) expresses one's identity long after one has permanently returned.

In other communities where agriculture was not conducive to mechanization—olives and grapes—the gentry retained a stronger family representation and continued to play a direct role in the economy and political life of all the local institutions. Here too, many of the day laborers participated in the migratory movement to Western Europe, although their numbers were smaller than in the wheat growing areas. Except for the migrants who spent nine months of the year in Switzerland, there was less of a migrant class or identity. *Emigrantes* were simply persons working abroad. Upon their return to the community they were expected to revert smoothly to their old status of *obrero* or *jornalero*. Only repeated emigration, for a second and third time, allowed them and their families to be distinguished from the other workers more clearly as *emigrantes*.

In the larger mountain villages, it is difficult to get a direct answer to the question: "Who is an *emigrante*?" Almost everyone has left for an extended period at one time or another. Migration is a more "universal" experience. The people of these sierras have always been more closely involved in subsistence agriculture and retained greater control over their lands and local businesses. Migration was always employed as an alternative or supplement similar in function to what is more commonly observed in Galicia. Migration is thought of less as a unique set of experiences that sets one family apart from another than as a loss of community members.

Throughout most of Andalusia, however, the majority of the families affected by emigration come from the lower classes. In a society where the family plays the major role in establishing one's social position, the migrant's class position is marked by the fact that the male heads of families are forced to work manually, often on a daily basis, for others.

The wives and children of the lower classes will also work if the situation presents itself. Although status is obtained primarily through the male head of the household, the employment of a man's wife and daughters can be instrumental in lowering the status of the family. All members of this lower stratum work with their hands; own an insignificant amount or no land at all; are unable to trace legitimate descent back to historically prestigious families in their communities; have the least dependable income; suffer from a lack of sufficient education at a time when education has become increasingly important in the larger Spanish society; have little prestige due to the lack of the refinement of a valued life-style which (especially in the 1950s and 1960s) was measured by ample housing, the ability to dress well every day of the week and self-imposed leisure time. Their political influence as a group until the mid-1970s was minimal; and most of the members of this class would never be able to realize any significant change in status for themselves or their families as long as they remained permanently in their home communities. The absence of occupational mobility for this group is highlighted in table 7.4, which indicates the profession of the migrants before departing for Western Europe, and in table 7.5, which indicates the type of profession they practiced upon their return.[5]

To repeat, the macroeconomic situation in Andalusia—analyzed in terms of occupation, employment possibilities, ownership of land, and agricultural

Table 7.4 Profession of Migrants Before Migrating to the Federal Republic of Germany

	N	%
Self-employed land owners	4	2,9
Specialized workers	1	0,7
Semi-specialized workers	7	5,1
Renters of small land holdings	2	1,5
Agricultural workers without a specialization	82	67,2
Manual workers in services and manufacturing	27	19,7
Don't understand	2	1,5
No answer	2	1,5
TOTAL	137	100,0

Source: Encuesta de Emigración de 1977.

Table 7.5 Profession Practiced by Returning Migrants

	N	%
Specialized services	6	4.4
Commercial agents	1	0.7
Self-employed land owners	5	3.6
Specialized workers	1	0.7
Semi-specialized workers	8	5.8
Renters of small land holdings	1	0.7
Civil Guard	1	0.7
Agricultural workers without a specialization	60	43.8
Manual workers in service and manufacturing	20	14.8
Retired	1	0.7
Don't understand	9	6.6
No answer	24	17.5
TOTAL	137	100.0

Source: Encuesta de Emigración de 1977.

operations—plays a major role in determining the way in which the poorer classes earn, or do not earn, their livelihood and influences a family's decision to seek new economic opportunities outside their community. This is especially true for those families who decide to make a permanent break and migrate internally to other regions of Spain.

The decisions of community members seeking only a provisional disengagement from their villages and towns, through what was supposed to be a temporary and short-term move into the labor markets of Western Europe, were equally influenced by the structure of their domestic group and the phase of its developmental cycle. In comparison with the internal migrants, the intra-European migrants were generally older, had more children, and shared a more traditional outlook on life.

The ideal structure toward which the organization of the domestic group strives is the nuclear, conjugal family based upon an overriding preference for setting up one's own household. While kin ties are reckoned bilaterally, an individual's paramount loyalties are to the nuclear family, where all adjustments in rights and obligations with kin should be mediated through the husband and wife. The father is primarily responsible for the economic survival of the family. He is also supposed to act as the ultimate patriarchal authority. The mother should not work outside the home, if at all possible, and has the primary responsibility of educating the children. The strong sense of familial independence is also supported in a positive manner by the idea that parents and relatives should have little choice in the ultimate selection of a marriage partner.

This ideal family type is seldom or only temporarily realized among the lower classes. In the countryside the three-generation extended family is at times closer to the structural realities of the domestic group. It usually is composed of one or both the older parents, their married daughters and sons-in-law, and their unmarried grandchildren. At times an unmarried or widowed brother or sister of the older parents is also present.

Applying the term "extended" to such a family grouping is meaningful only in the residential sense. The actual domestic group formed by such a three-generation extended family does not stand for in-group solidarity as is common in the areas of northern Spain. Among the lower strata, the individual nuclear families clustered together in a common residence lack any significant patrimony which might bind them together in a cooperative group for a longer period of time. Economic resources are rarely pooled and there is little sharing even in the consumption of everyday household goods.

The existence of the three-generation domestic group stands primarily for common residence. Its very structure is largely determined by scarce economic resources, a chronic shortage of housing and a residential preference for uxorilocality if neolocality is not possible. Housing has always been a problem. It was not uncommon for four to five families to live together. The parents would have the best part and other choice areas were designated to the daughter who married first. Since the oldest daughter usually married first and the youngest last, the latter usually received the least desirable location. Due to the larger number of children, however, the oldest was often the most cramped for space.

While living space is still a considerable problem (especially in the cities) and is aggravated by the continuing high birthrate in Andalusia, the situation radically improved in the late sixties and early seventies. During this period there was considerable government support to construct new living quarters for the lower classes. Migration, however, played the major role. Those who migrated internally would ultimately sell their houses. Those who migrated temporarily to Europe returned and used their earnings to construct new living quarters or improve old ones.

The average size of the domestic group, rather than the average size of the nuclear family composing the domestic group, is what created the actual pressures whose resolution was finally sought in external migration. For example, in one of the larger communities studied, the average family size for both nonmigrants and external migrants was 4.4. Average domestic group size for nonmigrants, however, was 5.3, while average domestic group size for the external migrants was 7.3.

The domestic groups of the external migrants pass through three phases, and it is in the second phase that the family of the first-term migrant finally make their decision. The first phase is a period in which the sons of the household are gradually replaced by sons-in-law. While most parents attempt to influence their children to marry into their own class in order to reinforce conjugal ties, the children in actuality have a great deal of freedom in the selection of a spouse. Children of the lower stratum become more seriously involved and form stronger attachments in courting relations at an earlier age (between 14 and 18 years) than do those of the gentry and middle classes. Their period of courtship is also relatively reduced.

The longer a couple remains engaged, however, the greater the obligation to marry. Long engagements that do not end in marriage are particularly harmful for the girl in that she will have difficulty in finding a second suitor. In the past the moral feelings of the community supplied a powerful sanction against faithlessness. But today the *noviazgo* (period of courtship and engagement) is in greater danger as the young men go off to work elsewhere for longer periods of time.

The men from the lower classes tend to marry at an earlier age (late 20s and early 30s) than do those of the middle classes. Women of all strata prefer to marry in their early or mid-20s. Therefore, the average age difference between couples of the working classes is less extreme. Younger marriages (couples in their mid-20s) became increasingly common in the 1970s. This was especially true among those youths from the lower stratum participating in internal migration. During Spain's boom years, better job opportunities existing outside the communities allowed the young to achieve greater independence from parental control at an earlier age. The average age at marriage of those men participating in external migration more closely paralleled traditional patterns.

As a rule, the main role of marriage is directed toward the formation of the nuclear family. The more extensive affinal ties which result are invariably of strained importance. Kinship ties formed by marriage merely provide a facultative tie in which relatives are assimilated to the position of "ascriptive" friends.

The most important factor leading to the temporary formation of the three-generation domestic group in this first phase of the developmental cycle among the lower stratum is an unstipulated rule of uxorilocal residence. As previously stated, the ideal is neolocal residence, which is expressed in the refrain *No casaré sin casa* (no marriage without house). But due to limited economic resources of the newly married couple and the traditional shortage of acceptable housing, the husband invariably goes to live in the house of his wife. It is generally conceded that uxorilocal residence for the newly married couple avoids putting a strain on the marriage which would be created by rivalry between a man's wife and his mother if virilocal residence were the rule.

The wife is not expected to relate closely to her husband's parents. Relationships between her and her in-laws before marriage are all but nonexistent. The man does all of the courting in the vicinity of her house. She remains distant to her fiance's parents while he gradually makes friends with her brothers, visits her mother when the father is out, and finally sits in the house and eats with both parents after he has asked to marry the girl. Even after marriage the wife's relationship to her in-laws is one of guarded formality.

Uxorilocal residence is also preferred because of the required cooperation needed between women to run the house while the men are away. During the early period of a man's married life he spends little time at home except for eating and sleeping. His days are filled with work or looking for work. Temporary employment on distant farms takes him away from his community for weeks at a time. His evenings are spent in the bars or in the streets with his male friends. Daughters are more familiar with the daily patterns in their natal homes and are used to their mother's authority; they can follow her direction with less resentment after marriage. Furthermore, a woman is invariably pregnant during her first year of marriage and receives greater emotional support and assistance from her own mother.

The jural basis for maintaining a household is the rights of maintenance and inheritance. The family formed by marriage is legally viewed as a single entity: the new families formed by the marriage of the daughters establish their singularity within the larger structure of the domestic group. The solidarity of the family is formally seen to rest in the authority of the father and is identified with the prerogative of the husband. Ideally, the wife is subject to her husband's control. After marriage he is supposed to assume control of her material property. Her ideal role should center around the education and rearing of the children. In all cases she is to be submissive, retiring, frugal, and uncritical.

While the men of the house are supposed to represent household interests to the wider society, in reality the mother and wives are often the real power within the home. They run the domestic group, make major decisions affecting the economy of their families, and direct the household labor force even to the degree of pressuring their husbands to seek temporary work though external migration. The woman commands in a manner that effectively preserves the illusion of male dominance. She insists that her children maintain a strict form of respect for their father and in public will seldom contradict or offer "learned commentary" to his opinions. The males are not unaware of her dual role. In discussing the woman's role, a husband will often stress the ability of the wife to command without the use of force: "No manda pero domina suavemente" ("She does not give [direct] commands but maintains the upper hand with gentleness"). The woman's role is further accentuated by the fact that it is considered far more tragic for the mother of the house to die than for the father—even though he is supposed to be the major means of economic support.

During the early part of phase 1, the core authority structure of the domestic group remains the active married older parents of the household. Sisters and mothers continue to form a close emotional bond. Sons-in-law get on rather well with their fathers-in-law and often establish freer and more open relationships with them than with their own fathers. Brothers-in-law form close ties of friendship during the early period of their marriages and attempt to work together during the day and drink together at night.

As children are born the husband-wife ties begin to predominate within the domestic group and the emotional balance swings more toward the conjugal family. Lineal ties are deemphasized. Loyalties between sisters are less easy to sustain as the women are confronted with choices which emphasize the welfare of their own family over that of the larger domestic group.

The source for potential disruption of the domestic group and the pressures to seek a solution through temporary migration to Western Europe occur during the second phase of the developmental cycle. The phase usually begins with the birth of the youngest sister's children, followed by the older parent's retirement from active economic life—often ending in the death of the father. Here, as elsewhere in Europe, women have a greater longevity than men. As during the end of phase 1, conjugal ties continue to receive increased emphasis over lineal ones. The simple demographic pressure upon the use of limited space within the household becomes a bitter focus of contention with the birth of each new child. As the older parents become part of the dependent population, the brothers-in-law (at the instigation of their wives) attempt to assume new roles of authority within the domestic group. Since each man derives his family's income from a daily wage, which rules out any common effort in earning money for the domestic group as a whole, there is no basis upon which one or the other of the brothers-in-law might actually base their claim.

With the death of the elder father and the weakening of the mother, the sororal joint family is strained by increasing rivalry between the sisters, whose potential for solidarity is less than what existed between them and their parents. Among the lower stratum this sororal joint family is less enduring due to the scarcity of economic resources and the laws of inheritance, which reduce the insignificant patrimony to nearly nothing. Property, which is paramount in strengthening familial and more extended kin ties among the elites (as witnessed by the markedly higher percentage of first cousin marriages), among the lower strata is usually reduced to the house and the material goods inside. The law of inheritance dictates that when a property owner dies (in this case the male owner of the house and land) the property is divided in half: half goes to the widow, the other half is to be divided equally among all the siblings. Because there is so little, it is usually impractical to divide the property at the death of the father. In that the heirs are usually unable to reach agreement, everything often remains in the hands of the mother until her death. Nevertheless, conflicts and disputes continue. The sororal joint family comes closer to the point of partition as some of the heirs try to buy out others while the mother is still alive.

One example of the complicated division that can take place is the case of Enrique. The house at one time belonged to Enrique's maternal grandparents. Enrique's father came from a barrio across town to live in his wife's house. Upon the death of Enrique's grandparents the house was divided between his mother and mother's sister; they walled up the middle and built two separate entrances to the street. Upon the death of Enrique's father, his mother was forced to sell his section to the father of Enrique's future wife, who had just returned from Argentina. When Enrique married, he moved back into his natal house, which was not the house of his wife.

Increasingly, the men caught up in these family struggles became aware of the wider opportunities for physical mobility and sought to migrate to Germany, Switzerland, or France. There they believed that they could earn enough money to erect their own house. It became quite common in some areas for brothers-in-law to attempt to escape the conflictual relations of the domestic group by migrating together.

The third phase of the developmental cycle is marked by the severance of female siblings from the domestic group. In many cases, the final break is perpetuated by the death of the mother. One sister will try to purchase the patrimonial share of the other siblings. If this cannot be accomplished, actual partition of the living space might occur. Today, however, purchase is easier than it has been in the past due to the effects of migration. The external migrant has anticipated the problems of phase 3 and has sought a solution during the end of phase 2. Furthermore, the fact that the returned migrant now has enough funds to construct a superior living space to anything he had previously makes him more agreeable to sell his or his wife's share at a more reasonable rate than he might have done otherwise.

Of course, partition can also take place during the advanced age of the mother. The daughter who agrees to support the dependent mother is the one who will invariably retain the house. Due to the fact that the aged parents prefer to be under the care of a daughter, the sons seldom acquire the parental home.

The independent nuclear families, once established in phase 3, soon unavoidably set out to re-create the structure of the multinucleated domestic group by repeating the pattern of the developmental cycle. At the time partition takes place, most of these families already have one or two children who will enter the marriage market within ten years.

During the first decade following the pivotal year 1959, the Andalusian migrants seeking "temporary" work in Western Europe shared an optimistic vision that through "steady" employment and higher wages abroad, they would be able to achieve a social, as well as an economic, transformation for their families at home. In contrast to the permanent internal migrants, this group's propensity to migrate was more influenced by their belief that they could somewhat improve their social status locally. While they rejected their perceived position in the traditional system of stratification, they on the whole continued to support many of the community's cultural values. They hoped that migration would first improve their poor housing situation, which in their eyes and the eyes of the community was an indicator of their low social standing. They sought improvement, however, not just in terms of architectural structure, furnishings, and appliances, but also in terms of greater familial independence.

After housing, their goal was to acquire enough capital to open a small enterprise not directly associated with agriculture, one that would provide "fixed" or permanent employment. Somehow, manual labor in Western Europe would teach them new skills that would allow them to change their occupational status and escape the low prestige associated with manual labor in agricultural activities in southern Spain.

While saddened by the potential separation, the family was used to months of separation under the traditional work system where the older males continually were forced to seek work outside their towns and provinces. Their miscalculation, however, was that they believed the family's goals were achievable within a year or two. At first the majority of the migrants were men who left the children at home with their mothers. The new wealth in the form of remittances allowed the mother to spend all of her time at home and provided the children with a better diet and clothing. As the temporary became extended into the indefinite, more and more men sent for their wives and older children of working age. The new calculations were based upon the greater earning powers of the couple, which should reduce the time spent living provisionally abroad. More and more the younger children were being left with grandparents, uncles, and aunts. While well cared for physically, the children's local education was often severely neglected by the grandparents. In the first instance, where the mother is forced to take on the roles of both father and mother, she often becomes more authoritarian and rigid with her children than is usually expected. In the second case, the grandparents lean toward greater permissiveness, always being in doubt of their ultimate authority within family structures which have traditionally emphasized the husband-wife-children bond over all others. This situation is further aggravated by the parents' return, when the children find themselves caught between the role models of the grandparents from another generation and those of their parents, slightly changed by their greater contact with urban industrial society.

THE MOVE TO WEST GERMANY

The early migration cohorts from Andalusia to Germany were recruited directly by industry. Their movement was primarily stimulated by demand. The German employers informed the Federal Employment Institute in Nuremberg how many workers were wanted, what their qualifications or professions should be, and what nationality was preferred. The Institute forwarded this information to their "German Commissions" in the sending countries, which were left with the responsibility of testing the professional qualifications and health of the migrants, arranging for work and residence permits, and transporting them to Germany. The more familiar anthropological patterns of family chain migration did not occur until much later.

After the demographic imbalances created by World War II, labor shortages in West Germany (from 1945 to 1961) had been filled by 10 million refugees from Eastern Europe and 3.5 million from East Germany. The steady demand for workers in West Germany next led to a search for manpower among non-German nationalities, resulting in the signing of various labor treaties: with Italy 1955, Spain 1960, Greece 1960, etc. By the the mid-sixties the West German government and industry had activated programs and relatively liberal policies that would facilitate the massive transfer and turnover of foreign labor. They developed an ingenious system of work and residence permits—one affecting the other and determined by length of stay. The permits could be used to check the continued usefulness of the foreign worker. If the residence permit expired (or was withdrawn), or if the worker stayed outside the country for more than three months, the work permit was automatically canceled. Residence permits for nonworking spouses and children under 18 were only obtainable after three years of work in Germany and proof of adequate housing. Naturalization depended on a minimum residence period of ten years.

Between 1959 and 1973 Germany received more immigrant labor, in both absolute and relative terms, than any other country in Western Europe (see tables 7.6 and 7.7).[6] During the height of the economic boom in 1964, the one millionth worker who stepped off the train in Germany was officially greeted with flowers and presented with a new motorbike. By September 1973 there were 2,596,630 foreigners in the active work force; including their dependents the total figure was over 4 million. By the early 1970s more than 800,000 foreign workers were migrating on a yearly basis from the developing countries of the Mediterranean to the industrialized regions of Western Europe. No other part of the contemporary world experienced such a large-scale movement of workers with temporary contracts. As late as 1976, 7.5 million migrants were included in the active work force of Western Europe; they were accompanied by 5.5 million dependents. Even these figures, however, are only a gross estimate of the magnitude of the transfer of human labor since the 1950s. There is no accurate way to include the millions more that illegally sought work for a few months or a year and unobtrusively returned to their native countries.

Officially, however, it was repeated with monotonous regularity in government circles that "Germany is not a country of immigration." Their use of the term "guest worker" implied that the migrant had no natural or acquired right to permanent admittance. For this and other reasons, Hans-Joachim Hofman-Nowontny (1978) believes that there was no real immigration policy in a country

Table 7.6 Foreign Population: Comparison between 1974, 1978, and 1979

	Foreign Population			Sept 1979/1974		Sept 1979/1978	
	Sept 1974	Sept 1978	Sept 1979	Abs.	%	Abs.	%
Turks	1,027,800	1,165,100	1,268,300	+240,500	+23.4	+103,200	+8.9
Yugoslavs	707,800	610,200	620,600	- 87,200	-12.3	+ 10,400	+1.7
Italians	629,600	572,500	594,400	- 35,200	- 5.6	+ 21,900	+3.8
Greeks	406,400	305,500	296,800	-109,600	-27.0	- 8,700	-2.9
Spanish	272,700	188,900	182,200	- 90,500	-33.2	- 6,700	-3.5
Portuguese	121,600	109,900	109,800	- 11,800	- 9.7	- 100	-0.1
Others	961,500	1,029,000	1,071,700	+110,200	+11.5	+ 42,700	+4.2
Total	4,127,400	3,981,100	4,143,800	+ 16,400	+ 0.4	+162,700	+4.1

Source: *Boletín de Información*, Octubre-Diciembre 1980.

Table 7.7 Evolution of the Spanish Population in the Federal Republic of Germany

Ano	Total Spanish Population	Active Spanish Population	Dependants
1950			
1951	1,600		
1952	1,700		
1953	1,800		
1954	1,900	400	1,500
1955	2,100	500	1,600
1956		700	
1957		1,000	
1958		1,500	
1959		2,200	
1960		16,500	
1961	61,800	44,200	17,600
1962		94,000	
1963		119,600	
1964		151,100	
1965		182,800	
1966		178,200	
1967	177,000	129,126	47,874
1968		115,900	
1969	206,900	143,100	63,800
1970	245,500	165,864	79,636
1971	270,400	183,020	87,380
1972		184,200	
1973	286,100	190,000	96,100
1974	272,700	149,718	122,982
1975	247,400	124,533	122,867
1976	219,400	107,518	111,882
1977	201,400	97,226	104,174
1978	188,900	90,875	98,025
1979	182,155	89,992	92,163
1980	180,000	86,500	93,500

Source: *Information Bulletin: Social Work with Spaniards*, June-August 1981; Körtc 1980.

like Germany, only an "alien policy." This alien policy, as well as the immigrant's own low level of education, made integration or assimilation of the immigrants very difficult. Nevertheless, the government's official position in declaring that they were seeking migratory labor rather than potential citizens was partially sustained by the migrant's own intentions to return home after a few years of work abroad. While the return has been significant, and became part of the pattern of contemporary labor migration, many of the Spaniards stayed longer than they had originally intended (see table 7.8). Most had planned to stay less than five years. By 1983, however, of the 173,526 Spaniards remaining in Germany, 126,374 had lived in the country for over ten years.

Back in the early 1960s nearly 90 percent of the Spanish immigrants were males between the ages of 20 and 45. The first wave came from the north of Spain; they

Table 7.8 Duration of Stay in the Federal Republic of Germany

	Total	from 1 ano	1 & 2 Years	2 & 3 Years	3 & 4 Years	4 & 5 Years	5 & 8 Years	8 & 10 Years	10 Years or more
Men	2,069,416	83,468	98,043	145,968	90,905	62,692	119,724	227,269	1,241,347
Women	1,414,298	60,403	65,594	80,440	62,778	54,929	153,254	194,622	742,278
Children	1,183,203	83,697	106,734	119,988	109,328	98,450	289,795	172,239	207,972
Total	4,666,917	227,568	270,371	346,936	263,011	216,071	557,773	594,130	2,191,597
		4.88%	5.79%	7.42%	5.64%	4.63%	11.95%	12.73%	46.96%
Turks	1,580,671	56,405	77,621	155,363	110,300	89,115	246,448	275,280	570,139
Yugoslavs	631,592	15,396	19,492	22,080	20,467	19,819	59,668	89,705	385,075
Italians	601,621	24,529	30,129	33,412	31,399	28,585	61,604	58,048	333,915
Greeks	300,824	9,318	9,188	7,853	7,503	7,739	26,670	28,717	203,836
Austrians	174,988	6,923	7,404	7,726	6,792	5,508	13,266	15,796	111,572
SPANISH	173,526	3,786	3,203	3,160	3,126	3,151	11,904	18,822	126,374
Dutch	108,975	3,554	3,447	3,193	2,847	2,529	7,914	6,984	78,507
Portuguese	105,005	2,128	2,757	3,210	3,539	3,527	15,551	26,821	48,472

Source: ''Ausländerpolitik,'' editada por el Ministro Federal del Interior, Bornn, enero 1983, *Boletín de Información*, Febrero-Abril 1983.

were soon outnumbered, however, by the steady flow up from Andalusia. These Spaniards contributed directly to the expansion of industry as the Germans moved into the services. They filled unskilled and semiskilled vacancies in manufacturing and construction and were heavily represented in those areas of mass production that were particularly repetitive and unhealthy. Unlike the Germans, they were often paid according to piecework or the bonus system. They put in more overtime, working as much as two shifts a day. Because of the long hours and the greater risks, they also appeared more regularly in the formal accident statistics (Körte 1980, 20).

Because of their intentions to return they generally left their families back in Spain. Their problems were initially those of most single men in a foreign culture: those created by sustained absence from close kin, language, food, provisional housing, discrimination, education, isolation, and the lack of social mobility. Even during the best of times the Spanish worker found it difficult to interpret the cultural patterns of his hosts. His knowledge of German was never a guide for interaction. All the Andalusian migrant sought was enough information on, or insight into, the chances or risks of working in the new country; and while he never tried to be permanently accepted, he at least tried to be tolerated. Regardless of their difficulties, the early cohorts manifested a positive dynamism and general optimism. They felt caught up in a purposeful struggle whose end would bring about a positive change in the life of their families. Gradually, as other members of their families joined them, and they formed a new separate social stratum at the bottom of Germany's social structure, their problems also changed. Their goals changed from dreams of achievement and an early return to an obsession with daily maintenance and survival.[7]

THE CRISIS

In the fall of 1973 a freeze was settling upon the vigorous economies of the Common Market countries, creating a bleak economic forecast. Rampant inflation, industrial stagnation, and technical bankruptcies shook public confidence. On November 9, 1974, the unit staff of the European Economic Community (EEC) projected an unemployment figure which would total 4.1 million by April 1975. On December 18 the Organization for Economic Cooperation and Development (OECD) came out with the most pessimistic report in its thirteen-year history, in which it stated that its member nations were facing economic problems unusual outside times of war and that inflation- and recession-caused layoffs would soon reach 6 million.

Ironically, when for the first time in contemporary history dictatorships were finally absent in all of Western and Southern Europe, the public lost faith in their governments, especially in their ability to manage the economic crisis. The working people of the Western nations were beginning to fear that their venerated system of growth was in danger of collapse. They were caught in a contradiction where their political system, whose ideology and structure were dependent upon the unfaltering growth of the economy, now had an economy that could not deliver. People's frustrations were repeatedly expressed in the ambiguous results of national elections. Each new government promised a reversal of trends. Once again, the OECD, the International Monetary Fund, and other prestigious economic institutions came out with some of their gloomiest economic forecasts in years. They implied that very little could be done to reverse the situation politically, especially the high unemployment rates, which the West Europeans were not used to.

Within the context of this international crisis, which strained both the integration of the world economic system and Western polity, political solutions continued to receive far more emphasis than economic ones. Two antiliberal political tendencies developed to protect the liberal societies: (a) growing protectionism and isolation; and (b) an incipient growth in racism and interethnic rivalry between the poorer classes competing for fewer jobs at the bottom. The first political attempt to deal with the problem was a search for an expedient way to bring about a shift in labor which would be politically attractive to the natives, even though it might not make the most economic sense. It was decided that the type of human capital most socially expendable was the temporary migrant worker.

Therefore, there was a swing back to more restrictive measures and a call for a new "orchestration" of manpower policies between receivers and senders in order to decrease the number of foreign workers in the host countries. On December 11, 1973, the German government put a stop to the contracting of workers not part of the Common Market. A comparison of the first six months of 1973 with the same period in 1974 shows that Spanish migration decreased by 33 percent.

In November 1974 new regulations were imposed concerning the government's subsidy of children *(Kindergeld),* which discriminated against workers who had maintained their children in their home country. This legislation also seemed contradictory in that it actually encouraged the migrants who remained to send for their children.

On December 11, 1974, a directive from the Federal Office of Labor suspended the issue or renewal of work permits to workers in Germany (not part of Common Market) if there were unemployed Germans capable of doing the work or learning how to do it. The fact is, however, that between 1974 and 1978 foreign workers submitted 6,370,000 requests for new, or the renewal of old, work permits. Only 2.5 percent were refused.

On March 3, 1975, the order was sent out prohibiting the settlement of recently arrived immigrants in cities or zones where their density had reached 10 percent or more. The reason given: "We don't have the infrastructure to take care of them." By 1982 the 4.65 million foreigners in West Germany composed 7.5 percent of the total population. They were 22 percent of the population in Frankfurt, 18 percent in Stuttgart, and 17 percent in Munich. There were more than 1 million children under 16 years of age (of which 46,000 were Spanish).

Nearly 47 percent of them were born in Germany. Over 70 percent failed to attend kindergarten. Of the other 485,000 children of school age, 20 percent were habitually absent. Of those who did attend, more than 50 percent failed to pass their final exams, which meant that they would never be able to obtain even an apprenticeship position.

In April of 1975, 4.7 percent unemployment among Germans in the work force (1,087,100) contrasted with 7.4 percent (178,424) for foreigners. The Spanish, however, approximated the Germans with 4.7 percent (7,858). By September of 1976, when we began our survey, 93,500 of the 898,900 unemployed were foreigners. By the end of the year total unemployment was again at 1,060,336 (938,069 Germans and 106,145 foreigners) despite the migration ban and the drift homeward of foreign workers. By February of 1982 the rate of unemployment among Germans reached 8.2 percent compared to 12 percent for foreigners.

The growing pressures affecting the migrants' sense of exclusion reached the point that an unpublished document prepared by Patrick Hillery for the EEC stated that the resulting frustration felt by the migrants was in the long term not only intolerable but dangerous to the EEC as whole. Since 1975, however, the debate concerning the immigrants' position in German society has become increasingly strident. A decade after the initial ban, fifteen doctors of law, medicine, and philosophy publicly expressed the opinion: "It is with great concern that we observe the undermining of the German people through the presence of several million foreigners and their families, and the de-Germanization of our language, our culture and our national character." They believed that migrants' return home would bring "the federal republic not only societal but ecological relief."

If the professors have their wish and the above opinion actually serves its purpose of blocking all new immigration, the West German population would decline from its current 62 million to 57 million by the end of the century. Since 1963 the German birthrate has fallen steadily. In 1972 deaths finally outnumbered births among German citizens. The population increases that did occur were directly attributable to a positive immigration balance. Between 1973 and 1975 the natural deficit of the German population (−624,000, or an average of −208,000 a year) was partly offset by the natural increase in the number of foreigners (+279,000, or +91,000 a year) (Kayser 1977, 236). It is currently calculated that one out of every six children in West Germany is a foreigner. Nearly 20 percent of all marriages in Germany are with foreigners. Most of these unions have been between German women and foreign men. Up until 1975, however, a child's nationality was still determined by that of his father.

Paradoxically, legislation developed in 1965 concerning family reunification was given new vigor. The reworked legislation stipulated that in order to bring their families, the migrants must have resided in Germany for a minimum of three years and be able to prove that they had good possibilities for long-term employment. They had to demonstrate that they had a decent place for the family to live, one that was similar to that of a German at a comparable income level. The legislation applied only to the reunion of spouses and children under 21 years of age, and the program gave only the right to a residence permit, not an automatic work permit.

Of course, the family reunion program was viewed with trepidation by the Germans even during the 1950s and 1960s. During this period it was estimated that only between 7 and 9 percent of the foreign workers lived with their families. Thirteen years later the situation had changed dramatically (see table 7.7). In the case of the Spaniards who remained, seven-tenths of the nuclear families were reunited in Germany.

The program of family reunification actually seems to be an attempt to structurally solidify Germany's foreign workers by assuring that the needed replenishment in the future will be made up by family members. The Germans had also begun to consider the fact that a family-based immigrant community would create fewer problems than the male-dominated rotation type. So like the first generation of migrants who filled demographic gaps in the 1960s, this second generation based upon family reunification will fill the gaps in the 1990s (Körte 1980).

The recruitment ban did not have an immediate effect. The foreign population began to slowly decrease only after 1976 and even then never reached the 1973 low. More significant than the actual change in numbers, however, was the change in the composition by nationality. The shift is explained by two factors: (a) changed composition of immigration and re-migration, and (b) excess of births among foreign residents (Hönekopp and Ullmann 1980, 6). The Spaniards in particular, who had reached a peak in 1968 (206,900, or 8.69 percent), slowly began to decline in numbers even before the 1973 ban (see table 7.7).

From 1975 to 1976 the Spanish workers decreased by nearly 17 percent (from 139,135 to 116,373). There are many sound economic reasons for this steady decline: a four- to five-day workweek with no overtime, an inflation rate that leveled the purchasing power of the migrant's family, unemployment, etc.

Gradually, the demographic structure of the temporary work force became less temporary and looked more like that of an immigrant population. The sex ratio of 63 men to 37 women of 1979 changed to 56:44 in 1977. The number of young children, adolescents, and people over 40 expanded the dependent population. Their housing became less provisional (which appears to be a function of the intended length of stay) as more than 80 percent of the migrants moved into individual apartments. There was the formation of new concentrations of foreign populations, not so much whole neighborhoods as entire streets or blocks. These "clan-like groups" consisted either of relations or at least of members from the same town or area.

New types of mutual aid societies began to take shape. Because of the increasing problems of the second generation, the largely recreational Spanish Clubs, run by Caritas, started to share their space with more effective and politically active groups like the Spanish Parents Association, composed of 114 associations representing 9,000 families, with a total of 17,000 children. The new problems focused on naturalization, housing, the right to vote, education, and job training. This group was particularly concerned with the education of their children. Between 40 to 50 percent of Spanish children in Germany abandon their schooling and never receive certification of graduation. Over 75 percent receive no, or inadequate, professional training.

The values and behavior of all the migration cohorts, those with as well as those without families, underwent significant changes. Most of the migrants came from villages or small towns. Even those who had left from the Spanish cities had initially migrated internally from the rural areas. They came for economic reasons: to work, to save, and to realize their sacrifice and investment upon their return to Andalusia. The majority soon discovered that their salaries were insufficient to allow them to reach their savings goals as soon as they had expected. Only around 5 percent of the Andalusians in Germany ever earned more than 2,000 marks a month. The average was closer to 1,500 marks. To maximize their earning potential and time, the men worked as many extra hours as they could. Their wives, many without work permits, worked as cleaning ladies. Life was lived provisionally, and everything was deferred for savings and the future purchase of a home in Spain.

The social assistants who worked with the Spanish family came to view its primary characteristic in Germany as one of insecurity. Husbands and wives saw very little of each other except on the weekends. The younger children were left to themselves and the television set. The older children spent long hours in school and part-time work.

The father was still thought of as the head of the family as he had been in the rural areas. He basically gave orders and was little concerned with the opinions of his children. The informal education of the children and running of the household economy was the responsibility of the mother. But she was now also an important wage earner who was obliged to work long hours outside the home. If the household was going to work at all, the men would have to begin helping their wives in domestic chores. It was difficult, however, for them to redefine their roles. The demands placed upon the mother made it difficult for her to meet the needs of both her husband and children. The conflicting roles of both parents often led to feelings of guilt and tension within the family. Their behavior toward their children oscillated between authoritarianism to hide their confusion and permissiveness to compensate for the lack of time spent as a family.

Invariably, the children spoke a more fluent German than their mother or father. The lack of basic education on the part of the parents impeded their learning the language and required that they depend upon their children for all the more complex transactions with the society. The father felt that this reversal of roles undermined his authority. The older children resented having to behave like Spaniards at home and Germans outside the home. They all understood, however, why their parents were in Germany: to acquire something that was blocked to them in Spain—a better life for the entire family. In this sense Germany, regardless of all its drawbacks, represented progress for them all.

THE PROPENSITY TO RETURN HOME

The exact figure of homecomers to Spain is at this point impossible to ascertain. Nevertheless, in comparing figures of earlier and more affluent periods one is left with an impression of the magnitude of this return. In 1970 one out of every ten Spaniards lived abroad. During the economically expansive decade of European development, from 1960 to 1970, the number of returnees actually exceeded the number that migrated. As early as 1964 a study by the Spanish Ministry of Labor estimated that 87 percent of the migrants to European countries returned after three years, but 46 percent re-emigrated. By 1979 the rate of return for all migrant workers in Germany reached two-thirds: 9 out of 10 Italians, 8 out of 10 Spaniards, 7 out of 10 Greeks, 5 out of 10 Yugoslavs and 3 out of 10 Turks (Böhning 1980, 3). Inasmuch as 42 out of every 100 Spanish migrants to Europe were Andalusians, the vast reverse flow was channeled back to the areas least capable of receiving them (see table 7.9).

What do these figures really mean? What is the primary impetus forcing the Spanish migrants home? Juan Manuel Aguirre, director of social assistance for the Spanish in West Germany since the early 1960s, thought that unemployment was overestimated as the major contributing factor. He found that many Spaniards with good jobs and relative security were in the vanguard of the return flow:

> "People are returning who should be staying. Spaniards with good jobs. There is an interesting demographic fact associated with their move. Namely, that the largest number of returnees are evacuating the smaller German villages and towns . . . not the larger cities. There is a type of contagion, almost a psychosis, which builds up over a fatalistic resignation: 'One day soon now they are going to throw us out. Why not go now?' They see their friends and neighbors packing their bags and saying goodbye. Their departure from the smaller towns is dramatic and obvious. Those remaining begin to make their own plans to return home. There is a fear based on: 'We don't want to be the last one's left here.' Many of these people have been working in the same factory for a least 10 years and their jobs are secure. No, it is not just economics. Rather, the economic uncertainties have opened up deep wells of fatigue. Finally, even their well planned future is uncertain. However, their uncertain future in Spain begins to hold more fascination for them than an uncertain future in Germany based upon more or worse of the same."

A similar pattern was observed in the area of Rüsselsheim, the manufacturing center for the Opel automobile. The automotive industry traditionally employed a large number of foreign workers. It was one of the earliest and hardest hit by the recession. Don Marcelo, a Spanish priest, has worked in Rüsselsheim since 1964. He exchanged his white collar for a blue turtleneck sweater, and his office became the key to an informal network of labor exchange. His position and influence place him in contact with a greater number of Spanish workers now than during the peak years of immigration. In commenting upon the situation, he said:

> "There are fewer Spanish, Greeks, Portuguese, Italians . . . all except the Turks. The Turks hang on, and the Germans can't shake them off. But the rest of our foreign legion of Mediterranean laborers is slowly going home and not being replaced. Of the 5,000 Spaniards who worked in this factory in 1968, less than 900 remain. In 1973 I baptized 71

Table 7.9 Net Migration, 1982

1. Foreigners arriving in the Federal Republic of Germany	321,682	
Foreigners abandoning F.R.G.	433,268	
Net migration		-111,586
2. Spanish arrivals in the F.R.G.	3,781	
Spanish departures from the F.R.G.	10,392	
Net migration		-6,661
3. Greek arrivals in the F.R.G.	12,838	
Greek departures from the F.R.G.	18,137	
Net migration		-5,299
4. Italian arrivals in the F.R.G.	41,367	
Italian departures from the F.R.G.	81,771	
Net migration		-40,404
5. Portuguese arrivals in the F.R.G.	1,891	
Portuguese departures from the F.R.G.	9,173	
Net migration		-7,282
6. Turkish arrivals in the F.R.G.	42,713	
Turkish departures from the F.R.G.	86,852	
Net migration		-44,139
7. Yugoslav arrivals in the F.R.G.	22,207	
Yugoslav departures from the F.R.G.	41,210	
Net migration		-19,003

Source: *Wirtschaft und Statistik* 1983.

Spanish children—this year less than 20. Most of the unmarried men have gone home—even those who didn't have to worry about their jobs."

Others returned because they began to feel tired and old; they realized that they were close to losing their youth in Germany. They wanted to return to Spain before they were useless. There is a cohort of men now 50 and older who tend to stay on. They realize that if they return it will be impossible for them to make a living if they have failed to achieve their savings target.

A second factor which played an important role in influencing the migrants' decision to return was the idealized image of Spain they carried back to Germany after their summer vacations. They journeyed back to Spain in August, during the local fiestas, and were shocked at how well those who had not gone to Germany were living. They saw workers like themselves who owned a secondhand car. In the bars they were the ones being treated to rounds of hard liquor and taken to dinners and dances. Those who had stayed behind in Spain were peeling off 1,000 peseta bills from wads of money stuffed in their wallets the way the migrants had once been able to do back in the 1960s.

The reversal in roles had its effect. In the 1960s the migrants were envied. They tried to impress those who had stayed behind with their new success by a heavy-handed, often superfluous, spending. But now with inflation everywhere, with less advantageous exchange rates, with shorter workweeks, the migrant returned to Spain during his vacation with a greater sense of economy. Those who stayed in Spain felt that it was their turn to show the migrants how well they could live. Of course, their spending was equally fictitious in that most of the migrants' friends had no money in the bank, were loaded down with debts, and the impressive sums that they pulled from their pockets were all they had earned that week.

THE FINAL RETURN TO SPAIN

As noted earlier, accurate information on the return flow of migrants after 1974 was difficult to obtain. Official figures were conservative, portraying the return as a trickle. Unofficial sources, however, estimated that between 300,000 and 400,000 migrants returned from Western Europe between 1973 and 1977. Between 1978 and 1980, 300,000 more migrants returned to Spain. More important than the figures, however, was the new way the migrants were viewed in Spain. For years they had been considered a solution to many of the country's problems. The architects of the Primer Plan de Desarrollo were acutely aware of the necessity of using migration as an instrument to deal with the problem of unemployment in regions like Andalusia, an area which lacked a sufficient industrial base or agricultural cycle to provide even minimum employment throughout most of the year. Therefore, they estimated that 64,000 Spaniards would have to seek work outside the nation to facilitate the plan's objectives. In 1959 the Instituto Español de Emigración raised the estimate to 81,350. The Spanish workers, however, had a more realistic grasp of their situation. Their numbers surpassed the estimates of the planners; the yearly average for external migration between 1959 and 1963 was over 90,000.

By 1974 "the solution" had become "the problem." The exportation of workers was supposed to have long-term benefits on unemployment, but joblessness remained at one of the highest levels in a decade. In December of 1974 Andalusia harbored 37 percent of Spain's total unemployment, and the number has climbed steadily since. When questioned as to the major problems faced by the migrants on their return, 60 percent of our rural sample accurately stated that it would be finding work, 12 percent thought it would be readaptation to the community, and 8 percent readjustment to family life.

The migrants' remittances were supposed to help develop the country and alleviate long-standing regional differences. Unfortunately, the money was not used to develop the poorer areas such as southern Spain, from which the majority of migrants had come, but rather supported the richest zones. The largest savings bank in the south invested in the region barely 1.5 percent of the money deposited by the migrants in its fourteen branches, while investing over 98 percent in Madrid, the Basque provinces, and Barcelona. Remittances, therefore, actually accentuated regional differences rather than alleviating them.

Neither was the role the return migrants played in creating new jobs very encouraging. Those who tried to return permanently to their rural villages and agrotowns were usually married men with families. They emigrated between the ages of 28 and 32 and stayed a minimum of five years—many much longer. The unmarried and married migrants 30 or younger returned only temporarily to their home communities before finally leaving for the urban areas within Spain. While the money saved could be considerable, it was invariably spent in a nonproductive manner. The information on our questionnaire directly related to personal earnings and savings was false. What was significant was the demonstration of a high degree of mistrust and privacy in all economic matters. Nevertheless, from over 160 case studies, there was a range of savings between a low of $1,000 to a high of $75,000 where the husband, wife, and three unmarried children worked and pooled their incomes. The average, however, was $14,000. The savings were usually deposited in a regular account drawing low interest rates and were quickly withdrawn upon the migrant's return, to be spent first on housing, next on a small owner-operated business, and finally upon work vehicles.

The renaissance in house construction during the past fifteen years has been referred to as "cosmetic development"—a superficial facelifting with no fundamental change in the local social or employment structure. Nearly 60 percent of the respondents to the questionnaire spent their savings on housing and furniture, 5 percent on a business, and another 5 percent on land not related to housing. When asked if they would spend their savings in the same manner if given another opportunity, 64 percent answered affirmatively.

The purchasing behavior of all the Andalusians has been strongly affected by the yearly flood of international tourists and the new material desires of the migrants returning from Western Europe. This trend in consumption was first noted in a 1967 market survey in which the researchers expressed considerable surprise at the high percentage of poor families that had acquired the more expensive domestic appliances such as refrigerators, washing machines, etc. The new patterns of consumption in Andalusia are indicative of the general change in the structure of households and the age composition of the population. Between 1967 and 1977 the number of Spanish households rose from 8 to 9.2 million. The average number of persons per household, however, dropped from 4 to 3.8, still one of the higher figures in Western Europe. The youth of these households can be seen in the population figures for 1977 in which 70 percent of Spain's 36 million inhabitants were under the age of 40. After decades of belt-tightening this young generation developed new consumption patterns that "are less governed by ecological or sociopolitical considerations" and have been referred to as "conspicuously unascetic." This 1977 business survey of the new Spanish markets drew a profile of a young, newly affluent, acquisitive generation where "the superfluous sells very well" (Business International 1977, 105–106). Regardless of the severe problems of unemployment, especially among those seeking jobs for the first time, many of those who had jobs considered their type of employment superior to that of their parents. Of course, a better job in Spain does not automatically mean a significant change in one's class position. It does, however, provide greater amounts of discretionary income to purchase the facade of luxury.

Migration was supposed to open new paths of social mobility for the workers by teaching them skills which would provide them with opportunities for social promotion upon their return to Spain. In Germany, however, these migrants filled the lower position in the work hierarchy, labored at relatively unskilled jobs, or were plugged into assembly lines as part of a specialized production force. A migrant who had worked in the Opel factory in Germany was not prepared to open a garage in his home community.

Around 87 percent of the migrants sampled in our 1977 questionnaire classified themselves before migrating as agricultural day laborers without a specialized skill. Upon their return 43.8 percent still placed themselves in the same basic category regardless of the fact that none of them had been employed in agricultural activities when working in West Germany. This is not to say that they personally believed that they had returned the same as they had left. They placed considerable value on their experience outside of Andalusia. When asked about what aspects of their life had changed the most, apart from their actual occupation back in Andalusia, 32.1 percent responded that the way they worked and their level of living had changed the most. Only 2.2 percent believed that their level had actually fallen.

The majority in each of the three groups sampled—elites, migrants, and nonmigrants—believed that the overall effects of migration were positive for the individuals and their communities. Most of the people considered the professional capacity of the migrants, compared to that of the nonmigrants, to be basically the same as before migration. When the migrants returned, they were seen as possessing an improved professional capacity and a higher level of initiative, particularly the elites (55 percent). However, when the migrants were asked if they had learned a new skill in Germany, only 27 percent noted a significant change. What seems to be a strong positive evaluation of the migrants and their initiative—a belief in their changed status and professional abilities—in many ways turns out to be a condemnation. Simply stated: yes, the migrants have changed and improved themselves. No, these improvements will be of little assistance to them in their home communities. Where might they realize their new potential? Outside the community to the north in the more industrialized regions. If the migrants do not readapt to the rhythm of their old lives, they soon discover that their families are against them, their friends are against them, and the local authorities are against them, and the individuals thought to have the most initiative will soon find that they have the least support.

In terms of assumptions concerning the significance of personal action and development in Andalusia, all three groups in our sample agreed that the condition of the Spanish worker depended more upon overall economic development of the country than upon workers' political activity. The returnees were somewhat more evenly divided between these two positions. When asked, however, if they knew of any workers who had become relatively prosperous on their own, there was a clear division between the elites who did and the migrants and nonmigrants who did not. While the elites attributed the workers' success to initiative and intelligence, the migrants and nonmigrants ranked simple hard work higher.

The most significant constraints in Spain which limit the migrants' initiative are of an economic nature. It is contradictory, but the migrants feel that a man with initiative must be "given" work, credit, and outside benefits if he is to succeed. In Andalusia, while the migrants consider the redistribution of land and a change of power holders to be one of the most pressing problems, the elites and nonmigrants only speak about changing the wealthy's mentality. When discussing agricultural reform in Andalusia, the returnees want land collectivization to ensure distribution to those who work it. The elites are primarily concerned with increased mechanization and better markets for their agricultural products. It is only the nonmigrant who places a greater emphasis upon creating local industries. Regardless of their differences, the three groups agree that Andalusia must find "union" and "work" if it is to prosper—two factors that outranked those of justice, order, peace, or liberty.

While the migrants changed their attitudes towards work, there appears to have been little or no change concerning their attitude toward the traditional structure of the family and a woman's role in the family; 72.3 percent expressed the opinion that everything had remained pretty much the same (see table 7.10). In fact, the male migrants' experience in Germany actually intensified their traditionally conservative position. The distribution of answers in table 7.11 indicates that of the three groups sampled, the return migrants were the most extreme in believing that the woman's place was in the home, that she was not equal to a man, and that she would never achieve that equality. These responses on the part of the mi-

Table 7.10 Life Changes Resulting from Emigration

Changes upon return	Great change		Little change		No change		Don't Understand		No Answer		TOTAL	
	N	%	N	%	N	%	N	%	N	%	N	%
Your living standards	43	31.4	51	37.2	39	28.5	1	0.7	3	2.2	137	100
Your form of work	44	32.1	33	24.1	56	40.9	1	0.7	3	2.2	137	100
Your friendships	20	14.6	32.	23.4	80	58.4	1	0.7	4	2.9	137	100
Your attitude toward local costumes	23	16.8	35	25.5	75	54.7	1	0.7	3	2.2	137	100
Your forms of amusements	20	14.6	33	24.1	79	57.7	1	0.7	4	2.9	137	100
Your family relations	9	6.6	24	17.5	99	72.3	1	0.7	4	2.9	137	100
The way you view social problems	26	19.0	32	23.4	69	50.4	5	3.6	5	3.6	137	100
Your attitudes toward politics	18	13.1	27	19.7	73	53.3	9	6.6	10	7.3	137	100
Your attitudes toward religion	9	6.6	20	14.6	92	67.2	6	4.4	10	7.3	137	100

Source: Encuesta de Emigración de 1977.

Table 7.11 Opinions Concerning Equality between the Sexes and the Effect of Labor Migration

Opinion concerning the women's roles	Elite		Mig-grants		Non Mig-grants		TOTAL	
	N	%	N	%	N	%	N	%
Women are equal to men	95	74,2	55	40,1	119	47,8	269	52,3
Women will never be considerd equal to men	12	9,4	13	9,5	23	9,2	48	9,3
A woman's place is in the home	14	10,9	61	44,5	92	36,9	167	32,5
Don't understand	2	1,6	4	2,9	11	4,4	17	3,3
No opinion	5	3,9	4	2,9	4	1,6	13	2,5
TOTAL	128	100	137	100	249	100	514	100

Source: Encuesta de Emigración de 1977.

grants, however, deal more with their values and reaction to a state of affairs in which their wives and daughters play an increasingly important role as wage earners outside the home and have made important inroads into the areas of decision making thought of as male prerogatives. The wives and daughters of the elite, whose responses are more egalitarian, are far more restricted in their actual behavior.

The case of Juan is similar to that of thousands of Andalusian migrants who left their rural communities for Germany in the mid-1960s. Juan saw his work in Germany as the only way to better himself at home. For six years he worked in the Teves-Thompson factory in Hanover. Twice monthly he sent a major part of his salary to his wife. She used it to purchase an old house in a better section of the town, demolished it, and reconstructed a new one in its place. She hung an overly large, expensive, cut glass chandelier in the front room. She bought a Formica bookcase on which to display the new 17-inch German television set, tape recorder, a row of leather-bound books, and a plastic doll in flamenco dress. A modern tile bathroom was erected where the mule shed had once stood. Finally, a three-foot wide stairway, with slabs of marble, was constructed leading up to two small sleeping rooms on the second floor.

When Juan finally tired of Germany and rationalized that he had realized his savings target, he returned home seeking the social validation he was unable to obtain earlier. He experienced nothing but problems after his decision to return permanently to Spain. He had particular difficulty understanding the bureaucratic papers sent to him from Madrid concerning his difficulties with the local labor syndicate which had canceled his social security.

"I don't understand any of it. They don't want us to live like persons. Ever since I've returned it's been trouble with work and my papers. The fat ones in the local labor syndicate keep on trying to take away the only insurance we migrants have—our agricultural cards. They say that because I worked in a factory in Germany I am no longer an agricultural laborer. I have to show them that I worked in the fields for 90 days."

During the first year of his return, Juan was able to find work for a total of only 58 days unloading trucks on the highway and picking olives. The money remaining after paying off the loans on the house was his family's major source of support while Juan looked for work. In discussing the political changes reforming Spain after Franco's death and Juan's return, Juan said:

"Nothing really changes here. All our money has gone into the pockets of the powerful—those with the land and those who control our papers. I don't care about politics. I care about work! I want a steady job here like I had in Germany. I want to work with people who respect me. My friends and I will go with those who give us real jobs . . . we don't care what they call themselves."

Many of the return migrants spoke of re-emigration, but re-emigration was impossible except for those few who still had their annual, nine-month contracts with Switzerland. There was no reentry into a country like Germany from which they had been absent over three months. Even the position of those with contracts, however, was tenuous. Federico had been working in Switzerland for eighteen years. He had a contract with a construction firm in Geneva which was building a nuclear power facility in the mountains on the French border. He saw his wife two or three months each year. During the years he had been away she had given birth to nine children, four of whom had survived.

In Geneva Federico lived in a prefabricated German barracks, used to house troops in France during World War II, which had been purchased by the Swiss construction firm and reassembled in Geneva to house their foreign work force. The barracks were depressing wooden structures. To brighten the gloom Federico painted landscapes of his village on the panels of his cabinets and door. In Spain, however, he lived in a new two-story house with a tiled bath, marble staircase, four bedrooms, and a refrigerator and washing machine.

When his children were younger, they knew their father only from his photograph. As they grew older and Federico returned for his vacations, the children were irritated with his exercise of authority and were often disrespectful. His wife said that the happiest time of the year was the two months before his return:

> "Then the house is filled with expectation that Papa is coming home. What will he bring? Should I buy a new dress and a little rouge for my cheeks? But then after the first two days, when we are all so very happy together, I begin to think that in two months he will have to return to Switzerland."

Her mood of discouragement affected the entire household, and Federico began to spend his days with the other migrants in the local bars. Once again he felt isolated, though this time it was within his own village. His situation was similar to that of the other dwindling numbers of migrants holding on to their jobs in Western Europe. It is an unending round of drudgery and frustration that continues until they stop migrating. Finding no work on their return to their villages and towns, many move for a last time to the provincial capitals. They sell the homes that they had sacrificed their youth to build and move in with their older children. They place their hope in these children, whose future role, they believe, is to support their aging parents.

CONCLUSION

There is an interesting relationship between the family, work in the agricultural areas of Andalusia, and migration. In 1950 there was a revival of agricultural activity. The new necessities of the postwar years created a situation in which there was a scramble to use as much valuable land as possible. The growth of the population, as well as its immobility, created a new demand for agricultural products. Even land above 1,500 meters in the sierras of Andalusia, which was generally used only for pasturage, started to be cultivated. In 1958 and 1959, with the opening up of new migration opportunities, a new phenomenon developed. With the outflow of labor, as well as its rising cost, the cultivation of marginal land slowly began to be abandoned. Migration opened up a new fount of riches for those remaining behind, and as a result of remittances, decreased the scale of their traditional agricultural activities. For the first time in decades, work had become profitable for the Andaluz, even though it was only profitable outside of his region.

Regardless of the prescriptions for cultural change correlated with the theories of motivation and adult socialization, there remains an existing economic structure in the south of Spain into which the migrants are born. It is formed by an agricultural elite that never really adapted itself to the investment and marketing procedures of the 20th century.

Looking at migration, the family, and its role in Andalusia, we are beginning to comprehend that their culture and behavior is really an adaptation to the lack of economic and social development in the south, not the cause, as has been postulated by the developmental economists. The many cultural stereotypes of the Andalusian, based upon his poor work habits, have their origins in an endemic system of underemployment and/or unemployment. The majority in Andalusia are adapting to the minority's failure to adapt its tightly controlled resources to modern capitalist procedures of investment and production.

When the Andalusians migrate out of the matrix of the traditional economic structure, where they are considered unproductive and lazy, their productivity increases dramatically. In countries like Germany, France, Switzerland, etc., they are highly valued by their employers, if not by the population at large. Their traditional behavior is challenged, new roles are learned, and new skills acquired. The immigration areas (both internal and external), where the migrants' behavior remains the same, are those areas where the cultural patterns and social system are determined by the traditional upper classes who control the economy and fill the bureaucracies.

Nevertheless, upon the migrants' return to Andalusia they must sooner or later adapt to the old realities, regardless of what was painfully learned outside their community and region. In a very real sense, when we speak about the migrants' return, we are speaking about their readaptation. How can their earnings and training have any value in areas which have not changed economically or socially since their original departure? Yes, there have been major political reforms. There have not been, however, any accompanying changes in the economic system. The economic structure continues to be dominated by a traditional elite concerned with neither regional nor national development. The continued increase in population offsets the temporary deficits created by out-migration. Investment opportunities are few. Work remains scarce. Therefore, the structure remains largely the same.

NOTES

1. This article is based upon a synthesis and summary of fieldwork and writing carried out in Western Europe from 1966 to 1978. The period from 1966 to 1968 was funded by

the Foreign Area Fellowship Program. For a comparison of the Spanish material with that concerning return migration to Portugal, see Gregory and Cazorla 1985.

2. In this section we have relied upon the following sources for our information pertaining to national economic and demographic trends in Spain: Baklanoff 1978; the Spanish Institute of Emigration's annual reports; the *OECD Economic Surveys* for Spain 1969–1979; FOESA 1975.

3. Two of Stuart Holland's works have made a thorough analysis of the reasons for the persistence of severe regional problems in capitalist economies. While we disagree with his solutions based on more direct state intervention, his works have been of great benefit to us in this paper (1976a; 1976b).

4. Much of the material in this section is based on a field study carried out in collaboration with Professor José Cazorla of the University of Granada, from 1976 to 1978. Comparative materials were gathered in the Algarve in southern Portugal by Professor Joan Neto. The project was funded by the Ford Foundation.

5. Professor Cazorla designed two questionnaires based upon an analysis of the field notes, interviews, and case study materials gathered from July 1976 through June 1977. Professor Gregory directed the field studies in Andalusia. For a more complete analysis of these questionnaires see Cazorla 1980. The first questionnaire sampled 129 elites (mayors, priests, notaries, large landowners, prominent business figures and politicians), 136 return migrants, and 246 nonmigrants (those members of the community with a social and economic background similar to that of the migrants, but who had rejected migration as a possible solution to local problems). The second questionnaire was administered to 248 delegates of the largest chain of savings banks in Andalusia. The object was to obtain a complementary picture of the flow of remittances into the areas, the levels of migrants' savings, and their types of investments. Throughout this study the source of our unpublished survey is referred to as Enquesta de Emigración de 1977.

6. The national figures for Spain are to be taken only as estimates. The statistical information for Germany is superior to that for Spain. In both cases, however, they must be read with a certain amount of care. Figures in the various tables do not always agree because of the different sources from which they were gathered. Nevertheless, they do give an accurate picture of the general trends.

7. We are indebted to Juan Manuel Aguirre, director of the network of social workers for Spanish migrants in Germany, for giving us access to the Social Centers throughout Germany. He also provided us with a wealth of unpublished and officially circulated comparative materials gathered by his staff in their "Boletín de Información."

REFERENCES

Anderson, Charles W.

1970 *The Political Economy of Modern Spain: Policy Making in an Authoritarian System*. Madison: University of Wisconsin Press.

Baklanoff, Eric N.

1978 *The Economic Transformation of Spain and Portugal*. New York: Praeger.

Banco de Bilbao

1975 *Annual Report*

Böhning, W. R.

1980 "Guest Worker Employment, with Special Reference to the Federal Republic of Germany, France and Switzerland—Lessons for the United States." Working Paper. Center for Philosophy and Public Policy, University of Maryland.

Bovenkerk, Frank
1974 *The Sociology of Return Migration: A Bibliographic Essay*. The Hague: Martinus Nijhoff.

Business International Research Report
1977 "The New Spain: Business Problems and Opportunities."

Castles, Stephen, and Kosack, Godula
1973 *Immigrant Workers and Class Structure in Western Europe*. London: Oxford University Press.

Cazorla, José
1965 *Factores de La Estructura Económica de Andalucia*. Publicaciones de la Caja de Ahorros de Granada.
1978 "Paro y Emigración, Los Males Endémicos de Andalucía: Algunas Sugerencias." *Revista de Estudios Regionales* no. 2: 17–37.
1979 "Emigración y Subdesarrollo: El Contexto Socio-Político de un Fenómeno Actual." *Agricultura y Sociedad* 11: 111–128.
1980 "Mentalidad Modernizante, Trabajo y Cambio en los Retornados Andaluces." *Revista Española de Investigaciones Sociológicas,* no. 11, Julio–Septiembre.

Council of Europe
1978 *Population Decline in Europe*. New York: St. Martin's.

FOESA, Fundación
1975 *Informe Sociológico sobre la Situación de España*. Madrid: Euramerica.

García Fernandez, Jesús
1965 *La Emigración Exterior de España*. Barcelona: Ariel.

Gendt, Rein van
1977 *Return Migration and Reintegration Services*. Paris: OECD.

Gregory, David
1975 "Extraños en su Propia Tierra: El Retorno." *Información Comercial Española* 503: 102–109.
1976 "Rural Exodus and the Perpetuation of Andalusia." In *Economic Transformation and Steady-State Values,* edited by Edward Hansen. New York: Queens College Press.
1978 *La Odisea Andaluza: Una Emigración Intereuropea*. Madrid: Tecnos.

Gregory, David, and Cazorla, José
1985 "Intra-European Migration and Regional Development: Spain and Portugal." In *Guests Come to Stay: The Effects of European Labor Migration on Sending and Receiving Countries,* edited by Rosemarie Rogers, 231–262. Boulder, Colo.: Westview Press.

Heckmann, Friedrich
1978 "Socio-Structural Analysis of Immigrant Worker Minorities: The Case of West-Germany." Sozialwissenschafliches Institut der Universitat Erlangen, Nürnberg. Xerox.
1980 "Temporary Labor Migration or Immigration? 'Guest Workers in the Federal Republic of Germany.' " Lehrstuhl für Soziologie und Sozialanthropologie, Nürnberg. Xerox.

Hermida, R.; Blasco, J.; and Guereca, L.
1959 *La Emigración Española y el Desarrollo Economica*. Madrid: Instituto Español de Emigración.

Hofmann-Nowotny, Hans-Joachim

1978 "European Migration after World War II." In *Human Migration Patterns and Policies,* edited by William McNeill and Ruth Adams, 85–105. Bloomington: University of Indiana Press.

Holland, Stuart

1976a *Capital versus the Regions.* New York: St. Martin's.

1976b *The Regional Problem.* London: Macmillan.

Hönekopp, Elmar, and Ullmann, Hans

1980 "The Effect of Immigration on Social Structure: Federal Republic of Germany." Institute for Labour Market Research, Nürnberg. Xerox.

Instituto Español de Emigración

1969–1980 *Estadísticas de Emigración Exterior.* Madrid: Minesterio de Trabajo.

Kayser, Bernard

1977 "European Migrations: The New Pattern." *International Migration Review* 11: 232–240.

Kayser, B., and dos Santos, Americo

1979 *Migration, Growth and Development.* Paris: OECD.

Körte, Hermann

1980 "The Development and Significance of Labor Migration and Employment of Foreigners in the Federal Republic of Germany between 1950 and 1979." Universität Bochum. Xerox.

Naylon, John

1975 *Andalusia.* London: Oxford University Press.

Organization for Economic Cooperation and Development

1966 *International Management Seminar on Emigrant Workers Returning to the Home Country, Athens.* Paris.

1969–1979 *OECD Economic Surveys: Spain.* Annual. Paris.

1976 *The Migratory Chain.* Paris.

1979 *Migration, Growth & Development.* Paris.

Paine, Suzanne

1977 "The Changing Role of Migrant Labour in the Advanced Capitalist Economies of Western Europe." In *Government, Business and Labor in European Capitalism,* edited by Richard Griffiths. London: Europotentials Press.

1979 "Replacement of the West European Migrant Labour System by Investment in the European Periphery." In *Underdeveloped Europe: Studies in Core-Periphery Relations,* edited by Dudley Seers, Bernard Schaffer, and Marja-Liisa Kiljunen, 65–75. New York: Humanities Press.

Piore, M.

1979 *Birds of Passage: Migrant Labor in Industrial Societies.* New York: Cambridge University Press.

Rhoades, Robert

1978 "Intra-European Return Migration and Rural Development: Lessons from the Spanish Case." *Human Organization* 37: 136–47.

Secretaria de Estado da Emigraçao

1974 *Boletim Anual.* Ministerio do Trabalho. Lisboa.

Tapinos, George, and Piotro, Phyllis
1978 *Six Billion People: Demographic Dilemmas and World Politics*. New York: McGraw-Hill.

Tilly, Charles
1978 "Migrations in Modern European History." In *Human Migration Patterns and Policies,* edited by William McNeill and Ruth Adams. Bloomington: University of Indiana Press.

Trivino, Villalain
1963 "Emigraciones Especiales." In *La Emigración Como Problema*. Seminarios 17, Madrid.

Vanhecke, Charles
1980 "Andalusia's Controversial Difference." *The Guardian* April 27: 12.

8 Factory and Community in a West German Immigrant Neighborhood

Ann H. L. Sontz

ABSTRACT. Sontz's article focuses on a more specific aspect of migration than do the previous contributions: the work setting and its influence on social relationships outside the factory context. She aims to demonstrate that the manner in which different migratory waves are integrated in different niches in the industrial edifice has a bearing on the totality of the migratory experience.

Sontz argues that changing relations of production may explain differences in the degree of assimilation of foreign workers into the host society: The early migrants of diverse ethnic backgrounds who were recruited in the mid-19th century filled skilled positions and enjoyed a social and economic status superior to many of the locals who engaged in the more menial tasks in the securing of raw materials and production. Consequently, they were rapidly accepted by their local counterparts and acted to further their joint interests through effective labor organization.

Since the turn of the century, however, a sharpening of the separation between management and workers, increasing state involvement in welfare functions, deskilling of many traditional positions, and round-the-clock operation have affected the work situation. The skilled glassblowers whose jobs were eliminated through automation were able to move laterally into other skilled jobs. With spiraling production after World War II, the factory began to hire workers again. However, the new jobs largely were for unskilled workers. Most of these were recruited from abroad. Already isolated from the local workers by their lowly position in the industrial hierarchy, these workers were also more likely to accept those jobs and work shifts that isolated them even further. This process contributed heavily to the ethnic segmentation of contemporary Nordstadt.

INTRODUCTION

Although the literature on many aspects of intra-European labor migration in the postwar era has proliferated during the past decade,[1] two general trends in the literature nevertheless appear prominent. First, a distinct focus on the role of intra-European labor migration in fostering regional unification has evolved.[2] The degree of both economic and cultural integration has been measured largely in terms of spurts and declines in transnational migration flows, or in rates of migrant entry into the industrial and manufacturing sectors of north European countries. Additionally, the historical existence of intra-European labor migration has been emphasized and has occasionally been depicted as but an early manifestation of a trend towards West European integration. Second, and on a similarly macrosocial level, the past decade has also seen a growth in the attempt to assess, through broad attitudinal surveys and the statistical elucidation of migrant residence and settlement, church memberships, and patterns of participation in industrial unions, the extent to which these migrants have adjusted to the north European "host" societies in which they now find themselves.

In what follows I have tried to draw together a few of these threads of concern in order to see how migratory movements in Europe and any possible tendencies towards cultural integration work out, or fail to work themselves out, in *one* north European industrial locality where industrial in-migration has long been integral to the course of community development. For whatever the contributions of intra-European labor migration to cultural or economic metamorphosis in regional or macroscopic perspective, the available literature continues to suffer from a relative paucity of detailed case studies of industrial migrants *sur place,* from a lack of a feel for happenings at the workplace, and from an absence of any clear sense of the actual impact of the industrial work in which migrants are involved on ties among migrants or between migrants and members of "host" localities. This, then—a sketch of the link between industry and the collective life of a West German neighborhood with a substantial Mediterranean migrant population—represents a small foray into the microscopic. At best only advisory with respect to configurations of regional integration, it is nonetheless specific local findings that provide a comparative basis for an understanding of the growing number of other pluralistic north European industrial localities which comprehend migrant populations of Mediterranean origin, and that will ultimately inform processes of integration within the European community at large.

I first present a brief outline of the history of Nordstadt—an industrial neighborhood located on the fringe of a large West German urban center—and of the growth of Nordstadt's sprawling glass manufacturing firm which was founded there in the late 10th century and which provoked a series of past and present in-migrations of transnational laborers and their families. How each wave of migrants was absorbed into differing niches in the glass factory's occupational structure and how work organization conditioned extrafactory relationships in Nordstadt's past and in the contemporary neighborhood are discussed. Though this paper is less analytical than documentary, a major aim has been to stress that in Nordstadt, at least, the adaptation of cross-national labor migrants cannot be fully understood without an examination of the nature and context of that very labor for which in-migration itself was often originally undertaken.

HISTORICAL SETTING

The contemporary industrial locality of Nordstadt was a small and independent agricultural marketing town for over 1,000 years.[3] Nordstadt was founded in 870 A.D. when a French knight established a convent and the still-standing Church of St. Anne's in the north of today's neighborhood. Late in the 13th century the convent was given the right to raise its own tariffs, and in the 14th century the small market town that had grown up around convent and church was elevated to the status of a "free" city. By 1400 Nordstadt had a town wall, an army, and its own currency. In the 1600s, however, Nordstadt apparently began to experience more turbulent times, for it was plundered by both the Dutch and the Swedes; at the end of the 18th century Nordstadt was again occupied by foreign troops after the town had become part of a French municipal district. Though Nordstadt soon came under Prussian rule, it remained a small, rural market town of less than 1,000 residents until a number of interrelated events significantly altered the course of Nordstadt's economic development.

The first of these events was the founding in the 1830s of the German railroad system which linked Nordstadt to several cities on the Rhine. This meant, among other things, that for the first time in its history Nordstadt could import and export goods on a large scale. The existence of efficient transportation links also constituted a major reason behind the establishment of a glassworks in the southern part of Nordstadt in the 1860s. It was this more crucial occurrence which prompted the eventual end of the town's century-old economic dependence on the marketing of agricultural products and closely wedded its future to the manufacturing and industrial way of life.

It is unfortunate that much of Nordstadt's past is represented by little more than a chronological accounting of dates and events and a limited amount of factual detail. Nordstadt was in existence during eras of extraordinary urban and economic resurgence and, especially in the Middle Ages, during increasing encroachment by burghers on the military and judicial authority of feudal lords. To a large extent, these were also times when for a variety of reasons—plague, trade, famine, and war among them—people, if not in the massive numbers with which we are familiar today, were definitely on the move. However modest an urban settlement Nordstadt was, it must have participated in these processes. Indeed, the consistent conquest of the town by foreign invaders appears to have been an undeniable facet of community life.

To suggest, therefore, that the founding of Nordstadt's glassworks signified the close of an isolated epoch in Nordstadt's history would be misleading. What did change with the establishment of the glass firm was that the town's links to the wider world as well as the tenor of its local ties were brought decisively under the sway of the evolving structures of industrial capitalism. In Nordstadt these structures ensured that future invasions by outsiders would be comparatively gentle ones, guided as much by the broad impersonal forces of the European economic or political scene as by the rational decision-making processes of a local managerial elite. The head of this elite and the founder of the glassworks was—like many before him—a stranger to the town as well. It was his successful business venture which ultimately hastened Nordstadt's already growing transformation from a small marketing town to an industrial community.

Nordstadt itself was in a highly advantageous position for both the manufacture and distribution of glass products (Seeling 1964, 16–17). The raw materials of glass production, including sand and potash, were to be found in the rural areas near Nordstadt's eastern limits; fuel to fire the glass ovens was readily available in the form of coal that was mined less than fifty miles away in the Ruhr Valley. Further, the newly formed German railway system connected the town directly to the Rhine city of Ebbesthal. From there, shipping facilities reached northward to Rotterdam and southward towards the vineyards of the Mosel. Since Ebbesthal and other European centers were themselves undergoing a process of rapid industrialization, Nordstadt was conveniently located at the nexus of an expanding national and international market for bottles and other materials made of glass.

What the glassworks' founder did not find in Nordstadt were experienced glassblowers. Unlike Bavaria, Saxony, and other regions in Germany, the Rhineland and the Ruhr had little tradition in the age-old art of glassmaking. Necessary workers were therefore recruited, initially on the basis of three-year, renewable contracts, from the east and south of Germany, from Russia and the Baltic states, and especially from Poland (Seeling 1964, 48). In these areas small glass foundries had evolved as adjuncts of large agricultural estates. When these estates began to decline in the 1860s, the glassblowers suffered severe unemployment and became a fertile field for the recruitment policies of Nordstadt's newly established glass firm. Between the early 1860s, or soon after the glassworks was founded, and the turn of the century, nearly 300 glassblowers and their families migrated to Nordstadt (Seeling 1964, 9). The scope of the demographic impact of the in-migrants is suggested by the fact that during these four decades, Nordstadt's population grew from slightly less than 800 inhabitants to almost 3,000 persons, a figure that approximates Nordstadt's present population numbers (Seeling 1964, 40–41). The rise in population indicates that in the relatively short space of forty years, the majority of Nordstadt's residents had come to be directly or indirectly associated with the town's most recently established, yet already by then, most economically promising industrial employer.

WORK INSTITUTIONS AND COMMUNITY: THE EARLY YEARS

In view of the sharp population increase, the relatively sudden growth of an ethnically heterogeneous work force, and the inexorable shift towards an industrial way of life, there is surprisingly little evidence that anything more serious than occasional verbal arguments among glassblowers ruffled the surface of

Nordstadt in the decades immediately following the establishment of the glassworks. The only jarring note in this comparatively tranquil period in Nordstadt's history appears to have been the participation of the majority of glassmakers in a brief work stoppage for better wages in the autumn of 1901 (Seeling 1964, 69–70), a year which also saw other types of craftsmen go out on short strikes throughout much of Germany. Some of the more relevant questions that can be asked of this period in Nordstadt's past are: How was this seeming unity of purpose achieved by an ethnically diverse population of glassmakers who had emigrated to Nordstadt only a few years before? Why did variability in language and national origin not serve to undermine a concerted action on the part of the immigrants? And was the experience of having a common trade or shared economic need mainly responsible for blunting these otherwise stark differences in background?

Certainly, as participants in an age-old craft, the immigrant glassblowers must have felt a commonality of experience. Yet as evidence from elsewhere in the industrializing world demonstrates, even though workers use the same technological mode of production and have similar status, they cannot always transform their shared interests into an active, organized quest for common goals. In the absence of other integrating forces, the differing ethnicity of skilled workers has constituted a serious threat to the maintenance of unity during industrial strikes (Brody 1960, 120–121; Epstein 1958, 30–31; Warner and Low 1947, 33). It may be useful, then, to survey some of the major local integrating processes in Nordstadt at the turn of the century. I would suggest that these comprehend processes inherent in the glassworks itself—the role of the immigrant glassmakers in the process of glass production, and the relationship between the institutions of the factory and the lives of Nordstadt's resident glassblowers and their families.

Glass production in Nordstadt at the turn of the century was dependent on the hallowed tradition of hand-blown glass by highly skilled glassblowers. Unskilled workers, drawn from Nordstadt's small indigenous population and from surrounding rural areas, mixed the raw materials and transferred them to the ovens where they were melted in the open heat. The glassblowers were then summoned from their company apartments in order to blow the mouth and body of the bottles with a thin-stemmed pipe. After the bottles had cooled, the glassblowers returned home, and unskilled laborers readied and packed the bottles for shipment in the loading areas. When the ovens were empty, a new mixture of raw materials was prepared by the unskilled workers, who transferred them to the ovens where this mixture or "batch" was once again melted in the open heat until ready for blowing. Within the framework of this general process of turn-of-the-century glass production, one glassmaker in Nordstadt was able to produce between 250 and 350 bottles during the course of an eight-hour period (Seeling 1964, 62–63).

The shared art of glassblowing might well have fostered a growing sense of common identity during the work stoppage and contributed to a unified stance during that time. Further, as even this brief sketch of early 20th-century glassmaking suggests, the experience of practicing a common craft might have been heightened by the fact that the glassblowers, because they formed a particular task-group, were functionally segregated from other workers at the plant and were the only skilled laborers involved in the production process. An additional integrating factor among the ethnically diverse glassblowers was that in comparison to the unskilled laborers at the firm, the glassmakers were a stable and settled work force. Their contracts had originally been of three-year duration. Yet a decline of employment opportunities in their homelands prompted the glassblowers to remain in the town and to bring their families to Nordstadt to reside with them. Unskilled laborers, in contrast, were often part-time agriculturalists, unmarried youths who moved easily to other sources of employment, or wandering workers with no specific trade (Seeling 1964, 66). A lack of desired employment opportunities as well as the practice of a traditional craft must have fostered both a strong commitment to the glass factory and to Nordstadt itself and rendered the glassblowers increasingly likely to voice any common grievances in some form of joint or concerted action.[4]

Yet another feature of the industrial context which provoked the unified stance of the glassmakers during the strike was the virtual absence of ethnically segregated task-groups at the plant (Seeling 1964, 70–77). Around each of the glassworks' nine ovens, thirty-five glassblowers used to stand. The glassblowers, however, were apparently assigned to particular ovens without reference to ethnicity. That task-groups were not organized along ethnic lines encouraged a high degree of daily contact among glassblowers of diverse origin and helped to break down potentially partisan ethnic barriers.

A final characteristic of the glassworks which may have speeded the integration process among the glassblowers lay in the relationship that existed between the factory's management personnel and the craftsmen and their families. The factory's owner involved himself directly in the lives of the immigrants, helping them to fill out and file citizenship papers and mediating personal disputes. Factory funds provided an old-age home for elderly glassmakers and a kindergarten for workers' children. Glassmakers were also provided with old-age, accident, and medical insurance (Seeling 1964, 74). Moreover, the factory erected ten blocks of company housing, with apartments available at a minimal cost, and initiated associations—a song club, smoking club, and sports club—which appear to have been organized for glassmakers largely without reference to national origin (Seeling 1964, 73). The ethnically based provincial clubs, regional associations, and *Landsmannschaften* so familiar from the urban anthropological literature on migrants never seem to have arisen in Nordstadt and therefore never became a divisive force in the glassblowers' way of life.[5]

In a variety of ways, therefore, the glassworks had by the turn of the century helped transform the agriculturally oriented marketing town of Nordstadt into a residential unit with what Epstein has termed a "unitary structure" (1958, 153)—a locality wherein the predominant factory organization has been designed to influence almost every aspect of its inhabitants' existence. With the major exception of Nordstadt's political offices, which remained in the hands of the indigenous local gentry (Seeling 1964, 81), there were few spheres of life in the town that by 1900 had not fallen under the ruling presence of the glass factory. This was especially true with respect to Nordstadt's immigrant glassblowers and their families who had come to make up the majority of the town's population. The unique position of the skilled glassmakers in the production process as well as the firm's influential role in providing the in-migrants with low-cost housing and welfare programs undoubtedly conditioned their permanent settlement in the town and set the stage for the growth of an ethnically heterogeneous immigrant population into an eventually homogeneous "German" community.

One reflection of the increasing integration of the immigrant community is indicated in the marriage register of St. Anne's, where it is recorded that between the years 1890 and 1900 more than half the marriages among children of the glassblowers were contracted between those whose parents had originally migrated to Nordstadt from different countries or from various provinces within Germany. Equally reflective of integrative tendencies in Nordstadt was the evolution there of a German dialect that mirrored the presence of migrants from eastern and northern German provinces, as well as from the eastern regions of the European continent, and that became the lingua franca among the glassmakers and their families (Seeling 1964, 42). The unanimity of the glassblowers during the short work stoppage was in itself a significant manifestation of an increasing state of integration within the ethnically diverse immigrant community, a state which appears to have been largely rooted in factory institutions and the local organization of labor.

WORK INSTITUTIONS AND TODAY'S COMMUNITY: IN-MIGRANTS FROM SOUTHERN ITALY

Nordstadt's second wave of immigrants began to arrive from southern Italy in the late 1950s. By the end of the 1960s Nordstadt's southern Italian population had grown to a little over 800 persons and comprehended unskilled workers at the glass plant along with a complement of their wives and children (see figures 8.1 and 8.2). Though the glass factory and its surrounding low-cost workers' housing had remained intact (Nordstadt's physical plant having escaped damage in the Allied bombing attacks during the Second World War), several significant changes in the local industrial environment had occurred during the fifty-odd years preceding the southern Italian settlement. These changes had engendered an increasing need for a pool of unskilled laborers just at a time when these were locally unavailable and when underemployment and unemployment in the more rural regions of the Mediterranean Basin were rife. Such changes in the local industrial context, however, had not acted to ensure the integration of Nordstadt's more recent industrial in-migrants into the ongoing life of the locality.

One shift in Nordstadt in the decades following the turn of the century involved corporate organization and corporation-community relations. In the late 1920s, shortly after Nordstadt had lost its independent political base and become part of

Figure 8.1 Age-Sex Structure of German Nordstadters

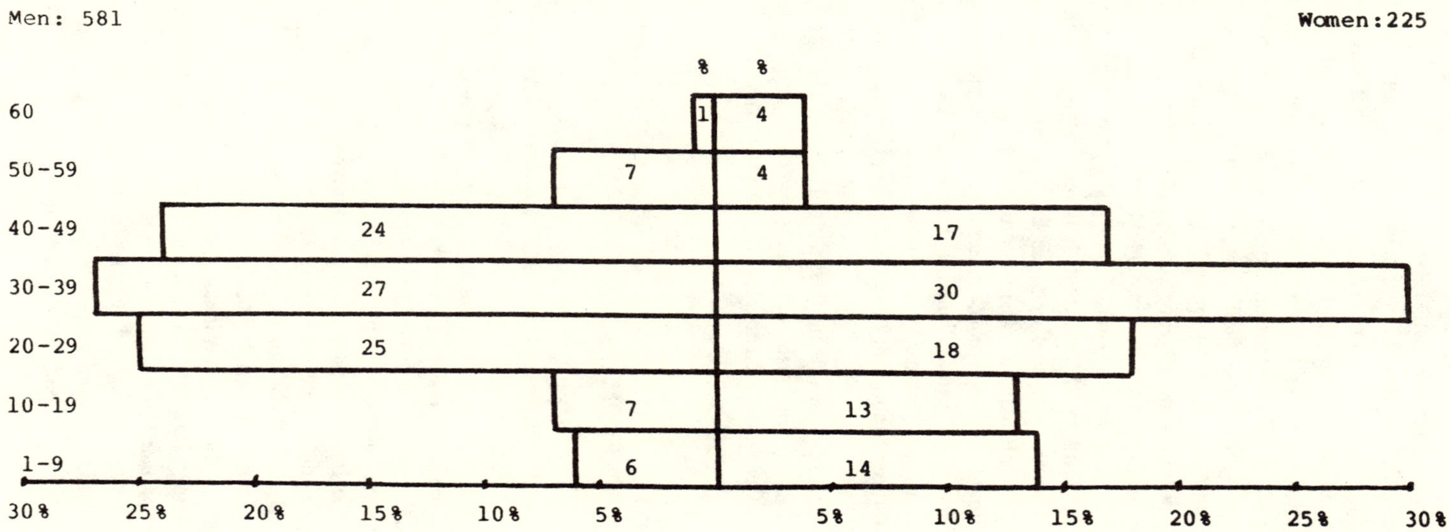

Figure 8.2 Age-Sex Structure of Italian Nordstadters

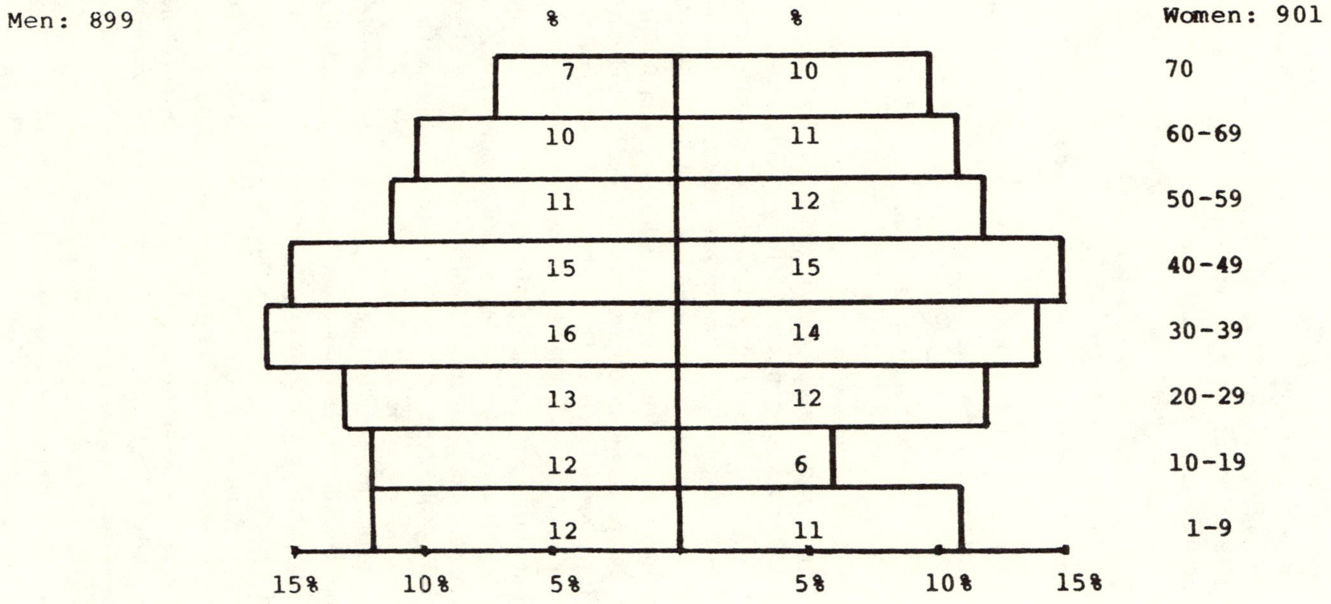

the expanding manufacturing city of Ebbesthal, the paternalistically run glassworks was transformed into a publicly owned corporation capitalized by the sale of stock and administered by a staff of middle- and upper-level managers. Personal intervention in family affairs and disputes among workers in extrafactory contexts by a single company owner and a small coterie of associates dissipated, and the factory associations and clubs originally sponsored and cultivated by the company's founder declined (Seeling 1964, 104–105). Further, though some administration of social welfare policies remained in the hands of the enterprise, the West German state effectively assumed control over medical, old-age, and accident insurance in the aftermath of the Second World War (Stolper 1967, 286–87).

A major effect of the half-century's trajectory of bureaucratic expansion and of the shift in corporate organization was a distinct widening of the organizational and social distance between management and workers. The smoothing over of difficulties among workers of divergent origins, if and when these occurred, could not always be expected of those with little contact with laborers on the factory floor, or of those potentially geographically mobile middle-echelon administrators who, unlike the plant's original founder, did not necessarily possess a similarly intense stake in the harmony of the work force. A survey we took during fieldwork in 1973–1974 of 109 southern Italian industrial workers at the plant indicated that a majority had never approached appropriate administrative personnel on questions concerning compulsory social and unemployment insurance. This was true even though these employees had been with the firm for ten or more years, knew the administrators by name or by sight, and translation aid was provided. A perceived social and cultural distance between workers and administrators that remained unmodified by the type of close and continuous contact which linked managerial staff and glass workers in the fledgling years of the firm must be among many possible reasons for this failure to seek out office staff. Instead, Italian employees turned to fellow countrymen for advice on matters of welfare policy still channeled through the firm, or sought out help at the Italian Consulate in the city center.

The greatest shift in Nordstadt during the first half of the century, however, was the automation of the glass production process. The gradual introduction of automated equipment in the plant revolutionized glass production and signaled an eventual end to the need for a large number of specialist glassblowers. One automatic glass manufacturing machine alone could produce 15,000 bottles in an eight-hour period, or the number of bottles that could be produced in the same amount of time by seventy-five glassblowers using traditional methods (Seeling 1964, 110). By the early 1950s glass production in this industrial neighborhood was entirely automated, and the skilled craft of glassblowing was replaced by rapid-paced molding and forming machines.

On the surface, the immediate impact of the automation of glass production on Nordstadt itself appears to have been circumscribed. The increasing, yet gradual, automation of glass manufacture, combined with drops in production levels during the two world wars occurred just at those times when Nordstadt's own manpower reserves were falling because of military drafts and war-related casualties. As a consequence, Nordstadt never fully experienced the disruptive effects of mass unemployment brought about elsewhere in the industrializing world by the relatively sudden introduction of automated techniques. Moreover, throughout the years the glassblowers and their descendants not affected by the wars were able to move laterally into other highly skilled jobs at the firm—either as mechanics, machinists, or electricians assigned to maintain the automated equipment, or as supervisory personnel in the newly founded machine service departments.

Glass automation nevertheless acted to deepen the already existent division between skilled and unskilled workers at the firm. One significant source of cleavage was that automated machines, unlike human glassblowers, could function around the clock. A series of rotating work shifts or "turns" were therefore instituted for the unskilled packers of finished bottles, since unlike skilled electricians and maintenance workers, the packers labored directly on the production line. Skilled workers, in contrast, were present on the factory floor only during daylight hours. As long as the majority of Nordstadt's male residents were skilled laborers at the plant and the number of unskilled local Nordstadters was restricted, this characteristic of labor organization did little to drive a divisive wedge between members of the still close-knit, local industrial community. It was only with a spiraling increase in production levels after World War II, and the concomitant need for an enlarged unskilled labor force, that the divisive potential of the temporal organization of work and other features of the more contemporary local industrial context became apparent.

The lack of a local unskilled labor force prompted another wave of in-migration to Nordstadt at the end of the 1950s. As in the 19th century, the glassworks found its labor supply in the economically underdeveloped areas of rural Europe. But with much of agrarian Europe enclosed within the Warsaw Pact, the southern provinces of Italy, as well as Sicily, became a fertile field for the company's recruitment policies.

Interested workers were contacted at rural Italian labor offices and signed nine-month contracts. The first 100 men arrived in Nordstadt in 1959 and were followed during the next year by an additional 350 workers. After their nine-month contracts had expired, some returned home; but fully one-half of the original group stayed in Nordstadt year after year, brought their families after them, and lived in the same factory apartments that were also home to the descendants of Nordstadt's glassblowers. These in-migrants then formed the nodal points around which later migrants—friends, relatives, and fellow townsmen—clustered, and over the years the newer migrants more than compensated numerically for the loss of a large portion of the original migrant group.[6] At the beginning of 1974 the 806 southern Italian men, women, and children resident in Nordstadt represented nearly one-third of the neighborhood's population. A little over 400 male members of this migrant population were unskilled operatives at the plant, while 650 male German Nordstadters, the great majority the descendants of the glassblowers, occupied skilled positions at the firm. Together, local Germans and in-migrant Italians constituted nearly 55 percent of the factory's manual labor force.

Each diverse group of Nordstadters is thus differentially absorbed into the firm's skill hierarchy, and we may better understand the implications of this differential allocation for in-plant and extrafactory ties by clarifying the spatial positioning of skilled and unskilled labor in the production process and the varying temporal organization of skilled and unskilled work. Glass production in today's neighborhood, for example, is based on the passage of viscous glass from the smelting ovens to a series of automatic forming machines, where bottles are shaped; the bottles then travel slowly through the cooling or annealing furnaces as well as through an automatic quality control system until they reach the end of the moving canal, which had been carrying them, and arrive at the packing area. Each oven and its associated canal has two packing areas for the bottles that are produced, and at least four men are placed at every packing station. Besides the oven mechanic, who is at the head of the long canal and out of sight of the packers, and an occasional machinist who comes to correct deviations in the angles of the forming machines, the largest contingent of canal workers are the packers. These load the finished bottles into cartons, which are then removed from the production floor for shipment.

Integral to the production of glass bottles but spatially separated from the production line itself are the machine service departments where toolmakers, locksmiths, and electricians are located. Their work entails the repair and maintenance of the automatic machines and molds, and these workers sit at individual tool banks in large enclosed areas some two minutes' walk from the production line. To an overwhelming extent, German Nordstadters are concentrated in the machine service departments' skilled occupational categories, while with few exceptions, local Italians hold the unskilled position of packer and labor directly on the production line. Differential absorption of Italian and German Nordstadters into unskilled and skilled labor categories, however, has not only brought with it a different spatial positioning in the production process. It has also encapsulated local residents within varying temporal patterns of work. Skilled German Nordstadters in the machine service departments work only on weekdays during the daytime. Where the machines function continuously on the production line, workers follow a rotating swing shift, so that every packer alternates between a morning, late afternoon, and all-night shift. These successive shift periods last seven days each and are separated by a one- to three-day rest, or holiday.

This differential absorption of Italian and German Nordstadters into alternative systems of employment characterized by varying temporal patterns of labor, levels of skill, and spatial location in the production process has conditioned the quality of on-the-job interaction among Nordstadt's diverse populations. Southern Italian workers are clustered together at the packing stations near the end of the canals, segregated by long distances from local German mechanics or machinists on the forms. Spatial distance and the division of labor also segregate packers from skilled local German workers in the service departments. It follows from this that there are only highly circumscribed amounts of in-plant contact among the local German and Italian manual labor force. Those contacts that exist occur primarily during short beverage or lunch breaks at tables located at a spatial midpoint between the canals and the machine service departments. However, these contacts are generally transient and are rendered superficial by the fact that the swing shift system that the Italian workers follow brings them into this already fleeting association with the same grouping of skilled German neighbors at the plant for less than a few weeks out of every month.

At work, unskilled Italian laborers are thus seemingly locked into patterns of social interaction with others on their own packing station and shift group while the factory-located ties of skilled German Nordstadters remain encapsulated within the service departments. The differential spatial positioning of the unskilled and skilled manual labor force within the plant's bottle glass divisions, as well as the two varying temporal configurations of labor, have greatly diminished the Nordstaders' capacity to construct a set of in-plant relationships across ethnic lines that might have anything more than a perfunctory quality.

The same features of contemporary work organization that set severe limits to interethnic relations at the glassworks appear to have put restrictions on interassociation among neighborhood laborers within the community at large. Primary among these features is the temporal organization of work. By assigning local skilled Germans to labor patterns that conform to what has been termed the familiar and accustomed notion of "mainstream time" (Lieber 1976, 326) while relegating unskilled in-migrants to the ever-changing rhythms of the shifts, the temporal arrangement of labor at the glass firm has done more to heighten existent ethnic divisions than to attenuate them. The "normal" working hours of local Germans and the changing nature of the migrants' shifts severely limit opportunities for association between members of the "host" community and the Italians, and restrict chances for interethnic contact largely to those times when a grouping of local in-migrants works an early morning "turn" and therefore, like local Germans, has the afternoon and evening free. For each unskilled Italian factory worker, however, the opportunity to labor and to have leisure hours at a time approximating that of a local skilled German occurs only one week out of every three. Encounters between neighborhood German workers and Italian in-migrant laborers are fleeting, take place primarily on the streets on the way to the factory or on the stairs of the factory housing complex, and have little chance to evolve into significant relationships. Local Italian and German workers live out their leisure hours as well as their working lives in time categories that rarely conjoin, their opportunities for extended association literally slipping by them despite common and close residence.[7]

The dominant industrial cleavage between local Germans and Italians appears to be at least partially mirrored in the ethnic segmentation of local life in yet another way. Since the majority of Nordstadt's population lacks the daily or even periodic forums for significant transethnic interaction—either at the plant or in the community at large—it is not surprising that the number of intermarriages between German and Italian Nordstadters has remained correspondingly low. From the outset of the Italian in-migration to Nordstadt in the 1950s to 1974, only eleven marriages between Italian men and German women took place in the neighborhood, and none between local German men and Italian women. Informal associations between unmarried Italian workers and single local German women were also few and apparently transient.

Undoubtedly, a variety of factors contributed to this ethnic distance. Many local Italian men were already married when they arrived in the neighborhood. Additionally, there were few single Italian women of marriageable age within Nordstadt's migrant community; the great majority were wives of immigrants or younger children. Moreover, unmarried Italian males tended to outnumber single local German women, a fact which added to these workers' already present desire to return to their homeland for wives who could then accompany them to Nordstadt.

Further, there was a belief, prevalent both locally and in the wider society, that Germans and Italians were too far apart in custom and temperament to make successful candidates for a long-term relationship (Leudesdorff and Zilessen 1971). Yet the separation of local Germans and in-migrants at the plant and, as a result, in their local lives, did little to break down ethnic stereotypes based on preconceived notions of cultural and social distinctions, and it may have at least aided in the continuing existence of these negative beliefs. The relative isolation of Nordstadt's "host" and migrant populations—mirrored in yet another way by the fact that few in-migrants had sufficient opportunity to learn the German language—and the absence of ramifying interethnic ties despite close residential propinquity, did not encourage the testing of beliefs in the crucible of everyday observable behavior and precluded the growth of a local climate that could possibly promote a rise in interethnic marriages or liaisons.

By way of summarizing the preceding data on the historical and contemporary link between Nordstadt's glass factory and the local immigrant labor force, it can be said that in the past the predominant industrial influence on immigrant life was the attenuation of distinct ethnic boundaries. This influence, as it appears from available information for that period, derives primarily from the fact that glassmakers of diverse national and cultural origin were integrated into basic task-groups at the fledgling 19th-century firm without reference to ethnicity. Similar work schedules helped ensure that interethnic associations in leisure-time situations would evolve as well. Today the industrial segregation of diverse groups of Nordstadters at the glass factory—a separation based mainly on placement in the production process and varying temporal schedules of labor—is recapitulated in the ethnic segmentation of the neighborhood itself. In large measure, ethnic boundaries in contemporary Nordstadt have industrial dimensions, and industrial boundaries have come to signify ethnic divisions.

CONCLUDING REMARKS

Nordstadt may well be an unusual community on the West German scene. Like other neighborhoods, it has been host to contemporary Mediterranean labor migrants. But Nordstadt was the definite locus of a specific historical labor in-migration at the end of the 19th century. And though the Polish in-migration to the Ruhr Valley at the turn of the century was also extensive, no community similar to Nordstadt—one with present-day southern European in-migrants as well as the descendants of an earlier migrant flow—has yet been examined. The mixture of past and present migrant groups, both of which were contingents of two historically distinct migrant waves, lends Nordstadt the cast of a migrant zone of long standing, a continuity of in-migration and immigrant adaptation which by virtue of its very existence may render Nordstadt unique and therefore unrepresentative of other contemporary foci of intra-European migratory movements.

Further, the link between the in-plant and extraindustrial adaptation of in-migrants and the changing organizational and technical structure of a single enterprise over time might not be able to be clarified by additional evidence from other industrial localities with long entrepreneurial histories, for the industrial plant in certain West German regions was damaged in the war era and has been superseded by modern constructions, equipment, and new and surrounding indigenous communities. With all this, life in Nordstadt still illuminates the manner in which the contemporary organization of Mediterranean migrant labor has managed to set significant parameters to the course of in-migrant adaptation to one industrial locality and the degree to which grass-roots integration, or indigene-migrant association, has taken place. The evidence of the strong relationship between factory organization and migrant community in turn-of-the-century Nordstadt only serves to underscore this view: that the nature of the integration of in-migrants and the attenuation or maintenance of ethnic boundaries in Nordstadt have been in large measure a response to processes emanating from the neighborhood's major industrial firm.

As the context of European anthropology has evolved from a concentration on the small village to a growing focus on West European industrial society and the link between national and regional processes and local communities, there has also been an increasing anthropological encounter with labor in-migrants from the European south in north European "host" neighborhoods. Nordstadt is by no means alone; and the extent to which local industrial systems impinge on migrant adaptation and on migrant interaction with local populations should, I think, become a crucial part of the research agenda of urban anthropologists of Europeanist persuasion. If in certain ways Nordstadt proves a unique local community, if other urban neighborhoods lack a historical base similar to this ancient locality, employer-provided housing near factories and indigenous settlements nevertheless remains the most usual form of accommodations for migrant workers and their families in today's Germany and in several other industrially developed West European states (Castles and Kosack 1973, 248ff.). These factories, along with their associated communities of indigenous and immigrant laborers, form a vivid social and spatial complex in Western Europe's industrial core. Additional inquiry into modern industrial institutions as possible mediating factors in immigrant adjustment as well as immigrant-indigene interaction may result in a more developed or holistic picture of south European migrant life in industrial north European localities. The industrial ethnology of transnational Mediterranean migrants could also contribute to a continuing dialogue in the social and political sciences on the role of intra-European labor transfers in promoting the integration of contemporary populations of divergent cultural traditions in north European metropolitan centers, and thus help lay bare some of the more human and informal aspects of that growing trend towards European community formation which has become recently manifest in the proliferation of transnational political and corporate bureaucratic entities.

NOTES

1. See especially Bouscaren (1969), Friedrich (1969), and Lindberg and Scheingold (1970).

2. Feldstein (1967) and particularly Friedrich (1969) have paid close attention to the possible contributions of intra-European labor migration to the emergence of an integrated Europe.

3. Most of Nordstadt's recent history is summarized in Seeling (1964), and its earlier years in Weidenhaupt (1970).

4. Kapferer (1972, 138) makes a similar point about the long-term employees of a Zambian factory, their commitment to the firm, and the link between this tie and their joint action in a strike against management.

5. Though voluntary associations have been shown to aid the integration of urban migrants, they can also serve to heighten ethnic distinctions among association members (Fallers 1967; Meillassoux 1968).

6. About 40 percent of male southern Italian laborers had their families with them in Nordstadt.

7. I have written largely of male Italian in-migrants and industrial workers, and not of their wives. However, since nearly 60 percent of female in-migrants and over 40 percent of local German women worked outside their homes, either full- or part-time in other sections of the city, I found little evidence that the circumscribed leisure-time schedules of these women permitted them to establish the type of close neighborly relations that could override existent local tendencies towards ethnic segregation.

REFERENCES

Bouscaren, A. J.
1969 *European Economic Community Migrations*. The Hague: Martinus Nijhoff.
Brody, D.
1960 *Steelworkers in America: The Nonunion Era*. New York: Harper and Row.

Castles, S., and Kosack, G.
1973 *Immigrant Workers and Class Structure in Western Europe*. London: Oxford University Press.

Epstein, A. L.
1958 *Politics in an Urban African Community*. Manchester: Manchester University Press.

Fallers, L. A., ed.
1967 *Immigrants and Associations*. The Hague: Mouton.

Feldstein, H. S.
1967 "A Study of Transactional Political Integration." *Journal of Common Market Studies* 6: 24–55.

Friedrich, C. J.
1969 *Europe: An Emergent Nation?* New York: Harper and Row.

Kapferer, B.
1972 *Strategy and Transaction in an African Factory*. Manchester: Manchester University Press.

Leudesdorff, R., and Zilessen, H., ed.
1971 *Gastarbeiter-Mitbürger*. Geimhausen: Burkharthaus Verlag.

Lieber, M.
1976 " 'Liming' and Other Concerns." *Urban Anthropology* 5, no. 4: 319–34.

Lindberg, L., and Scheingold, S. A.
1970 *Europe's Would-Be Polity*. Englewood Cliffs, N. J.: Prentice-Hall.

Meillassoux, C.
1968 *Urbanization of an African Community: Voluntary Associations in Banako*. Seattle: University of Washington Press.

Seeling, H.
1964 *Geschichte der Gerresheimer Glashütte*. Düsseldorf: Geschichtsverein Düsseldorf.

Stolper, G.
1967 *The German Economy 1870 to the Present*. New York: Harcourt, Brace and World.

Warner, L. W., and Low, J. O.
1947 *The Social System of the Modern Factory*. New Haven: Yale University Press.

Weidenhaupt, H.
1970 *Gerresheim: 870–1970*. Düsseldorf: Verlag L. Schwann.

9 A Day in the Life of a Single Spanish Woman in West Germany

Charity Goodman

ABSTRACT. Like Sontz, Goodman deals with life as an immigrant factory worker in Germany. Her focus is on the plight of single women. She argues that women should be regarded as economic decision makers in their own right, rather than as appendages to male migrants whom they eventually follow to the host country. Goodman's argument applies to married women as well (see also Goodman 1984). Decisions about which family members should migrate must be regarded as an integral part of family strategies in which women and men have equal input, rather than as parts in life plays masterminded by men.

Goodman also shows how ephemeral migration policies may lead to the formation of cohorts of migrants with unique characteristics, in this case a higher percentage of single women than in subsequent cohorts.

INTRODUCTION

There is a pervasive stereotype of migrant women in much of the social science literature on the guest worker migration in post–World War II Western Europe. Women are depicted as remnants of a backward rural culture and are seen as appendages or servants of their men folk (see Castles and Kosack 1973; Kosack 1976; Morokvasic 1983). To a certain extent this stereotype is also present in the thinking of migrants (Brandt 1977). By focusing on the little-researched case of single women recruitees, I hope to dispel this image of women as only passive participants in the migration process.

In the social science literature of this period (1960 to the present) little has been written on the case of single migrant women recruited to work from the Mediterranean nations. The main focus has been on married women who migrated to be with their husbands or families. Although foreign single women are presently not in the majority in West Germany, single Spanish women were recruited in greater numbers than married women in the earlier recruitment years, 1960–1971 (Mediavilla 1980).

The methodology used is that of a case study of one Spanish woman. This type of life-history approach adds to anthropologists' traditional community study approach (Buechler and Buechler 1981). We are able to see the changes in attitudes over time as a migrant woman describes her immigration experience. In larger community studies, such life histories are often gathered by ethnographers, but then they are lost when they are consolidated into a composite analysis of a community. One purpose of this study is to show how the individual may be reinstated into community studies.

Fieldwork for this project was conducted in 1979-1980 and the winter of 1982 as part of my dissertation research. It is based on participant observation at the workplaces and homes of Spanish women living in "Rheinstadt," West Germany, a pseudonym for a city of 110,000.

West Germany is the size of the state of Oregon and has a population of approximately 60 million, of which 4 million are foreigners (German Information Center 1983). Approximately 31 percent of all foreign workers are women (Statistical Year Book 1983, 104).

REASONS FOR FEMALE MIGRATION

Why and when women decide to migrate are often attributed to their particular marital status or life cycle stage (Moch and Tilly 1979; Brettel 1978; Arizpe 1978). Previous researchers only analyzed the case of married women as the typical woman in the post–World War II migration to Western Europe (Weber and Schultze 1979; Münschner 1979; Brandt 1977). This is undoubtedly related to two important facts. In West Germany the majority (77.5 percent) of employed migrant women 18 and over are married (Nolkensmeier 1980, 14; Mediavilla 1980; Moch and Tilly 1979), and a strong bias in the literature assumes that women, particularly from Mediterranean- and/or Moslem-based cultures, are followers of men (Brandt 1977; Brettel 1978; Morokvasic 1979). For example, C. Brettel found that women migrants decide to migrate only after the men's labor market positions are already secure in the foreign countries (1978, 212). Migration of women is seen only in the context of the functions of women as attached "wives," not as breadwinners (for a review of this literature see Morokvasic 1983).

One exception to the literature is Morokvasic's study of Yugoslavian women in which she finds that women are not passively following their men but are responding to specific international labor market demands. For instance, she concluded that Yugoslavian women in West Germany tend to come from regions which are underdeveloped industrially and have a low female labor force participation rate (1977, 83).

Some authors suggest that other migrants and residents in the home village think that single migrant women are opposing village norms by migrating. For example, Brandt (1977) found that some West German migrants describe single migrant women as morally loose. Single migrant women are even seen as prostitutes.

Many Turkish and Moroccan Muslims in West Germany believe that women who are not married should remain confined to prevent them from being "spoiled" and thus unmarriageable (Moch and Tilly 1979, 25). For example, in Rheinstadt it was difficult for Muslim teenage girls to attend German classes when boys were present. In rural southern Spain, an area where many immigrants originate, single women are not expected to ride in cars with men or go walking alone in the countryside (Masur 1981).

Single women are also seen as less attached to their families (Moch and Tilly 1979). Some are reported to move to another nation in order to remove themselves from their homes for either social or economic reasons (Lequin 1977; Moch 1974, as cited in Moch and Tilly 1979; Douglass 1976). After living in a more cosmopolitan and urban environment, single migrant women may prefer to marry outside the village. Single women may also wish to migrate in order to free themselves from the strict rules they are expected to follow in their villages (Brettel 1978). Or single women may be asked to migrate before their fathers (or wives before husbands) when the labor market has openings in jobs that are designated as women's employment. (This happened during the 1967 recession in West Germany when jobs in the electronic industry were more available than jobs in, for instance, the auto industry [see Abadan-Unat 1977].)

MIGRATION AND MARITAL STATUS

There is a controversy in the literature as to the exact effect migration has on women. Nermin Abadan-Unat (1977) and G. Kosack (1976) suggest that women gain authority and independence upon immigrating and entering wage labor for the first time. Abadan-Unat measures this by women earning their own wages and having savings accounts and investments and labels it "pseudo-emancipation." Kosack (1976) finds that there are two types of immigrant women: nonworking women, who are isolated and solely conducting household chores for their families, and wage-earning women, who gain a new independence by their participation in unions. On the other hand, L. Brouwer and M. Priester (1983) find that men still retain authority over immigrant women.

The effects of state immigration legislation on whether married or single men or women immigrate are also not well known. The state selects workers by marital status, gender, age, and ethnicity. For example, in the earlier West German recruitment era (1960–1973), only wage earners were allowed entrance. Nonworking women (i.e., dependents) were not permitted until 1972. Single wage earners were likewise excluded from the work force in the postrecruitment era (1973-present).

Let us turn to the case of Cari, a Spanish woman living in Rheinstadt. I worked with her on a factory team packaging candies as part of a factory internship. I had a series of two factory internships in West Germany that were arranged through the American Embassy in West Germany and the textile and clothing union of West Germany. Workers were accustomed to factory apprentices and therefore adjusted to my presence rapidly. Cari also invited me to her home, where I interviewed her about her work and home life. Therefore, this vignette is presented in an interview-like format.

Cari first entered the Federal Republic of Germany on a tourist visa and worked illegally. Later she reentered as a recruited worker, employed legally in a West German factory.

CARI, A SINGLE WOMAN RECRUITEE

"Why don't you come back with me to Germany and earn a little money?" Cari's older sister asked Cari. Her sister had been living for several years in West Germany and was home in Spain on a summer visit. At that time Cari was living at home helping her mother run the village bread bakery and care for the household. Her mother had been in charge of the bakery since her father's death.

In 1965, at the age of 29 years, Cari did decide to go with her sister to West Germany. She thought her eight brothers and sisters could help out her mother in the shop.

Cari is now 46 years old and has lived in Rheinstadt, West Germany, for seventeen years. "Life here," she says, "is very hard." For the last thirteen years she has worked in a candy factory in Rheinstadt. But when I visited her and her roommate for tea one Sunday afternoon, she recalled her first year in West Germany with vivid detail:

"I first came with my sister on a tourist visa. We worked on the 'Lorelei,' a Rhine river boat that cruises between Cologne and Mainz. I worked 'privately,' or illegally, for six months cleaning the halls and decks as a maid. My sister worked the cloakroom. Since I studied sewing at home I would periodically sew for an American on the boat. I had a nice room on the bottom floor of the boat. Mosquitos did bother us at night during the summer.

"I was proud of my earnings of 2.49 DM [$1.08] an hour and saved 1,000 DM [$435.00] in seven months. On my first vacation back to Spain I took new clothes for all my eight brothers and sisters at home. It was like Christmas. They thought Germany was terrific.

"My sister, after her fourteen years of work on the boat, returned to live in Spain. Then I was left to work the boat alone. Nights on the boat people made lots of noise. There was rowdy drinking and fighting. One night a man had a knife and slit another man's throat. I left for Spain that year vowing never again to work the 'Lorelei' boat.

"After I returned to Spain from the boat experience, I realized I really did want to continue to work in Germany. This time I went to the Spanish Institute of Immigration and they signed me up for a job in a canning factory thirty kilometers north of Cologne. At the end of the summer, nine women from the Granada area and I boarded a train en route to Cologne through Paris. I can still remember that train ride. We were all pretty nervous and excited. We spent a day in Paris wandering around and then, in Cologne, a representative of the factory met us at the station with a Spanish translator. We were brought to the factory dormitory. There were two of us to a room.

"The work at the canning factory was very difficult and uncomfortable, with long hours. We had to wear big hip boots and gloves and stand in water washing fruit all day. We worked from 6:00 A.M. to 6:00 P.M., twelve hours a day Monday through Saturday. Our pay included room and board. My present roommate, Maria, and I worked there for three and a half years. Then Maria's cousin knew of a candy factory in Rheinstadt. Both Maria and I moved there and have been working at the 'Bon-Bon' [pseudonym] candy factory for the last thirteen years."

A Day in the Candy Factory

Cari begins her day at six o'clock in the morning, preparing sandwiches for her lunch and breakfast at the factory. She drinks a quick cup of *café con leche* and, with her roommate Maria, walks the ten-minute walk to the Bon-Bon factory.

For the last three years Cari and her roommate have shared a small two-room apartment under the rafters of a large mansion-like home. They share the top floor with Maria's relatives, who live in the apartment across the hall. Germans live on the first and second floors, which are better maintained. Prior to having this apartment, the two women lived in factory dormitory housing provided by Bon-Bon. There, Spanish women lived six to a room in double-decker bunk beds.

They reached Bon-Bon, the factory, and chatted in Spanish quickly with coworkers as they placed the rolls of plastic bags onto the packing machines. Maria, Cari's roommate, was also her packing partner in her work group. They were paid a piecework rate based on the work group's accomplishments. Next to them on the other eight packing machines were other single Spanish women who still lived in the factory dormitory. Two Turkish women were also included in the work unit with the fifteen Spanish women. One helped in the packing work groups, and the other took check orders from the factory delivery men, who were also Spaniards from the same Granada area as the female Spanish workers.[1]

The bell to start the assembly line rang a harsh, loud tone, and the women were barely in place before the multicolored licorice candies were shooting out in sealed plastic bags. Cari grabbed each sealed bag with an open hand as it came out the chute and packed it into a carton. Neatly, she placed thirty bags face up so the labels could be read and her supervisor would not complain. When the box was full she sealed and placed a label on the whole box. The candies were continuously coming down the chute with no pause or lapse in the flow. Cari fell behind by five or six bags and hurried to catch up with the machine. She caught up with the machine just as she again had to stop filling the box in order to seal and label it. Then she was again behind the machine that continuously expelled the plastic bags of candy.

Cari has worked on this machine for nine and three-quarters years. In 1979 she was earning 1,300 DM, or $565.22, a month. I asked Cari about her work. "I like it, but it is very hard work and makes me nervous. At least I get to work with my friends. We work well together."

"This work is very hard work," she stated to me several times. "It is bad for your nerves and I have rheumatism from the cold water in the previous canning factory."

At lunchtime the topic of vacations back in Spain came up. It was March and the women felt that summer was approaching. The conversations about vacations saddened Cari. She thought of her mother, who was well into her eighties, and said to me, "In the back of my mind all I think about is my mother, and if she gets sick I will return to Spain immediately."

Cari talked about women's work and family ties in the Federal Republic of Germany (FRG). She said that women with small children in the FRG have to help their husbands earn a living, implying that the cost of living here is too high for a single wage earner to support a family. She also said that Spanish men and women in the FRG do not keep the morals of the village life. "A lot goes on here that would not in Spain," she said.

At lunchtime the women in each group sat around their packing machine and used the base of the machine as their table. They ripped open the plastic bags from the candies and spread them out as a temporary tablecloth. They ate their lunch of tuna and tomatoes in fifteen minutes. Right after they had eaten the women all began to sweep and clean up around their work areas. One woman explained to me that it was a Friday and therefore cleanup day. She said that when the machines went back on, the woman would be too busy to clean up, so they had to do it on their lunch hour. After first carefully wiping off the machines, they swept, dusted, and washed the floor. They had just finished when the bell rang and they scurried to their places as the bags of candy again began to rapidly drop down the chute.

From a distance one could see German women who were managers eating their hot lunches that were delivered to them in their glassed-in room on the factory floor.

On the way home at a quarter past four o'clock I asked Cari what she did in her free time. "I have very little free time because I only have time to work. The little time I have, I sew, go to church, and after church I go to the church *local*. [This is a social club where Spanish church members gather for coffee, wine, or Coca-Cola in the basement of a church building. Here the men play cards in one room and the women and children talk in the other.] I also call home for news of my mother and sister."

The last question I asked Cari was what she would do if she won the lottery. Her answer reflected how, despite her nineteen years in FRG, she still felt split from her family in Granada.

> "First I would go home to my people. Secondly, I would divide up the money between my brothers and sisters. They all have jobs, but they could use the money. I like to give it out, divide it up. I'll save a little for my retirement, but not more. The rest is for the family. We'll buy new clothes and shoes. I'll go home and say, 'This is for all of us.' I won't go to the candy factory anymore."

ANALYSIS

Cari is representative of a set of single women who were recruited through bilateral contracts to work in the northern factories or in domestic service in West Germany. For most of her seventeen years in West Germany she has lived in factory-owned housing. In the past, the factory where she worked had three dormitories; one for single Spanish men, one for single Spanish women, and the third for Spanish married couples. Only the dormitory for single women has remained open. The other workers had either returned to Spain or lived off the factory premises in private housing.

Like the other women who still lived in factory housing, Cari entered in the recruitment period and has lived for about half her adult life in West Germany. As can be seen in table 9.1, the average length of stay for the recruited women is fifteen years. Despite the fact that only 22.5 percent of the foreign women over 18 are single (Nolkensmeier 1980, 14), their particular characteristic of migration gives us new insight about single women's purposes for migration and their migration patterns.

Cari and other single women recruited to work demonstrate women choosing to earn cash incomes. They left their home villages for cities, languages, cultures, and peoples unknown to them. Cari followed her sister's advice and came with her to West Germany. But after her sister returned, she continued to live without kin in West Germany for another sixteen years.

Besides single recruited women, several other categories of single women

Table 9.1 Spanish Single Women Entering the FRG as Recruits

PRESENT AGE	AGE UPON ARRIVAL	NUMBER OF YRS. IN FRG	YEAR OF ARRIVAL	YEARS MARRIED	LEGISLATIVE PERIOD
60	N/A	N/A	N/A	0	
35	20	15	1965	0	Recruitment
60	41	19	1963	0	Recruitment
35	18	17	1965	0	Recruitment
46	29	17	1965	0	Recruitment
33	18	15	1964	14	Recruitment
29	21	8	1972	3	Family Reunion
42*	24*	15*	1965*		

*Averages

Source: Author's field research 1979–1980; 1982.

Table 9.2 Spanish Single Women Entering the FRG to Join Their Families

PRESENT AGE	AGE UPON ARRIVAL	NUMBER OF YRS. IN FRG	YEAR OF ARRIVAL	LEGISLATIVE PERIOD
16	10	6	1974	Post-Recruitment
14	6	8	1972	Family Reunion
17	9	8	1973	Post-Recruitment
16	11	5	1975	Post-Recruitment
18	14	4	1976	Post-Recruitment
15	11	4	1976	Post-Recruitment
16*	10*	6*	1974*	

Note: 1972 was the first year Family Reunion Guest Workers' relatives were permitted and the last year of the recruitment period.

*Averages.

Source: Author's field research 1979–1980; 1982.

exist. Single girls born in West Germany are one such type. The second and third generations that were born on West German soil are not considered German citizens because West Germany does not have a naturalization law (i.e., citizenship by virtue of one's birth on the nation's soil is not granted). The negative stigma associated with immigrants as guest workers is being passed on to third and fourth generations.

The other category of single women is called in German *Nachgeholte,* or youth brought in after their parents. Table 9.2 demonstrates the characteristics of this labor stream. These women tend to be between the ages of 12 and 16 and are not permitted entrance after the age of 16. They were most likely raised by grandparents in the home country in order to obtain a grammar or junior high school diploma there. According to the German chancellor, it is this particular group of youth, the *Nachgeholte,* who are the hardest to integrate and the most likely to end up as criminals or on the German unemployment rosters (German Information Center 1983).[2]

Married women, in contrast to single ones, had a different set of options under the German laws. These laws directly reflect the changes in the economy and West Germany's labor needs. In the recruitment period (1960-1973), married women could remain in Spain while their husbands migrated without them, or as dual wage earners, husbands and wives could both migrate. (See table 9.3.)

Many wives were recruited to different regions of West Germany. Leonor Mediavilla (1980) suggests that one reason for married women's separation from their husbands is that many women were not familiar enough with the geography

Table 9.3 Spanish Married Women Entering the FRG

PRESENT AGE	AGE UPON ARRIVAL	NUMBER OF YRS. IN FRG	YEAR OF ARRIVAL	YEARS MARRIED	LEGISLATIVE PERIOD
44	34	10	1972	22	Family Reunion
40	30	10	1972	14	Family Reunion
42	34	8	1972	9	Family Reunion
45	34	11	1969	15	Recruitment
54	43	11	1969	17	Recruitment
20	18	2	1978	2	Post-Recruitment
21	16	5	1975	5	Post-Recruitment
38*	29*	8*	1972*	12*	

*Averages.

Source: Author's field research 1979–1980; 1982.

of West Germany to write on the form the correct region where their husbands were located. Also, many of the women were illiterate and therefore not able to comprehend the forms they were signing. Respect for family unification did not appear in the migration laws until the Family Reunion Policy of 1972, the very last year of the recruitment period. In the recruitment period the West German state brought in labor in order to fill their own need for unskilled laborers but also because they wanted cheaper labor than native workers. Migrants' dependents raise the costs to the infrastructure with their educational and medical costs. Therefore, single men and women were the ideal workers in this recruitment period.

The postrecruitment policies reflect a different economic climate, one of recession in which the German state attempted to halt the growth of the foreign dependent population and encourage repatriation. Work restrictions on dependents, tightening up of illegal work, and repatriation funds are all part of this postrecruitment policy package.

In the recruitment period, single women like Cari have lived more years in West Germany than have the married women because the single women entered in the earlier stages of the recruitment period. Yet single women remain less integrated into the German population than, for instance, Spanish men. This is perhaps why factory housing continues to be available for single women, but not for single men or married couples. It is also possible that single women's decisions to migrate may have actually diminished their chances of marrying.

The lives of single women in factory-based housing are different from those of single women who live in private housing off factory premises. Abadan-Unat

(1977) suggests that women in factory housing have little chance to be affected by their new urban environment and do not have the beneficial influence that creates, in her words, "pseudo-emancipation," which she defines as the effects of women's ability to earn wages and obtain savings and investment accounts. I would argue that factory housing may inhibit women from meeting men, German or Spanish, and possibly reduce their chance of marriage. This conclusion is substantiated by W. Douglass (1976). He found that Spanish men residing in French factory housing also did not have the opportunity to marry during their stints abroad.

Women's decisions to migrate do not center around their attachment to men. Single recruited women did not come to West Germany following men or because they were pushed out of households by men. Neither did they come in search of husbands. They were specifically recruited by German employers in cooperation with the West German state at a particular time in history when West Germany was experiencing an economic boom and in need of unskilled, cheap labor. Single women came to earn their own wages and bring cash into their Andalusian households. This is reflected in the life of Cari, who actively made decisions about her own migration. It is necessary to see women's migration differently than the literature has previously shown it. The purpose of immigration for single women is *not* to follow men or to get married; they are not just appendages of men. Single women came to West Germany to seek a badly needed income and to better contribute to their households in Spain.

NOTES

1. Work units in factories tend to be either foreigners or Germans and are rarely integrated. One manager of a German factory reported to me that he integrated work groups, but they did not work well together and he disbanded them.
2. See also Barou (chap. 4).

REFERENCES

Abadan-Unat, Nermin

1977 "Implications of Migration on Emancipation and Pseudo-Emancipation of Turkish Women." *International Migration Review* 11, no. 1: 31–57.

Arizpe, L.

1978 *Etnicismo y cambio económico (un estudio sobre migrantes campesinos en la ciudad de México).* Mexico City: El Colegio de Mexico.

1979 "Rotating Urban Labor Relaying Migration as a Strategy for Survival among Peasant Households." Unpublished paper.

Benería, L.

1976 "Women's Participation in Paid Production under Capitalism: The Spanish Experience." *Review of Radical Political Economics* 8, no. 1: 18–33.

Berger, H.; Hessler, M.; and Kaveman, B.
1978 *Brot für heute, Hunger für morgen. Landarbeiter in Südspanien*. Frankfurt: M. Suhrkamp Verlag.

Bloch, H.
1976 "Changing Domestic Roles among Polish Immigrant Women." *Anthropological Quarterly* 49: 3–10.

Brandt, F.
1977 *Situationanalyse nicht erwerbstätiger Ehefrauen ausländischer Arbeitnehmer in der Bundesrepublik Deutschland*. Bonn-Bad Godesberg: Der Bundesminister für Jugend, Familie und Gesundheit.

Brettel, C.
1978 *Hope and Nostalgia: The Migration of Portuguese Women to Paris*. Ph.D. diss., Brown University.
1982 *We Have Already Cried Many Tears: Portuguese Women and Migration*. Cambridge, Mass.: Schenkman.

Brouwer, L., and Preister, M.
1983 "Living in Between: Turkish Women in Their Homeland and the Netherlands." In *One Way Ticket: Migration and Female Labour*, edited by A. Phizacklea, 115–29. London: Routledge and Kegan Paul.

Buechler, H. C., and Buechler, J-M.
1975 "Los Suizos: Galician Migration to Switzerland." In *Migration and Development: Implications for Ethnic Identity and Political Conflict*, edited by H. I. Safa and B. M. DuToit, 17–31. The Hague: Mouton.
1981 *Carmen: The Autobiography of a Spanish Galician Woman*. Cambridge, Mass.: Schenkman.

Bundesanstalt für Arbeit
1973 *Reprasentätiveuntersuchung 1972: Beschäftigung Ausländischer Arbeitnehmer*. Nürnberg.

Bundesminister des Innern
1983 Aufzeichnung zur Ausländerpolitik und zum Ausländerrecht in der Bundesrepublik Deutschland. October, V, II, 1–937, 029/19.

Busia, K. A.
1950 Social Survey of Sekondi-Taroradi, Accra.

Castles, Stephen, and Kosack, Godula
1973 *Immigrant Workers and Class Structure in Western Europe*. London: Oxford University Press.

Cornelisen, Ann
1977 *Woman of the Shadows: The Wives and Mothers of Southern Italy*. New York: Vintage.

Douglass, W.
1976 "Serving Girls and Sheepherders: Emigration and Continuity in a Spanish Basque Village." In *The Changing Faces of Rural Spain*, edited by J. B. Aceves and W. A. Douglass, 45–62. New York: John Wiley.

Foner, N.
1975 "Women, Work and Migration: Jamaicans in London." *Urban Anthropology* 4: 229–249.

German Information Center
1983 Focus on Minorities in Germany. No. 6, December.

Goodman, C.
1984 *The Decision Makers: Spanish Migrant Women in West Germany*. Ph.D. diss., Rutgers University.

Gregory, D.
1976 "Migration and Demographic Change in Andalusia." In *The Changing Faces of Rural Spain,* edited by J. B. Aceves and W. A. Douglass, 63–96. New York: John Wiley.

Heldman, H. H.
1980 *Ausländerrecht*. Köln: Paul-Rugenstein Verlag.

Hönekopp, Elmar, and Olle, W.
1980 *The Effect of Immigration on Social Structures*. Paris: UNESCO.

Kosack, G.
1976 "Migrant Women: The Move to Western Europe—A Step Toward Emancipation." *Race and Class* 17: 370–79.

Lequin, Y.
1977 *Les ouvriers de la région lyonnaise*. Lyon: Press Univ. de Lyon.

Levi, A.
1977 "Evolution of Portuguese Women Migrants." *Migration News,* no. 2: 2–11.

Little, K.
1971 *West African Urbanization: A Study of Voluntary Association in Social Change*. Cambridge: Cambridge University Press.

Mandelbaum, D. C.
1973 "The Study of Life History: Gandhi." *Current Anthropology* 14: 177–96.

Martinez, Alier
1971 *Laborers and Landowners in Southern Spain*. Totowa, N.J.: Rowman and Littlefield.

Masur, J.
1981 *Work, Leisure and Obligation in an Andalusian Town*. Ph.D. diss., University of Chicago.
1981 Personal comments from anthropological fieldwork in southern Spain.

Mediavilla, Leonor
1980 "Die spanischen Frauen in der BRD." *Dossier Europa Emigrazione* 1, no. 3: 38–40.

Moch, L., and Tilly, L.
1979 "Immigrant Women in the City: Comparative Perspectives." Center for Research on Social Organization. Working Paper No. 205.

Morokvasic, M.
1976 "Yugoslavic Migrant Women in France and the Federal Republic of Germany." *Migration News* 3 no. 4: 27–30.
1977 "Die Yugoslavischen Frauen in Frankreich und der Bundesrepublik Deutschland. Materialization zum Projektbereich." *Ausländische Arbeiter,* no. 17: 75–104.
1979 "Migration of Women in Europe." Presented at the conference on Creation of Relative Surplus Population, Immigration, and Urbanization, workshop no. 4.
1983 "Women in Migration: Beyond the Reductionist Outlook." In *One Way Ticket: Migration and Female Labor,* edited by A. Phizacklea, 15–22. London: Routledge and Kegan Paul.

Münschner, A.
1979 "Ausländische Familien in der Bundesrepublik Deutschland Familiennachzug und generatives Verhalten, Materialien zum dritten Familienbericht der Bundesregierung." München: Verlag Deutsches Jugendinstitut.

Nikolinakos, M.
1973 *Politische Ökonomie der Gastarbeiterfrage: Migration und Kapitalismus.* Reinbeck bei Hamburg, Rowohlt.

Nölkensmeier, I.
1980 "Ausländische Frauen in der BRD." *Dossier Europa Emigrazione* 1, no. 3: 13–24

Padres de Familia
1982 Press Release.

Phizacklea, A., ed.
1983 *One Way Ticket: Migration and Female Labor.* Boston: Routledge and Kegan Paul.

Presse und Informationsamt der Bundesregierung
1978 "Frauen: Informationen, Tip und Ideen zum Nachschlagen und Weitersagen." Pamphlet published by the Federal Republic of Germany.

Rist, R.
1978 *Guestworkers in Germany: The Prospects for Pluralism.* New York: Praeger.

Statistical Year Book
1983 Federal Republic of Germany Press.

Weber, Oranna, and Schultze, Dorothea
1979 "Kulturschock und Identitätskrise Spanischer Ehefrauen in der BRD-unter Berücksichtigung ihres sozio-kulturellen Hintergrundes in Spanien." Graduierungsarbeit für die staatliche Abschlussprüfung für Sozialarbeit. Katch, Fachhochschule, N. W. Aachen.

10 Spanish Galician Migration to Switzerland: Demographic Processes and Family Dynamics

Hans Christian Buechler

ABSTRACT. Buechler views migration simultaneously from the perspective of the place of origin—Spanish Galicia—and of migrants in the place of destination, in this case Switzerland. Using both quantitative and qualitative data, he focuses on the family and its transformation both historically and as a result of recent migrations. Like Gregory and Cazorla (chap. 7), he shows that the stage in the family cycle has a major bearing on the family and its migrant and nonmigrant members. Finally, like Barou (chap. 4), he examines how stages in the development of a migratory movement and changing migration patterns affect the options of different age cohorts.

INTRODUCTION

This chapter views migration as an integral part of the lives of Spanish Galicians: both those who migrated to other European countries, particularly Switzerland, and those who remained at home.

Galicians have long depended on migration to alleviate land pressure. In addition to relatively high population densities, land shortages came about because a large percentage of arable land was kept out of production by wealthier farmers (see Buechler and Buechler 1975, 18). In the late 19th and early 20th centuries, migration to Latin America reached massive proportions. It subsided again in the 1930s as a result of the Spanish Civil War and its aftermath, but became a veritable exodus again when industrialized West European countries opened their doors to workers from the south in the 1960s and 1970s. Thus, in the Galician parish studied by the authors "ninety-six or 62 percent of the households included members or children of members who were or who had been out of the country. If one adds migrant siblings and parents of household heads, this figure would be much higher still" (Buechler and Buechler 1975, 19).

Much of the earlier migration and most of the recent migration have been temporary. Even those migrants who have worked abroad since the early sixties expect to return to Spain, and most migrants return home for a few weeks to several months every year or two. Migration of entire families is the exception rather than the rule. Children, wives, and aging parents depend on migrant remittances, while migrants depend on the services of their kin at home to take care of their children and property. So an analysis of the dynamics of interpersonal relationships among closer kin cannot be confined to the host country. Rather, it must include ties with family members and other kin back home. The process of migration is thus not something that is added onto an established structure. Rather, family structure and migration are intricately interlinked in a single system and must be analyzed as such.

An approach which focuses on the family rather than on the individual is crucial to an understanding of migrant strategies as well as the effects of demographic processes on social relationships. The concept of "life course" provides a useful tool for such an analysis, for "it encompasses individual development as well as the collective development of the family unit" (Hareven 1978, 5). Instead of treating individuals as isolates, this concept plots individual life histories, stages in an individual's life cycle, and crucial events or periods in an individual's life (such as the migratory experience) against those of other members of a family, the development and composition of the family as a whole, and specific historical events or conditions.

The complexity of these processes requires an approach that relies neither exclusively on statistical data, where the interaction of multiple variables may become clouded, nor entirely on qualitative data, where the representativeness of the experiences of small numbers of informants may be questioned. We shall therefore base our analysis on both quantitative and qualitative data.

Qualitative data including topical interviews and life histories were gathered in 1972–1973 and the summers of 1974 and 1978 mainly in one Galician parish, which we shall call Santa Maria, located halfway between La Coruña and Santiago de Compostela, and among migrants from Santa Maria and adjacent parishes who migrated to Geneva, Berne, and Thoune, Switzerland. Some of these migrants were interviewed in Switzerland and some in both the place of origin and the place of destination. Nonmigrant members of their families were also interviewed. In addition, we carried out a census of a number of hamlets in the parish; copied birth, marriage, and death records of the parish and the entire municipality in which it is located (which we shall call Castiñeiro), and data from the personal files of individual migrants from Castiñeiro and adjacent municipalities both in the province capital and in the three Swiss host localities. Finally, the semi-computerized system in Thoune permitted us to obtain comparative data on all Spanish migrants in that city for four years between 1972 and 1978.

Our analysis will begin with a comparison of the household composition in Santa Maria in the 18th century (based on a census undertaken in 1761) and present-day households (based on our own census). Such an approach prevents possible biases which may result from projecting short-term processes observed in the present into the more distant past and serves to underline continuities and major long-term transformations in Galician households, particularly those associated with migration. Then, we shall present concrete examples of Santa Maria households in order to depict different types of household structure and illustrate the influence of migration in shaping them. We shall move on to a quantitative analysis of the missing segment of the Santa Maria population residing in Switzerland. Finally, we shall make these figures come to life by following the development of Galician households in Switzerland and the networks the migrants establish.

EFFECTS OF MIGRATION IN THE AREA OF ORIGIN

Migration and Family Composition: A Comparison of Santa Maria in 1761 and in 1973

A comparison between modern families and 18th-century families may serve as a basis for understanding certain demographic changes which may have influenced migration and others which are a result of increased migration, for it appears that in 1761 migration from the community was much lower than at present: only one spouse is listed as "fuera de este reyno" (absent from the kingdom) at the time the census was taken.[1]

Eighteenth-century households were significantly smaller than modern ones. The size of households headed by men had an average number of 4.3 members in 1761 (see table 10.1) versus 5.06 in 1973 (see table 10.2).[2] The most obvious reason for this difference in size is the larger number of children in modern households—an average of 2.16 in 1973 versus 1.69 (1.81 including all *criados* or servants) in 1761—which in all likelihood reflects a general decrease in infant mortality.[3] But the larger size of modern households is also due to a much higher percentage of extended households in 1973 (26.2 percent versus 19.5 percent in 1761) which in turn is related to greater longevity (see tables 10.3 and 10.4).[4] Although a lower percentage of men over 60 headed extended households in 1973 (36.2 percent of all men that age) than in 1761 (when they represented 53.6 percent), they constituted a larger proportion of all the household heads (12.4 percent as opposed to 9.5 percent in 1761). In addition, extended households headed by men in their forties and fifties were proportionately more frequent in 1973 (when they headed 48.8 percent of all households) than in 1761 (when they headed 44 percent of the households) (see table 10.3). Men in their forties and fifties were also three times as likely to head extended households in 1973 than in 1761.[5] This is due to the somewhat higher percentage of widows in 1973 (17.3 per 100 households versus 13.8 in 1761) combined with the fact that widows were more likely to live in extended households in 1973 (66.7 percent) than in 1761 (52 percent) (see table 10.3).

A decrease in infant mortality and greater longevity are not the only factors that have influenced the composition of Galician households. Migration has also had a major impact. Couples who migrate often leave their children with either set of

Table 10.1 Relationship of Household Members to the Oldest Married Male, 1761

Age of House-hold Head	% of House-hold Members	Self	W	S	SW	D	DH	SS	SD	DS	DD	M	WM	AUNT	Z	MZ	CRIA-DO *	CRIA-DA	NIECE OR NEPHEW	OTHER	TOTALS	% OF MEM-BERS	AVE SIZE
10-19	0.6%	1	1											1							3	0.4%	(3)
20-29	17.0%	27	26	10		14						5	3	1	5	1					92	13.1%	3.4
30-39	20.8%	33	33	32		37						1	1		2		1	4	1		146	20.8%	4.42
40-49	24.5%	39	39	50	1	52									1		2	4	1	WZ,WZS	191	27.2%	4.9
50-59	19.5%	31	30	26	3	26		2	2	1	2						1	3		2 WZ	129	18.4%	4.16
60-69	12.6%	20	15	12	5	13	4	5	2	2	6							3			87	12.4%	4.35
70-79	4.4%	7	3	6	2	9	4	2	2	8	5							1			49	7.0%	7.
80-89																							
90-99	0.6%	1					(grandson + W = 2)											1			4	0.6%	(4)
Sub Totals		159	147	136	12	151	8	9	6	11	13	6	4	2	8	1	4	16	2	3WZ,1WZS	701		4.4
% Household		22.7%	21%	19.4%	1.7%	21.5%	1.1%	1.3%	0.9%	1.6%	1.3%	0.9%	0.6%	0.3%	1.1%	0.1%	0.5%	2.3%	0.3%	0.4%			
																					681		4.3
% of Kin		23.3%	21.6%	20%	1.8%	22.2%	1.2%	1.3%	0.9%	1.6%	1.9%	0.9%	0.6%	0.3%	1.2%	0.1%			0.3%	0.4%			
		M Head	F Head																				
Rel. to Widow Household Head			14	5	2	10		1	1										1	1 "Widow"	35		
Rel. to Spinster Household Head			7												2				2		11		
Bachelor Household Head		1																			1		
TOTAL		160	168	141	14	161	8	10	7	11	13	6	4	2	10	1	1	3	19	2 5	748		4.1

KEY: S = son, B = brother, D = daughter, Z = sister, H = Husband, W = Wife, * servants - 3 listed as minors

Table 10.2 Relationship of Household Members to the Oldest Married Male, 1973
(Including Households Where Husband Is Away)

No. of House-hold	Age of House-hold Head	Self	W	S	SW	Mar. D	Non-Mar. D	DH	SS	SD	DS	DD	M	WM	B	Z	OTHER KIN		NO.	%	AVE SIZE
	10-19																				
1 0.7%	20-29	1	1				1												3	0.4%	(3)
22 16.1%	30-39	21	22	35			27						1	3			2(WB, WZD)		111	16.3%	5
32 23.4%	40-49	31	32	50	1		43					1	3	3			2(WFZ,WZ)		166	24.3%	5.2
35 25.5%	50-59	35	35	51	2	2	44	1			2	4	2	2		1	1(WMB)		182	26.4%	5.2
22 16.1%	60-69	22	19	23	2	3	13	3	3	4	5	4	1		2	3			107	15.6%	4.3
17 12.4%	70-79	17	10	15	4	4	5	2	3	6	10	3		1	1				81	11.8%	4.9
6 4.4%	80-89	6	4	4	1	1	3	1	1	1	1								23	3.4%	2.8
2	90-99	2	1			1		1			1	3					2(WBS,WZSW)		11	1.6%	(5.5)
137 100%	Total	135 19.8%	124 18.2%	178 26.1%	10 1.5%	11 1.5%	136 19.9%	8 1.2%	7 1.0%	11 1.6%	19 2.8%	15 2.2%	7 1.0%	9 1.3%	3 0.4%	4 0.6%	7 1.0%		684 100%		5.06
Bachelors		2													2	2	1(FBS)				
Widows		8		3			6			2	1	1						1*			
Spinsters		2																			
?		3	3	9			7				1		1								
TOTALS		150	127	190	10	11	149	8	7	13	21	16	8	9	5	6	8	1	739		4.92

KEY: S = son; B = brother; D = daughter; Z = sister; H = Husband; W = Wife; * hired hand

Table 10.3 Types of Households in 1761 and 1973*

Age	Widowers as oldest Married Males	1761 Nuclear or with distant Kin	1973	1766 Extended + SW	1973	1761 Extended + DH	1973	1761 Extended + Married D (H away)	1973	1761 Extended + Married D	1973	1761 Extended + M	1973	1761 Extended + WM	1973	1761 TOTAL EXTENDED	1973
10–19	1973	1 100%															
20–29		19 70%	1 100%									5 18.5%		3 11.1%		8 29.6%	
30–39		30 91%	18 82%	1 3%								1 3%	1 4.8%	1 3%	3 14.3%	3 9%	4 18%
40–49		38 97.4%	25 78%	1 2.6%	1 3.1%								3 9.4%		3 9.4%	1 2.6%	7 22%
50–59	1	27 87%	27 77.1%	3 9.7%	2 5.7%		1 2.9%	1 3.2%	1 2.0%	1 3.2%	2 5.7%		2 5.7%		2 5.7%	4 13.1%	8 32.9%
60–69	2	11 55%	16 72.7%	5 25%	2 3.1%	4 20%	3 13.6			4 20%	3 13.6%		1 4.5%			3 45%	6 27.3%
70–79	5	1 14.3%	9 52.9%	2 28.6%	4 23.5%	4 57.1%	2 11.5%		1 5.9%	4 57.1%	3 17.6%				1 5.9%	6 85.7%	8 47%
80–89	2		4 66.7%		1 16.7%		1 16.7%				1 16.7%						2 33.3%
90–99	1	1 (100%)	1 (50%)				1 (50%)				1 (50%)						1 (50%)
		128 80.5%	101 73.7%	12 7.5%	10 7.3%	8 5.0%	8 5.8%	1 0.6%	2 1.5%	9 5.7%	10 7.3%	6 3.8%	7 5.1%	4 2.5%	9 6.6%	31 19.5%	36 26.5%

KEY: S = son, B = brother, D = daughter, H = Husband, W = Wife

* male headed where age of head was given

Table 10.4 Type of Household

	NUCLEAR				EXTENDED			
	1761		1973		1761		1973	
	N	%	N	%	N	%*	N	%*
10-19	1	0.8%					N	
20-29	19	14.8%	1	1.0%	8	25.8%		
30-39	30	23.4%	18	17.8%	3	3.8%	4	11.1%
40-49	38	29.7%	25	24.8%	1	3.2%	7	13.4%
50-59	27	21.1%	27	26.7%	4	12.9%	8	22.2%
60-69	11	8.6%	16	15.8%	9	29.0%	6	16.7%
70-79	1	0.8%	9	8.9%	6	19.4%	8	22.2%
80-89			4	3.9%			2	5.5%
90-99	1	0.8%	1	1.0%			1	2.8%
	128	73.8%	101	73.6%	31	19.5%	36	26.2%

parents.[6] This fact, together with greater longevity, may account for the increase in the percentage of grandchildren in Galician households (7.6 percent in 1973 versus 5.8 percent in 1761), and the fact that there were grandchildren in 42 percent of all households in 1973 versus 15.3 percent in 1761 (tables 10.1 and 10.2).

The demographic impact of migration becomes most apparent, however, when family composition is viewed over its developmental cycle. In 1973 only one household (0.7 percent of all households) was headed by a male under 30 versus 28 (15.5 percent) in 1761. Households headed by males between 30 and 39 still represented only 14 percent in 1973 versus 18.2 percent in 1761. The percentage of male-headed households peaked at the age of 50-59 in 1973 versus 40-49 in 1761. Finally, while in 1973 16.7 percent of all households included married males over 70, only 4.4 percent did so in 1761. In addition to showing greater longevity in 1973, these figures clearly indicate the importance of migration, especially in the 20-29 age bracket and to a lesser extent in the 30-39 age bracket. More young people of both sexes have moved to towns and cities, or have migrated abroad, leaving their parents alone or with the remaining unmarried siblings. Since building a house of their own is a major priority, many of these migrants—in many families perhaps even all children—may eventually establish their own nuclear households rather than join those of their parents. Whether widows will then also be more likely to live alone is another matter. They may well move in with their children again in return for a larger share of the inheritance, as is often already the case. I shall return to these issues later.

In part, the age composition of the 1973 households is also the result of later marriage age. This can also be deducted from the fact that the age curve for parents of unmarried children is much flatter than in 1761. Thus in 1973 almost the same number of fathers were between 50 and 60 years and between 40 and 50, while the percentage of unmarried children with 50-60-year-old parents is sharply lower in 1761. Again migration plays a role (tables 10.1 and 10.2). Records of Santa Maria marriages between 1964 (when migration regained importance) and 1972 do not show a significant difference in marriage age between individuals with migratory experience and nonmigrants. However, our census indicates that at least the older migrant couples (i.e., those between 31 and 40), where both have migratory experience, appear to have waited longer to have children than either nonmigrants or couples where only one spouse (almost invariably the husband) migrated. In this same age bracket, the average number of children is also lowest (1.84) for those cases where both parents have migratory experience. In this age bracket nonmigrants have an average of 2.57 children and couples where only one spouse emigrated have an average of 3.16 (see table 10.5). Low postponement and high numbers of children may have been one of the motive forces for men in the latter category to migrate in order to provide for their larger-than-average families and enable them to save for such major items as houses (see table 10.6).[7]

The migrants we interviewed on the subject were well aware of different methods of contraception including the pill (see Buechler and Buechler 1981,

Table 10.5 Average Number of Children of Santa Maria Migrant and Nonmigrant Couples (Census 1973)

	ALL AGES		21 - 25		26 - 30		31 - 35		36 - 40		41 - 45		46 - 50	
	N	AV	N	AV	N	AV	N	AV	N	AV	N	AV	N	AV
Both Parents Emigrated	52	1.84	12	0.92	17	1.47	9	1.78	10	1.90	2	4.00	2	4.5
One Parent Emigrated	46	3.16	--	----	11	1.64	6	3.00	18	3.22	7	4.14	4	3.25
Neither Parent Emigrated	83	2.57	12	1.25	12	1.50	7	1.70	16	2.93	21	2.76	15	4.13

N = Number of couples. AV = Average number of children.

Table 10.6 Number of Children of Migrants from Castiñeiro in Berne Correlated with Age of the Father

AGE BRACKET	16-20	21-25	26-30	31-35	36-40	41-45	46-50	+50
A. WIFE RESIDES IN BERNE								
Number of cases	6	10	21	11	5	4	0	1
Average number of Children	0.17	0.6	0.81	1.27	1.2	1.25		
B. WIFE RESIDES IN SPAIN								
Number of cases		2	5	7	5	9	8	3
Average number of children		0.5	1.4	2	3	2.4	2.5	0.7

xvi). Many, however, seemed to use less safe methods than the pill. One woman said that she did not use the pill because of health hazards. Swiss doctors were reluctant to provide details about birth control—after all, the Spaniards come from a Catholic country which frowns upon the practice—but it became apparent that advice about such matters was given frequently. One doctor said that sterilizations were quite frequent among women from Mediterranean countries with many children.[8]

What are the overall effects of migration and lower birthrates on births in Castiñeiro? Certainly, the absolute number of live births in the municipality has decreased considerably since 1912 (see figures 10.1 and 10.2). In that year the total number of births was 449 and in 1972 only 374, a drop of 16.7 percent. Since the municipal capital attracts migrants from neighboring municipalities as well, the drop is even more significant; for in rural areas the decrease was 35.9 percent. The impact of this drop on long-term population trends will depend on the number of children born to migrants outside of Spain who will eventually return to the municipality.

Second, what are the implications of these demographic changes we have discussed on interaction patterns within households in Galicia? The increase in the number of siblings increases the number of sibling relationships. There is a similar increase in grandparent-grandchild interaction in general and grandmother-grandchild relationships in particular. In contrast, there is a decrease in daily interaction between young adult family members (who constitute the bulk of the migrants) on the one hand and their parents and younger siblings on the other. As we shall see, though, this is compensated by a greater dependency of younger siblings on older ones during migration. Migration also occasions a decrease in interaction between parents and their immature children, with the most drastic decrease in the frequency of interaction between fathers and their older children and between mothers and their first- and second-born children. Later, we shall see that these patterns are modified by the permeable nature of households. In addition, we cannot necessarily predict the content or intensity of interaction from the frequency with which it takes place.

Marriage and Residence Patterns

Migration and the decreasing role of agriculture in the life strategies of Galicians may also have a significant impact on postmarital residence patterns. Between 1912 and 1977 parish endogamy in the entire municipality of Castiñeiro generally decreased. This is especially true for rural parishes, where the only time there was an increase in endogamous unions since 1912 was between 1922 and 1932.[9] This trend reflects increasing contacts between rural parishes. Migration has definitely contributed to these contacts. Thus, visiting migrants attend religious festivals at considerable distances and, as we shall see later, meet and marry persons from other localities while abroad.

Traditionally, according to C. Lisón-Tolosana (1971), three different types of

Figure 10.1 Place of Birth in Relation to That of the Parents: Rural Communities in the Municipality of Castiñeiro (1912=387; 1972=248)

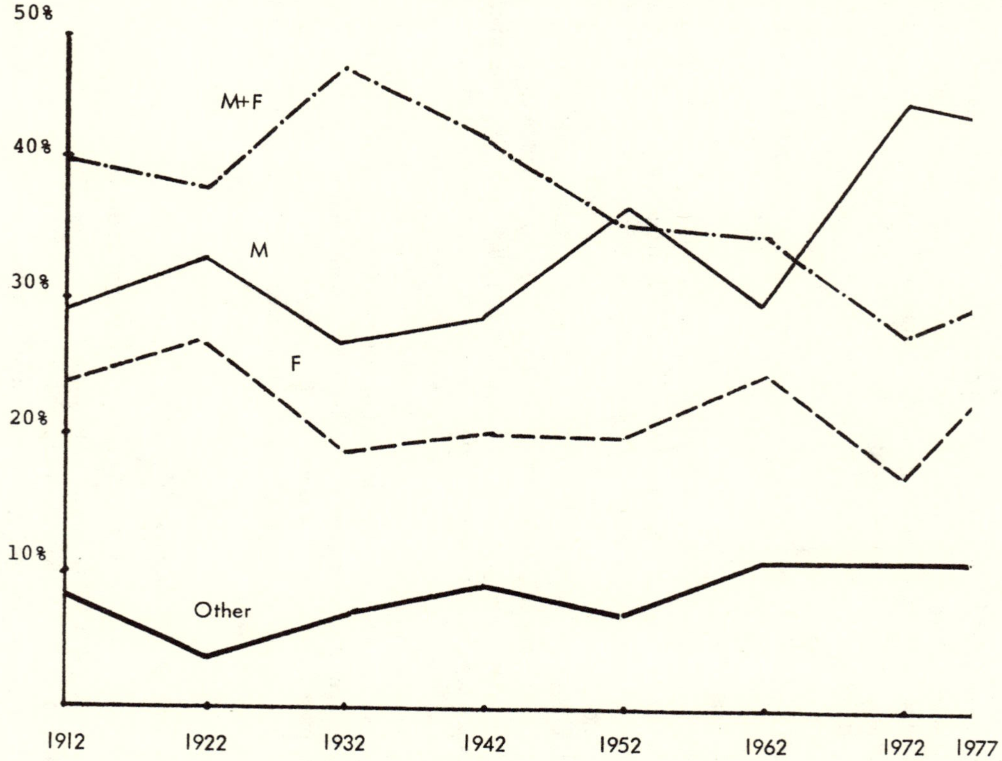

Key: M = Mother born in the same locality as the child.
F = Father born in the same locality as the child.

Figure 10.2 Place of Birth in Relation to That of the Parents: Town of Castiñeiro (1912=387; 1972=248)

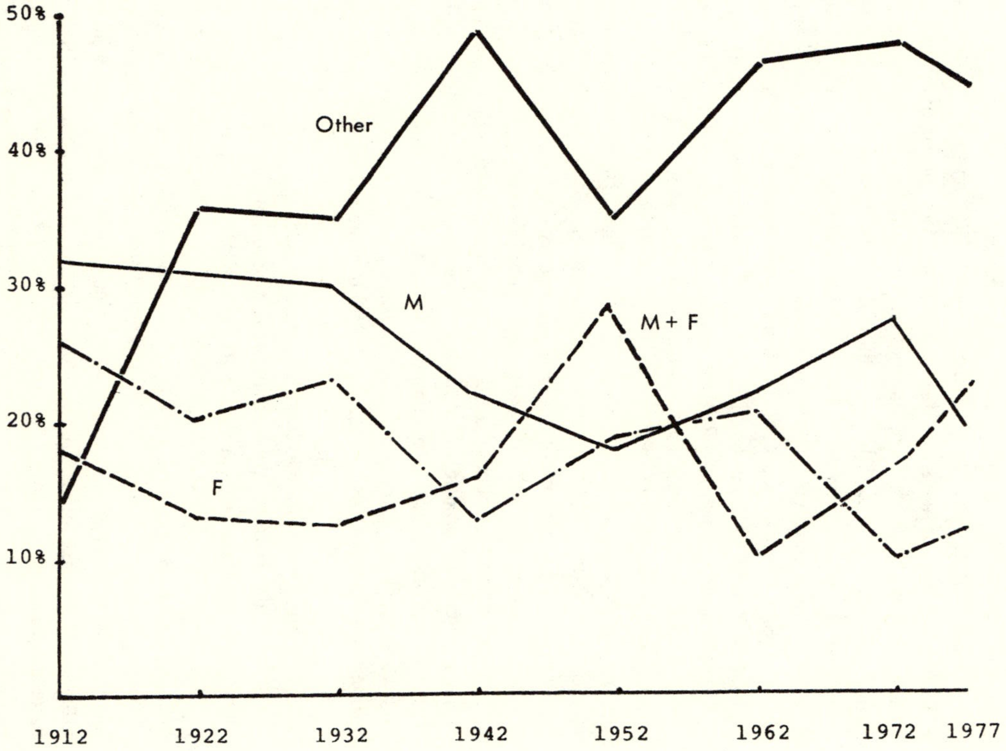

Key: See figure 10.1

residence patterns could be found in Galicia. Inland farming communities tended to encourage patrilocal residence; fishing communities, where men were often away at sea, were characterized by matrilocal residence; while in the province of Orense, in the south of Galicia, married men and women remained in their respective paternal homes. He attributes the recent increase in matrilocality in inland communities to emigration, which also takes males away from home more frequently than females (1971, 272, 348, 350).[10]

An examination of the birth records between 1912 and 1977 in the municipality of Castiñeiro does in fact show that an increasing proportion of children were born in the community of origin of the mother, even though this trend is not entirely consistent (figs. 10.1 and 10.2). Santa Maria occupies a somewhat special position within the *ayuntamiento*. In contrast to other parishes, where uxorilocality has been higher than virilocality at least since 1912, the trend towards uxorilocality in Santa Maria has been of more recent origin. According to our 1973 census, fifty-four couples lived in the wife's hamlet and seventy-seven in the husband's hamlet. Similarly 7.2 percent of all households included married sons and only 5.8 percent included married daughters. However, 41.2 percent of all marriages which took place between 1973 and 1977 were followed by uxorilocal and only 19.6 percent by virilocal residence.[11] The difference from other parishes in the municipality may arise from the fact that Santa Maria is considered a relatively wealthy community. There is some evidence that, at least in the past, wealthier peasants preferred to pass on the family house and with it a larger share of the land to a son. Indeed, residence in a hamlet where there are a number of houses which still belong to an absentee landlord is predominantly uxorilocal. However, uxorilocality also characterizes the settlements along the principal highway which leads to the municipal capital. Many of the men and some of the women commute to work to this town and to nearby cities. It would appear that in this case parents gave their daughters choice pieces of land with ready access to transportation in order to keep them close by.

Interestingly, both residence patterns are regarded as normative. Virilocality is viewed as resulting from a desire to keep the family name associated with a particular farm, while women who brought their husbands into their parents' households insist that men have no choice but to follow an uxorilocal rule.

Changes in residence patterns undoubtedly did result from recent changes in local economies which, in turn, were often directly associated with or at least influenced by migration. But it would be wrong to conclude that residence patterns were once more consistent. The 1761 census shows almost identical residence patterns in extended households as in 1973. Given the recent changes in the parish, this means that residence in Santa Maria became more patrilocal before it shifted towards matrilocality. It would appear, then, that residence patterns were always subject to situational choices. The fact that in 1761 all widows lived either alone or in households which included close female blood relatives (usually daughters) lends support to this hypothesis.

Neolocality

Migration is also a major contributor to neolocality (see Buechler and Buechler 1981, 199; H. Buechler 1983). Migrants purchase houses or apartments in towns and cities, planning to live there upon their return. The trend towards urban residence is well apparent from the birth statistics of the municipal capital. While in 1912 only 14 percent of the children born there had parents who were both immigrants, 49 percent fell in this category in 1942 and 48 percent in 1972 (fig. 10.2). Should the migrants be forced to return, this percentage might rise even further, for the town, which had a population of just under 10,000 in 1972, had at least 361 unfinished apartment buildings with some 3,000 apartments in 1978.[12]

In contrast, few persons move to rural parishes other than those of their parents, although there has been a slight increase in such moves over the years. Migrants who have accumulated cash abroad but have no access to land at home are among the buyers of rural properties offered for sale in the newspapers.

Examples of Santa Maria Families

The cross-sectional approach employed in the comparison between the two censuses freezes households at particular moments in their development. It does not show how the composition of specific households changes over time, nor the degree of patterning of succession within family lines. An exhaustive analysis of such processes by means of an analysis of longitudinal data is beyond the scope of this chapter. However, the following profiles of Santa Maria families will give an indication of the range of succession possibilities within families. They also show other means of establishing a household, including the role played by migration money. At the same time they give an idea of the reasons why kin live together.

The first case exemplifies three-generation extended households and both patrilocal and matrilocal residence. José inherited his parental home because his older brother contracted tuberculosis in Montevideo and died young, while his two sisters were crippled. They remained at home and contributed to the household economy by sewing, but remained single. Today José and his wife live with his married daughter, his son-in-law, who works as a mason in the area, and his four grandchildren. Another daughter lives nearby. This daughter's small son also feels as much at home at his grandparents' house as in his own parents' home. In addition to the adaptability of residence patterns within the same kindred over generations and the manner in which invalid family members are provided for, the case shows that the very boundaries of a household can be flexible as grandchildren come and go at will. As we shall see, this is by no means an isolated instance of such permeability.

The next three cases exemplify variants of grandparent-grandchild households.

In each case migration has played a major role in the composition of the household, its establishment, and in one case the financing of a small business.

Avelina, age 72, and Jesús, age 75, live in a house which was originally rented and was passed on through matrilineal succession for three generations. Avelina's father had migrated to Cuba and abandoned his family. Her two sisters then migrated to Montevideo and sent money to purchase the house outright. The elderly couple has seven living children, two of whom were in Switzerland at the time we took the census and two had been there earlier. At present Avelina and Jesús live with two of their grandchildren. One is 19 and works in construction. The other is 3 and was left in their care by a daughter who is in Switzerland. In addition to the older grandson, the couple can count on the assistance of some of their children who have not emigrated, as well as of the migrant children when they return home for Christmas.[13] The migrant parents of the younger grandchild contribute to the household by sending remittances from abroad.

Two generations of migrants have thus contributed to the economy of this household, but the extended family has also suffered from the failure of a migrant belonging to yet another generation to fulfill normal expectations. The victims include siblings in Montevideo who had to compensate for the delinquency of Avelina's father by going beyond the normal call of duty of supporting kinsmen back home.

While in the previous example kinsmen assisted in the establishment of the household, Roberto, who is 50, founded his entirely on his own. Before marriage he worked as a tailor. After marriage he and his wife rented a small house in a neighboring parish and opened a cloth and notions store. Later he requested a small plot of land (a little more than a hectare) from the municipality,[14] built a house there, and slowly improved the practically worthless land by carting in good soil. Then he worked in the nearby mines for nine years until migration opened to Germany and Switzerland, where he worked during the next five years. At present he sells fish, fruit, and vegetables from a small delivery truck. One of his sons who is a mechanic is investing his savings in a building constructed on his father's land where he hopes to open a service station. This son and three daughters are all working in Switzerland. A 2-year-old child of one of the daughters also lives with Roberto, and on some weekends his youngest daughter, who is studying to become a secretary in the city of La Coruña, comes home as well.

Roberto's case is thus the diametric opposite of the previous example. He *successfully* established a household *before* migrating. Roberto would have been too young to emigrate when migration was still open to Latin America, and his household was perhaps at too advanced a stage in its development for him to go to Venezuela in the fifties. But later, by migrating to Switzerland, he was able to both improve his own economic position and lay the foundations for his son's return from abroad and the establishment of his own small industry.

Finally, Mario (who is in his sixties) provides an example of the importance of migration in establishing a household: the classical goal-migration pattern. He built his house on his in-laws' land. But previously he had gone to work in Cuba for twelve years when he was only 16 and married soon upon his return. At first he opened a tavern in a nearby parish, but then the Civil War came and he opened a bakery across the road from his parents-in-law. Later he worked in tin and tungsten mines in the area, including a small one owned by his brother, until he decided to open a brick kiln. With his savings he bought more land and finally switched to farming altogether. In addition, his wife inherited some farmland and house plots along the main road. Some of these were passed on to daughters.

The couple has taken in Ricardo, the 6-year-old grandson of one of the daughters. He was born in the grandparental home and remained there when their daughter and her husband migrated to England in order to earn money to build their own house, thereby repeating Mario's goal-migration. His parents have returned to Spain, but Ricardo prefers to stay with his grandparents (he visits his parents for only a few hours on end and then returns). Since his parents have three other children, everyone seemed happy with the arrangements. In addition, Mario has two other daughters in Santa Maria, one son in Venezuela, and one in Switzerland.

The couple do most of their farm work alone. As he puts it: "The children have their own work and have little time. The daughter who helped most was the mother of the boy who lives with us, but since she has three other children, if she brings them here, my wife has to take care of them and we haven't gained anything."

The final two examples are of nuclear families whose heads represent different generations. Jesús (who is 52 years old) moved into his in-laws' house upon marriage. He and his wife Maria (who is 46) lived there for twenty-one years. When the landowner whose land they rented sold off his vast estate, the couple purchased part of the land and built their own house. Three of their daughters have emigrated and one of the sons is serving in the military, but there are still two single children at home, a 19-year-old son and an 18-year-old daughter.

Upon marriage, Mario, who is 28 years old, and his wife Ortencia, who is 31, first lived in the province of León where Mario worked as a miner. When the couple returned to Santa Maria they first lived with Ortencia's mother, a poor day laborer who never married. However, Ortencia's mother also had another illegitimate daughter living with her, and soon the young couple rented a home nearby. Later the house Ortencia's mother had rented collapsed and she rented a house across the road from Ortencia. Mario and Ortencia have seven children. He is presently working in Germany, but with so many children it would be impractical for her to join him.

As these two examples show, cross-sectional data on household composition can be misleading. Both nuclear families passed through an extended phase which in the first instance lasted over twenty years. In the second case, the family remains very closely linked to the wife's mother, who lives just across the road.

In conclusion, one can only understand household composition and functioning by viewing the household in the context of its development over time and its relationship with contemporary households of other close kin both in Spain and abroad. The life choices made by the members of these families must, in turn, be seen in the context of intermittent opportunities to migrate, the risk of being abandoned by a migrant breadwinner, and the timing of these opportunities relative to the stage of each household member and the stage in his or her life. Later we shall see that the migrant households themselves must be viewed both in relationship to those of kinsmen back home and those of fellow migrants of the same as well as different age cohorts.

THE MIGRANTS IN SWITZERLAND

A complete analysis of the structure of Galician migrant households would, at the very least, have to include past and present households in Cuba, Montevideo, Buenos Aires, Caracas, and the United States in addition to those in various countries in Western Europe. In each case, accessibility to Spain, the age of the diaspora community, the nature of the opportunities abroad (e.g., the possibilities of establishing one's own family enterprise), settlement policies in the host countries, and other factors could influence household forms and, more generally, help shape kin networks. Here we shall limit ourselves to an examination of the development of households in Switzerland.

The flow of migrants to the more industrialized European countries has fluctuated considerably over the years. In Switzerland the latest wave of migrants gained momentum in the 1950s. Spanish migrants became a major component of this wave in the early sixties. In Switzerland immigration peaked in 1964, but the number of foreigners continued to rise until 1974. After that year the foreign population began to drop rapidly.[15] While the total population of Spaniards residing in Switzerland or working there with a seasonal permit does not seem to have dropped between 1972 and 1977, in Thoune, where we followed the changes in the Spanish migrant population during this period, the decline was very marked. Their number dropped from 413 in 1972 to 271 in 1977.

Age of Migrants

The demographic characteristics of the Spanish migrants in Switzerland confirm that they are indeed the segment of the population pyramid missing in the place of origin. In Switzerland as a whole, 20.4 percent of the Spaniards with annual or permanent permits were between 20 and 29, and 24.6 percent were between 30 and 39 in 1976.[16] A comparison with migrants to Switzerland of all origins shows that there were many more migrants between 20 and 49 among Spaniards than among all migrants in the above categories (see table 10.7), a difference that had all but disappeared by 1984 as fewer younger Spaniards went to Switzerland, while the older, more established ones (and presumably some of their by now older children) remained. During the five-year study period, most Spanish migrants in Thoune were under fifty (see table 10.8). In 1972 the age bracket with the largest proportion of both male and female migrants was between

Table 10.7 Age Structure of Annual and Permanent Migrants in Switzerland, December 1976 and 1984

	All Migrants			Spaniards		
	1976	1984	Change	1976	1984	Change
0 - 9 yrs	20.1%	12.4%	-7.7%	18.4%	14.3%	-4.1%
10 - 19 "	14.3%	15.5%	+1.2%	11.3%	14.1%	+2.8%
20 - 29 "	15.8%	16.4%	+0.6%	20.4%	15.7%	-4.7%
30 - 39 "	22.3%	19.2%	-3.1%	24.6%	23.2%	-1.4%
40 - 49 "	15.0%	18.6%	+3.6%	17.7%	17.6%	-0.1%
50 - 59 "	6.5%	10.7%	+4.2%	6.0%	11.7%	+5.7%
60 + "	6.0%	7.2%	+1.2%	1.6%	3.4%	+1.8%

Source: *Die Volkswirtschaft* April 1977, 185; April 1985, 187.

21 and 30: 42.9 percent of all Spanish men and 50.8 percent of the women fell into this category.[17] For Galicia as a whole this age bracket predominated even more for both sexes: 45.7 percent of the Galician men and 62.2 percent of the women were between 21 and 30, while only 37.8 percent of the male and 39 percent of the female non-Galicians were that age. Five years later this difference had maintained itself, although there had been substantial changes in the size and other characteristics of both subpopulations. All four Galician provinces exhibited this feature, but in both years it was most marked in the subpopulation from the province of La Coruña.

During the study period, the average age of the total adult Galician population in Thoune increased by 0.4 years for men and 1.6 years for women, indicating both the continued turnover of migrants but also, as we shall see later, a lengthening of the average stay. Galician and rural non-Galician men were very different in this respect. While the average age of rural non-Galician men actually fell by 0.2 years, that of the Galician men rose by 0.6 years (see tables 10.8 and 10.9). In contrast, the average age of *all* women increased, albeit more than double for Galicians: by 0.8 years for rural non-Galician women and by 2.2 for Galician women.

Initially, Spanish men had a markedly wider age spread than women. In 1972 those above 40 represented 20.1 percent, while the percentage of the women in this category was only 13.5 percent (table 10.8). Migrants from the province of La Coruña differed from the Spanish population as a whole by their lower average age. There was a lower percentage of both men (15.7 percent) and women (6.9 percent) over 40.[18] Over the years, the age distribution of men and women in the total Spanish population became more similar and by 1977 it was practically the same (20.2 percent of the men and 21.5 percent of the women were over 40, and similar proportions were present in all other age brackets). In contrast, this was not the case for La Coruña migrants (11.9 percent men over 40 versus 5.6 percent women).[19]

It was more difficult to ascertain how many Spanish migrants had children in the three localities studied. Nationally, as table 10.7 indicates, the percentage of children between 0 and 19 years (29.7 percent of annual and permanent migrants) was significantly lower for Spaniards than for other migrants (34.4 percent in 1976 (see also table 10.10). However, these figures already represent a substantial lessening of the difference in the percentage of Spanish children in the population of Spanish annual and permanent permit holders in comparison with the migrant population as a whole since 1971.

Unfortunately, foreign registration records in Thoune give only the number of children residing in Spain. In 1973, of the 87 Spanish couples in Thoune, half had children in Spain and the other half either had no children or had them in Thoune. Married men from La Corũna with wives in Thoune were somewhat more likely to fall into the latter category (see table 10.11). In the same year eleven couples (i.e., 12.6 percent of the couples in Thoune) had a total of sixteen children in

Table 10.8 Age of Registered Spaniards in Thoune (%), 1972 and 1977

	1972						1977					
	Spaniards		Galicians		From LaCoruña		Spaniards		Galicians		From LaCoruña	
Age	Men	Women	Men	Women	Men	Women	Men	Women	Men	Women	Men	Women
Under 20	10.7	10.5	12.0	12.2	11.8	24.1	6.4	7.1	6.2	8.2	9.0	11.1
21-30	42.9	50.8	45.7	62.2	41.2	58.6	44.4	44.0	47.3	53.1	53.7	66.7
31-40	26.3	25.0	25.0	21.6	31.4	10.3	28.9	27.4	29.5	28.6	25.4	16.7
41-50	15.2	8.1	13.0	2.7	10.8	3.4	17.6	16.7	16.1	10.2	11.9	5.6
51-60	4.2	0.8	4.3	1.4	4.9	3.4	2.1	2.4	0.9	0.0		
61-70	0.7	1.6					0.5	1.2				
over 70	0.0	1.6					0.0	1.2				
Sum (N)	289	124	184	74	102	29	187	84	112	49	67	18
Ave. Age	31.8	31.1	30.9	27.9	30.8	26.4	32.2	32.8	31.5	30.1	29.8	27.4

*Most children are not registered separately and do not appear in these figures.

Table 10.9 Age of Registered Non-Galician Spaniards in Thoune (%), 1972 and 1977 (by Rural and Urban Origin)

	1972								1977							
	Rural Non-Galicians				Urban Non-Galicians				Rural Non-Galicians				Urban Non-Galicians			
	Men		Women		Men		Women		Men		Women		Men		Women	
Under 20	9	10.0	2	4.9	0	0.0	2	22.2	5	7.7	2	6.1	0		0	0.0
21 - 30	34	37.8	16	39.0	6	40.0	1	11.1	25	38.5	11	33.3	6	50.0	1	33.3
31 - 40	24	26.7	11	26.8	6	40.0	4	44.4	18	27.7	8	24.2	3	25.0	1	33.3
41 - 50	17	18.9	7	17.1	3	20.0	1	11.1	14	21.5	8	24.2	2	16.7	1	33.3
51 - 60	4	4.4	0	0.0	0	0.0	0	0.0	2	3.1	2	6.1	1	8.3	0	
61 - 70	2	2.2	4	9.8	0	0.0	0	0.0	1	1.5	1	3.0			0	
over 70			1	2.4			1	11.1			1	3.0			0	
Sum (N)	90		41		15		9		65		33		12		3	
Average Age	33.5		35.8		32.7		35.6		33.3		36.6		32.4		35.7	

schools in that city: four in kindergarten, ten in elementary school, and two in secondary school. School-age children thus represented only 5.7 percent of the recorded Spanish migrant population.[20]

For Berne the figures are more complete. In 1973 the percentage of married women from Castiñeiro either with no children or with children in Berne was similar to the Thoune figures for all Spaniards. Of these women 29.2 percent had no children, 50.8 percent had children in Spain,[21] and 20 percent had children in Berne (table 10.11). Finally, in Geneva about a third of the couples from Castiñeiro with annual and permanent permits (in practice, a prerequisite for being allowed to have children in Switzerland) had children in Geneva (table 10.11).

Sex and Marital Status

In any given year around 70 percent of all adult Spanish migrants in Thoune were men. The ratio fluctuated only slightly between 1972 and 1977 (70 percent in 1972 and 69 percent in 1977).[22] The percentage of adult Spanish men was substantially higher in Thoune than in the country as a whole: 72.4 percent of the working annual and seasonal permit holders in 1977 were men versus 65.7 percent for the following year in the country as a whole (*Volkswirtschaft*, June 1978).[23] By comparison, among adult migrants from Castiñeiro in Berne, there was a smaller proportion of men (64.1 percent) than in Thoune, perhaps because there may be more employment opportunities for women in a larger city.

There were always more married than single adult migrants in Thoune (61.8 percent were married in 1972 and 68.6 percent in 1977), a difference which is particularly marked for women. Over the study period there were no major changes in these proportions for men in the Spanish population as a whole, but a slight decrease in married men (from 58.8 percent to 55.3 percent) among migrants from La Coruña. In contrast, the percentage of married women in the total adult female population increased steadily from 64.5 percent in 1972 to 83.3 percent in 1977 and among La Coruña women from 58.6 percent to 88.9 per-

Table 10.10 Percentage of the Migrants in Switzerland with Annual and Permanent Permits under 16 Years of Age*

	December 1971	December 1976
Spaniards	22.2%	25.7%
All migrants	28.0%	30.0%

Source: *Die Volkswirtschaft*, April 1972 and April 1977.

Table 10.11 Residence of Children of Spanish Migrants to Switzerland, 1973

Locality in Switzerland	Place of Origin	Number of Couples	Couples with Children in Spain	Couples without Children	Couples with Children in Switzerland	Couples without children or with children in Switzerland
Thoune	Spain	87	44 (50.6%)			43 (49.4%)
	La Coruña Province	24	9 (37.5%)			15 (62.5%)
Berne	Castiñeiro	65 (married women)	33 (50.8%)	19 (29.2%)	13 (20%)	32 (49.2%)
Geneva	Castiñeiro (annual and permanent permits *)	88			32 (36.4%)	

cent.[24] Correspondingly, since married women rarely migrate alone, the proportion of men whose wives reside in Thoune increased from 44 percent of all married men to 64.7 percent (26.6 percent to 40.7 percent of all adult men). This ratio is consistently lower for migrants from the province of La Coruña: 36.7 percent of the married men had wives in Thoune in 1972 and 54.1 percent in 1977 (21.6 percent to 29.9 percent of all adult men). This indicates that there was a greater tendency towards goal-migration among these migrants than for the Spaniards as a whole: men would migrate alone for as long as it took to accumulate savings for a specific purpose such as building a house.[25]

Length of Residence

The increase in the percentage of men with wives in Thoune seems to reflect a degree of stabilization of the migrant population. This is confirmed by the average length of time migrants have held annual or residency permits.[26] In 1972 the average duration for the entire Spanish population of this period was 3.1 years; in 1977 it was 4.6 years.

Another way of measuring this stabilization is by ascertaining in which year of the study period migrants who were in Thoune in 1977 are recorded for the first time. Of the 85 migrants from La Coruña who were in Thoune in 1977, 24 (28.2 percent) had been there in 1972, 6 (7.1 percent) had come originally in 1973, and 5 (5.9 percent) had come originally in 1974; therefore, 35 (41.2 percent) had been in Thoune for three years or more and 30 (35.3 percent) had been in Thoune for four years or more. It should be noted that 21 (24.7 percent) of these migrants had also lived in other localities in Switzerland (usually in neighboring Steffisburg), so actual residence in Switzerland was longer.[27]

The increase in the proportion of long-term residents is true for Spaniards in Switzerland as a whole. A good measure of this change is in the ratio of holders of annual permits to permanent residents, for permanent permits are normally given to migrants who have been in Switzerland for ten years.[28] In the five-year period between 1971 and 1976 the percentage of permanent Spanish residents grew from 17.1 percent to 48.4 percent of the migrants from that country with annual and permanent permits and from 10.1 percent to 40 percent of all Spanish migrants.[29] The corresponding increase of permanent residents among migrants of all nationalities to Switzerland with annual and permanent permits was from 43.4 percent in 1971 to 68.3 percent in 1976, which corresponded to a change from 35.4 percent to 62.4 percent in the percentage of permanent residents of migrants in all categories. The Spaniards, who at the time were relative newcomers, had thus made considerable gains in terms of permanence vis-à-vis the migrant population as a whole, but they still had a long way to go to catch up. By 1984, however, they had more than caught up: 79.7 percent of the 105,983 Spaniards with annual and permanent permits fell into the latter category, versus 78.6 percent among migrants of all origins, while 70.4 percent of all Spanish migrants had permanent permits (versus 73.8 percent of migrants of all nationalities). The

Spanish population had come of age. The newer migrants included an increasing percentage of Yugoslavs, Turks, and Portuguese (e.g., 28.8 percent of all Turks with annual and permanent permits held permanent ones [*Volkswirtschaft,* April 1985]).

The rate of conversions of annual permits held by Spaniards to permanent ones accelerated between 1971 and 1976. In 1971 9.97 percent of the annual permits were converted, while in 1976 the conversion rate was 11.14 percent. By 1984 this rate had reached 21.3 percent! Thus while rotation is substantial even among the reduced number of migrants of the latter part of the seventies, many Spanish migrants have stayed on, often much longer than they had initially intended.

Family Relationships in Switzerland

We shall now analyze the meaning of the foregoing demographic characteristics of migrant workers in terms of concrete interpersonal behavior. We shall begin our analysis with an example of a married man who migrated alone, which as we have seen is a very frequent migratory mode. The examples will also demonstrate differences in the lives of migrants that are related to the age cohort to which they belong[30] and the interrelationship between different cohorts.

Early migrants found life in Switzerland particularly isolating. At that time, many of the men worked as agricultural laborers on small farms where they were often the only foreigners. To a degree these migrants became integrated in the farm family life. As Miguel explained, "In the beginning I communicated with my boss through signs. But I played a lot with his children who even wanted to sleep in my bed. They were closer to me than anyone else in the household and so I soon learned the language." On their day off, these men would visit one another by bicycle, thereby establishing new migrant networks.

The single women were often even more dependent than the men upon the Swiss families who employed them, for they were more reticent to venture out to find comigrants. Some established close emotional attachments to the host families and became fluent in the Swiss dialect or in French. As Sabina explained:

"The doctor's wife for whom I worked treated me like a daughter. My, what a good person she was. I was liked wherever I worked and always was sad to leave. A week or two after leaving a place where I had worked, I would always return to visit. I knew other Spanish women who complained that they didn't eat well and other things like that, but I was always lucky. They always wanted me to eat well and see me happy and so I came to like them. After the first year other neighbors from my hamlet came and I saw more of them, but the first year I was closer to the Swiss families for whom I worked because I was afraid to go out for fear that people would talk. On the Saturdays and Sundays I had off, I would go to the tearoom of the boss who employed me during the summer and would be there helping on occasion, if there was a lot of work. Otherwise, I would just sit there. Even in winter (when I worked for the doctor) this man asked me to come so I wouldn't lose my attachment to the family and return for the next season."

Even today, with many more opportunities for recreation, especially in larger cities and well-established migrant communities even in small villages, life for bachelors and married men whose wives remained in Spain is a lonely experience. A recent example of a married migrant is Juan. Juan began migrating to Switzerland late in his life, when he was already 38 and had two children of 14 and 10 years. He had been working in construction in Galicia, often very far from home, and could only come home for weekends. After a while he got fed up and asked his cousin, who was already in Berne, to find him a job. How else could he save up for a new house? If he couldn't see much of his family anyway, why not at least earn more?

In Berne Juan worked for a construction firm and shared a decrepit, bedbug-infested room with two fellow Spaniards, for which he was charged Fr 300 a month, an amount which represented much more per square meter of living area than most Swiss apartments would have cost. The noise from other people drinking and gambling in the middle of the night was often almost unbearable.[31] On his days off Juan sometimes visited his cousins, who lived in barracks owned by a construction company. But when we visited him, Juan was sick in bed and feeling lonely and depressed. At times during our conversation, he could not hold back tears of bitterness and solitude while he described the filthy conditions he was forced to put up with and the lack of opportunities in Spain. He expressed a fierce loyalty to his extended family. One of his roommates was lying on his bed wondering whether he should call his wife, from whom he had just received a letter telling him that her mother was ill. When the roommate left the room, Juan commented with disdain: "He told me that he didn't like his mother-in-law at all, but was afraid that his wife and in-laws would criticize him if he didn't express his concern. So I answered: 'Do what you wish, but if this happened to me, I would certainly call because my mother-in-law has been very kind to me.' " In contrast, Juan likes to treat his mother-in-law fairly: "Last year she would have given me a plot of land which was up for sale. But I didn't accept her offer, because it would have been like a falsehood, for if by any chance we don't get along in the future, I would pick up and leave anyhow (and she would feel cheated)."

Sharing a room with strangers is wrought with tension or at least apprehension. When Juan was scheduled to move in with three men who were related to one another, they were extremely unhappy about the intrusion. After three days they accepted Juan, however, and they soon became "like brothers."

Young bachelors who did not have members of their immediate family nearby also continued to spend many lonely hours at the time of our research. One young bachelor who had worked in Geneva for two seasons expressed this fact eloquently when he explained why he worked on Saturdays and often even on Sunday mornings:

"If one spends Saturday and Sunday here in the barracks it is more lonely ("se hace más pesado"). Because you don't go out until the evening anyway because there is nothing to do and so you get bored, but when you work on Saturdays [until four] and on Sunday mornings you feel liberated. After working you come home and you say to yourself: 'Well, now I am going to go out,' and you eat and leave and amuse yourself, so it's a lot more fun."

Most men who do not live in barracks with food service cook individually for themselves, although occasionally the wife of a migrant may cook for a number of kinsmen. Unmarried women usually live with kinsfolk or in a room provided by the institution: hotel, restaurant, private home, or hospital where they work.

Young singles do, however, have considerable opportunities to meet, and although the majority of the young couples we interviewed had met in Spain, quite a few met and married in Switzerland. Often, a young man gets to know a young woman through a male friend who is related to her. Restaurant and hotel workers may meet girls through their employment, and especially in more recent years, Swiss dance halls and Spanish clubs have become a means of social contact between the sexes. Thus, Carmen met her husband through their common participation in an ethnic dance group organized by the Spanish-Helvetic Club in Berne.

Initially, courtship abroad led to an extension of the geographical area from which spouses were chosen. Early migrants often made friends with individuals from distant localities and even other regions of Spain. The small size of the migrant community made an expansion of one's social horizons imperative. Thus, Alfonso, an early migrant from Santa Maria, came to know his wife, Alicia, a Castilian, in Thoune because in the beginning his network of friends and acquaintances included migrants from all over Spain. At that time the mere fact of hearing someone speak Spanish on the street or in a restaurant was a good enough reason to start a conversation and become acquainted. Even at this time, however, spouses mostly came from localities separated by twenty kilometers or less. Presently, marriages between individuals from widely distant points of origin are less likely to occur, for the geographical span of an individual's network has shrunk again and has come to include mostly migrants from the same locality and, among these, mostly kinsmen.

Couples in which the partners are from distant localities may be the most likely to remain in Switzerland or to move to a third locality, such as a city in Spain. For neither spouse feels at home in the other's region, while they do at least share both a familiarity with the host country and their Spanish identity. We were aware of only very few marriages between individuals of different countries. In one case we were able to document, the wife's mother had already been a migrant, but there had been considerable resistance on the part of the parents of both. However, they now visited both sets of parents and were well accepted. The Italian husband spoke a flawless Spanish and seemed both interested in and accepting of Spanish customs. In another case, a Galician woman married a Turkish man. The couple purchased real estate in Istanbul as well as in Jijón, a Spanish city in another province where some of her relatives have settled. It is unlikely that they will return to either of their rural communities of origin to live permanently.

The opportunities for meeting members of the opposite sex often instill in the wives who have remained in Spain the fear of abandonment by their husbands. We encountered two women in Santa Maria who had been abandoned by husbands who had migrated to Latin America, and we heard stories about a number of other cases. Our informants recalled only one case of abandonment by a migrant to another West European country and one case of suspected marital infidelity. In addition to the divorce laws in force in Spain at the time of our research, close networks of fellow villagers and kinsmen provided a safeguard against such occurrences, as did the greater ease and frequency of visits to the home country. In the instance of marital infidelity just mentioned, the husband was forced by his kinsmen to return home and was not allowed to re-emigrate. However, the fear of abandonment persists. Thus, Cecilia called her husband back from Germany because his former sweetheart had also emigrated there and she was afraid that the girlfriend had gone to be with her husband (Buechler and Buechler 1981, 133).

Young Couples and Families

Life in Switzerland is perhaps most agreeable and the opportunities to save for the future most advantageous for young childless couples. Most continue to live in cheap studio apartments, in rooms provided by the employer, or in larger apartments shared with other couples. Although they miss their extended families, they often have more leisure time than at home and they often see more of their relatives and fellow villagers than they do at home.

More difficult times and often serious hardship begin when children are born. Some Spanish women prefer to give birth in Spain where they can count on the assistance and support of their families. But since it is obligatory for all migrants to have medical insurance, and migrants often prefer the health care services provided in Switzerland to those they receive in Spain, many have their children in a Swiss hospital. Although their parents might not be around, they can still count on visits from their kinsmen and friends. Indeed they might be visited by people they have never met, for hospital visiting is a favorite pastime. Maria complained that the hospital permitted visits by only two persons at a time.

''If a wife goes to visit her sick husband and they have three children, only one can go along. That shouldn't be the case. Of course sometimes people go for a hospital visit as though they were going to a meeting or to a fiesta. Once a friend was operated on her appendix and we counted 35 visitors. All Galicia came to visit her. The nurse protested that if everyone brought that many people along there wouldn't be space to put them. But it means we aren't all that bad: we still have friends who come to see us. When I was in the hospital with a nervous breakdown, people came to see me that I had never met before. I didn't know whether they were a husband or a wife of a friend. And when I was having my daughter a woman came whom I couldn't place at all. Then, finally, I remembered that she was working for the same employer as I. And all the visitors were like that. I barely knew them, but they came to see me."

As we have seen earlier, there are relatively few Spanish children in Switzerland. A major reason for this is the fact that migrants are not automatically permitted to keep their children in Switzerland. Stringent rules apply to family migration. Workers must have an annual permit to be allowed to bring nonworking members of their families to Switzerland. In other words, a seasonal worker must wait for four years. Annual migrants must wait fifteen months after their arrival except under special circumstances. A sympathetic Swiss staff manager recounted how she attempted to persuade the authorities to permit a woman who had just had a child to keep it in Switzerland. The response was a flat negative and the mother was forced to send her child to Spain only two weeks after it was born. The pain entailed by this solution is all too evident when the mothers talk about their children (see Buechler and Buechler 1981, 188–189, 199–200).

Second, cantonal authorities often require couples to have a separate room for a child. With the scarcity of housing in major cities, it may be next to impossible to find an apartment for a reasonable rent, making it even more difficult to keep children in Switzerland. When cheaper housing is available at all, the outgoing renters often charge an exorbitant price, ostensibly for their furniture, but in fact as a fee for ceding their rental rights. High fees and often bribes also go to rental agencies.

Third, the lack of day-care facilities in Switzerland makes it difficult for women with children to work. Even when children go to school, the erratic school schedules and the fact that children return home for lunch impede many women from holding full-time jobs.

The experiences of Sabina, whose early years in Switzerland we have followed above, and her husband Carlos exemplify these difficulties. Carlos had already lived in France near a sister who had preceded him there.[32] After three years he found employment in Lausanne through an ad in the newspaper. Later he married Sabina, a migrant from a neighboring parish, whom he had regularly visited in Thoune, some two hours by train from Lausanne. Sabina in turn had gone to Thoune because her neighbors in Santa Maria had migrated there. A year after their marriage, their son José was born. Since they both were long-term residents, they had the right to keep him with them in Switzerland. Sabina remained at home for the first one and a half years, then began working for three days a week in a supermarket and finally full-time in an institute.

Carlos took care of their son on Saturdays. It was readily apparent from the nature of the interaction with the child that Carlos's involvement in child care was much greater than it would have been had the couple remained in Spain. On the days when both worked, an Italian neighbor with three children of her own took care of José. Sabina had found her through an ad in the newspaper. Although she would in some ways have preferred her son to speak more Spanish, she didn't switch to a Spanish baby-sitter when one became available, for José adored his baby-sitter's son and made a scene every time he had to go home. At the age of two José understood Spanish, Italian, and French equally well, but spoke little.

Child care may present more serious problems, however. One couple we interviewed in Geneva discovered that their sitter neglected to feed their child. When they became worried that their daughter did not eat when she was with them, the baby-sitter replied that the child had already eaten. In reality, the sitter, a Spanish woman who worked at night, fell asleep as soon as she came home. After four months the child's lips turned black and she went into a coma. At the hospital they were told that her stomach had shrunk so much that she couldn't eat properly. Fortunately, the child regained its health.

Now that the daughter is three, she can go along when her mother works in the laundry. The laundry provides plenty of space, including the whole attic and an extra room. Although the daughter has all her toys there, she often plays at working: she sweeps the floor, irons, etc. She tells her mother very seriously that she has to do one kind of work or the other. When she is told that it is time to go to work, this even makes waking up very early in the morning easier. Now that Maria is pregnant and tires more easily, the child sometimes tells her: "Mother, why don't you sit down; I will do the work."

Ultimately, the fear of leaving a child with a stranger has led many informants to make other kinds of arrangements. Thus, when their son was born, Juan and his wife, who worked together in the same restaurant, switched to another restaurant where one could work during the day and the other at night. Since lodgings were provided by the restaurant in the same building, the arrangement proved quite satisfactory.

In one instance a grandfather and in another a grandmother were called to Switzerland to help with child care. However, Swiss authorities only rarely permit such arrangements.[33] Even with their children present, the elderly feel very isolated, miss their work in the fields, and rarely even venture out on the street. The grandmother soon returned to Spain. In another case two sisters-in-law who worked part-time and a neighbor took turns taking care of their children. Many such informal arrangements may not be condoned by Swiss authorities. At least in the canton of Berne a law was enacted that prohibited child-care arrangements with private individuals. Since there are not enough child-care centers and many of them are too expensive for migrant families, this law has forced migrant women to send their children home, cut short their own stay in Switzerland, stop working, or break the law. One informant petitioned to have her cousin who was staying at home with her own two children take care of her infant son. When her request was denied, she approached the Spanish mission that runs a day-care center. Since the mission had no openings, they agreed to accept the child officially but allowed the cousin to actually take care of it. The family who took care of the child admitted to us that they would never have agreed to the arrangement if they had planned to stay on in Switzerland. As things were, they had decided to return permanently to Spain anyway and could therefore afford the risk of discovery.

Due to these difficulties, some Spanish women stopped working altogether or worked only during odd hours when their husbands were at home. Women with more than one child, where the difficulty and cost of child care was compounded, were particularly likely to choose this solution. Maria, in our example above, was fortunate because her boss had already told her that she could bring both children to work, but as she herself pointed out, "How many women are as fortunate in this regard?"

The importance of limiting family size while abroad is clearly recognized. Thus, Manuel, one of the early migrants to a small village near Thoune, found it easy to decide to bring his child to Switzerland once he was legally entitled to do so. His wife works in a hotel and restaurant where they were given two rooms on the condition that they not invite friends in order not to disturb the guests. But he admitted that things would be worse if they had more than one child: "This son one can take along easily, even in your pocket, but if we had two, three or four, that would be quite a different matter."

It is indeed at the point when a woman has three children that she is most likely to return to Spain. Child care becomes too complicated and expensive abroad, so that a woman's added earning capacity as a migrant may scarcely be worth the cost and hassle (see Buechler and Buechler 1981, 191). Sending the children home to Spain may be equally expensive if they are sent to a boarding school or too much of a burden on kinsmen if they are left in their care. For the same reason, men who migrate late generally do not take their wives along if they already have three children (see Buechler and Buechler 1981, xvi and 133n.), a fact that provides one explanation for the high average number of children in families where only the husband has migratory experience.

The lack of adequate housing, the need for companionship, the desire to save as much as possible, and—in rare instances—the need to have someone around to take care of small children have led to complex apartment-sharing arrangements among migrants, especially kinsmen. Single siblings or a single and a married sibling frequently share a room or an apartment. In addition, when space is available, all sorts of other kinsmen may spend their first weeks or months in Switzerland with established migrants. In one household a niece and a young bachelor whose sister is married to the nephew of the household head were both sleeping in the large living room, one on the couch, the other in a partition neatly made out of curtains. In another, the sister of the household head, his wife's sister, and her husband lived together until the latter's child was born and they decided to return to Spain for good. In yet another instance, two married children and their spouses shared an apartment with their widowed mother, who took care of their two children.

In addition, relatives, especially those who first want to see what life in Switzerland is really like before making a final commitment to migrate, may stay for short visits. Thus, Alberto, who was visiting Spain on a vacation from Australia, spent two weeks with his Gallega but Uruguayan-born wife, whose parents had also moved to Australia, at his cousin's apartment in Berne. He had bought a plot for an apartment building in Castiñeiro and wondered whether it might not be better to find employment closer to Spain. Although it was April, it snowed constantly and Alberto's wife stayed inside most of the time. Five years later they were still in Australia and had taken Alberto's brother along with them.[34]

Apartments are also gathering places for kinsmen and friends: they generally afford much more privacy than the mess halls in barracks or rooms that might be provided to them by hotels. Only a few are as lucky as Ramón, who meets with his friends and relatives in the spacious casino where he works, which is closed to the public during the day. Siblings spend their weekends and, when they are not too tired, evenings, together. Women leave their children in the care of kinsmen when they are invited to a party, and the more established migrants use the telephone to overcome the physical distance that often separates them from their kinsmen in a larger city.

The demands on working women lead to a somewhat more egalitarian relationship between husbands and wives than is the case in Spain. As Carlos put it: "I have worked in a restaurant and have done all sorts of work there. Even if I have to clean house like a woman, I don't mind, because I am accustomed to it from the time I worked in the restaurant. When I pass over the floor with the vacuum cleaner, why should I mind? I do so just as she would and it is the same with other things." Sabina added: "Yes, the men in Spain have the bad custom of not helping their wives at home, but when they come here to Switzerland, they get a bit more used to helping their wives. Since the wife works, it is only normal that they should help a bit. . . . No, in this respect, my husband is good, because when the two of us were in the restaurant, we helped each other until we were finished with everything and it was time to go home." "That is true," replied Carlos, "but in those times I didn't do anything at home. But then I was in the military service and there I learned because there you have to do those things." Men may also take over child care when they are on vacation and have decided not to spend their vacation in Spain.

Social life in Switzerland also appeared to be more couple-oriented than in Spain. Migrants, especially married ones, rarely visited bars, for frequent drinking could have an effect on their ability to save. Rather, they would postpone such indulgences until their vacations in Spain. The most frequent form of entertainment was mutual visiting, mostly among Galicians. Thus, Sabina and Carlos have some contact with two senile Frenchmen and a Swiss family who live on the same floor. But kinsmen remain the most important source of contact. Carlos's sister and her husband, who lived in Orbe and owned a car, visited them frequently, or they all got together in one of the three localities where they lived.[35] Women took part freely in the conversations, even if the visitors were male. However, in larger gatherings (e.g., at celebrations) sex-segrated groupings formed again after meals. It is interesting to note, too, that the Spanish center in Geneva was frequented almost exclusively by men. Similarly, sports organized by these clubs (e.g., soccer) were male-oriented. However, some clubs organized ethnic dance groups in which both men and women participated and excursions to other parts of Switzerland and even to Spain.

The Improvised Nature of Migrant Living

In spite of the fact that migrants have made profound alterations in their life-style as an adaptation to the conditions they face in the host countries, their lives still have a distinctly improvised quality. The uncertainty of being allowed to stay, heightened by the frequent referenda to limit the migrant population sponsored by ultranationalist groups, and the general downturn in the economics of West European countries have inhibited migrants from making any long-range plans to remain in Switzerland (see Buechler and Buechler 1978). Thus, few migrants make a concerted effort to learn the language, preferring instead to work extra hours and enhance their *present* earning capacity. Any move by a spouse (often the husband) to make long-range plans to remain abroad usually encounters heavy opposition from the mate. Thus, Maria feels very threatened by her husband's toying with the idea of building a house in France across the border from Geneva, even though she is one of the few Spaniards we mistook for a Swiss because of her perfect fluency in French. Even her husband's argument that the move would make good economic sense as a short-term investment has not swayed her.

The resistance to making any long-term commitment to a migratory existence strongly affects plans for the education of children. Many migrants who have children in Switzerland simply send them home when they reach school age, often to boarding schools. A number, however, are impressed by the quality of Swiss education and would like their children to be educated there. Some, however, are dissuaded from such a move when there is no Spanish program in the locality where they live which would enable Spanish children to adapt more rapidly to the Spanish system, should they return home.[36] An example of the quandry in which parents find themselves regarding the future of their children is the case of Jorge's family. Jorge had owned a small mine near Santa Maria but was cheated out of his share by an unscrupulous partner. In Switzerland, like most of his fellow migrants, he worked in menial jobs but eventually attracted the attention of a travel agent, where he ordered tickets for his Spanish friends, who were confused by the intricacies of making travel plans. When we interviewed him, he was working part-time for the agent. His two daughters were sent to secondary schools in Spain but have learned French there. He would like one to join the travel agency he is working for and the other to study at a Swiss university. This, however, would necessitate two years of further language training in Switzerland and thus require considerable long-term commitment to remain in Switzerland. Jorge's wife is afraid that if she and her husband should return to Spain, they would be separated from their children once more. The fact that they have built a handsome home near Castiñeiro indicates that they have always planned to return there.

In contrast, Ramón and his wife have made a medium-range adjustment which includes long stays in both Spain and Switzerland every year. They both work in a casino during its seven-month season and then leave for Spain, where he is building a dance hall and restaurant with two brothers in a town near his wife's community. This arrangement makes the long separation from their daughter more bearable, and, since the daughter can visit her grandparents frequently, prevents the need for a major adjustment every time they leave again. Ramón thinks that he might continue this arrangement even when his business is operating, but his wife would return to Spain permanently and take care of his interests while he is away. Most migrants, however, plan to return home after having accomplished certain major goals, such as building a home and perhaps establishing a comfortable nest egg in a bank, but some simply continue to live abroad with vague plans of returning.

The Second Generation in Switzerland

How second-generation Spanish migrants will fare in Switzerland if they choose to remain there is to a large extent still an open question because of the shallow time depth of Spanish migration to Switzerland. As far as adjustment to life in Switzerland is concerned, small children who went to Swiss nursery schools and kindergartens had the easiest time. As remarked by Sister Rosemarie—a Swiss woman with many years of experience with foreign children in Switzerland, France, and Italy who heads a nursery school for hospital employees in an idyllic setting in Berne—one of the problems faced by migrant children who are brought to Switzerland after spending the first few years of their lives with their grandparents or other relatives in Spain is the adjustment to living with their parents (see Buechler and Buechler 1981, 187–189). "The parents are often distraught," she remarked, "because they can't understand why their children don't accept them immediately after they had lived with other relatives for long periods. As they are not well educated they expected an immediate response from the child." One of the children in this situation that Sister Rosemarie has taken care of became despondent upon its arrival in Switzerland and simply watched the other children play. After five or six months, however, the child's behavior became normal. Interestingly, even in this nursery school the children had some contact with a Spanish adult. The Spanish woman who cleaned the school became a surrogate grandmother figure to all associated with the child-care center. The mothers would stop to chat with her as well, and when one of the staff was absent, she would pitch in and help with diapering. Most of the Spanish children under her care are very small because, as Sister Rosemarie remarked, they generally go home to Spain after two or three years. "The first time a child goes home, the parents of the mother start working on her to keep the child there. Generally they return once more with the child but then they bring it to Spain permanently the next time they go."

Sister Rosemarie is a person of rare understanding and tolerance of differences; however, our experience with visits in school classes that included Spanish children was that the teachers expected foreign children to adapt fully to Swiss customs and even adopt their worldview. Indeed, they took a moral stand on such issues and argued that children who experienced the world differently from Swiss children were somehow deprived. Thus, one lamented the lack of interest which Spanish parents have in taking nature walks; and a vocabulary lesson we observed examined all the creatures in the forest, an exercise to which the Spanish children could not contribute at all. It may not have occurred to the teacher that a topic of interest to both Swiss and foreigners might have elicited a more positive response.[37] Similarly, when we sent our own twin daughters to a nursery school on the Lake of Thoune while we were undertaking fieldwork there, the teacher asked neither them nor a little Italian girl to contribute a song or a story from their own backgrounds.

By the time they reach primary school age, Spanish children who have attended kindergarten seem to have few problems in school. Those who come into Swiss schools directly from Spain have greater difficulties. Although the larger cities provide extra classes, they are badly attended. Also, one class we visited contained children of all ages, a mixture that did not seem very conducive to rapid learning. A little half-Spanish girl who seemed to follow classes with great difficulty had nevertheless been allowed to graduate to the next grade. The teacher observed that she was very neat and organized and was, therefore, on the right track. Indeed, she copied numbers from her neighbor, very neatly placing each one into a separate square on her checked blackboard. In contrast, a little boy who was quite proficient at multiplication was criticized because of the untidy appearance of his calculations.[38] The reaction of many teachers was simply to have the foreign children struggle along as well as they could in the belief that they would be able to perform more or less adequately after about two years. Often the children themselves would help one another. Schoolteachers used the old-timers as interpreters when they had difficulty understanding a recently immigrated pupil. And in one instance we observed a close symbiosis develop between a Spanish and an Italian boy. The latter, whom the teacher considered somewhat maladjusted himself, took the Spanish boy under his wing and explained what the teacher said in Italian. During a class we visited, two Swiss boys refused the Spaniard's request to play chess, but the Italian accepted immediately, walked to the front of the class with a swagger (and a glance in our direction), and animatedly explained to his friend how to play the game.

Some of the teachers were quite resentful of the foreigners. A kindergarten teacher in Berne complained that she was given all the foreign children because no one else could get along with them, and a young teacher was resentful because he felt that the foreign children were dumped on the younger teachers.

How Spanish children will manage when they get out of school is more difficult to answer, for adolescents in this age group are still rare. One young man who had received most of his education in Switzerland had a Swiss girlfriend and seemed well adjusted and happy about living in Switzerland, a view substantiated by his conversations with Swiss visiting the hotel where he and his family lived. However, he did not receive encouragement from his teacher (whom we met briefly) to enter a formal apprenticeship, which in Switzerland also entails taking evening courses at a trade school, in spite of the fact that most Swiss either receive some schooling beyond primary school or enter an apprenticeship. Instead, he became a semiskilled worker in the construction industry. Our conversation with the teacher left us with the impression that the young man's migrant identity had a lot to do with the teacher's failure to provide encouragement.

CONCLUSIONS

Migration must be studied from both ends, that is, as a system, in order to understand the dynamics involved. We must take into account the options in and policies of the host country as well as the possibilities and limitations at home (see Leeds, chap. 2). Simultaneously, we must take into account the fact that the lives of both migrants and nonmigrants are transformed by the demographic changes that result from emigration; for migration affects individuals of different sex, age, marital status, economic status, and other characteristics unequally, resulting in both migrant and nonmigrant populations with new characteristics. We are thus dealing with two types of adaptations at once: adaptations to original (or preceding) imbalances and adaptations to the effects of the solutions taken. As our demographic analysis has shown, migration has a profound influence on the age structure in the community of origin in general and in the remaining households in particular; it reduces the percentage of households headed by younger individuals and the number of single adults within their families. It also decreases the birth ratio, since the most fertile segment is away. In turn, the migrant population tends to be young and relatively homogeneous in age. This homogeneity is increased by the fact that migrant families reduce the number of children they bear, at least during their stint abroad, and frequently send their children, especially older ones, home to live with relatives or in boarding schools. Males predominate, as some occupations such as construction and certain industries are open to them alone and are often better paid.

At home these trends, combined with the increasing rural-urban migration of young people who might otherwise have remained on the farm longer and the commuting of husbands, manifest themselves in a greater burden placed on women and older people who must run the family farm with little assistance from younger men. This in turn leads to greater use of extensive techniques and mechanization of agriculture (see Zimmerman 1969; Buechler and Buechler 1978, 132, and 1981, 215–217). For the migrants themselves the same trends translate into a life which is often lonely, particularly for men who migrate alone, a greater dependence on relationships with individuals belonging to the same generation, and a special role for couples who often provide a substitute for extended households at home by inviting lone migrants to eat with them on their days off, and in some instances even provide lodgings.

Our task, however, does not end with an analysis of the characteristics of two distinct populations or subpopulations at a given point in time. First, these populations remain in dynamic interaction beyond the initial move. For an as yet undefined proportion of the migrants, migration constitutes a temporary segment of the life cycle. Indeed, even those who may eventually remain abroad almost invariably view their diaspora as impermanent; for not only is it difficult to attain the status of permanent resident in such countries as Switzerland, but it is impossible to predict future job opportunities and new restrictions imposed by their governments. In addition, government authorities in Switzerland make few longer-term provisions for migrants in educational and other infrastructural planning. This orientation in turn explains the nature of the migrants' stay abroad. It constitutes a stage in their lives in which personal comfort and leisure time are sacrificed for a better future at home: a time of struggle to maximize savings by living extremely frugally, if possible working in two jobs, and sending one's children home—either alone or with their mother—rather than renting a larger, more expensive apartment as dictated by migration regulations. Also like Leeds's Portuguese migrants (chap. 2), the life choices of Spanish nonmigrants are themselves strongly affected by such migrant inputs as remittances and investments in the region of origin. Migrant remittances secure a more comfortable existence for those who remain behind, particularly the elderly. They provide work in the construction of houses and apartments the migrants live in. Finally, upon their return, the migrants contribute to the demographical and occupational changes taking place in Spain: they often move to towns or cities rather than remaining in their rural hamlets or use the latter as bases from which to commute to urban jobs.

Second, the characteristics of the two subpopulations are themselves subject to change with the needs of the host countries, developments in the regions of origin, and the maturation of a migratory wave. These dynamics may in turn alter the relationships between migrants and nonmigrants. We have seen how over a period of six years the average age of migrants in Thoune increased, as did the age spread particularly of women, who were also increasingly likely to be married, and how the percentage of children in the Spanish migrant population in Switzerland as a whole increased. Combined with the lengthening in the average duration of their sojourn abroad and the changing numbers of migrants, these factors have influenced the nature of social interaction among migrants. The social networks of migrants decreased in geographical span but became denser (i.e., more interconnected). Most recently, however, particularly in smaller Swiss towns, migrant rotation and the reduction of migration may again lead to social isolation of those who stay on, as more and more of their fellow villagers return to Spain.

The changes that accompany the maturation of a migratory wave have important implications for the study of the life course of different cohorts. In recent years family development studies have moved away from their previous emphasis on invariant properties of life cycles to the effects of long-term historical transformations as well as specific historical events on the life course of individuals. Such studies recognize the fact that different age cohorts are influenced differently by the same historical events. Thus, an individual's experience of the Depression and the part it played in his or her life depended on his or her age during that period (Elder 1978, 35). At present, such studies treat history as an independent variable (e.g., Hareven 1977, 348, and 1978, 1–2), and with the exception perhaps of cross-generational influences, they tend to treat each cohort in isolation. Applied to the study of migration, such an approach would lead to serious distortions; for once a migratory wave is set in motion, family and kin dynamics become an integral part of the migratory process and must be included in any definition of history. For the same reason, the experiences of different age cohorts cannot be treated in isolation, for the earlier migrants alter the social environment entered by later—and hence generally younger—migrants in significant ways.

Thus, we may summarize the life course of the cohort of Galicians who migrated to Western Europe soon after migration to the region became possible (i.e., in the early and mid-sixties) as follows. Typically, these migrants were born around 1940 and experienced a childhood and adolescence during which Spain was relatively isolated from the rest of the world. They were mostly engaged in agriculture at an early age, the poorer ones working as indentured farm laborers. Few had more than six years of education, and many had only two years. Some of their parents could have had migratory experience, especially in Cuba and Montevideo, but this would have occurred in the relatively distant past in the 1910s and 1920s. Many of the migrants came from large families and were likely to have older siblings who migrated to Venezuela when that country became a prime destination for migrants in the 1950s. Other siblings could have participated in the wave of migration to Spanish cities. Born too late to avail themselves of the opportunities in Venezuela, many of this cohort had their first migratory experience within Spain. They formed the bulk of pioneer migrants, mostly recruited through official channels, to France and later to other European countries, especially Germany and Switzerland. Many were initially recruited for agricultural labor. Isolated from their kinsmen and fellow villagers, they were forced to create new social networks, usually among Spaniards. Some also became acquainted with Italian migrants and established fairly close ties with Swiss employers and more rarely Swiss coworkers. However, they soon transformed their social environment, first by moving into cities where they could earn more and where contacts with other Spaniards were more readily possible and then by facilitating the migration of kin, friends, and fellow villagers.

The more recent migrants thus entered a situation which had been substantially modified by their predecessors. Let us follow the life course of the cohort of migrants and their nonmigrant fellow villagers born around 1950. Some are the youngest members of families where all other siblings either have moved away to form separate households or have migrated abroad. They are under considerable pressure to remain at home and assist their parents in agriculture and/or commute to a job in a nearby town or city. Since they entered the job market at a time when construction increased, fueled by migrant investment in new housing, this is a feasible option. Those who decide to emigrate can count on the support of the old-timers to find jobs and lodgings. The latter have also established voluntary associations and provide ready-made networks of persons to socialize with. The newcomers look up to their pioneer predecessors, who enjoy a degree of centrality in these social networks which they would not have had at home. On the negative side, the younger cohort is more subject to the influences of inflation in construction costs occasioned by the increasing flow of migrant remittances and many become victims of progressive restrictions on migration to West European countries.

Differences in the migratory experiences of the two age cohorts may influence their long-term life options. Those who were able to invest in a business in Spain early enough may have an advantage over late-comers. On the other hand, some might take advantage of their more established position abroad to avoid the increasing competition for scarce jobs in Spain which is resulting from the contraction of the labor market in the more industrialized European countries. Many may increasingly come to view their country of origin as a place to spend vacations and perhaps to retire, rather than as a place where they will return permanently to spend the rest of their working lives or even where they may try to establish themselves with the option of re-emigrating if things do not work out as planned.

In conclusion, cross-sectional comparisons based on censuses taken in 1761 and 1973 contribute to an understanding of the effects of population growth, migration, urbanization, and incipient industrialization in Spanish Galicia. The analysis of birth and marriage records over a period of sixty-five years provides some correctives to this comparison and demonstrates recent transformations in residence patterns. A combination of cross-sectional and longitudinal analyses of migration records over a period of six years shows major changes in such variables as age, sex distribution, and length of residence abroad. However, only holistic longitudinal perspectives provided by the life histories of migrants enable the social scientist to visualize what the demographic changes mean concretely. They show the complex interconnections between demographic variables, the interdependencies between migrants and those who remain at home, and the interplay between "history" and family dynamics. The integration of numerical and qualitative data facilitates interdisciplinary research and can lead to more flexible definitions of such social scientific fields of inquiry as "migration," "international relations," and even "historical process." In order to reach its full potential such an endeavor will require an increasing effort to close the gap between macrostatistics and detailed ethnographic data. The present study is intended as a small step in this direction.

NOTES

1. The census which I found in the parish archives and gained access to, thanks to the kindness of the parish priest, covers the entire parish, which according to the official 1970 census was almost exactly double the size of the unit covered by our own 1973 census. However, this should not significantly distort the comparison. The 1761 census includes the ages of all male household heads as well as the sex and relationship to the household head of all other members. Since, with a few exceptions, the head is the oldest married

male or in his absence a widow, I have arranged data from my own census accordingly to make the comparison possible. In this study the term "household head" therefore does not imply authority. (In addition, the census contains the occupation of household heads and economic data which I have not made use of here.)

2. If one includes households headed by widows and bachelors, the figures are 4.1 in 1761 and 4.92 in 1973. Even if one includes servants living in the household as members, the average number of household members in male-headed households was still only 4.4 in 1761. It should be noted, however, that the average household size in the hamlets covered by my census is significantly lower according to the figures of the official 1970 census, namely, 4.58 members (de jure population).

3. This conclusion is further supported by the fact that, in 1973, the number of unmarried children was higher in households headed by men of all age groups.

4. Greater longevity in 1973 becomes particularly evident when one compares three-generation households where both grandparents are still alive with those where one has died. In 1761, 81.5 percent of the three-generation households included a widowed grandparent versus 35.7 percent in 1973.

5. Of the men between the ages of 40 and 60, 22.4 percent headed extended households in 1973 versus 7.1 percent in 1761.

6. Fosterage by grandparents is practiced in nonmigrant families as well but is much rarer.

7. The lower birthrate among migrant women is confirmed by the fact that the average number of children of sixteen migrant women in the 31-40 age bracket from the municipality of Castiñeiro residing in Berne, Switzerland, was only 1.25 compared to 2.4 for the wives of twelve men (the records give only the age of the migrants themselves) in the same age bracket, whose wives remained in Spain. The lower number of children among migrant couples in the Berne sample compared to migrant couples in the Santa Maria census can be explained by the fact that the latter included returnees, who may have borne children after their return, as well as couples still abroad (table 10.6).

8. This same doctor was strongly against abortion. In one instance of an abortion request by a mother who already had two children, the hospital denied the request but provided diapers and a nurse after the child's birth and saw to it that the employer gave the father a raise.

9. In the municipal capital, a town of some 10,000 inhabitants, endogamy was always lower, but there was a slight rise between 1942 and 1972. More recently (1972–1977) there has been a slight rise in endogamy in both rural and urban areas of the municipality.

10. Lisón-Tolosana notes, however, that ultimately, when both men and women emigrate, either sex may inherit the paternal home, or it may be sold and no child given preferred treatment (1971, 353).

11. Neolocal residence followed 25.5 percent of the marriages, while in 13.7 percent of the cases, husband and wife were still abroad. Correspondingly, according to baptismal records between 1972 and 1977, 39 percent of the children were born in the mother's community, 26.5 percent in the father's community, 30.7 percent in that of both parents, and 4.2 percent in that of neither.

12. In addition, 205 buildings were finished with the exception of the ground floor, which is usually reserved for small business enterprises. Finally, many of the finished apartments may have been vacant.

13. But they pay the son who owns a tractor every time he works for them.

14. An option many poor landless families were able to take advantage of.

15. In December 1974 the number of foreigners in Switzerland peaked at 1,065,000 (not including seasonal migrants and international functionaries), but their number had dropped to 933,000 by December 1977 (*Die Volkswirtschaft)*. After dropping further to a low of 883,837 in 1979 (*Die Volkswirtschaft,* March 1982), the number of foreigners in this category regained the 1977 level by December 1984, when it stood at 932,386 (*Die Volkswirtschaft,* April 1985). This increase was due to higher immigration than emigration rates, rather than to an increase in the number of births.

16. This breakdown is not available for earlier years; neither, by 1984, is a breakdown by sex.

17. The records do not include young children of migrants living in Thoune.

18. In 1973 the corresponding figures for migrants from the municipality of Castiñeiro in Berne were 21.1 percent for men and 8.7 percent for women. (In the same year, 15.4 percent of the men and 7.6 percent of the women in Thoune were over 40.) The men thus resembled the Spanish population in Thoune as a whole, while the women followed the pattern of their province mates.

19. The four Galician provinces followed the pattern of Spain as a whole, but there were never more than five women over 40 from all of Galicia in Thoune.

20. Registered migrants plus schoolchildren. Only four of these were Galicians. However, all three married women from Santa Maria had children in Thoune in 1973.

21. Of these, seven had their children in Berne and sent or brought them home after a period of between three weeks and nine months.

22. Among migrants from La Coruña in Thoune, the men represented an even higher percentage and this percentage increased slightly over the years (77.9 percent in 1972, 78.8 percent in 1977). In other cities, the percentages of men and women varied. In Geneva 67.1 percent of the Spanish seasonal workers and those with annual permits were men (the inclusion of permanent residents would have decreased the proportion of men slightly). Again this percentage remained fairly constant over time. In August 1963, 67.5 percent of the Spanish workers in these categories were men. By contrast, in the tourist-oriented town of Interlaken only 57.5 percent of the 313 Spanish migrants in these same categories in August 1971 were men.

23. In April 1978, 67.9 percent of the seasonal and annual migrants of all origins working in Switzerland were male.

24. In the country as a whole, 74.3 percent of all Spanish workers with annual permits in December 1976 were married (*Die Volkswirtschaft,* April 1977). The corresponding figure, but for Spanish workers with annual *and* permanent permits for 1984, was 74.8 percent. (In Thoune 73.8 percent of the Spanish workers with annual permits in 1977 were married.) Male and female annual workers in 1976 were almost equally likely to be married: 74.7 percent of the men and 73.7 percent of the women were married.

25. In contrast, in Berne the percentage of men with wives in Switzerland was already much higher in 1973. In that year 65 out of 102 (63.8 percent) of the married individuals from Castiñeiro residing in that city, and all but one of those with annual or permanent permits, had their spouses with them. In Geneva, of 103 cases of married couples with annual or permanent permits, 56 (54.4 percent) had their spouses with them.

26. The period includes the years the migrants had one or the other of these permits but were working in other localities in Switzerland. The number of seasons these migrants have held seasonal permits was not available. However, most of the later migrants had to have held seasonal permits for five years before they became eligible for an annual permit. There were no cases of Spanish migrants obtaining Swiss citizenship.

27. Of these twenty migrants, eight appeared in Thoune for the first time after 1974, four in 1974 (or late 1973), two in 1973, and seven in 1972 or earlier.

28. Seasonal employment is included in this period.

29. That is, those with annual and resident permits who lived in Switzerland in December 1971 and December 1976, plus those who obtained seasonal permits sometime during that year (*Die Volkswirtschaft* April 1972, April 1977, and April 1984).

30. Or, more precisely, cohorts of individuals who migrated at the same time.

31. House owners often let old houses disintegrate entirely, for if the building reaches a certain point of decay, they are allowed to demolish it and replace it with a new high-rent apartment building.

32. She in turn had followed another married sister who had been brought there by a friend of her husband.

33. The children of an elderly person must prove that there would be no one left in the family who could take care of the parent.

34. It would have taken Alberto many years of working in unskilled jobs before he would have even been allowed to accept employment in his specialty, carpentry.

35. In contrast, Carlos visited the Galician center in Lausanne only once, because one cannot take children there.

36. In principle, it is obligatory for Spanish children to attend these Spanish programs run by the Spanish government. Where such programs exist, Spanish parents must make a special petition to the Swiss school authorities for dispensation, if they do not wish their children to attend. They are then told that they must bear the full responsibility, should the family return to Spain and the children have difficulty adapting to the Spanish school system.

37. Interestingly, the same teacher showed considerable sensitivity and insight in devising a technique for improving a Spanish pupil's mathematical skills. Since the boy's father was a waiter, she translated the mathematics problems into calculations regarding tips. The boy became interested and soon was doing very well in math.

38. When the author attended a Swiss school after growing up in Bolivia, the teachers were equally aghast at the untidy handwriting and the imprecise draftsmanship.

REFERENCES

Beiras, X.

1970 *Estructura y problemas de la poblacion gallega.* La Coruña: Grafinsa.

1972 *O atraso económico de Galicia.* Vigo, Spain: Galaxia.

Buechler, H.

1983 "Spanish Urbanization from a Grass-roots Perspective." In *Urban Life in Mediterranean Europe: Anthropological Perspectives,* edited by M. Kenny and D. Kertzer, 135–61. Urbana: University of Illinois Press.

Buechler, H., and Buechler, J-M.

1975 "Los Suizos: Galician Migration to Switzerland." In *Migration and Development: Implications for Ethnic Identity and Political Conflict,* edited by H. Safa and B. DuToit, 17–31. The Hague: Mouton.

1978 "Social Class, Conflict and Unequal Development in Spanish Galicia." *Review of Radical Political Economics* 10: 130–35.

1981 *Carmen: The Autobiography of a Spanish Galician Woman.* Cambridge, Mass.: Schenkman.

1984 ''Four Generations in Spanish Galicia: A Developmental Analysis of Socio-economic Options.'' In *Culture and Community in Europe: Essays in Honor of Conrad Arensberg,* edited by O. Lynch, 150–72. New Delhi: Hindustani Press.

Elder, G.

1978 ''Family History and the Life Course.'' In *Transitions: The Family and the Life Course in Historical Perspective,* edited by T. Hareven, 21–64. New York: Academic Press.

Hareven, T.

1977 ''The Family Cycle in Historical Perspective: A Proposal for a Developmental Approach.'' In *The Family Life Cycle in European Societies,* edited by J. Cuisenier, 339–352. The Hague: Mouton.

1978 ''Introduction: The Historical Study of the Life Course.'' In *Transitions: The Family and the Life Course in Historical Perspective,* edited by T. Hareven, 1–16. New York: Academic Press.

Lisón-Tolosana, C.

1971 *Antropologia cultural de Galicia.* Madrid: Siglo XXI.

1973 ''Some Aspects of Moral Structure in Galician Hamlets.'' *American Anthropologist* 75: 823–83.

Die Volkswirtschaft: Wirtschaftliche und sozialstatistische Mitteilungen.

(various) Monatsschrift mit Beilagen der Kommission für Konjunkturfragen. Bern: Eidgenössisches Volkswirtschaftsdepartament.

Zimmermann, G.

1969 *Die bäuerliche Kulturlandschaft in Südgalicien.* Das Geographische Institut der Universität Heidelberg.

11 Return Migration to Rural Ireland

George Gmelch

ABSTRACT. Gmelch takes us to the only non-Mediterranean country of Western Europe with a high emigration rate: Ireland. His focus is on return migration to the western counties from both North America and England. He explores the consequences of moving from primarily urban contexts in the countries of destination to primarily rural ones back home.

Gmelch concludes that in contrast to the predominantly economic reasons for emigration from Ireland, those that are most influential in the return are noneconomic in nature. Although most return migrants eventually adjust to conditions back home, many find it difficult to cope with the slow pace of life and widespread inefficiency. They feel that their nonmigrant compatriots are nosy, "narrow-minded," parochial, and inward-looking. Such attitudes often make it difficult for migrants to renew contacts even with old friends and relatives. In addition, wages and work conditions in Ireland are often inferior to those in the host countries.

INTRODUCTION

Return migration, the movement back to one's previous place of residence, has long been an elusive and little understood aspect of the migration process. Despite enormous increases in return migration in southern Europe, the Caribbean, and several other regions of the world, relatively little attention was given to this process until the 1970s.

Robert Rhoades (1978) has suggested several reasons for the neglect of return migration by social scientists, particularly anthropologists. The massive urbanization occurring in most parts of the world led to a "rural-urban" analytical framework in which geographical movements were viewed as occurring in one direction only—rural to urban. The nature of traditional anthropological fieldwork that involved research for a limited period of time (customarily one year) in a limited space (a single community) may also have led to a view of migration as a static event. Finally, return is the most difficult aspect of the migration cycle to quantify. While most countries gather information on incoming aliens, they do not do so for returning citizens.

This chapter concerns return migration to western Ireland.[1] The chapter briefly describes the demographic characteristics of Irish return migrants and then examines (1) their reasons for returning to their homelands and (2) their readjustment at home after having spent years abroad in an urban-industrial society.

THE SETTING AND OUT-MIGRATION

The eight western counties (Cork, Kerry, Clare, Galway, Mayo, Sligo, Leitrim, and Donegal) in which this study was conducted constitute the poorest and least developed region of Ireland. The area is predominantly rural with more than half the population living on farms or in settlements of less than 1,500 population. Family farms, the majority under thirty acres in size and carved into small parcels separated by hedgerows and stone fences, form a quiltlike pattern across the landscape. The rural economy is based largely on cattle and sheep farming. Specialization in the form of commercial livestock farming is increasing, yet a sizable proportion of the population still practices mixed cottage farming aimed at producing just enough to meet household subsistence needs. For all but the large landowners, agricultural opportunities are limited by low-fertility soils, widespread blanket bog, and a wet and windy climate.

The expansion of nonagricultural employment has not been able to keep pace with the surplus farm population or the natural population increase of the towns. The lack of adequate economic opportunities at home coupled with a growing desire for a higher standard of living has sent many young people abroad. Emigration is a fact of life in the west of Ireland; in some way it touches every family. In the period 1951–1971 net emigration from Ireland totaled 543,000, or about half the Irish labor force at the end of the period (Walsh 1974). In the last century the population of the rural areas and small towns of the west has declined by half. In the present study 59 percent of the men ($N = 2{,}206$) and 64 percent of the women ($N = 1{,}920$) in the families in which the respondents or their spouses were raised had emigrated.

A study of the attitudes toward emigration among young people in one Irish county (Cavan) found that 36 percent of the youths surveyed definitely intended to emigrate and an additional 40 percent were seriously thinking of it (Hannan 1970). The primary reason was their belief that their home region would not be able to satisfy their occupational and income aspirations. Among the return migrants in my survey, 76 percent of the men and 67 percent of the women gave economic factors as the main reason for their emigration from Ireland. Several studies, however, point to factors other than economic ones as also being important causes of Irish emigration. In her work in the Gaeltacht areas of western Ireland, E. Kane (1969) found emigration to be a rite of passage—one means by which young people make the transition to adulthood. Emigration is also an opportunity for a profitable, mildly adventurous change. F. Bovenkerk (1973) in a study conducted in one of our sample communities (Castleisland, county Kerry) found that the desire for adventure—"to see the world," "to travel," "to see how other people live," and "wanting change in life"—was nearly as important in promoting emigration as economic motives. In several studies the lack of social/recreational facilities was found to be an important motive, especially for women (Kane 1969; McNabb 1964; Hannan 1970).

Emigration from Ireland has, however, fallen in recent years as economic prospects have improved and work opportunities for emigrants in Europe and North America have tightened (Walsh 1974). While young people are still noticeably few in number on the streets and in the fields, emigration is declining and the return flow increasing. Emigration has dropped from an average 17.2 per 1,000 population in the 1950s to 5.0 per 1,000 in 1971.[2] Return migration to the region averaged 5.07 persons returning per 1,000 population in 1971, a rate far exceeding the 3.62 for the rest of the country. County Donegal had the highest rate of return (6.4) in the country, while the other Atlantic seaboard counties of Clare, Sligo, Kerry, and Galway ranked third, fourth, fifth, and sixth. The only county outside the survey area with a comparable rate of return migration was Wicklow (6.0), which borders Dublin on the east coast of Ireland.

METHODS

The fieldwork on which this study is based was carried out over two summers in 1977 and 1978; a return visit was made in 1985.[3] Data were gathered principally through a questionnaire survey and open-ended interviews. The questionnaire contained ninety-eight items and was divided into four main parts: the circumstances of the migrant before emigration, the emigration experience, the reasons for return, and the postreturn adjustment.

A sample of 606 migrants were interviewed by a team of twelve interviewers in communities along the western seaboard, beginning in county Cork in the south and stretching to county Donegal in the north. The sample was selected opportunistically with the names and addresses of return migrants being obtained from postmen, shopkeepers, clergy, teachers, and from the returnees themselves, who at the conclusion of each interview were asked to provide names of other migrants in their neighborhood. In small communities an attempt was made to interview all the known migrants in the locale. Most migrants were interviewed at home, although some interviews were conducted in the workplace. The response to the survey was good: about 85 percent of the migrants approached agreed to be interviewed. Only in areas of heavy tourism such as the Ring of Kerry and Connemara were there many refusals. As a general rule, the more remote a community was from the major tourist routes, the more cooperative were the returnees and the higher the response rate.

In-depth interviews, some tape-recorded, were conducted with about fifteen returnees. Also interviewed were staff at the United States Embassy, the organizers of two American-Irish associations, and other individuals who had regular dealings with returnees and were familiar with their situation.

CHARACTERISTICS OF THE RETURN MIGRANTS

Of the returnees in the survey sample, 51 percent were men and 49 percent were women. The mean age at which they had first migrated from Ireland was 22. At the time of their emigration all but 11 percent were single; by the time they returned 57 percent had married. Ninety percent of the returnees had married other Irish. This rate of endogamy is much higher than that found among expatriate Irish populations. For example, Breandan Caulfield and Askok Bhat (1979) report that the endogamy rate for Irish-born living in Britain, based on 1971 census returns, was 31 percent ($N = 6{,}730$). That is, less than one-third of the emigrants married individuals who were also born in Ireland. The considerable difference suggests that migrants who marry noncompatriots are less likely to return. Conversely, migrants who take spouses from their own group are more likely to return home than migrants who do not.

One-third of the returnees married individuals from the same home parish, and another 12 percent married people from the same county. Thus almost half the emigrants who married while abroad selected not only an Irish mate but also a mate from close to home.

A comparison of the place of residence of the migrants before and after their return reveals that return migration for the majority was an urban-to-rural movement. Over 74 percent of the Irish had left cities in the United States and Britain with populations of more than one million. Of those returning from the United States 58 percent had left New York City, while 51 percent of those returning from the United Kingdom had come from London. Less than 10 percent of the sample returned from places with a population under 100,000, that is, from small cities and towns.

A majority of the household heads in the sample had returned to their home communities. This pattern is less true of white-collar migrants, who are inclined to resettle in urban areas where the employment opportunities they desire are based.

REASONS FOR RETURN MIGRATION

Why do Irish migrants return home? Why are they willing to leave comparatively prosperous, industrialized areas with high living standards to return to less developed rural communities where unemployment is high and services limited?

The procedure used in our study was to ask respondents how much influence each of a series of factors had had on their decision to return. This enabled us to minimize problems inherent in the common method of asking respondents directly why they returned (standard motive), which assumes that people know what motivates them and will state it when asked and that there are one or two

Table 11.1 Reasons for Return Migration to Ireland

Reasons for Migration*	Percentages of Migrants (N = 590) No Influence	Some Influence	Much Influence
1. Ireland is my homeland	20	10	60
2. To live with people of my own background (culture)	42	11	38
3. To be near family and friends	47	12	41
4. Personal reasons (in Ireland) (e.g. need to care for elderly parents)	61	5	34
5. Chance to own my own business or farm	73	4	23
6. Too much crime and violence abroad	77	8	15
7. Job opportunities at home	77	3	18
8. Many things I did not like about the host society	80	8	12
9. Felt like a stranger abroad	89	4	7
10. Household head did not like his job	93	3	4
11. Household head was unemployed	96	2	2
12. Personal reasons/problems abroad	94	5	1

*The number to the left of each item indicates its individual rank among all twelve reasons for return migration.

overriding factors that influence their decision. First, a list was compiled of all the reasons for return migration elicited in a pilot study. The responses were then classified into three broad categories: (1) patriotic-social, (2) economic-occupational, and (3) familial-personal.

Within each category the reasons were further divided into "push" and "pull" factors. Push factors (as seen by the actor) are those that tend to drive the person away from the host society, while pull factors are those which draw him to the homeland. The former tend to be negative (crime, unemployment, prejudice, etc.), while the latter are usually positive (proximity to family, new opportunities, better climate, etc.). In all, twelve factors representing the strongest in each of the crosscutting categories were selected for testing.

Each factor was converted into a question in which the respondent was asked to indicate on a three-point scale (much, some, or none) how much influence the particular factor had on his or her decision to return to Ireland. The results are shown in tables 11.1 and 11.2. In table 11.1 twelve individual motives for return migration are shown in their rank order of importance. In table 11.2 the rank order of the six categories of motives (e.g., economic-occupational) is shown.

Table 11.2 Reasons for Return Migration to Ireland by Category of Reasons

Categories of Reasons for Return Migration	Percentages of Migrants (N = 590)
Patriotic-Social Pull	55%
Familial-Personal Pull	41
Economic-Occupational Pull	16
Patriotic-Social Push	11
Familial-Personal Push	7
Economic-Occupational Push	4

The first step in the analysis of the migrants' motives was to assess the strength of different "push" and "pull" factors in their decision to return. As table 11.2 shows, the pull factors, or attractions of the homeland, were decisively more important in the migration decisions of the returnees than their push factors: the respondents cited pull factors as having "very great" or "much" influence on their decisions to return five times more frequently than push factors.

Taking the categories individually, the patriotic-social category for both groups was found to be predominant, with 55 percent of the sample citing one or both of its two reasons as having a strong influence on their decision to return. Clearly, the returnees have a strong emotional attachment and identification with their homeland. Also very strong were familial-personal pull factors, primarily the desire to live near friends and relatives. The migrants have strong ties with relatives; during the time away they maintained regular correspondence.

Next in importance, although far behind the first two categories, are the economic-occupational pull factors. These included good job opportunities at home and/or a chance to be self-employed. The emphasis here, given an unfavorable employment situation in Ireland, was on self-employment, as many migrants who had been engaged in wage labor while abroad, often in construction or bartending, hoped to set up their own businesses at home. It was not uncommon for returnees to buy and operate a pub.

As noted earlier, the push factors had considerably less influence. However, crime and violence in the host society was an important consideration for some. This was most frequently cited by respondents who had children. They expressed various fears including the possibility of their children being harmed or molested, or taking drugs. Also, they were anxious about the sexual permissiveness of adolescents in the host society and its possible influence on their children. There was also concern about racial integration in schools and neighborhoods.

Within the broad category of familial-personal push factors were respondents who had returned to escape problems caused by the death of a spouse, separation, divorce, or poor health. They hoped that returning home would be an escape from painful memories and offer the chance to start a new life; and the ill hoped to regain their health.

Overall, economic factors were found to be less important in return decisions than were the other categories. This contrasts sharply with the overriding importance of economic concerns in out-migration: 71 percent of the respondents cited either lack of employment or desire for a better job as the primary reason for migrating. For migrants to return to their homelands while there is still higher unemployment than in the host societies attests to the importance of the noneconomic motives in Irish return migration.

In studies where economic considerations were found to predominate in return migration decisions, there were usually strong push incentives. J. Hernandez-Alvarez (1968) reports that many Puerto Rican migrants returned home from the United States only when they lost their jobs due to mechanization and automation. Similarly, scores of European guest workers, or *Gastarbeiter,* returned to their Mediterranean homelands from Germany, Switzerland, and France when economic recessions (1966–1967, 1972–1973, 1982–1983) sharply reduced employment opportunities.

We must also consider that while there is still high unemployment, and goods and services are more expensive than in the host societies, rural Ireland does have a quasi subsistence and barter economy that can considerably reduce the cost of living and make return migration affordable. Some foodstuffs and services that were paid for in cash in the host urban setting may be produced or obtained through barter at home.

The relative unimportance of economic considerations in Irish return migration suggests that econometric models of migration may be of limited benefit in explaining return migration. The primary variables considered in econometric studies of migration are income and unemployment differentials between the sending and host societies. Using census data and multiple regression analysis, econometric studies portray population movements largely as a function of labor supply: individuals seeking jobs and the available job openings are brought together by a movement of workers, self-selected according to demands. For example, in an econometric study of Irish migration to Britain, Brendan Walsh (1974) examines the following variables: average weekly earnings of male industrial workers in Ireland, deflated by the Irish consumer price index; average weekly earnings of male industrial workers in the United Kingdom (UK), deflated by the UK consumer price index; annual average percentage of nonagricultural workers registered as unemployed in Ireland; and the annual average percentage of nonagricultural workers registered as unemployed in Great Britain. The structural equation constructed with these variables, which measures economic conditions in both Ireland and Britain (push and pull), was able to explain fluctuations in the net emigration rate over the twenty-one-year period examined. Walsh's model, however, does not tell us much about the causes of return migration to Ireland, which in this case are largely independent of differentials in weekly earnings and levels of unemployment. Simply, return migration for most Irish migrants was not toward, but rather away from, the area where the demands of the labor market were greatest.

In most cases the migrants' decision to return involved a number of considerations: only 11 percent of the migrants indicated a single overriding motive. On average, they acknowledged 3.5 factors on the twelve-point scale as having played a role in their decision to return, and these figures probably understate the complexity and range of issues considered by the returnees.

Was the decision to return arrived at abruptly or was it considered over a long period of time? Respondents were asked how long they had been planning to return before they actually moved. The majority (55 percent) had been planning their return home for at least one year. About a fifth of these said they had "always" intended to return; for them return migration was merely the fulfillment of what they had always intended to do. Forty-five percent of the returnees said their decision to return was made abruptly, without planning. Many of the abrupt movers had returned in response to a family crisis at home that required their assistance, such as the death or illness of a parent.

For most migrants, however, the decision to return was neither sudden nor clear-cut. There was much ambivalence and soul-searching among the returnees. That they had chosen to emigrate from their homelands in the first place meant there was one or more serious drawbacks to the place, which probably had not been remedied during their absence. But the host society also has its disadvantages. As H. R. Bernard and S. Ashton-Vouyoucalos (1976) concluded for Greek returnees, the decision to return is often "triggered by adding one or more factors to either side of the balance." A migrant whose child is failing in school or mixing with the wrong crowd may finally feel pushed to return. Or a migrant whose parents are ailing at home may feel pulled back to be with them.

RETURN MIGRANT READJUSTMENT

How well do the Irish returnees readjust to rural life after having spent many years away in an urban-industrial society? What problems, if any, do they have? The experiences of the returnees surveyed suggest that readjustment may be difficult for some. When asked how satisfied they were with their lives in Ireland during their first year back, over half (51 percent) of the returnees said that they were not satisfied and would have been happier had they stayed abroad. The first year appears to be particularly difficult; it is a time when many returnees wonder if they have made the right decision. Most individuals eventually do learn how to cope with the problems they experience upon returning; among the returnees surveyed just one in five still regretted, at the end of their second year at home in Ireland, their decision to return.

Problems in Readjustment

What poses the greatest difficulty for the return migrants when they first come back? Fully one-fifth (21 percent) of the returnees interviewed said that readjusting to the slow pace of life in Ireland and coping with widespread inefficiency had been their biggest problem. Everything seemed to happen so slowly or take so long to accomplish that they often became impatient and frustrated. Most respondents expressed this problem in concrete terms. Clerks and checkout girls, for example, were described as moving at a snail's pace compared to their counterparts in America and England. In the larger stores there were long waits in the checkout aisles as checkers casually carried on conversations with other customers and employees. Plumbers, electricians, carpenters, and other workmen failed to come at appointed times or did not come at all. The paperwork and legal delays in buying a house dragged on for months, in some cases for years. One middle-aged woman whose husband had died of a heart attack attributed his death to the frustrations and aggravations he experienced in trying to build his own home in Ireland.

Another exasperated returnee, the owner of a laundromat in a small town in county Mayo, encountered so many delays in ordering replacement parts for his washing machines from Dublin that he now orders from a firm in Cleveland. Giving an illustration of the problems he believes are commonplace for returnees running businesses in Ireland, he recounted how he had ordered the same part, a small plastic cog, from the American and Irish firms:

> "Three weeks ago the part arrived from Cleveland. And do you know what I've heard from the people in Dublin? Nothing! Nothing for five weeks, till this morning. Would you believe, they want me to send them a money order before they'll send the part? The part costs less than a pound, and they want a feckin' money order. Five weeks to tell me they want a money order, and the machine'd be out of use all that time."

Somewhat later in reflecting upon his situation he explained: "The problem is that I've seen another system, where people do their work and things get done. The people here that have never left Ireland don't know any better. And if you don't know another way, you're happy with what you have."

Another informant described his eventual adjustment as a process of slowing down to the Irish pace and radically changing his expectations:

> "It took me two years to settle, the pace was too slow. Time doesn't mean anything to people here. If you wanted someone to paint the house, they'd say they'd come at ten o'clock and not come till two or maybe they mightn't come at all. At first I was angry but now I don't mind. I don't expect them to carry through with what they say, with what they promise. That way, you're not disappointed."

The second most frequently mentioned readjustment problem involved relationships with local people. Fourteen percent of the returnees felt that the attitudes and worldview of local people had been the single most difficult aspect of their return. Local people were described as "narrow-minded" and "backward," as inflexible and inward-looking. They were criticized for being preoccupied with the lives of others in the community. After experiencing the anonymity of big city life in America or Britain, these returnees felt that their lives were being closely monitored by neighbors. They felt that their actions—what they wore, what they bought, or who their daughter was seen holding hands with at a school outing—were always under public scrutiny and gossiped about. Some returnees perceived this as a loss of personal freedom: "In America you could do anything you want, and nobody would bother you or take notice. In Ireland people are gossipy, nosey, always interested in the other people's affairs. You don't have that sense of freedom. Not freedom like you find in America." According to another repatriate:

"People here are very cagey about what they say. People here worry too much about what other people think of them. Americans have more freedom to say and do what they want. In America people talk out loud in public, they are free and easy in their talk. Here you have to keep your voice down. You never know who's listening."

Some return migrants also felt that they no longer shared many interests with local people. Their own interests tended to transcend the local community and were more cosmopolitan in nature. Local sporting events, for example, did not hold the same fascination for them as they did for other community members. Having spent a good part of their lives in America or Britain, they remained interested in the current events of their host countries and were disappointed when their neighbors did not express the same interest or were openly disinterested.

Other migrants had returned expecting to resume relationships with friends and relatives at the same level of intimacy they had shared years before. Not infrequently they were disappointed. The first few visits during which they reminisced and exchanged memories were pleasant, but later visits revealed that they no longer had much in common. A 35-year-old school teacher who had been away four years recalled some of the difficulties of meeting old friends:

"Initially, in the first three months at home, you meet all the friends and acquaintances that you had and were friends of yours four or five years earlier. Some of them have been married and their partner is less obviously going to be a friend. Or they have changed circumstances enormously or changed interests enormously. You've got to realize that you've changed and that they've changed, you can't just pretend that four years didn't exist."

The problems encountered in reestablishing former relationships increase with the amount of time returnees have spent abroad. And it is partly because of the difficulties returnees face in trying to resume past relationships that they come to realize just how much they have changed during their years away. We asked returnees if they felt they were different from Irish people who had never lived abroad and, if so, how? Fully 85 percent felt that they were different; some felt that they had been so changed by their overseas experience that they now had more in common with citizens of the host country than with their own countrymen. Seventy percent believed that they were "broader in their outlook" than those who had never left Ireland. They had been exposed to many different ethnic groups and life-styles and had come to understand, to a certain extent, that culture is relative, that the Irish way of doing things is only one of many ways and that others are equally valid. As one informant explained about returnees:

> "They have experience of a different society, whether it's successful or unsuccessful it doesn't matter. They have experience of a different kind of way of life, different kind of environment and they've got to bring that back with them. It just widens the worldview, so you've got to be different. . . . For me, it gives me much greater understanding and tolerance for the ambiguities of people."

Returnees also felt that they were better educated (35 percent) than nonmigrants and that they worked harder or were more ambitious (28 percent).

Closely related to the problem of divergent attitudes and interests was that of developing a satisfactory "social life." Over 13 percent of the respondents cited this as the single most difficult aspect of their readjustment. The difficulty in making friends was mentioned most often by women (17 percent versus 9 percent for men). This is partially explained by the fact that few married women, especially those living in rural areas and small towns, are able to find jobs in Ireland. Women who had worked while living abroad and who had made many contacts through their jobs were now stuck at home. Also, many of them did not have a car, which would enable them to get out and visit. Some younger women returnees complained that neighboring women whom they might have been able to socialize with were overly family-oriented and were not interested in or did not make time for activities outside the home.

Since the failure to achieve a good social life is closely related to the lack of shared interests and the perceived "narrow-mindedness" of local people, the two variables could be lumped together. When this is done, it becomes the single most important adjustment difficulty faced by return migrants (27 percent compared to 21 percent citing the slow pace of life).

The Irish climate also posed a major problem for 14 percent of the sample, particularly the elderly and those who had returned from America. Irish winters are damp, the sky is gray much of the time, and daylight hours are short. Due to the dampness and the absence of central heating in many homes, the cold is penetrating. Although the temperatures do not dip below freezing for long (mean temperature for January is 42°F) and there is very little snow, older returnees find the weather more uncomfortable than the bitter but less humid winters of the northern U.S. cities—New York, Boston, and Chicago—which most of the American returnees had left. The psychological effect of the dreary Irish winter is compounded by the fact that most returnees while living abroad had only visited Ireland during the pleasant months of summer. Thus many had forgotten what the climate was like during the rest of the year. We interviewed several returnees who were considering re-emigrating to a sunnier and drier climate. One returnee advised emigrants thinking of resettling in Ireland:

> "Take time off and really see the country and spend a winter here. They must spend a winter here before they give up their homes. When they come on a vacation during the summer the weather is beautiful, and you think the weather is always good. We lived here last winter, and it wasn't the same Ireland we saw on our visits. It was very depressing. It was cold and the dampness seeps into your bones."

One-tenth of the returnees found the unfavorable economic situation the most difficult aspect of their readjustment. Some who had set up their own businesses, most commonly pubs and small construction firms, had been overly optimistic when estimating the income they would be able to earn from these enterprises. Publicans, for example, often found that they were making less money owning and running their own pub in Ireland than they had made tending bar for someone else in New York City. To make matters worse, the hours were longer. Instead of working an eight-hour day, most returnees with businesses were working twelve hours a day, six days a week. Retired people with fixed pensions from the United States were hurt by the declining value of the dollar and the high rate of inflation in Ireland.

Other factors mentioned by returnees but of less consequence were the absence of modern conveniences ranging from household appliances such as dishwashers to public transportation. The lack of variety in shopping which had become a favorite pastime of some women while abroad was also missed.

In many cases the problems of readjustment, especially during the first year back, can be attributed to the returnees' false or unrealistic expectations about life in Ireland. Many returned without up-to-date information on living conditions, the economic climate, and other factors which impinge upon their lives. Some basic fact-finding and more thoughtful questioning would have in many cases enabled returnees to avoid serious disappointment. For example, if one elderly couple planning retirement in a remote part of Connemara had considered in advance the infrequency of bus service in the area, they might not have returned and found themselves isolated and confined to home six days of the week.

Emigrants err in both directions in their expectations about Ireland. Most expect to find the same level and range of amenities and services that they enjoyed in America or Britain and are disappointed. Others expect to find Ireland as undeveloped as when they left many years before. They too are disappointed when they discover that Ireland is no longer the traditional, close-knit, folk society of memory. One Mayo publican complained about several of the returnee families in his community: "They think it has stood still all these years they were away. They still believed the streets were unpaved, thatched cottages, and all. . . . They should have been aware that Ireland today is a modern society."

To a large extent, the problems return emigrants experience can be attributed to differences in the scale of the communities they have returned to. Nearly three-quarters of the sample had left large cities in Britain and America and returned to small villages and towns in western Ireland. Their complaints that neighbors seem narrow-minded and provincial would probably be the same had they moved to rural areas within North America or Britain. In other words, many of their complaints about life in small communities in rural Ireland are true of small communities everywhere.

While most returnees adjust to the changes demanded of them, some features of Irish life continue to bother them well after the initial period of readjustment. The returnees were asked what they felt were the major disadvantages of life in Ireland. Among the respondents who had been back three years or more, 38 percent considered low wages and poor working conditions to be a major disadvantage of life in Ireland. For some the difficulties of making a good living in Ireland were not apparent during their first year back when they had savings to fall back on and were hopeful of new opportunities at home. The excitement of being home and among old friends and relatives and of planning for a new life overshadowed early financial difficulties. By the third or fourth year many who were still unable to find a well-paying job or any job at all had begun to discover the economic costs of return migration. The "bad" climate continued to be an annoyance for nearly one-third of the migrants. About an equal number complained that even after several years at home they had still not developed a good social life.

With time the majority of returnees learn to cope with such disappointments; they learn to bring their own expectations into line with the realities of life in Ireland. While over half (51 percent) were dissatisfied during their first year back, only 21 percent still felt that way after two or more years at home. And among those who had been back for more than five years, the number who were maladjusted or felt dissatisfied dropped to 17 percent. Not included in this figure, however, are the estimated 5 to 10 percent who were so unhappy that they had already re-emigrated.

Predictors of Readjustment

What factors are related to successful readjustment? Is a person who spent many years abroad less likely to adjust well than someone who has been away for a shorter period of time? Do men adjust better than women? In order to test these propositions and others, the relationship between the level of adjustment and seven independent variables—sex, age, education, length of time abroad, job satisfaction, housing satisfaction, and satisfaction with social life—were examined. Zero order correlations between adjustment and each of the independent or explanatory variables were computed. The results are presented in table 11.3.

No relationship was found between adjustment and education ($r = .01$). A weak but statistically significant relationship was found between sex ($r = .10$) and adjustment, with men being more satisfied than women. Several factors

Table 11.3 Correlations of Variables with Readjustment

Variable	Correlations with Adjustment*
Sex	.10
Age	.13
Education	.01
Length of Time Abroad	.18
Job (satisfaction with)	.26
Housing (satisfaction with)	.25
Social Life (satisfaction with)	.37

*$p < .05$ or better

probably contribute to this. Married women who enjoyed working abroad are often unable to find jobs in Ireland, which eliminates an important arena in which they can make friendships. Second, nonworking women in rural areas, particularly those without automobiles, are confined at home much of the time. Third, women more than men miss the modern conveniences they had abroad which make housework easier. And finally, returnees more often return to the husband's home community where the wife does not have a support group or old friends. Given the disadvantaged position of returnee women in Ireland, it is somewhat surprising that the relationship between sex and adjustment is not stronger.

The relationship between age and adjustment is also weak ($r = -.13$), and if we control for years spent abroad, this relationship is reduced to .00, indicating that the reason older returnees are less satisfied is that they have been away from Ireland longer.

An inverse relationship was hypothesized between the length of time spent abroad and adjustment. It was reasoned that the longer the period spent in another society, the higher the level of acculturation in that society and the more divergent the migrants' attitudes and values would have become from those of their native society. The hypothesis was supported ($r = .18$); controlling for age reduces but does not eliminate the relationship ($r = .12$).

A moderate relationship was found between readjustment and both housing and job satisfaction ($r = .25$ and $r = .26$, respectively). That is, respondents who found their jobs and housing in Ireland better or about as good as what they had abroad tended to be well adjusted.

The variable most strongly related to adjustment was satisfaction with social life ($r = .37$). Returnees who felt their social life in Ireland was as good as or better than what they had abroad tended to be better adjusted than those who did not feel this way. Here we see again the importance of developing friendships, of gaining acceptance among local people. And a key factor in gaining acceptance appears to be *conformity*. That is, returnees must not appear to think or behave too differently from local people, nor should they dwell on their life abroad. The factor that probably hinders the acceptance of returnees more than any other is their temptation to make comparisons between Ireland and the host countries they have left. Irish people are naturally sensitive and at times defensive when their small country is compared with America or Britain; they do not wish to hear that wages, medical services, public transportation, or vegetables are poorer in Ireland. They have heard it all before and do not wish to hear it again. One informant's response to the question "What advice would you give future returnees?" expresses the sentiment of many: "Settle down and get to know your neighbors. Answer their questions but don't keep talking about the country you came from. They don't like to hear it."

The term "Return Yank" is applied, often derogatorily, to the returnee who has not changed his foreign ways, who has retained his foreign accent, idioms, and expressions. At the opposite end of the spectrum from the stereotypic Return Yank, however, are a minority of returnees who have so successfully embraced the traditional rural Irish life-style that the outsider would never guess they have been out of the country.

CONCLUSIONS

In summary, the bulk of migrants left home in their early 20s and settled in large metropolitan areas of the United States, Great Britain, and Canada. There they remained for a period of years during which they married, selecting spouses from within the overseas migrant community.

The migrants' reasons for returning were assessed using a push-pull model. The results revealed that the positive features of the homeland (pull factors) exerted far more influence in the decision to return than did attributes of the host society. Returnees had not been dissatisfied with their lives abroad, but rather they thought life at home would be better. The considerations that caused them to return were different from those that had led them to emigrate. Furthermore, their return was motivated primarily by patriotic, social, and familial concerns—identification with the homeland and its traditional values and the desire to live close to kin and people who share the same culture.

The economic factors that were the primary reasons for their out-migration were found to be less important in return decisions. However, income and employment variables are important in providing a minimum threshold for return migration to become feasible, at least for all those who do not have fixed pensions or fat bankrolls. With only dim prospects of finding a job, inadequate housing, and primitive services, only a trickle of migrants will return, no matter how strong family ties and loyalty to country may be. Also, it should be noted that the motivations of migrants returning to urban areas may be different. One might expect, for example, that migrants returning to Irish cities would have higher socioeconomic status and attach more importance to occupational-economic concerns and less to social benefits than migrants returning to a rural community.

The return migration represented in this survey was primarily an urban-to-rural movement in which the migrants left the large metropolitan areas in which they had settled abroad and returned to rural areas. Many migrants experienced difficulty in readjusting: during their first year half the respondents were dissatisfied and thought they would have been better off had they stayed abroad. The major problems encountered by the returnees were differences in the pace of life, inefficiency, lack of shared interests with local people, difficulty in making friends, unemployment, and a sluggish economy. The cause of dissatisfaction among many migrants was the lack of fit between their expectations and the reality. Dissatisfied migrants were often unrealistic about what Ireland could provide them. Gradually, the migrants learned to cope with the inefficiency, slow pace, and other annoyances of rural and small-town Irish life, so that by the end of their second year at home only one-fifth of the sample was still dissatisfied. Nevertheless, about one in every seven migrants never fully readjusted, and some were so dissatisfied that they eventually re-emigrated.

NOTES

1. This chapter was written expressly for this volume, but it is based on two previous publications (Gmelch 1983; Gmelch 1986).

2. Figures were obtained from volume 7 of the Central Statistics Office's *Census of Population of Ireland, 1981*.

3. The research on which this paper is based was generously supported by the Irish Foundation for Human Development, Earthwatch and the Center for Field Research, and Union College. I wish to acknowledge the assistance of Theresa Brannick and John Cullen in the planning of the survey, the twelve Earthwatch volunteers who helped conduct interviews, Larry Delaney and Richard Felson in the data analysis, and Jack Brady and Sharon Gmelch for comments on an earlier draft of this chapter.

REFERENCES

Bernard, H. R., and Ashton-Vouyoucalos, S.
1976 "Return Migration to Greece." *Journal of the Steward Anthropological Society* 8: 30–52.

Bovenkerk, F.
1973 "On the Causes of Irish Emigration." *Sociologia Ruralis* 3: 263–275.
1974 *The Sociology of Return Migration: A Bibliographic Essay*. The Hague: Martinus Nijhoff.

Brannick, T.
1977 *A Study of Return Emigrants in a Rural Parish*. M.A. thesis, University College Dublin, Dublin.

Caulfield, Breandan, and Bhat, Askok
1980 "The Irish in Britain: Trends in Intermarriage and Fertility Levels 1971–1976." Unpublished manuscript.

DaVanzo, J.
1976 "Differences between Out and Return Migration: An Econometric Analysis." *International Migration Review,* 10: 13–27.

Gmelch, G.
1980 "Return Migration." In *Annual Review of Anthropology,* edited by B. Siegel, 135–59. Menlo Park, Calif.: Annual Reviews.
1983 "Who Returns and Why: Return Migration Behavior in Two North Atlantic Societies." *Human Organization* 42: 46–54.
1986 "The Readjustment of Return Migrants in Western Ireland." In *Return Migration and Regional Economic Problems,* edited by Russell King, 152–70. London: Croom Helm.

Hannan, D.
1970 *Rural Exodus*. London: Geoffrey Chapman.

Hernandez-Alverez, J.
1968 *Return Migration to Puerto Rico*. Berkeley, California: Institute of International Studies.

Hughes, J., and Whelan, B.
1976 *Emigration from Ireland: An Overview*. The Economic and Social Research Institute, Dublin. Mimeograph.

Kane, E.
1969 *A Gaeltacht Report*. Dublin: Comhairle Gaeilge.

McNabb, P.
1964 "Social Structure." In *The Limerick Rural Survey, 1958–1964,* edited by J. Newman. Tipperary: Muintir Na Tire Rural Publications.

Rhoades, R.
1978 "Intra-European Return Migration and Rural Development: Lessons from the Spanish Case." *Human Organization* 37, no. 2: 136–47.

Schrier, A.
1955 *Ireland and the American Emigration: 1850–1900*. Minneapolis: University of Minnesota Press.

Taylor, R. C.
1969 "Migration and Motivations: A Study of Determinants and Types." In *Migration,* edited by J. A. Jackson, 99–133. Cambridge: Cambridge University Press.

Walsh, Brendan
1974 "Expectations, Information, and Human Migration: Specifying an Econometric Model of Irish Migration to Britain." *Journal of Regional Science* 14, no. 1: 107–20.

12 A Review—Guest, Intruder, Settler, Ethnic Minority, or Citizen: The Sense and Nonsense of Borders

Judith-Maria Buechler

A review of the social science literature on migrants in Europe is a formidable task, given the sheer volume of persons involved, the uneven quality and type of data available, and the complexity of the problem. An exhaustive summary lies outside the scope of this article. Rather, I wish to focus on those aspects of recent models or general theories of migration, surveys and descriptions that seem most relevant to the understanding of one of our main problems: the effect of changing legislation or policies formulated in the last two decades on the lives of migrant families in their host countries and at home. Such an inquiry by its very nature is multidisciplinary. It attempts to wed the insights of political economists, sociologists, and geographers (among others) to the more data-oriented descriptions of field-workers: anthropologists, educators, social workers, and journalists. It is based on the premise that migration is an ongoing phenomenon that is embedded in complex international relationships.

Explanatory models of European migration have ranged from single-variable through multiple-factor treatments to those that involve complex group dynamics and structural relationships in partial or total systems. Among the single-variable models are those based on distance between the place of origin and the place of destination or spatial distribution (Clark 1975) or on psychological tolerance level (Freeman 1979). Others are based on multiple economic factors that push or pull migrants from their homelands to their destinations (e.g., Gmelch chap. 11), or those based on complex cost-benefit calculations of the import or export of labor. These factorial models have given way to ones based on group dynamics, or nonassimilation and ethnic interaction (Buechler and Buechler 1972; Foner 1977), or of chain migration (Palmer 1977) and social network formation (Buechler J-M. 1976; Leeds, n.d., see chap. 2; Anwar 1979; Yücel, chap. 6). The changes brought about by these massive population movements have also been analyzed in terms of world systems, economic and political crises, and demographic trends (Castells 1975; Gorz 1970; Freeman 1979).

The immigration of ''alien labor'' is not a new phenomenon in Western Europe. The latter part of the 19th century witnessed the entrance of Irish, Poles,

Jews, and Sikhs (among others) into Great Britain; Poles into Germany; Belgians and northern Italians into France and neighboring Germany; Austrians, French, and Italians to Switzerland. However, the magnitude of the movement greatly accelerated after World War II. In this chapter I am particularly interested in describing the impact of policies during the last twenty years, especially on the part of the "labor importing countries," to restrict immigration, accompanied by the attempts of some "labor exporting countries," such as Portugal, Turkey, and Algeria, to curb the outflow of laborers. Such policies, based on economic fluctuations, real or perceived labor needs, long-term colonial or neocolonial ties, more immediate diplomatic relations, international prescriptions, and the internal pressures of various constituents, have become more restrictive and closed with major intended and unintended consequences for the migrant populations both at home and abroad.

Unlike other European states, Great Britain recruited from three reserve pools of labor: the Anglicized West Indies and Ireland (see Gmelch, chap. 11), and then from India, Pakistan, and Africa (who expected full political and social rights), and also South Europeans, a large proportion of whom were female, skilled, and middle-class. Since 1962 successive governments, Tory and Labour alike, passed four immigration control and three race relations acts, that have gradually withdrawn citizenship rights to persons from the former colonies and Commonwealth, and imposed controls, such as surveillance pass laws and voucher systems, in the attempt to terminate black settler immigration and to induce repatriation (Sivanandan 1976). Such policies, described as domestic forms of neocolonialism, and other "measures to promote integration" have created at least six categories of foreigners with various rights to enter Great Britain (Studlar 1979; Rees 1979).

Restrictive labor migration legislation seems to have had unintended consequences. The Commonwealth Immigrations Act of 1962 and the subsequent restrictive laws seem to have had the effect of turning temporary labor migration of primarily men into the relatively permanent immigration of families, thereby increasing the total annual rate of migration.

In spite of this trend, the sex ratio in the Asian population remains uneven (Anwar 1979; Ballard and Ballard 1977; Watson 1977). Family reunion was a difficult process. For Pakistanis, it involved cumbersome, humiliating, complex, and slow entry procedures. But these did not prevent the formation of extended and joint families or the creation of complex social networks of patrilineal descent groups and exchange systems that linked families in Great Britain to Pakistan. Similarly, the pressures of the new laws and the uncertain future of Hong Kong seem to be associated with the use of family emigration among the Chinese. In this case, kin groups in Britain are favored, and by reducing the socialization of grandparents, the kinship networks which tie the English community to its home villages are threatened. However, younger migrants continue to return to the new territories to marry (Watson 1977).

Like the migration of Asians, the annual rate of West Indian migration seems to have increased as well, but in this case, a high proportion of the migrants are women. For the West Indies, migration has been accompanied by earlier legalization of marriage, but with the continuation of grandparental fostering of children. With the continued rise of dependents arriving in Great Britain, such fostering may become curtailed and the sex ratio equalized.

In sharp contrast to the previously mentioned groups, the Greek Cypriot population was always composed primarily of families, and their numbers have declined from the early 1960s. A very large proportion emigrated as whole families during a limited time from 1955 to 1962. When young single women arrived to work in the developing dress industry and young men returned to Cyprus in search of suitable brides, the balanced sex ratio of the community continued. Pamela Constantinides (1977) attributes the subsequent decline in the population less to the Commonwealth Immigrations Act than to the decline in economic opportunities in service industries in Britain. In a similar fashion, Ladbury (1977) gives priority to the history of migration and interethnic relations for understanding of Turkish Cypriots in London. They too arrived early, from mixed villages, before the 1967 fighting and the 1974 war. In both cases, then, the profile of the immigrant community seems to be a response to changes both in England and in Cyprus. The form and structure of migrant communities in England, then, reflect legislation and economic conditions.

Since the Second World War the Federal Republic of Germany has continued its long-term policy of labor importation begun in 1871 (Rhoades 1978b; Goodman 1984, chap. 9; Gregory and Cazorla, chap. 7; Sontz, chap. 8; Yücel). From 1955 until 1968 Germany initiated a series of treaties with Italy, Spain, Greece, Turkey, Portugal, Yugoslavia, Tunisia, and Morocco for laborers. Since November 1973, however, by a series of bilateral agreements and unilateral measures, Germany has suspended all labor recruiting abroad, severely restricting the numbers of foreign workers (now said to be 60 percent of the work force). The reunion of families and issuing of residence permits were curtailed. As in the case of Great Britain, the earlier migrants had been predominantly male, but after 1973 the percentage of women increased in some groups. The sex imbalance seems to be higher for Turks and Yugoslavs than for Spaniards, Greeks, and Italians (Mehrländer 1979b). In 1968 less than half of the Turkish workers were accompanied by their wives (Paine 1974, 78).

Family reunions were discouraged by abrogating work permits for dependents and by regulating housing and residency (Goodman 1984; Gregory and Cazorla). The policies have been described as a "mixture of covert rotation and the principle of limited integration whereby a majority of guest workers were expected to return voluntarily after some years while a minority remained as permanent residents" (Reimann and Reimann 1979, 75). Local governments and police also tried to enforce stricter control of employers by raiding establishments, by raising fees for alien workers employed and penalties for illegal or "spontaneous" employment and by enforcing the adequate housing of "guest workers" (see Yücel). Departure premiums or incentives, "training courses," and further restrictions in residence permits (often dependent on the needs of particular industries), have not met with much support by either migrants or employers.

As in England, recent data seems to indicate that in Germany migrants are trying to "beat the ban," too. The trend seems to be in favor of family reunification. In addition, there seems to be an increase in the numbers of migrant women, even some single women working in labor-intensive multinational electronics and textile plants and national metal industries (Morokvasic 1976; Kudat 1975; Paine 1974; Goodman, chap. 9). More commonly, married women seem to join their husbands, bringing with them some if not necessarily all of the children (Cornelisen 1980). Whether migrants come singly, as couples, or as families seems to be a function not only of legislation but of the availability of work, housing, child care, and education in Germany as well as the conditions at home, but in recent years the fear that migration might cease altogether has been a powerful incentive for family reunification.

With migrant workers representing 8.5 percent of the total labor force, France has followed much the same path as Great Britain and Germany. From 1945 to 1967 the policy can be characterized as control in theory but laissez-faire or spontaneous in fact, with increasing control and regulation thereafter. Like those of Great Britain, France's policies reflected its colonial heritage and charter membership in the European community. Favored nation status was extended to former French colonies and administrative territories in North and sub-Saharan Africa, and to some French Caribbean islands. France also entered into special accords with Italy, Germany, Greece, Spain, Morocco, Mali, Mauritania, Tunisia, Portugal, Senegal, Yugoslavia, and Turkey. However, from 1968-1969 on, there has been a decided shift to restrict new immigration by "regularizing" (i.e., legalizing) migrants who entered as tourists, but also by establishing quotas and enforcing residence permits. These progressive restrictions came at a time of massive immigration, 80 percent of which was legalized post facto (Miller 1982). It seems to have been difficult to implement these restrictions, however, given the exemptions for Portuguese and Spanish domestics and some skilled workers. Caroline Bretell (1970) writes that two-thirds of all Portuguese immigrants to France from 1950 to 1970 came clandestinely. Since the two countries were close by, the possibility for legalization post facto was simple, and the rigid emigration laws in Portugal and the lengthy military obligation in African wars made legal emigration difficult (see also Callier Boisvert, chap. 3).

After the introduction of the Fontanet "circulaires" of 1972, the position of immigrant laborers in France became even more insecure and dependent on employers, who were liable for housing and required to coordinate residence and work permits. Thus, actually, a temporary contract labor system was created (Freeman 1979, 3). In July of 1974 a full halt to immigration was declared (even for dependents for a short while). The general trend was to actively discourage the settlement of migrants, especially those regarded as "unassimilable" like the North Africans. Regions and enterprises employing a "disproportionate" number of foreign workers were punished by withdrawing subsidies and investment write-offs (Moulier and Tapinos 1979).

As a further discouragement, in 1976 some deportations and police identity controls were instituted, and a year later repatriation and cash incentive return programs were initiated. However, here as in Germany the former were ineffective and the latter met with only a weak response. French policies, unlike those of Great Britain and Germany, reflect the decline in population since the 18th century and the continued importance of agriculture in the total economy along with the growth of both smaller and larger enterprises. Both population decline and the bimodal industrial growth seem to favor family migration at least from certain areas. Brettell (1970) estimates that 60 percent of all Portuguese emigration between 1964 and 1974 was familial, with an increasing number of single women leaving for Paris, where they were employed as domestics. After 1974 members of separated nuclear families were permitted to join each other (Callier Boisvert).

French migration policies are also embedded in complex international relationships. Specific cases, such as the Franco-Algerian and Franco-Tunisian relationships between 1962 and 1979, reveal that these complex, "delicate," often volatile arrangements were certainly as much an expression of energy dependency and third-party conflicts as the need for labor (Koelstra and Simon 1979). The French figures may also reflect the mostly unsuccessful attempts by such countries as Portugal, Algeria, Turkey, and Tunisia to control or prohibit outmigration.

Switzerland, with the highest percentage of aliens in the total population (16 percent in 1975), has consistently maximized the import of foreign workers, but minimized their chances of integration into Swiss society (Hoffman-Nowotny and Killias 1979; Buechler, H., chap. 10). With a backdrop of five referenda from 1960 to 1977, which attempted unsuccessfully to curtail migration, the Swiss government has pursued a "stabilization policy" to attempt to balance the numbers permitted to enter by those leaving. First, a series of measures froze the number of annual permit holders and reduced the time limit for changing jobs, occupations, or cantonal residence. Then, by 1975 all annual permit holders were able to stay for just one year. In spite of these measures, the number of immigrant workers has not been reduced appreciably; rather, as elsewhere, there seems to be a more significant restructuring of the foreign population (Kayser 1977).

In contrast to the countries described previously, Sweden has a smaller foreign labor force: 5.5 percent of the total. Swedish policy shares with France and Great Britain the recognition of the permanent nature of immigration. But Swedish policy, unlike French, is less a reaction to demographic pressures and historical allegiances than a positive support for cultural pluralism and a social welfare ideology. The latter favors family reunion, decent living conditions, and the recognition of the rights of sending countries (Widgren 1979). Further, such policies allow for greater flexibility on the part of migrants as to migration strategy. As Ulla-Britt Engelbrektsson's study (1978) of Turkish migrants from two villages in Central Anatola to Sweden demonstrates, differences in ideology and power relations at home, rather than restrictive laws, were the most significant factor in determining whether men migrated alone or with their wives.

The foreign worker policies of the nations discussed above appear to reflect divergent notions concerning the migrant work force in the host society. Migrants are seen either as a primarily temporary, cheap, mobile, alien, and easily expendable reserve army or as a permanent work force. They are viewed either as a threat to cultural purity (especially when the numbers or proportions of aliens in the workplace, neighborhood, or school rise above a given number) or as a welcome addition to cultural pluralism and national enrichment. In spite of avowals for the greater integration of migrants into the national life of the nations discussed, the trends seem to point to policies that promote rotation rather than settlement, ethnic and racial discrimination rather than integration. If we were to rank the nations according to the relative importance of the two notions above, Switzerland would fall at one end of the continuum and Sweden at the other. In spite of the general ideological commitments of all these host countries to family reunion, the new laws in fact make family reunion more difficult to achieve by requiring assured work and residence. Ironically, family reunions are occurring in record numbers in spite of these laws.

MIGRANT EMPLOYMENT

Regardless of their prior skills, the migrants in question work predominantly in poorly paid manual, unskilled, or semiskilled occupations vacated by "native" workers who refuse such work, even in times of recession and unemployment. In Great Britain, compared with other countries, the employment pattern of migrants seems more varied but also relatively disadvantageous. Regardless of their background, West Indian men are concentrated in unskilled or semiskilled transport or factory work and West Indian women are found in service or textile-clothing industries (Philpott 1977; Foner 1977); the Chinese run the family restaurant trade (Watson 1977) and the Italians are involved in catering, specialized crafts, and small businesses (Palmer 1977); while Greek and Turkish Cypriot men work in services and manufacturing, the women are engaged at home in piecework in the garment industry. Some long-term migrants have been able to fulfill their dreams of self-employment.

The reasons for the predominance of migrants in work shunned by others is made very clear by Muhammad Anwar (1979). The Pakistani men he studied in Rochdale suffered discrimination but were willing to work night and other difficult shifts in the highly competitive textile industry. The women and children were also sometimes employed in the mills, but more frequently they sewed and packed at home.

Work possibilities seem somewhat more promising in Germany. Male migrants are concentrated in metal production, engineering, building, and manufacturing, while females are to be found in manufacturing, especially in textiles, clothing, metals, and electrical goods and electronics. A relatively small percentage work in agriculture or services (Castles and Kosack 1973; Paine 1974; Goodman 1984; Kudat 1975). The Italian men in Germany studied by Sontz were concentrated primarily in undesirable night-shift factory work. Cornelisen (1980) describes some upward mobility for the women and men from Torregreca, a southern Italian town, who were mainly engaged in domestic service and menial construction jobs in Freiburg, Offenbach, and Düsseldrof; and Paine (1974) shows some upward mobility for Turkish workers from mining to factory work. Yücel illustrates the strategies for Turkish entrepreneurs who establish their own workshops.

In contrast to Britain and Germany, a relatively large proportion of male migrants work in agriculture in France, even though they also rank high in building, public works, engineering, and commerce. The women predominate in private and public domestic and personal services (Castles and Kosack 1973; Brettell 1970). Color and ethnic origin seem to define the types of jobs in France. Some North Africans, the Algerians and Moroccans, seem to be concentrated in strenuous, monotonous, and dangerous fields such as mining, while others like the Tunisians work primarily in the tertiary sector (Miller 1979). Migrants from Italy, Spain, and Yugoslavia in Switzerland are similarly assigned work in private and public services, construction, and factories.

It is difficult to estimate the effect of recent legislation on the work life of migrants. To begin with, although most migrants may think of themselves as temporary and most governments expect them to be so, the evidence seems to indicate that migrant workers are, in fact, relatively permanent and certainly form a crucial part of the economic structure in the postindustrial host countries (Castles and Kosack 1973). As Ray Rist (1978, 215) puts it: "Thus the migrants have become a key component of the current economic arrangements and have themselves become a structural phenomenon that could be dislodged only at the peril of the entire economic apparatus now in place."

The number of registered foreign workers in certain countries such as the Netherlands, Sweden, and Belgium have increased while those in Germany, France, and Switzerland have decreased although, according to Lebon and Falchi (1980), the figures do not justify "speaking of a sharp drop." In Switzerland, more migrants work with A, or seasonal, permits. Also, the official figures do not include the 200,000 to 600,000 illegal immigrants estimated by the European Economic Community and others (Power 1979; Rist 1978, 1979).

Contrary to predictions, the recession of 1975–1976 did not give rise to any massive returns (Kayser 1977). Such monetary incentives as those offered in Germany and France seem to have been largely ineffective, for only those migrants who were planning to leave in any case took advantage of these bonuses (see Callier Boisvert). The fact that certain groups such as the Italians, Spanish, and Greeks returned at a highter rate than the Turks and Portuguese seems to have had less to do with government incentives than with the economic conditions in the home countries (Kayser 1977).

Those migrants who stay seem to be staying longer. Even groups who maintain the "myth of return," like the Portuguese in France or the Commonwealth immigrants in Great Britain, actually return "permanently" in very small numbers. Further, the Turkish data suggests that many skilled workers who came early on wish to and tend to remain abroad longer. Some even remain "permanently." Such seems to be the case for Italians in Germany as well. When Michele's family, in *Strangers and Pilgrims*, waxes nostalgic about home, he asks them, "Which one of you wants to be the first to give up eating? . . . Get into your heads now Torregreca is a place to die not to live" (Cornelisen 1980, 53). However, Gmelch (chap. 11) documents a high rate of return migration for Ireland.

The data points again and again to the extraordinary vulnerability of migrants in the host country. First, they perform tasks considered socially degrading, physically taxing, and detrimental to their health. Second, new labor legislation which prevents changes in occupation and residence makes migrant workers more vulnerable and dependent on employers. The industries like textiles, mining, and construction that employ migrants are also very sensitive to recession.

Economic cycles affected migrants in a variety of ways. The extent to which they have been successful in coping with the series of recessions since 1966 seems to have depended on the length of tenure in the host country. In some cases women fared better (as in services in Germany) and in others they fared worse. In England Cypriot and Pakistani women were employed in putting out systems of garment industries which are particularly endangered during periodic or seasonal slack periods. In Germany, by 1975, workers with longer tenure had been joined by families who presumably worked and were able to collect unemployment. In one family observed by Ann Cornelisen (1980), unemployment for the husband, though deeply disturbing, was short-lived. The family was able to make do on unemployment insurance, the contribution of the wife's and son's wages, and odd jobs picked up by the husband on the side. Nonetheless, for most migrants the unemployment rate at the height of the recessions was higher than among indigenous workers, and it might have been higher still if some had not returned home. Some more recent information suggests that the unemployment situation may be worsening (Salt 1981).

In such difficult times, women and children who might not otherwise have been recruited to the work force begin to work for target savings as well. The most striking example in this regard is the recruitment of Moslem women, Turks and Pakistanis who engaged in wage work in factories (Anwar 1979; Engelbrektsson 1978). Further, there is some indication of the increased use of child labor, both at home and in casual work. These women and children were doubly burdened by work "at home" and in the workplace.

The series of recessions has affected savings and remittances crucial to the well-being of family members at home and abroad. On the one hand, the amount saved seems to depend on marital status (e.g., single workers save less than married ones). On the other hand, the presence of family members may either add to or detract from the ability to save (Lohrmann and Manfrass 1974, 151). The percentage of income remitted also depends on the origin of the migrant, the number of dependents at home (especially the children and the aged), and exchange rates. Castles and Kosack (1973) claim that the average foreign worker in Germany sent a third of his wages home if he was unaccompanied by his family. In many cases, migrants seem to have been caught in a double bind of inflation, both at home and abroad, which affected both their ability to save and their ability to invest their savings.

The contrasting experience of the Sikhs and Pakistanis is instructive with regard to the changing nature and kind of savings and remittance patterns. For Sikhs in the early days of migration, men living in all-male households "sent money home almost as soon as they earned it" to cover family debts and passage; but later they retained as much as possible in order to invest in housing in Britain or to take home a lump sum (Ballard and Ballard 1977, 31). In contrast, the obligations to joint families in Pakistan and Great Britain led Pakistani migrants to support and invest in land, property, and small businesses both at home and abroad (Anwar 1979).

Families within a migrant community vary in their life-style, orientation, and plans. Cornelisen describes one Italian family in Germany that invested in the present by living in a well-furnished apartment, and eating and dressing well, much to the distress of another (Cornelisen 1980). Similar variations are described for the Gallegos in Switzerland and the Turks in Sweden (Buechler and Buechler 1972, 1984; Engelbrektsson 1978).

The relationship of remittance obligations to social networks, ideology, and economic structure is most vividly described by Stuart Philpott (1977). Although he expects less than 20 percent of Montserratian migrants presently in the British Isles to return, their ideology of return and their sense of obligation towards kin at home continue over time and have created an interdependent social system in which the home island is particularly vulnerable.

Information from long-term migrants may be suggestive for future trends. Many migrants aspire to self-employment in private enterprises wherever possible. This seems most possible in England and least possible in Switzerland. Direct remittances may become reduced with time, but there may be a continuation of keeping one's options open by investing in retirement or vacation homes in the country of origin, if not necessarily the home community (see Halpern, chap. 5). Such investments are, of course, dependent on options in the host country as well.

In addition to private enterprises and property, migrants also invest in education, marriage, and public works to enhance their own status or that of family members. Thus, Jamaican migrants to England initially sought the education of their children as social security (Foner 1977), while Turks in Sweden invested heavily in bride wealth (Engelbrektsson 1978), and Italians and Soninké sent money home for public works (Cornelisen 1980; Barou, chap. 4). Even seemingly irrational investments in monuments (rather than traditional agricultural technology as the Chinese and Italians have done) make sense in the long term (Watson 1977; Palmer 1977). Robin Palmer describes the contributions of Italian migrants in London to the construction of these monuments at home. With the decline of agriculture, the out-migration of the local youth, and the proximity of urban centers, the Inglesi (Italian English) hope that their monuments will help develop tourism (combined with intensive dairying) in their hilly region of origin.

Among Montserratians, unemployment, inflation, and personal crises like illness may prevent migrants from sending remittances home or limit the amount they are able to send to the island. At the same time, these very factors may force a return. Restrictive legislation curtails the numbers who are able to go abroad at all, further shrinking the flow of remittances upon which members at home have become increasingly dependent. The decline in remittances has seriously curtailed commercial activities and subsistence agricultural production on the island (Philpott 1977). Similar dependence on remittances has been described for villages near Hong Kong (Watson 1977), Turkey (Magnarella 1979; Paine 1974) and Spain (Rhoades 1978a; Gregory and Cazorla; Buechler and Buechler 1972, 1984; Buechler, H., chap. 10; Buechler, J-M., 1976).

On the national level, the possible reduction of remittances due to immigration bans has been of considerable concern to sending countries who depend on such cash flows for a sizable proportion of the GNP. It is subject to debate whether such foreign capital serves as a source of investment capital or as a source for the balance of trade, since it is argued that very large portions are expended on imported consumer goods, which aggravate trade deficits and do not contribute to productive enterprises.

The literature on return migrants is replete with criticism that migrants invest in housing, consumer durables, and nonproductive redundant enterprises (Rhoades 1978a; Gmelch 1980). Such criticism "blames the victim." In the few cases on record where labor-exporting countries and/or hosts have provided support for productive investment, the migrants have been quick and eager to respond. Gallegos invested in dairy cooperatives and Turks have taken advantage of reduced import taxes on machinery for agriculture, manufacture and service (Engelbrektsson 1978). Local industries, such as those involved in construction, have also profited in some areas such as Galicia and Portugal (Leeds, chap. 2). Where there are opportunities, migrants have also effectively used their foreign language and organizational skills.

Capital earned abroad is rarely controlled by migrants. Different groups vie for migrant savings to support various development strategies. One good example is the debate in Turkey. The Justice Party, supported to some extent by business, is promoting investment in privately owned firms and the establishment of a State Industry and Workers Investment Bank. The opposing National Action Party decries the export of skilled manpower and hopes to invest migrant reserves in state projects like armaments, while the militantly Islamic National Salvation Party prefers state investments in regional and locally oriented industries. The Republican Peoples Party, which stands in opposition to the ruling coalition, is calling for the investment of migrant savings in agricultural and industrial cooperative enterprises, with guaranteed jobs for return migrants (Lieberman and Gitmez 1979).

The benefits of migratory labor are distributed unequally among the classes and regions of sending countries. They often are associated with the intensification of regional differences (Gregory and Cazorla; Buechler and Buechler 1978). Even in nations like Yugoslavia, with parties who favor more equitable regional and class distribution of wealth, and where there have been some systematic attempts to favor migrants in terms of interest on capital, jobs, and housing, the general outlook does not seem encouraging (Taníc 1979; Halpern).

SOCIAL STRUCTURE AND REPERCUSSIONS

The economic hardship engendered by recent migration legislation has had serious social structural repercussions. The "call of kin" to host countries has altered the dynamics of sex and generation. Kinsmen often provide the initial capital for migration and the information and connections required for jobs, housing, and permits. The extent of these kin-based migration networks is illustrated by one Montserratian migrant, Thomas Fenton, who, over a period of twelve years, brought twenty-two persons to London, among whom were actual and potential spouses, children, siblings, nieces, and nephews (Philpott 1977).

Similar chain migration by pioneer Pakistanis is described by Anwar (1979, 21). These sponsored later Pakistani migrants, providing them with air tickets, necessary paperwork, work vouchers, and initial accommodations. Such sponsorship became even more crucial, Anwar claims, when immigration restrictions after 1962 led to the migration of persons who might never have come to Britain but "who did not want to lose the opportunity in case of further restrictions in the future." The difficulties of entry and reentry for returning migrants have forced many to bring over their families and take British citizenship, particularly after Pakistan left the Commonwealth in 1973 (Anwar 1979, 258). Barou describes a similar process for the Soninké.

In other cases, official avenues of migration were closed and only family members were permitted to join established workers. In some cases, illegal or clandestine migration became the only possible avenue (see Yücel). Official statistics are often misleading. For example, in Turkey official statistics and surveys claim that more migrants use official rather than informal channels to migrate, but Engelbrektsson (1978) found that less than 4 percent of the migrants from her two villages in Turkey used the official labor exchanges. Arriving as tourists in Sweden, most kinsmen or persons claiming kinship arranged for work or marriage with a Swede in order to obtain residence. She relates how, in 1966, four young "tourists" took a train to Stockholm, using money borrowed or given by relatives and saved from wage work and land sales. In the following ten years they brought ten related men, three women, and five children to Sweden. Their persistence and ability to manipulate Koranic and Swedish marriage laws in order to circumvent restrictions are particularly telling.

Kinship ties are extraordinarily important for migrants who wish to return home. This is especially the case when good permanent jobs or housing at home are scarce. One of Cornelisen's (1980, 182) informants, Vincenzo, just couldn't stand it in Germany anymore, so he joined a contractor in central Italy where there was work. But in order to find housing, he had to become engaged to the contractor's sister.

The second major area of family life affected by migration is the care of dependents. As we have noted for Galicia and others from the West Indies, Africa, and the Middle East, a good proportion of wages are sent home to provide care for children or for spouses, siblings, and aged parents (Barou; Buechler and Buechler 1972; Philpott 1977; Goody 1977; Kudat 1975). In spite of an ideology of family reunion, recent legislation seems to have made it increasingly difficult to bring in minor children or siblings (see Buechler, chap. 10). Given the nature of housing, child care, and education for migrant children, some families choose to leave their children at home with kin and may thus become estranged from their children. However, children taken along may also reject the language and culture of their parents and become progressively alienated from their roots and their present position.

In all the countries studied, a waiting period is imposed before dependents (usually defined as spouses and unmarried children under 21) are permitted to join relatives. Often "adequate" housing and sometimes work permits are required for the reunion. For example, A. Sivanandan writes with some passion about the report of the House of Commons Select Committee on Race Relations and Immigration: "It is here in the matter of dependents that the axe really falls." The report recommends that

> children over 12 years old born abroad to those settled here should not be allowed to join their parents and it may well be necessary on social grounds to adjust the immigration rules in the future to insure that children are only admitted if they are below school age. Dependents such as parents, grandparents and children over 18 should not be allowed to join families unless accommodation and means of support by the sponsor is approved by the authorities.

The message is clearly that unproductive additions to working-class black families are unwanted. If you want family life, "go home." Similarly, for Turks in Berlin, "Reasons for denial [by the police] are frequently not made explicit and few aliens seek legal advice to insure the unity of their families" (Kudat 1975, 89).

Such formal and informal means to prevent family reunions often preceded the recent recessions. They were attempts to curtail the cost of social services for migrants in the host countries (i.e., for housing, medical attention, and education), which rose as dependents joined kin. Judging from the description of migrant housing, often in costly overcrowded and dilapidated *bidonvilles,* the rate of occupational illnesses—including the common "fear syndrome," the "mis-education" or inadequate training of migrant children, and the lack of child-care facilities—the cost to host countries appears very low and the price paid by the workers very high (Buechler, H., chap. 10; Gregory and Cazorla; Mehrländer 1979a, 1979b; Moulier and Tapinos 1979).

The impression gained is that recent legislation has led to a general worsening of conditions for dependents. The resort to illegal entry forces dependents into illegal work, the nonregistration of children in school, the use of crisis-fostering by older siblings who are then also not educated, and nonuse of social services in general. One German study found that one-fifth of all foreign parents evaded sending their children to school (Mehrländer 1979a). Estimates in Switzerland are 25 percent, and in France children living in shantytowns are rejected in schools since their parents fake addresses elsewhere in order to remain in the country (Castles and Kosack 1973, 210).

There is some controversy as to the impact of these conditions on kin patterns. Some authors predict the demise and failure of traditional family life (Castles and Kosack 1973, 365), while others maintain that the migratory situation may serve to strengthen families, for it provides individuals some freedom from the burdens of extended kinship obligations (Cornelisen 1980). Obligations to wide kin networks seem to continue the maintenance of these strong families, and ethnic ties are, at least in part, supported by the ideology of return in the short or long term held by migrants and reinforced by hosts' expectations. They serve as a defense against discrimination and an insurance in an increasingly hostile environment. They are adapted to fit new situations and are mobilized for new ends.

In migration, the nature and dynamics of patterns of control are altered. Reports indicate that the traditional power or authority of older men over younger ones, men over women, and parents over adolescent children undergoes changes abroad which carry over to the return home. In Göteborg, the dominance of the Turkish patriarch declined, a decline which was already underway in Turkey as some established residences in town, away from the village (Engelbrektsson 1978). Other reports document the continued importance of age, although control of resources by the aged may be more superficial than real (Samuel 1978; Anwar 1979). Younger male Soninké are restructuring the *foyers* in Paris (Barou).

There is also contradictory, or rather noncomplementary, evidence regarding the extent to which the migratory experience contributes to significant changes in the relationship between men and women. Cornelisen describes "liberation" for her female friends. For once, the men were not off in some dark café "together, bored and restless. The women were not at home with waiting babies and drying laundry. . . . We were all bunched in together, the women as much a part of the discussions and the jokes as the men were part of the preparation of meals" (1980, 174). What will happen back in Torregreca?

Studies of other women—Turks in Germany and Turkey, Gallegas in Switzerland and Spain—show that changes in status, division of labor in the household, and social life in the host country may not carry over upon return. At the same time, women who have had experience controlling resources, as in Portugal and Galicia, and women in some villages in Turkey who had "a high degree of intimacy and communication with men" were able to influence major decisions and enjoy a somewhat more egalitarian relationship (Bretell 1970; Buechler and Buechler 1972; Buechler, H., chap. 10; Engelbrektsson 1978).

Differences in social interaction patterns are as much a reflection of differences in the villages and towns of origin as they are expressions of modernization under the impact of migration or urbanization. Migrants are not assimilating to more egalitarian roles in the host society. For one thing, the percentage of foreign women who work for wages is higher than the percentage of native women who do so. My Galician female informants were often amazed that Swiss women did not work outside the home, and the Gallego men pitied their Swiss coworkers because they did not have the help of their wives and would thus probably never be able to own their own homes.

The strain between male and female migrant workers has been interpreted as resulting from conservative rural women joining their more cosmopolitan husbands. I would rather attribute such conflict to the abysmal conditions of life and work in the host country. Publicly financed housing where it exists is inadequate, paternalistic, and restrictive, while private accommodations continue to be appalling: unsanitary, crowded, dangerous, and costly.

The fact that many migrants work night shifts puts additional strain on couples and families (Sontz; Anwar 1979; Cornelisen 1980). Dual worker families find it difficult to organize household chores, child care, and recreation. When these are compounded by irregular shifts, eating, sleeping, and shopping become even more difficult and women often become even more burdened. With the influx of new clandestine workers, the possibility for further exploitation, both at work and in housing conditions, becomes alarming. This is especially the case since plans to ameliorate conditions are based on inadequate statistics.

Inadequate child-care facilities also put a strain on couples. Migrants are sometimes forced to abandon traditional fostering arrangements and some are beginning to rely on strangers or newer boarding schools at home (Kudat 1979; Buechler and Buechler 1972; Buechler, H., chap. 10).

With longer-term settlement the "problem of the second generation" has gained some attention. These youth, often born and raised abroad, said to be situated "between two cultures" or alienated from both, rejected by peers and teachers alike, miseducated for failure, unable to find work, or unwilling to work in the same jobs under the same conditions as their parents, face a number of unenviable options. Some "go native," others flee "home," and yet others join peers in alienated marginalized groups. To guard against the dual dangers of geographic separation or cultural assimilation, some parents increase their ethnic encapsulation. Other parents seem more open. Our own experiences are similar to those of Alan James (1974, 18), who writes:

> Immigrant parents might to some extent sympathize with the aspiration of their sons and (more particularly) daughters for the "freedom" enjoyed by western teenagers; they are not entirely tyranous or reactionary, they have themselves "broken away" to some extent and are aware of the attractions of a different way of life. But they are subject to pressure from their own elders, and fear for the good name of their family in the Punjab amongst people who know little about life in Western cities. And there is always the fear at the back

of the parents' minds, that their daughter's chances of a good marriage will be ruined if there are rumours in the villages near their own that she has succumbed to "western" behavior. The sanctions on an individual's behavior that exist in the extended family household are maintained when the family is split up.

Barou mentions the shame felt by a Malian mother when her children behaved in an unacceptable French manner at home in Africa.

Two recent articles place the pain and anger of these young second-generation migrants in the political context of host countries. The hustler culture of the young unemployed Surinamers in urban Holland is analyzed as comparable to their young Dutch counterparts—the long-term unemployed and "beats" who establish irregular channels to acquire status in an environment of economic exclusion and racial discrimination (Biervleit 1975). Similarly, in England, Paul Gilroy 1981–1982 places the problem of the second generation squarely in the context of migrant conditions. He criticized the notion that a respectable and hard-working first generation of black parents are locked in conflict with their deviant, pathological, identityless children. Rather, he claims that generational conflict, when it occurs, is about political strategy, not familial strife.

MIGRANT RIGHTS

Since 1968 the insecurity of employment and residency, housing, education, racism, and discrimination have become increasingly salient political issues. The legal status of foreign workers ranges from member in the privileged European Economic Community to least favored seasonal worker, or worse yet, undocumented or illegal alien. Yet all suffer legally sanctioned discrimination and are denied many rights of citizenship.

The struggle of migrants must be seen in the context of increasing discrimination as well as international concern for human rights. On the one hand, the last ten years have witnessed a rise in antiforeign repression, racism, and xenophobia (particularly in England, France, Germany, and Switzerland) at the same time that official and unofficial attempts were made to strengthen migrant worker rights.

Neither voiceless nor powerless, migrants became "an emerging political force, a population group that already has significant dimensions of political investment which will likely become more important in the future" (Miller 1982, 30). This new political voice has threatened not only host countries but home countries as well. Migrant associations, sponsored by home governments, influence policies about social security, education, and recreation, and may also serve as instruments for political control. The cessation or control of out-migration is also often the way in which home governments control emigrants whose political participation abroad is seen as a threat to current regimes (Miller 1982; Lohrmann and Manfrass 1974).

For example, Mark J. Miller (1982) sees the 1973–1974 ban on further emigration from Algeria to France not merely as outrage directed against anti-Algerian terrorism but concern that the violence would be turned against the home regime. Turkish national opposition may similarly be transferred to German, French, and Swiss soil. Foreign parties may also establish bases in host countries and thus influence politics at home. For instance, in Germany and elsewhere, Greek, Croatian, Turkish, and Spanish workers have fought internal conflicts on foreign soil (Lohrmann 1980; Halpern), and in England, Indian and Pakistani settlers joined resistance movements in reaction to authoritarianism "at home" (Sivanandan 1978).

One cannot but be impressed by the institutional and noninstitutional channels employed by "alien labor" in their political struggle against increasingly coercive, repressive, local and national state intervention and the rise of nationalist racist movements such as Powellism in Great Britain, the Schwarzenbach initiative in Switzerland, and the Ordre Nouveau in France. The interaction between the struggle at work and in the community is illustrated particularly well by Gilroy (1981–1982) in his analysis of the politicization of Asian, Afro-Caribbean, and white youth in Britain. For our purposes, his quote from Ira Katznelson is particularly useful: " 'The making of classes at work is complemented by the making of classes where people live; in both places adaptive and rebellious responses to the class situation are inevitably closely intertwined' " (213). The struggle seems to take its form both within trade unions' work councils in collective bargaining and in limited institutionalized consultation; through foreign worker participation and representation on the local level by leftist political parties, church and civil rights groups, citizen and legal aid organizations and ethnic associations, but more significantly in work stoppages, boycotts, protests, housing and work strikes, petitioning, and the establishment of alternative educational projects (Miller 1982; Sivanandan 1981–1982).

The politics of the polls, parties, and workplace penetrate the home and community to form a new consciousness of class and ethnicity. In all the major European countries, foreign workers have joined together in strikes and other forms of resistance. These are geared specifically against social policies which affect family life: housing, vacations, schooling, and personal safety. For example, the wildcat strike called by Portuguese workers at the Karmann factory in Osnabrück dealt specifically with vacations. Another case in point was the four-year rent strike led by Algerian workers in France who live in overcrowded, dilapidated housing and are "disproportionally victims of fatal fires and gas leakages" (Miller 1979, 230). The protest dealt with living conditions in government dormitories, subsidized largely by differences in dependent allocations for those left in Algeria. Similar housing protests have been reported in Frankfurt and Geneva (Miller 1979, 1982).

The riots in recent years in Britain's inner cities are to be explained, in part, by the severe cuts in social welfare spending for housing and the monetarist policies of recent governments (Bridges 1981–1982). Strikers—supported by community organizations, temples, grocers, and landlords—protested work conditions (Sivanandan 1981–1982, 127). Migrants also organized rotating credit unions and mortgage clubs to buy houses. Where legal housing is unavailable, extralegal residences have been established; thus the rise of squatter settlements in France may be viewed as a form of protest as well.

In both informal and formal ways, migrant communities have tried to bring pressure on agencies at home and abroad to end discrimination in education and make it more responsive to the needs of immigrant children. Rist (1978) documents the less than successful experiments by different German *Länder*. It is thus not surprising that some parents, like the Turks, kept their children out of school. For the 70,000 Turkish children in Germany in 1972 only German and Christian schools were available. To fight the categorization, or tracking, of their children, other migrant groups such as the Afro-Caribbean community in England established alternative schools (Sivanandan 1981–1982; Fuller 1976). Others try to supplement national schooling with language courses. Migrant associations, like the Moroccan and Tunisian *amicale,* try to establish Arab language courses because, as one boy who wanted to learn Arabic wrote: "j'aime mon pays, j'aimerai y retourner après avoir acquis un bon métier. J' y construirai un petit pavilion" (Ouzzani 1976, 208). (I love my country. I would like to return after having learned a profession or skill and want to build a little house there.)

Migrants have protested and organized peaceably and violently against the rise of violence against them. Bans, entry certificates, stop and search arrests, "sus" (arrests "on suspicion" of loitering with intent to commit an arrestable offense) detentions, virginity tests on female entrants, beatings, and killings have been met by protests, rebellion, and the rise of Rastafari among Asians and blacks in England. In France violence, particularly against Arabs and black Africans, has led to work stoppages and protest demonstrations. One such demonstration by migrants and their supporters to protest police identity controls in the Paris metro took the form of wearing the yellow Star of David because such tactics were thought to resemble the Nazis' (Miller 1979, 227). Migrants have also gained some support from union civil rights organizations and parties. However, their struggle for human rights and citizenship in Europe will be long and arduous and will, in the last analysis, depend partially upon the way in which Western Europe restructures its economies and its states (Sivanandan 1981–1982; Böhning 1979).

REFERENCES

Anwar, Muhammad

1979 *The Myth of Return. The Pakistanis in Britain.* London: Heinemann Educational Books.

Ballard, Roger, and Ballard, Catherine

1977 "The Sikhs: The Development of South Asian Settlements in Britain." In *Between Two Cultures,* edited by J. Watson, 21–57. Oxford: Basil Blackwell.

Biervleit, W. E.

1975 "The Hustler Culture of Young Unemployed Surinamers." In *Adaptation of Migrants from the Caribbean in the European & American Metropolis,* edited by H. E. Lamur and J. Speckmann, 191–201. Leiden: University of Amsterdam Press.

Böhning, W. R.

1976 "The ILO & Contemporary International Economic Migration." *International Migration Review,* 10: 147–156.

1979 "International Migration and the International Economic Order." *Journal of International Affairs,* 33: 187–200.

Bovenkerk, Frank

1974 *The Sociology of Return Migration: A Bibliographic Essay.* The Hague: Martinus Nyhoff.

Brettell, Caroline

1970 "Portuguese Emigration to France, 1950–1974: A Brief Demographic Report." *European Demographic Information Bulletin* 7: 85–91.

Bridges, Lee

1981–1982 "Keeping the Lid On: British Urban Social Policy 1765–1981." *Race & Class* 23: 171–187.

Buechler, Judith-Maria

1975 "The Eurogallegas: Female Spanish Migration." In *Being Female: Reproduction, Power, and Change,* edited by D. Raphael, 207–14. The Hague: Mouton.

1976 "Introduction" and "Something Funny Happened on the Way to the Agora: A Comparison of Bolivian and Spanish Galician Migrants." *Anthropological Quarterly* 49, No. 1: 1–3, 62–69.

Buechler, J-M., and Buechler, Hans C.

1972 "El Aymara Boliviano y el cambio social: reevaluacion del concepto de intermediario cultural." *Estudios Andinos* 11, no. 3: 137–49.

1975 "Los Suizos: Galician Migration to Switzerland." In *Migration and Development: Implications for Ethnic Identity and Political Conflict,* edited by H. I. Safa and B. M. DuToit, 17–31. The Hague: Mouton.

1978 "Social Class, Conflict and Unequal Development in Spanish Galicia." *Review of Radical Political Economics* 10: 130–35.

1981 *Carmen: The Autobiography of a Spanish Galician Woman.* Cambridge, Mass.: Schenkman.

1984 "Four Generations in Spanish Galicia: A Developmental Analysis of Socioeconomic Options." In *Culture and Community in Europe: Essays in Honor of Conrad Arensberg,* edited by O. Lynch, 150–72. New Delhi: Hindustani Press.

Castells, Manuel

1975 "Immigrant Workers & Class Struggles in Advanced Capitalism: The Western European Experience." *Politics and Society* 15, no. 1: 33–66.

Castles, Stephen, and Kosack, Godula

1973 *Immigrant Workers and Class Structure in Western Europe.* London: Oxford University Press.

Clark, John
1975 "Residential Patterns & Social Integration of Turks in Cologne." In *Manpower Mobility Across Cultural Boundaries,* edited by R. E. Krane, 61–77. Leiden: E. J. Brill.

Constantinides, Pamela
1977 "The Greek Cypriots: Ethnic Relations in London & Cyprus." In *Between Two Cultures,* edited by J. Watson, 269–300. Oxford: Basil Blackwell.

Cornelisen, Ann
1980 *Strangers and Pilgrims: The Last Italian Migration.* New York: Holt, Rinehart and Winston.

Engelbrektsson, Ulla-Britt
1978 *The Force of Tradition: Turkish Migrants at Home & Abroad.* Göteborg: University of Göteborg Press.

Foner, Nancy
1975 "The Meaning of Education to Jamaicans at Home and in London." *New Community* 4: 229–49.
1976 "Male and Female Jamaican Migrants in London." *Anthropological Quarterly* 49: 28–35.
1977 "The Jamaican Cultural & Social Change Among Migrants in Britain." In *Between Two Cultures,* edited by J. Watson, 120–50. Oxford: Basil Blackwell.

Freeman, Gary
1979 *Immigrant Labor and Racial Conflict in Industrial Societies: The French & British Experience 1945-1975.* Princeton: Princeton University Press.

Fuller, Mary
1976 "Experiences of Adolescents from Ethnic Minorities in the British State Education System." In *Les Travailleurs Étrangers en Europe Occidentale,* edited by P. J. Bernard, 173–93. Paris: Mouton.

Gilroy, Paul
1981–1982 "You Can't Fool the Youths . . . Race & Class Formation in the 1980's." *Race & Class* 23: 187–207.

Gmelch, George
1980 "Return Migration." In *Annual Review of Anthropology,* edited by B. Siegel, 135–59. Menlo Park, Calif.: Annual Reviews.

Goodman, Charity
1984 *The Decision-Makers: Spanish Migrant Women in West Germany.* Ph.D. diss., Rutgers University.

Goody, Ester, and Groothues, Christine Muir
1977 "The West Africans: The Quest for Education." In *Between Two Cultures,* edited by J. Watson, 151–80. Oxford: Basil Blackwell.

Gorz, André
1970 "Immigrant Labour." *New Left Review* 6: 1.

Hoffman-Nowotny, Hans-Joachim, and Killias, Martin
1979 "Switzerland." In *International Labor Migration in Europe,* edited by R. E. Krane, 47–63. New York: Praeger.

James, Alan
1974 *Sikh Children in Britain.* London: Oxford.

Kayser, Bernard

1977 "European Migrations: The New Pattern." *International Migration Review* 11: 232–40.

Koelstra, Rein, and Simon, Gildas

1979 "France." In *International Labor Migration in Europe,* edited by R. E. Krane, 133–47. New York: Praeger.

Kubat, Daniel

1979 *The Politics of Migration Policies: The First World in the 1970's*. New York: Center for Migration Studies.

Kudat, Ayse

1975 "Structural Change in the Migrant Turkish Family." In *Manpower Mobility across Cultural Boundaries: Social, Economic & Legal Aspects, The Case of Turkey and West Germany,* edited by R. E. Krane, 77–95. Leiden: E. J. Brill.

Ladbury, Sarah

1977 "The Turkish Cypriots: Ethnic Relations in London and Cyprus." In *Between Two Cultures,* edited by J. Watson, 301–31. Oxford: Basil Blackwell.

Lebon, A., and Falchi, G.

1980 "New Developments in Intra-European Migration since 1974." *International Migration Review* 14: 539–79.

Leeds, Anthony

n.d. "Portuguese & Portuguese French Labor Migration." Mimeograph.

Lieberman, Samuel, and Gitmez, Ali

1979 "Turkey." In *International Labor Migration in Europe,* edited by R. E. Krane, 201–20. New York: Praeger.

Lohrmann, Reinhard, and Manfrass, Claus, ed.

1974 *Ausländerbeschäftigung und Internationale Politik*. Munich: Oldenburg.

Magnarella, P. J.

1979 *The Peasant Venture*. Cambridge, Mass.: Schenkman.

Mehrländer, Ursula

1979a "Problèmes scolaires et formation professionelle des travailleurs étrangers et leurs enfants en République Fédérale d'Allemagne." In *Les Travailleurs Étrangers en Europe Occidentale,* edited by P. J. Bernard, 193–202. Paris: Mouton

1979b "Federal Republic of Germany." In *The Politics of Migration Policies: The First World in the 1970s,* edited by Daniel Kubat, 145–63. New York: Center for Migration Studies.

Miller, Mark J.

1979 "Reluctant Partnership: Foreign Workers in Franco-Algerian Relations, 1962–1979." *Journal of International Affairs* 33: 219–236.

1981 *Foreign Workers in Western Europe: An Emerging Political Force*. New York: Praeger.

1982 "The Political Impact of Foreign Labor. A Revaluation of the Western European Experience." *International Migration Review* 16: 27–60.

Moulier, Yann, and Tapinos, Georges

1979 "France." In *The Politics of Migration Policies: The First World in the 1970's,* edited by Daniel Kubat, 127–145. New York: Center for Migration Studies.

Ouzzani, Mustapha

1976 "Défense et developpement des cultures d'origine." In *Les Travailleurs Étrangers en Europe Occidentale,* edited by P. J. Bernard, 203–209. Paris: Mouton.

Paine, Suzanne

1974 *Exporting Workers: The Turkish Case.* Cambridge: Cambridge University Press.

Palmer, Robin

1977 "The Italians: Patterns of Migration to London." In *Between Two Cultures,* edited by J. L. Watson, 242–269. Oxford: Basil Blackwell.

Philpott, Stuart

1977 "The Montserratians: Migration Dependency and the Maintenance of Island Ties on England." In *Between Two Cultures,* edited by J. L. Watson, 90–120. Oxford: Basil Blackwell.

Power, Jonathan

1979 *Migrant Workers in Western Europe & the United States.* New York: Pergamon.

Rees, Tom

1979 "The United Kingdom." In *The Politics of Migration Policies,* edited by Daniel Kubat, 67–95. New York: Center for Migration Studies.

Reimann, Horst, and Reimann, Helga

1979 "Federal Republic of Germany." In *International Labor Migration in Europe,* edited by R. E. Krane, 63–86. New York: Praeger.

Rhoades, Robert

1977 "Intra-European Migration and Development in the Mediterranean Basin." *Current Anthropology* 18: 539–540.

1978a "Intra-European Return Migration and Rural Development: Lessons from the Spanish Case." *Human Organization* 37: 136–147.

1978b "Foreign Labor & German Industrial Capitalism 1871–1978: The Evolution of a Migratory System." *American Ethnologist* 5: 553–574.

Rist, Ray

1978 *Guestworkers in Germany: The Prospects for Pluralism.* New York: Praeger.

1979 "The European Economic Community and Manpower Migrations Policies & Prospects." *Journal of International Affairs* 33: 201–217.

Salt, John

1981 "International Labor Migration in Western Europe: A Geographical Review." In *Global Trends in Migration Theory & Research on International Population Movements,* edited by M. Kritz et al., 133–58. New York: Center for Migration Studies.

Samuel, Michel

1978 *Le Prolélariat Africain Noir en France.* Paris: François Maspéro.

Sivanandan, A.

1976 "Race, Class & The State: The Black Experience in Britain." *Race & Class* 27: 350–367.

1978 "From Immigration Control to Induced Repatriation." *Race & Class* 20: 1–8.

1981–1982 "From Resistance to Rebellion: Asian & Afro-Caribbean Struggles in Britain." *Race & Class* 23: 111–153.

Studlar, Donley
1979 "Great Britain." In *International Labor Migration in Europe,* edited by R. E. Krane, 88–118. New York: Praeger.

Taníc, Zwan
1979 "Yugoslavia." In *International Labor Migration in Europe,* edited by R. E. Krane, 173–86. New York: Praeger.

Watson, James, ed.
1977 *Between Two Cultures: Migrants & Minorities in Britain.* Oxford: Brasil Blackwell.

Widgren, Jonas
1979 "Sweden." In *International Labor Migration in Europe,* edited by R. E. Krane, 19–44. New York: Praeger.

Author Index

Subject Index

Contributors

Jacques Barou is currently both the director of the Agence Inter Face Migrants, an agency that specializes in immigration problems, and a lecturer at the University of Paris IV. He has undertaken research and published extensively on African, Portuguese, and Yugoslav migration in France, addressing problems of housing, ethnic relations, and the role of Islam in African migrant communities. He is the author of *Travailleurs Africains en France: Rôle des Cultures d'origine* (1978).

Hans Christian Buechler is a professor of anthropology at Syracuse University. He received his Ph.D. in anthropology at Columbia University. In addition to his fieldwork on migration from Spanish Galicia to Switzerland, he has undertaken long-term research in Bolivia on a variety of topics, including land tenure, agrarian reform, rural-urban migration, ritual, and small-scale industries. He has authored and coauthored four books and many articles on these topics.

Judith-Maria Buechler is a professor of anthropology at Hobart and William Smith Colleges. She received a Ph.D. in anthropology from McGill University. In addition to having done fieldwork in Spain and Switzerland, she has undertaken long-term research in Bolivia on child-rearing practices, rural and urban marketing, and small urban industries. Her publications include *The Bolivian Aymara* and *Carmen: The Autobiography of a Spanish Galician Woman* (both with Hans Christian Buechler) and several articles on women, work, and politics in Bolivia and Spanish Galicia as well as on the effects of the international debt crisis on Bolivia.

Collette Callier Boisvert received a doctorate in anthropology at the Sorbonne and has written many articles on rural-urban migration in Brazil, migration from Portugal to France, and the effects of migration on a rural Portuguese community.

Her interests include family structure, female roles, and social networks. At present, she lives in Paris.

José Cazorla has a chair in political science at the University of Granada, where he has also acted as dean of the university's law school and as vice-rector. He holds a doctorate in law from the University of Granada. He has authored and coauthored eight books and numerous articles on political theory, the sociopolitical structure of Spain, and international migration. Presently, he is finishing a project on return migrants in Andalusia.

George Gmelch is a professor of anthropology at Union College. He was educated at Stanford University and the University of California at Santa Barbara, where he received his doctorate. He has done research on return migration in Ireland, Newfoundland, and Barbados. In addition, he has done major research on tinkers in Ireland and nomadic or "long-distance" travellers in England and Wales. Most recently, he has studied resource use in coastal southeast Alaska. Gmelch has published four books and numerous articles on travellers, poverty, urban anthropology, and return migration.

Charity Goodman is currently working as a social science analyst at the Fogarty International Center, National Institutes of Health. Her major fields of interest include international migration, women and employment, and medical anthropology. She has worked as a consultant at the Women's Bureau of the U.S. Department of Labor and at various medical institutions in Washington, D.C. Goodman has also lectured at the University of Maryland, Hood College, and George Washington University. She has published on migration in Germany as well as on medical anthropology. She received a Ph.D. from Rutgers University.

David D. Gregory is a professor of anthropology at Dartmouth College and a board member of the U.S.-Mexican Studies Center at the University of California, San Diego. He received his Ph.D. at the University of Pittsburgh. In addition to having conducted extensive research in Spain, partially in collaboration with Professor Cazorla, he has acted as a consultant for foreign and U.S. governments and private firms regarding opportunities and prospects for international business and labor. Among his publications are *Andalusian Odyssey* as well as reports on Spanish and Mexican migration.

Joel Martin Halpern is a professor of anthropology at the University of Massachussetts at Amherst. He received a Ph.D. in anthropology from Columbia University and has undertaken long-term research in Yugoslavia since 1953. His books include *A Serbian Village* (1967), *The Changing Peasantry of Eastern Europe* (1972), and, with Barbara Kerensky-Halpern, *A Serbian Village in Historical Perspective* (1972).

Anthony Leeds is a professor of anthropology at Boston University. He received his Ph.D. in anthropology at Columbia University. In addition to his work in Portugal, he has extensive field experience in Brazil, Peru, Venezuela, and the United States. His interests include theoretical issues in human ecology, scientific ideology, and rural-urban systems, topics on which he has published prolifically. Leeds is also an accomplished photographer and poet. At present he is undertaking labor market studies in six cities in Brazil.

Ann H. L. Sontz is the director of the Brunswick Institute on Aging. She received a Ph.D. in anthropology from Columbia University. In addition to her research on migration and interethnic relationships in Germany, she has studied ethnicity in relation to health care service delivery for elder adults, the social network relationships of the elderly, resettlement of older refugees, and other issues regarding the elderly. She has published several articles on these and related topics.

A. Ersan Yücel received his Ph.D. degree in anthropology at the University of Durham, England. His research on Turkish migrants in Germany combines both sociological and anthropological approaches. At present, he is working in the private sector in Saudi Arabia.